39-95

C000142698

NEUROBEHAVIOURAL DISABILITY AND SOCIAL HANDICAP FOLLOWING TRAUMATIC BRAIN INJURY

Brain Damage, Behaviour and Cognition:
Developments in Clinical Neuropsychology
Titles in Series

A MURRAY

Neurobehavioural disability and social handicap following traumatic brain injury

edited by

Rodger Ll. Wood
Brain Injury Rehabilitation Trust

Tom M. McMillan
University of Glasgow

First published 2001 by Psychology Press
27 Church Road, Hove, East Sussex, BN3 2FA

http:///www.psypress.co.uk

Simultaneously published in the USA and Canada
by Taylor & Francis Inc
325 Chestnut Street, 8th Floor, Philadelphia PA 19106

Psychology Press is part of the Taylor & Francis Group

© 2001 Psychology Press Ltd

All rights reserved. No part of this book may be reprinted or reproduced or utilised in any
form or by any electronic, mechanical, or other means, now known or hereafter invented,
including photocopying and recording, or in any information storage or retrieval system,
without permission in writing from the publishers.

British Library Cataloguing in Publication Data
A catalogue record for this book is available from the British Library

Library of Congress Cataloging in Publication Data
Neurobehavioural disability and social handicap following traumatic brain injury/
[edited by] R.Ll. Wood and T.M. McMillan.
     p. cm.—(Brain damage, behaviour, and cognition)
  Includes bibliographical references and index.
  ISBN 0-86377-889-5
   1. Brain damage—Patients—Rehabilitation. 2. Brain damage—Social aspects. 3. Brain
damage—Social aspects. I. Wood, Rodger Ll. (Rodger Llewellyn) II. McMillan, T.M.
(Tom M.) III. Series.

RC387.5.N46 2000
616.8'043—dc21   00-041521

ISBN 0-86377-889-5 (hbk)
ISSN 0967-9944

Cover design by Joyce Chester
Typeset in Times by Facing Pages, Southwick, West Sussex
Printed and bound in the United Kingdom by Biddles Ltd, www.biddles.co.uk

Contents

List of contributors

Nick Alderman, M App Sci, PhD, C Psych. Consultant Clinical Neuropsychologist, Kemsley Division, St Andrew's Hospital, Billing Road, Northampton, NN1 5DG, UK.

Sylvie Coallier, PhD. Neuropsychologist, Charles LeMoyne Hospital, Montreal, PQ, Canada.

Peter G. Eames, MA, MSc, MB, MRCP, MRC Psych, DPM. Consultant Neuropsychiatrist, Grafton Manor Brain Injury Rehabilitation Unit, Grafton Regis, Towcester, Northants, NN12 7SS, UK.

Dale E. Eazell, PhD, FACH. Former Chief Executive Officer, Casa Colina Hospital for Rehabilitation Medicine, Pomona, California. Past Chairman, American Medical Rehabilitation Providers Association, USA.

Jonathan J. Evans, BSc (Hons), Dip Clin Psych, C Psych. Consultant Clinical Psychologist, Associate Director of Research, Oliver Zangwill Centre for Neuropsychological Rehabilitation, Princess of Wales Hospital, Ely, Cambs, CB6 1DN, UK.

Patricia M. Flaherty, MEd. Educator, Acquired Brain Injury Program, G.F. Strong Rehabilitation Centre, Vancouver, BC, Canada.

Gordon Muir Giles, MA, PhD, Dip Cot, OTR. Director Neurobehavioral Programs, Crestwood Behavioral Health Inc., Assistant Professor, Samuel Merrit College, Hawthorne Avenue, Oakland, CA 94609, USA.

Denzil Lush, LLB. Master, Court of Protection, Stewart House, 24 Kingsway, London, WC2B 6JX, UK.

David Manchester, BSc (Hons), M Clin Psych, C Psych, AFBPsS. Consultant Clinical Neuropsychologist, TRU, Margaret House, 342 Haydock Lane, Haydock, St Helens, WA11 9UY, UK.

Tom M. McMillan, M App Sci, PhD, FBPsS. Professor of Clinical Neuropsychology, Department of Psychological Medicine, University of Glasgow, Gartnavel Royal Hospital, 1055 Great Western Road, Glasgow, G12 0XH, UK

Michael Oddy, MA, MSc, PhD, FBPsS. Consultant Clinical Neuropsychologist, Clinical Director, Brain Injury Rehabilitation Unit, Ticehurst House Hospital, Ticehurst, Wadhurst, East Sussex, TN5 7HU, UK

Jennie L. Ponsford BA (Hons), MA, PhD, MAPsS. Director of Research, Monash University and Bethesda Rehabilitation Centre, Melbourne, Australia.

Graham E. Powell, M Phil, PhD, C Psychol, FBPsS. Chartered Clinical Psychologist, 9 Devonshire Place, London, W1N 1PB, UK.

Barry Willer PhD. Professor, Department of Psychiatry, State University of New York at Buffalo, Buffalo, New York, USA.

Rodger Ll. Wood, BA (Hons), DCP, PhD, C Psych, FBPsS. Consultant Clinical Neuropsychologist, Clinical Director, Brain Injury Rehabilitation Trust, West Heath House, Ivy House Road, Birmingham, B38 8JW, UK.

Andrew D. Worthington PhD, C Psych. Consultant Clinical Neuropsychologist, Brain Injury Rehabilitation Trust, West Heath House, Ivy House Road, Birmingham, B38 8JW, UK.

Series preface

From being an area primarily on the periphery of mainstream behavioural and cognitive science, neuropsychology has developed in recent years into an area of central concern for a range of disciplines. We are witnessing not only a revolution in the way in which brain-behaviour-cognition relationships are viewed, but a widening of interest concerning developments in neuropsychology on the part of a range of workers in a variety of fields. Major advances in brain-imaging techniques and the cognitive modelling of the impairments following brain damage promise a wider understanding of the nature of the representation of cognition and behaviour in the damage and undamaged brain.

Neuropsychology is now centrally important for those working with brain-damaged people, but the very rate of expansion in the area makes it difficult to keep up with findings from the current research. The aim of the *Brain Damage, Behaviour and Cognition* series is to publish a wide range of books that present comprehensive and up-to-date overviews of current developments in specific areas of interest.

These books will be of particular interest to those working with the brain-damaged. It is the editors' intention that undergraduates, postgraduates, clinicians and researchers in psychology, speech pathology and medicine will find this series a useful source of information on important current developments. The authors and editors of the books in this series are experts in their respective fields, working at the forefront of contemporary research. They have produced texts that are accessible and scholarly. We thank them for their contribution and their hard work in fulfilling the aims of the series.

CC and GH
Sydney, Australia and Birmingham, UK
Series Editors

Preface

A growing number of people are surviving serious traumatic brain injury. This book addresses the constellation of cognitive and behavioural difficulties most frequently associated with damage to the frontal structures and the pathways that link these structures with other areas of the brain that are involved in human social behaviour. We recognise that many forms of brain injury can have an impact upon those personality and cognitive functions which support social behaviour and the ability to learn functional skills. The content of the book is therefore relevant to acquired brain injury resulting from causes such as cerebral hypoxia, brain infections, intracerebral haemorrhage, and certain types of brain tumour. However, traumatic brain injury produces the highest prevalence of persisting cognitive and behavioural problems in young adults. Consequently, it is used as the principal frame of reference throughout the book.

Many people who survive serious head trauma experience persisting cognitive and emotional problems (impairments) that lead to long-term neurobehavioural disability. In turn, this interferes with a person's ability to participate in various social roles, acting as a major constraint on social independence and leading directly to serious social handicap. This book is about the nature and assessment of adults who display neurobehavioural disability after acquired brain injury and explores some of the methods employed to reduce consequent forms of social handicap.

We suggest that rehabilitation services are often not organised in ways that address the needs of people with such disability and relatively few professionals are experienced in the clinical management of complex disability patterns which follow frontal injury. Consequently, most of the chapters are written by clinicians who work in specialist post-acute brain injury rehabilitation centres that address the needs of people with neurobehavioural disability.

The cardinal features of neurobehavioural disability are presented in Chapter 1, linking disability characteristics and different aspects of frontal dysfunction to the social handicap produced by such disability. The aim of Chapter 2 is to discriminate aspects of abnormal behaviour that are organically based from those that are reactions to disability. Chapter 3 concentrates on the impact of neurobehavioural disability on relatives and other carers. Chapter 4 addresses problems in assessing neurobehavioural disability, including the limitations of current neuropsychological tests, and suggests a broader approach to the assessment of social handicap associated with frontal brain injury. Chapter 5 is written by a lawyer rather than a clinician. The role of the Court of Protection in the UK, or similar agencies in other countries, is vital to ensure the long-term welfare of those who are not able to manage their own affairs after brain injury. The rules pertaining to a person becoming a "patient" or protected by the courts are outlined in this chapter.

Chapters 6 to 10 discuss different approaches to the rehabilitation of neurobehavioural disability. These chapters offer a theoretical framework for rehabilitation procedures as well as describing methods used to ameliorate different forms of social handicap caused by disability. Chapter 11 considers the effectiveness of post-acute rehabilitation both in terms of clinical and cost-effectiveness. The final two chapters explore service provision for brain injury rehabilitation and consider future directions in research and in service provision, given our expanding knowledge about brain injury and its consequences. The editors recognise that the chapters dealing with service provision and assessment of capacity have a UK bias. Whilst not necessarily desirable, this is somewhat inevitable because most of the authors practise in the UK. We acknowledge that a range of social rehabilitation services exists in different countries and recognise the need to organise rehabilitation within the context of local service provision. Hence, to further inform the readership there are commentaries on the chapter about model services from an Australian and an American perspective.

Some European countries remain traditionally "medical" in their approach to brain injury rehabilitation. Most of these services are hospital-based, focus on acute recovery, and often emphasise neurological recovery rather than neuro-psychological rehabilitation and the implications of the injury for persisting social handicap in the community. In contrast, post-acute services in the USA have become largely community-based and often work with brain injured people at home. This approach has been largely determined by financial restrictions on clinical (hospital-based) rehabilitation imposed by the health insurance industry in response to poor social outcomes of rehabilitation programmes during the 1980s. International differences in service provision are also related to different roles of professional disciplines. For example, in America and the UK, clinical psychologists are relatively autonomous and influential at all levels of service provision, whereas this is less common in Europe, Australia, and New Zealand. These differences have an impact on how disability is construed and how clinical services are emphasised and deployed. We hope that the information provided in this book will lead to a greater awareness of the need for specialist post-acute rehabilitation and social support so that a long overdue systematic structure for brain injured people with long-term complex disability will be created.

The editors believe that the book will be of help to the broad range of people working in brain injury rehabilitation, as well as to lawyers and relatives of brain injured people who seek to broaden their knowledge base and understand neurobehavioural disability. In addition, the book should be useful to the growing numbers of case managers, therapy care assistants and support workers, who have responsibility for the day-to-day care of brain injured people in the community.

R.Ll. Wood and T.M. McMillan
March 2000

PART ONE

The nature and impact of neurobehavioural disability

CHAPTER ONE

Understanding neurobehavioural disability

R.Ll. Wood
Brain Injury Rehabilitation Trust, Birmingham, UK

INTRODUCTION

People who suffer brain injury often experience the loss of their social role. The World Health Organization (WHO, 1980) provided a framework to understand the social consequences of serious injury when it published the *International Classification of Impairments, Disabilities and Handicaps*. After brain injury, *impairment* results from a loss of either physical or mental function caused by cerebral damage. This will *disable* the person in some way, by preventing or diminishing his or her ability to participate in certain activities. In turn, this can lead to a loss of some social role, defined as a *handicap*. Recently (WHO, 1997), there has been an attempt to clarify how people can be disadvantaged because of an inability to engage or interact at a social level. In this proposed revision of the nomenclature surrounding the social consequences of serious injury, *disability* is referred to in terms of the *activities* in which a person would normally engage and how performance in the abilities can be compromised. *Handicap* is referred to in terms of *participation*, describing how the opportunity for social interaction can be compromised, leading to social disadvantage. It is not yet clear whether these revised terms will be accepted into the jargon of rehabilitation medicine or whether they will apply equally to those with psychological problems as to those with physical problems. Whatever terms are used, Greenwood (1999) points to the fact that social disadvantage is a particular problem after brain injury. He examines how the revised language of disability reflects the disabilities implicit to a brain injured population, especially in respect of the role of mental functions in the control of how, when, and where activities are conducted. He suggests that cognitive and emotional factors are central to understanding the management of many forms of physical disability, an argument used throughout the chapters of this book.

Many forms of disability after brain injury are based on some form of cognitive impairment. The aphasias, agnosias, apraxias, and amnesic disorders can act as constraints on how skills are learned or applied. Consequently, many types of neuropsychological impairment can have a major impact on a person's capacity for social independence. These cognitive syndromes have been extensively researched over the last 20 years in respect of their primary characteristics, underlying cerebral pathology, and impact on social behaviour (see Cummings, 1985; Meir, Benton, & Diller, 1987; Robertson, 1993, for reviews). The influence of this research is probably most noticeable in the development of stroke rehabilitation which, during the 1970s and 80s, became viewed by many as representative of *neurorehabilitation*. However, the focus of brain injury rehabilitation has expanded over the last 20 years. This is partly a result of improved methods in neurotraumatology, helping more people survive serious traumatic brain injury, and partly because of a growing interest in the range of problems produced by traumatic brain injury. Unlike stroke patients, many of those who suffer serious head trauma make a good neurological and physical recovery and only spend brief periods, if any time at all, on neurorehabilitation units. It is only later in recovery that problems emerge which have a serious impact on social recovery, measured in terms of the individual resuming work, maintaining his or her position in the family, and relating to others in an appropriate and meaningful way.

Over the last 10 years, there has been a growing awareness of long-term (often permanent) cognitive, emotional, behavioural, and personality changes resulting from brain injury. The term that has grown in use to denote this complex, subtle, yet pervasive constellation of cognitive–behaviour changes is "*neurobehavioural disability*". It comprises elements of executive dysfunction, deficits of attention, diminished insight, poor social judgement, labile mood, problems of impulse control, and a range of personality changes that, when combined with specific cognitive problems and pre-morbid personality characteristics, can lead to serious *social handicap,* undermining a person's capacity for independent social behaviour.

Clinical experience has shown that the range of problems that comprise neurobehavioural disability require different treatment approaches and rehabilitation structures than exist in acute neurorehabilitation units. Post-acute *neurobehavioural rehabilitation* has therefore evolved over the last 10 years, as a sub-speciality of brain injury rehabilitation, to address the long-term sequelae of brain injury. This chapter attempts to elucidate the nature of neurobehavioural disability in respect of its underlying cerebral pathology and the social impact caused by its behavioural manifestations and underlying cognitive impairment. It is hoped that a greater awareness of this serious legacy of brain injury will provide the basis of a rationale for the rehabilitation of this complex disorder.

THE CEREBRAL BASIS OF NEUROBEHAVIOURAL DISABILITY

The neural underpinnings of social cognition and behaviour, both in humans and other primates, has been a topic of research in the neurosciences for some time. Studies have shown that damage to the frontal lobes can disrupt performance on tasks that require intentional control over behaviour (Milner, 1963; Milner & Petrides, 1984). Frontal structures and their complex connections with a range of cortical and subcortical centres are also considered to play a key role in the mediation of cerebral systems important to social and functional behaviour (Eslinger, 1999; Stuss & Benson, 1986). In particular, the ventromedial frontal cortex, somatosensory cortex, and amygdala are structures that appear to mediate between our perceptions of socially relevant stimuli and the behaviour such perceptions elicit (Adolphs, 1999).

A neural explanation of social behaviour in humans largely originates in the anecdotal studies of social changes following brain damage. The case of Phineas Gage (see Kimble, 1963) is probably the best-known example. He sustained a large bilateral lesion of the ventromedial prefrontal cortex (Damasio 1994) when an iron bar penetrated his brain, following an explosion. The personality and social changes exhibited by Gage, apparently in the absence of intellectual damage, has been noted in more recent case examples of patients with similar injuries (see Dimitrov, Phipps, Zahn, & Grafman, 1999). The alterations of behaviour and personality reported by the families of those who display characteristics of neurobehavioural disability (Brooks & McKinley, 1983; Lezak, 1978) closely resemble psychological changes associated with frontal lobe injury and represent some of the cardinal features we now refer to as neurobehavioural disability.

The term *frontal lobe syndrome* (Walsh, 1985) is not favoured by many neurologists or neuropsychologists. Eslinger and Damasio (1985) cautioned against its use because they felt that different clusters of behaviour and personality abnormalities after brain injury are likely to have different underlying mechanisms that could require different treatments. To some extent the notion of a frontal syndrome is beginning to be fractionated in terms of its major elements. The dysexecutive syndrome (Baddeley, 1986) is now used to emphasise the loss of intentional, goal-directed behaviour after brain injury. Humphreys and Forde (1998) have recently proposed the term *action disorganisation syndrome* to describe the functional deficits associated with executive disability, whilst behaviour disorders are usually described in relation to their primary characteristic, often using neuropsychiatric nosology. However, irrespective of the labels used to describe the cognitive and behavioural changes that constitute this pattern of disability, it remains closely associated with damage to, or dysfunction of, those systems of the brain associated with the fronto-temporal structures. Lezak (1995), for example, comments that the impulsive, labile, acting-out, apathetic, disinterested, non-initiating legacies of brain injury are organic features of frontal lobe damage.

The majority of people who display this pattern of disability after brain injury have suffered head trauma, largely because of the high incidence of road traffic accidents in the aetiology of acquired brain injury. The mechanisms of acceleration–deceleration that occur in moving vehicle accidents have the greatest impact on frontal structures (Pang, 1989) and form the largest category of those admitted to specialist post-acute brain injury rehabilitation units (see Eames & Wood, 1984; Eames, Cotterill, & Kneale, 1995; Wood, McCrea, Wood, & Merriman, 1999). However, other forms of cerebral pathology can be involved. The case of patient EVR (Eslinger & Damasio, 1985) is an example of executive dysfunction as a result of frontal damage following removal of a large left orbitofrontal meningioma. The four cases described by Humphreys and Forde (1998) include two with diffuse cortical injuries as a result of cerebral hypoxia and two who suffered cerebrovascular accident (CVA). CVA is also associated with alteration in mood, especially when the left frontal area is damaged (Lipsey et al., 1983; Starkstein & Robinson, 1989). Grafman and his colleagues (Grafman, Vance, & Weingarter, 1986) also showed mood disorders to be associated with orbitofrontal injury caused by missile wounds. They associated right frontal damage with agitated anxiety and depression, whilst left frontal damage led to increased anger and hostility. Case studies of patients with brainstem lesions have been noted to produce labile mood, irritability, loss of motivation, and disinhibition (Trimble & Cummings, 1981). Similar characteristics have been observed after recovery from herpes simplex encephalitis. Greenwood, Bhalla, Gordon, and Roberts (1983) report aggressive rage reactions, motivational changes, and other "frontal" behaviours in four patients who recovered from this neurological disease.

In the author's experience, there is a strong empirical relationship between various patterns of neurobehavioural disability and cerebral pathology or dysfunction associated with fronto-temporal structures. The cognitive, behaviour and personality changes associated with frontal injury represent the most prominent range of problems encountered in a rehabilitation setting. Because the majority of people receiving rehabilitation have suffered decelerative head trauma and therefore diffuse axonal injury (DAI), the precise location of cerebral lesions is often unclear. In many cases there is no radiological evidence of a lesion and where such evidence of frontal injury does exist, it is often contusional or haemorrhagic injury which has resolved by the time later brain scans have been obtained. Injuries to other areas of the brain can of course produce abnormalities consistent with neurobehavioural disability. It seems reasonable to assume, however, that whilst such lesions do not involve the frontal lobes *per se*, systems that interact with frontal structures are damaged in a way that affects their integrative nature (Eslinger, 1999; Rolls, 1999). Consequently, the control normally exerted by the frontal systems has been lost or damaged in some way.

THE SOCIAL IMPACT OF NEUROBEHAVIOURAL DISABILITY

Neurobehavioural disabilities can adversely influence social recovery by undermining learning processes central to social rehabilitation and community independence, or by preventing the social application of what has been learned because of a dislocation between knowledge itself and the ability to use knowledge to guide thinking and regulate behaviour. Neurobehavioural disorders may appear as challenging behaviours which prevent meaningful rehabilitation taking place, or as functionally ineffective habit patterns that are difficult to replace with socially adaptive behaviours. This can occur in the absence of physical or neurological abnormality *per se*. People with neurobehavioural disability may not show measurable impairment of intelligence or memory (see Shallice & Burgess, 1991) yet fail to use intelligence in a meaningful and socially adaptive way, such as to monitor, inhibit, or alter behaviours which others find offensive, threatening, or embarrassing. However, the influence of neurobehavioural disability on a person's capacity for clear thinking and social judgement is not always easy to detect, especially in a consulting room interview which often only lasts an hour or less (see Chapter 4). The structure implicit in formal clinical interviews can mask many neurobehavioural weaknesses, the impact of which are often subtle yet pervasive in respect of adaptive social behaviour. In order to promote a brain injured person's potential for social recovery and independence it is therefore necessary for rehabilitation practitioners to understand how cerebral impairment can lead to neurobehavioural disability, so that any organic constraints upon learning, or the application of learned skills in the context of social behaviour, can be minimised.

Behaviour disorders after brain injury can be considered in the context of the following categories: (1) Disorders of drive, arousal, and motivation, (2) diminished inhibitory or regulatory control, and (3) altered personality. These categories are not mutually exclusive and usually combine in ways that undermine a person's capacity to interact reliably with the social environment. Consequently they all have the potential to impose serious social handicap. These categories (whilst not exhaustive) offer reasonably good operational distinctions for an examination of the complex neurobehavioural problems that act as a barrier to community living.

Disorders of drive, arousal, and motivation

The "clinical picture" of frontal pathology painted by Lishman (1978) points to a "Lack of initiative and spontaneity, usually coupled with a general diminution of motor activity" (p. 95) as one of the cardinal behaviour changes affecting social independence. Lishman continues by describing the frontal patient's sluggish responses, pointing out that tasks are often neglected and new initiatives rarely undertaken. He contrasts this with the changes that occur when such patients are "vigorously urged" into some activity. Providing the impetus for the activity is externally controlled (e.g., by a therapist) a person may perform normally on a task, only to lapse back into inactivity when the external stimulation has been withdrawn. This description of frontal behavioural pathology refers to several distinct (but not necessarily mutually exclusive) neurobehavioural conditions—an arousal disorder, a problem of drive, plus an executive (initiating) weakness, illustrating how behaviours reflecting frontal pathology comprise different components of neurobehavioural disability which may need to be addressed separately in the context of a rehabilitation programme.

Wood and Eames (1981) discussed problems of arousal, drive, and motivation in terms of their impact on brain injury rehabilitation. They described drive as a "property of the organism", later referred to by Stuss and Benson (1986) as a "force that activates human impulses". This helps distinguish *drive*, a physiological state, from *motivation*, a psychological state (see Chapter 2). Wood and Eames defined motivation as "the amount of effort an individual with a given level of drive is prepared and able to exert in order to achieve a certain goal" (Wood & Eames, 1981, p. 88). This definition draws attention to the complex interrelationship between drive and hedonic responsiveness as mediators of motivational behaviour. In a "normal" individual, one would expect the strength of a need to determine the amount of effort (strength of the drive) exerted to satisfy the need. For example, a *need state* (hunger) establishes a *motivational incentive* (the acquisition of food). The strength of the need state will determine how much *effort* a person will make to locate food (shopping) and prepare a meal (cooking) so that the goal (reduction of hunger) can be achieved.

However, people with drive disorders often show an interesting dislocation between a need state and the behaviour required to satisfy that need. For example, many clients in rehabilitation have a well-developed smoking habit. One would normally expect that such people would show agitation and other signs of withdrawal if the supply of cigarettes ceased. Also, one might reasonably expect that if the only way a person could access cigarettes is through participation in a rehabilitation activity (one which is designed to be well within the client's ability), the client would generate the effort (drive) to participate and achieve the reward. In people with drive disorders, however, this presumed relationship between need state, motivational incentive, and drive (effort) does not always exist. Behaviour programmes designed to reward initiative, spontaneity, or some specific form of purposeful action often fail because the client does not exhibit the targeted behaviour, fails to earn the "reward" of a cigarette, yet shows no signs of distress, even after several days without smoking, during which the need state presumably increases. This indicates some relationship between drive disorders and disorders of hedonic responsiveness in the initiation and direction of behaviour.

The relationship between arousal and drive is less straightforward and beyond the scope of this chapter. It must not be assumed, however, that people with a drive disorder necessarily appear as *underaroused*. Stuss and Benson (1986) describe arousal as "the ability to be awakened, to maintain wakefulness, and to follow signals and commands" (p. 98). Wood (1992) points to the importance of arousal to maintain alertness, mediating both focused and selective attention. This makes arousal an important factor in rehabilitation because of the way it mediates the process of learning. Eames and Wood (1984) refer to arousal deficits improving as a result of vestibular stimulation. However, the improvements in motor control and cognitive functioning produced by increased arousal are maintained only for relatively short periods after the period of stimulation. Unfortunately, such phasic improvements in arousal do not have any impact on drive itself. Luria (1973) refers to an extreme form of drive disorder which incorporates arousal problems. He describes an *apathetico-akinetico-abulic syndrome*, in which a person remains completely passive, expresses no wishes or desires, makes no requests and refuses to seek food, even in the case of extreme hunger. He indicates that this condition is usually associated with serious bilateral frontal damage, but implies that less serious injury can have a similar but less intrusive impact on behaviour.

Schefft, Malec, Lehr, and Kanfer (1991) point out that less severe abulic disorders are often mistaken for depression, even when a person shows little evidence of emotional distress. Drive disorders are similarly misconstrued as reflecting poor motivation. This stems from a misinterpretation of behaviours which accompany drive disorders. People often appear as "lazy", lethargic and disinterested, lacking both initiative and spontaneity. This pattern of behaviour is often interpreted as reflecting a lack of motivation, implying that the person is unwilling to engage in meaningful behaviour. However, when asked, people with drive disorders may express interests, desires, needs, etc., but seem unable to impel themselves to achieve the objects of their desires. The majority of people with drive disorders are happy to follow prompts and will co-operate with others in the pursuit of some interest, but appear unable to sustain such behaviour of their own volition (cf. Lishman's observations earlier).

Consequently, many people with a drive disorder become much more purposeful when they enter a rehabilitation unit because their activities are structured and directed by others. Once support is removed, the individual with a drive disorder reverts to a lethargic, inactive or aimless, stereotyped pattern of behaviour. In contrast, those with motivational deficits often react antagonistically to being prompted because they perceive this as pressure to achieve something for which they have no sense of need. Organic disorders of motivation can therefore be even more of an obstacle to social functioning than drive disorders. Whereas a person with a drive disorder is often willing to co-operate, if properly supported and encouraged, and capable of expressing ideas or interests which can form the basis of an activity programme, someone with a motivational deficit may have little or no interest in a constructive activity and will actively resist, or be disruptive if encouraged to participate.

It is often necessary to distinguish those disorders of motivation that are organically based from those that are a psychological reaction to personal and social circumstances (see Chapter 2). Psychologically based problems of motivation usually reflect signs of phobic avoidance in the context of helpless, despondent behaviour. These reactions are often found in people with serious physical disability who worked hard during acute rehabilitation to diminish the social disability caused by cerebral impairment, yet without much success. This often leads to feelings of helplessness—nothing I do will change the way I am—and an attempt to avoid activities that have previously been associated with effort, fatigue, discomfort—but no perceptible improvement of function. Demotivation as a result of earlier experiences in rehabilitation can usually be overcome by the introduction of cognitive–behaviour therapy and the adoption of sensible (achievable) rehabilitation goals which form the basis for further goal achievement (see Chapters 7 and 8).

Some psychological reactions have a much greater impact on motivational incentive and one must be careful to distinguish motivational *deficits* from *abnormal motivation*. The former reflects a loss of motivational incentive of the kind associated with drive disorders or feelings of helplessness, whilst the latter implies that a person has retained a sense of motivational incentive but one which is directed not towards reducing disability but to maintaining it (a presumably unconscious desire to retain the status quo). These conditions are referred to as *dissociative* and reflect a form of hysteria. It is probably a consequence of damage to cerebral mechanisms regulating aspects of goal-directed behaviour. Serious traumatic brain injury can disrupt hypothalamic mechanisms responsible for hedonistic experiences relating to pleasure or pain (Rolls, 1975) which will directly influence a person's sense of value or need for achievement, satisfaction, etc. Consequently, the incentive value of a goal will be diminished, together with the amount of effort made by an individual to achieve a goal. (This is discussed more fully in the section on personality disorders and in Chapter 2.)

Jahanshahi and Frith (1998) propose that many disorders of drive and motivation should be construed as an *impairment of willed action*. They base the concept of a willed action system on a network of frontal cortical (dorsolateral, prefrontal, anterior cingulate, and supplementary motor area) and subcortical (thalamus and basal ganglia) systems. They present evidence to show that willed actions are controlled in a different way from routine, stereotyped actions and suggest that motivational disorders in general, plus the more specific disorders of apathy, abulia, and obsessional slowness, can be considered as impairments of willed actions. Whatever the underlying mechanism, the significance of disorders of motivation, both in respect of determining a person's rehabilitation potential, as well the ability to function in life generally, should never be underestimated. Organic disorders of drive and motivation often act as a poor prognostic indicator for rehabilitation and a person's capacity for social independence.

Disorders of inhibitory and regulatory control

Many clinical practitioners believe that persistent, intrusive, and disruptive behaviours are most frequently found in the context of frontal pathology (or in association with mechanical trauma that increases the likelihood of frontal pathology). There are a number of historical precedents for this opinion (Jastrowitz, 1888; Kleist, 1931; Welt, 1888). These authors reported behaviour and personality changes in relation to frontal damage (primarily orbitofrontal damage). They describe restlessness, euphoria, pressure of speech, puerile comments, obscene language, and a loss of ethical and moral standards which Kleist referred to as *"moral insanity"*. More recently, Blumer and Benson (1975) used the term *"pseudo-psychopathic"* as a frame of reference for orbitofrontal injuries leading to irritable and facetious behaviour, lack of tact and restraint, hyperactivity, hypersexuality, antisocial acts, and paranoid or grandiose thinking. Lezak (1989) comments that the orbitofrontal cortex is concerned with behavioural control and that damage to this area can lead to impulsive, disinhibited behaviour which is "out of touch with social values" (p.127). Even when skills and abilities remain essentially intact there can be defects in how they are expressed in the context of social activities.

Starkstein and Robinson (1991), commenting on mania after frontal injury, propose an orbito-temporal-limbic feedback loop by which cognitive functions influence instinctive emotional reactions at the level of the amygdala. They suggest that damage to orbitofrontal or inferior temporal regions disrupts the inhibitory influence of the cortex over the amygdala, releasing emotions from intellectual control. Support for this opinion is found in forensic studies of violent offenders. Raine, Meloy, Bihrle, and Stoddard (1998) used positron emission tomography (PET) scanning methods to study the brains of murderers. They report low glucose metabolism in nine "affective" murderers compared to a group of 41 control subjects. The "affective" murderers were described as those who displayed impulsive aggression. They conclude that PET scan results suggest a loss of frontal regulation, implying that emotional, unplanned, impulsive murderers are less able to control aggressive impulses generated from subcortical structures due to deficient prefrontal perfusion.

Problems of self-control.   A lack of self-control is one of the most common complaints made by families and carers of brain injured people. It incorporates such traits as:

1. Social and/or sexual disinhibition which may range from tactless and facetious remarks that cause offence and embarrassment, to inappropriate and unacceptable advances, comprising sexual touching, lewd comments, public masturbation, even sexual assault.
2. Impulsiveness, low tolerance and emotional reactivity, which often escalates out of control, resulting in displays of angry, emotional, and assaultive behaviour, which is often out of proportion to events which elicit them.

Adolphs (1999) and Davidson and Irwin (1999) report that people with bilateral amygdala damage tend to be excessively friendly towards others and seem to lack the ability to recognise when such behaviour is unwelcome and needs to be inhibited. This is a frequent observation of staff working in specialist neurobehavioural rehabilitation centres. Clients who are socially disinhibited seem unable to recognise when their attempts at conversation or social advances to strangers, especially in public places, are unwelcome, upsetting, or intimidating. They seem impervious to the "body language" and facial expressions that normally signal social disapproval and force one to change one's style of behaviour. Adolphs argues that the connections between the amygdala and the temporal lobes allow the processing of emotionally and socially salient stimuli from facial expressions, especially negative emotions such as fear. Damage to these structures or their connecting pathways results in a loss of social awareness because of the failure to emotionally interpret social signals.

Such legacies of brain injury have a damaging impact on interpersonal relationships, and compliance with, or participation in, rehabilitation and can seriously undermine the role of rehabilitation staff or support workers. The physical proximity associated with rehabilitation or nursing care activities, combined with the friendly attitude displayed by staff, can provoke over-familiar advances that may be perceived as threatening and intimidating by staff. This can prevent meaningful relationships being established at a working (professional) level of interaction. It also increases the risk of conflict because when such advances are politely but firmly rejected the protagonist may react angrily, a response that can gain momentum if not handled properly and result in an outpouring of verbal abuse, even physical assault. In many cases the protagonist later shows remorse and apologises but this rarely leads to the development of better self-control.

Unstable mood and temperament. Labile mood frequently occurs in association with problems of inhibitory control, and represents a pattern of behavioural instability which often follows frontal injury (Cummings, 1985; Stuss & Benson, 1986), usually in the context of decelerative concussion. Emotional lability imposes considerable stress on relatives and is an important factor contributing to relationship failure (Wood & Yurdakul, 1997). Shifts of mood are described as being sudden and frequent, without any obvious pattern or cycle. The content of mood varies from individual to individual. It may be mildly euphoric and out of keeping with the prevailing social situation, or restless, tense and agitated, oversensitive and reactive (see Chapter 2). Depressive phases may be included. These are usually short-lived, lasting no more than a few days, during which the person appears withdrawn and sullen, has little to say, and often retreats to the bedroom or otherwise remains apart from the family unit. A sense of fatigue is often reported in association with episodes of low, agitated mood.

Although not a true clinical depression, low mood is often the characteristic most easily articulated when questioned by a doctor. Consequently, many family doctors, or psychiatrists unfamiliar with post-traumatic or other organic disorders of mood, respond by prescribing antidepressant medication. This may elevate but not regulate mood. Antidepressants often mask the underlying disorder of mood without actually preventing the lability that results in excessive and inappropriate emotional reactions. The combination of low tolerance, impulsivity, and fragile mood is a volatile mixture, leading to explosive outbursts of temper which relatives find difficult to understand and tolerate. Noisy children or minor frustrations which are ignored and tolerated one day can lead to volatile outbursts the next. Relatives cannot understand this kind of behavioural inconsistency and often remark that the unpredictability of such outbursts acts as a major source of stress ("it's like living with a time bomb" or "it's like living with Dr Jekyl and Mr Hyde"), leading to family disharmony and eventual rejection by the partner.

An extreme example of an explosive form of aggressive behaviour is episodic dyscontrol (Mark & Ervin, 1970). This is characterised by sudden aggressive rages over which the individual has little or no control (and sometimes little awareness). These outbursts can occur in any setting with little or no provocation. They are sometimes associated with quasi-epileptic phenomena (Lishman, 1978), especially in the temporal areas (Trimble, 1981). Wood (1987) described these episodic reactions as usually lasting one or two minutes, being quite frenzied, with a primitive form of aggression (biting, scratching, kicking), which is usually directed at whatever object or person is nearest. Between episodes, the person appears friendly and co-operative and one does not have the "walking on eggshells" feeling associated with people who have the self-control problems described earlier. Eames (1990) points out that whilst the classical emotional outbursts associated with episodic dyscontrol can be dangerous the majority are not severe, even though they may be perceived as very threatening and stressful by those to whom the behaviour is directed.

The condition often does not become evident until several months post-injury (Gualtieri & Cox, 1991). Eames (1990) suggests that the temporal distribution of onset post-trauma may be similar to that of post-traumatic epilepsy. In the first five years of recovery, the condition does not show a trend towards spontaneous improvement, of the kind associated with some other neurobehavioural sequelae. Indeed, there is often a worsening of the condition because what may start as a purely organic (epileptic) phenomenon acquires characteristics of learned behaviour, when a person acquires a tendency to respond explosively to any form of frustration. This type of behaviour disorder rarely responds to purely psychological therapy, although cognitive–behaviour therapy can be used successfully to help people recognise prodromal signs of an incipient temper outburst in order to take some avoiding action. Fortunately the majority of sufferers respond to treatment with the anticonvulsant carbamazepine (see Post, Denicoff, Frye, & Leverich, 1997).

Altered personality

The term "personality change" is inevitably vague. It indicates a change from some assumed pre-morbid condition, without pointing to the nature of the change itself.

Lishman (1997) suggests that the term implies an alteration in a person's habitual attitudes and pattern of behaviour, so that reactions to people and events differ from pre-morbid behaviour. The role of pre-morbid personality is important not only because this will influence the nature of personality change but also because people who suffer brain injury present an infinitely diverse set of pre-morbid personality traits. This means that post-injury personality change will have the same diverse character. Bond (1984) points out that pre-morbid constitutional factors often shape post-injury emotional reactions. Lezak (1989) also mentions this, suggesting that a person who was meticulous pre-injury may become obsessional post-injury. However, personality changes are not simply extensions of pre-injury traits. Bond refers to occasions when there is a reversal of previous traits, when an extravert becomes an introvert, or a person shows a moderation of some objectionable pre-injury behaviour. He acknowledges, however, that this tendency is less common than an exacerbation of pre-morbid traits.

The characteristics that comprise the notion of personality change include all the cognitive and behaviour changes referred to in the previous sections of this chapter plus changes in emotional expression, cognitive interpretation, and behavioural disposition that are not easily included in the above categories of neurobehavioural disability. When considering personality change we must also try and distinguish primary from secondary emotional disorder (Lezak, 1989). Primary emotional disorders occur directly as a result of damage to cerebral structures or neurohumoral systems mediating the experience of, or expression of, emotion. Secondary disorders are reactions to mental or physical disorders and imply adjustment difficulties, heavily influenced by pre-morbid characteristics.

Emotional expression.   Indifference to the well-being of others, loss of warmth, lack of empathy, and an egocentric attitude are hallmarks of the emotional changes that families find difficult to accept. These changes in emotional expression have been reported in cases of ventromedial frontal injury (Damasio, 1994; Damasio, Tranel, & Damasio, 1990). These studies describe how individuals with this type of brain damage develop sociopathic behaviour and fail to respond autonomically to emotional stimuli. Damasio suggests that such individuals are incapable of evaluating actions of self and others.

A loving husband and father can become aloof, uncaring, even dismissive of those nearest to him whilst sometimes showing enthusiasm for things external to family interests. This is confusing and distressing to children who feel alienated from parental affection and security. Often, the brain injured person displays a childish petulance, or a demanding, dependent and immature disposition. This can be very stressful for the partner and elicits such comments as "It's like I've got three children now, not two". Changes in a couple's sexual relationship are common in such circumstances. This is not because a loss of sex drive often accompanies brain injury (low sexual arousal is more likely than high arousal) but because the partner sees him or herself in a different role, that of a minder rather than a partner.

Also, the emotional shallowness displayed by injured people means they become less sexually attractive to their partner.

Compulsive and ritualistic behaviours.   A rigid, concrete style of thinking may dominate the way a brain injured person responds to social situations. They can be dogmatic, pedantic, unreasonable, and adopt a "black or white" attitude to everything, making them impervious to reason and impossible to argue with because they seem incapable of seeing another person's point of view. This type of personality change can include obsessional or compulsive patterns of behaviour, such as compulsive checking behaviours or hoarding papers, magazines, empty egg boxes, etc., generally cluttering the living space with materials that could and should be discarded.

Compulsive behaviour may include the need to have a place for everything and to have everything in its place, what Bond (1984) refers to as "organic orderliness". If anything is out of its prescribed place the person with this disorder becomes very distressed, sometimes to the point of flying into a rage. Obsessive thinking may also comprise a ritualistic behaviour pattern, represented by stereotypical responses. This makes it difficult for family members to vary their lifestyle because their brain injured relative feels compelled to maintain a routine pattern of behaviour, in which certain days are devoted to specific activities. Luria (1973) suggests these behaviour patterns emerge because frontal injury prevents flexible thinking and the deployment of actions that are central to adaptive social behaviour.

Observations of compulsive behaviour patterns in neurobehavioural rehabilitation centres are relatively common, yet the reported incidence of obsessive–compulsive disorder after head injury has always been low. Grimshaw (1964) in a review of 50 patients referred to a psychiatric clinic found that 19% with obsessional disorders also had a history of neurological disorder. Lishman (1968) remarked that whilst frank obsessional neuroses linked to brain injury were uncommon, they were more likely to occur after more severe injuries. McKeon, Guffin, and Robinson (1984) reported on four patients who had developed obsessional symptoms after head injury. Three were identified from a series of 25 patients referred because of obsessionality and one other who was one of a pair of monozygotic twins discordant for the disorder.

"Disordered perceptions".   Much depends upon the person's ability to recognise personality changes that are detrimental to family life and social relationships generally. Many brain injured people are unaware of character changes yet are willing to accept that the complaints made by family members are genuine. Lishman (1997) points out that even when aware of such changes the individual seems incapable of acting to change or moderate them. In less serious cases, problems often develop as a result of the person's awareness of a change in ability or personality. This leads to feelings of insecurity, alienation, demoralisation, anxiety, and depression. However, cognitive changes may alter a person's

perception of events in more sinister ways which lead to *attribution errors* based upon a suspicious, even paranoid attitude, often involving accusations of infidelity towards one's partner, presumably in response to some recognition of changes in the quality of the relationship. People who experience such problems often have unrealistic aspirations and attitudes to life post-injury, even presenting grandiose ideas that border on being delusional.

Dissociative disorders.   These represent a serious form of avoidance behaviour, often characterised by pseudo-seizures; disproportionate memory loss; disturbance of speech, vision, or hearing; motor paralysis; paraesthesias; even disorders of arousal and drive. The term *"dissociative"* relates to the notion that symptoms result from a lack of co-ordination in different psychological functions. An alternative name for the condition is *"hysteria"* but recent nomenclature in DSM-IV and ICD10 prefers the term *"dissociation"*. The essence of the condition is that physical or cognitive symptoms exist in the absence of relevant brain pathology.

Mathews, Shaw, and Klove (1966) used the term *"pseudo-neurologic"* to refer to brain injured patients displaying cognitive deficits which were inconsistent with the nature and severity of brain injury. They include in this definition any pattern of disturbance that approximates a neurological aetiology but is actually psychologically based. The relationship between head injury and dissociative states is well known but not necessarily well understood. Whitlock (1967) reports on 56 patients admitted to a psychiatric unit with a diagnosis of hysterical conversion disorder. He found that two thirds of this group had suffered some kind of "brain disorder". Head injury had preceded the onset of hysterical symptoms within 6 months in 21% of these patients. Eames (1992) reported on 54 patients who presented hysterical behaviours after brain injury, in particular, hypoglycaemia and various types of hypoxia. Superficially, the behaviour patterns of these patients represented the syndrome of *"gross hysteria"* described by Charcot (1889) but closer analysis suggested the behaviours resembled the *"childhood pathological demand syndrome"* (Newson, 1989; see Chapter 2).

People who present with such conditions usually do not have pre-accident histories of such behaviour; indeed Eames' cohort did not show any correlations with family, personal, or psychiatric history. Clinical experience has shown that people who develop dissociative disorders often have pre-morbid personalities that can be described as driving, achievement orientated, or ambitious, rather than weak or "neurotic" in any way. Eames could not find evidence to support the view that the behaviour of his cohort represented an emotional reaction to the psychological stresses of brain injury. However, the psychological impact of brain injury can alter motivation in a way that adversely influences the person's prospects for recovery.

A psychological explanation for dissociation after brain injury can be formed on the notion of an *avoidance reaction*. In many cases, the realisation that brain injury has prevented a person fulfilling personal expectations or living life in a certain way seems to generate an attitude of avoidance—"If I can't live my life in the way I want to then I don't want to live life at all". This can lead to an unwillingness to try and regain old skills or acquire new skills to ameliorate disabilities. Wood (1987) suggested that, in cases of dissociation, motivation was not absent but present in a *negative* sense, i.e., the person seems to want to retain the *status quo* and lacks the *will* to overcome disability. In such cases the person's motivation is to remain a *patient* and he or she may try to embellish the impact of the disability; even resisting or actually sabotaging attempts at rehabilitative therapy. It is for this reason that the notion of *will* as a factor underpinning motivation and awareness is so important. Wood (1987) suggests that a remark made by Paget (1873) is particularly apt in this sense – "They say, 'I cannot', it looks like, 'I will not', but it is, 'I cannot will' ", meaning that they are unable to find the conviction or drive to overcome some form of adversity. The degree to which the person is "conscious" of their unwillingness to overcome disability is always difficult to judge and distinguishes dissociative states from malingering. It is probable that we will only really understand the mechanisms underlying dissociative states when we are able to disentangle the complex relationship between motivation and will.

COGNITIVE EXPLANATIONS OF NEUROBEHAVIOURAL DISABILITY

The role of attention

Cognition is the product of mediational and integrative functions of the cortex. It is *mediated* by arousal which maintains alertness and prepares a person to respond to social stimuli. Information is *integrated* by attentional mechanisms which, in turn, are controlled by conscious effort (*vigilance*). Brain injury can therefore disrupt cognition in a number of ways. It can either reduce a person's capacity for alertness, diminishing the quality and quantity of information being processed; or, it can disrupt the attention control mechanisms, weakening the ability to control the focus of attention, increasing distractibility, and making it difficult to switch fluently between different attentional sets. This makes it likely that people with brain injury will lose track when reading or conversing, preventing them absorbing meaningful units of information.

Many social problems experienced by brain damaged people occur because they do not perceive relevant social cues—what van Zomeren and Brouwer (1994) describe as *social inattentiveness*. Attentional mechanisms play a central role in controlling what information is processed and thereby influence how social situations are evaluated. In real life we are continuously exposed to a complex array of information, from different sensory modalities, at different intensities, in different forms, and with different meanings. What we perceive, how much we perceive, and how we interpret what we perceive (in terms of life experience) depends on our attentional capability. This comprises focused, sustained, and divided attention, speed of, and capacity for, information processing, and finally depth of processing (which determines the emphasis we give to information and how much we are likely to remember).

Attention as a control process.   To appreciate the vulnerability of adaptive social behaviour and its reliance on an intact cognitive system, one must first try to conceptualise the role of attention as a controller of cognitive processes (van Zomeren and Brouwer, 1994). Shallice (1982) proposed an information processing model in which a *supervisory attentional system* (SAS) monitors familiar routines *(schemas)*. These are overlearned actions or skills (habits), such as morning washing routines, making tea, dressing, etc., which are activated by social stimuli. Therefore, the activation of any schema depends on (1) being aware of the stimulus, and (2) interpreting it correctly in order for the most appropriate response pattern to be triggered.

Everyday life requires many schema to be activated in quick succession. This is not something that we can do consciously because the process would fully occupy our mental processes, leaving little room for any other cognitive activity. Therefore, the process is largely automatic, controlled by a system Shallice called *contention scheduling*. This process is the essence of mental flexibility because it allows us to activate a selected number of compatible schemas (actions) at any one time, switching to alternative schemas when circumstances change. However, in the event that an inappropriate action schema is triggered, or in novel situations for which no schema exists, the SAS comes into play, either to override the action schema already in place or to select new combinations of schema appropriate to the new situation. As such, the SAS is responsible for controlled processing of information: a slower and more deliberate system of information processing and response selection.

Burgess and Wood (1990) use this model to explain frontal deficits such as loss of insight, inappropriate conversational habit patterns, and lack of regulatory control over behaviour. The SAS model also explains the observations of Reason (1979, 1984). He described attentional lapses of behaviour, referred to as "*actions not as planned*" (e.g., putting frozen food in the oven instead of the freezer; putting things down and losing them within minutes; going into a room to get something then "forgetting" what one is looking for). Such incidents are part of everyone's experience but are much more frequent and intrusive after head trauma and can disrupt a person's lifestyle, leading to anxiety and distress.

Attention, awareness, and judgement.   Attention plays an important role in both promoting and maintaining awareness. William James (1890) remarked, "My experience is what I agree to attend to. Only those items I notice shape my mind" (p. 87). This eloquently determines the relationship between attention as a mechanism of cognitive control, and awareness as a higher order information processing system responsible for storing and evaluating social experiences.

Frontal injury leads to a reduction of insight or self-awareness that results in diminished ability to evaluate and judge one's actions. Good social judgement depends upon the capacity for awareness of self and others. Awareness of others relies on the ability to monitor and evaluate the impact of one's actions on the social or physical environment. The integration of self and other awareness is therefore essential for adaptive social behaviour. It involves the ability to divide attention in order simultaneously to (1) process incoming information, (2) monitor one's response, (3) evaluate its social impact, and (4) decide whether the response is appropriate or needs to be changed. The attentional demands of this everyday cognitive process are immense yet proceed without a great deal of conscious effort. Consequently, we only become aware of its complexity when something happens (like a brain injury) to disrupt the fluent processing of information from ever changing and often noisy social situations.

The poor long-term social consequences of diminished awareness have been commented upon in the social follow-up studies of Brooks and McKinlay (1983) and Thomsen (1989). Awareness implies judgement, the capacity to evaluate the social impact of our actions. Without judgement we cannot learn from experience and our capacity for decision making is seriously compromised. It is an important factor in maturational development and in the application of intelligence, which is one reason why adolescents who suffer brain injury have a higher risk of late behavioural and social sequelae (Thomsen, 1989). She felt that young people with head injuries remained immature because they lacked insight and a "down to earth attitude", which was responsible for delayed and incomplete maturational development.

Executive disorders

The nature and treatment of executive dysfunction will be addressed in Chapters 7 and 10. However, the role of organisational and planning abilities to structure and sequence activities; the employment of reasoning in the choice of social options and strategies; and the use of initiative to decide when an action should be implemented, all need to be addressed in this chapter, from the perspective of neurobehavioural disability.

The ability to regulate and adapt actions in response to changing circumstances lies at the heart of social independence and is central to the notion of "executive behaviour". Executive dysfunction is probably the most pervasive of all the neurobehavioural legacies, yet when the disability is mild or moderate it often escapes recognition. This is because many executive difficulties are quite subtle and people who experience them often appear physically and cognitively intact. They can give a good account of themselves when interviewed (see Chapter 4), and display a good level of measured intelligence and memory. Walsh (1985) refers to this as the "frontal lobe paradox" and remarks on how "persons with seemingly preserved intelligence fail to cope with demands of their occupation or profession".

This becomes difficult to understand when a person can verbalise how to carry out a task yet still be unable to execute the actions required. This was illustrated by one of my own patients, a lawyer who sustained frontal contusional injuries in a skiing accident. He made a complete physical and neurological recovery and did not present any obvious cognitive weaknesses as far as his family and friends were concerned. He returned to work as a senior partner in a law firm approximately three months post-injury but proved incapable of carrying out his duties effectively. He was unaware of the increasing concern experienced by his colleagues and members of his family and supplied a series of plausible explanations (excuses) when his poor performance at work was pointed out to him. His partners could not understand how someone who retained such a good grasp of the law and legal procedure could be so unreliable and inefficient in the application of his knowledge. By the time he was admitted to a post-acute neurobehavioural rehabilitation unit, his family recognised that he was incapable of looking after himself from day to day. He could not plan, initiate or sustain any type of goal-directed behaviour and needed frequent prompting from staff to complete even basic activities of daily living. His level of executive disability was independent of any form of measured cognitive deficit. He performed in the superior range of the WAIS-R (IQ = 126) and only displayed minor deficits on tests of memory and measures of frontal ability, such as the Wisconsin Card Sorting Test. He also retained the ability to complete *The Times* cryptic crossword before lunch every day.

Lezak (1989) provides four categories of functioning as a conceptual framework for understanding executive disorders. These comprise: (1) *volition*: the ability to initiate, to generate spontaneously motives and goals, and to sustain goal-orientated activities; (2) *planning*: the ability to sequence and organise thoughts and actions, to conceptualise options in response to simultaneously presenting ideas or events; (3) *self-regulation*: the capacity to start and stop activities, or switch from one activity to another in response to feedback, to modulate the intensity of an action, and to maintain a flexible attitude in response to changing conditions; (4) *quality control*: the ability to monitor one's actions and correct performance on the basis of this feedback.

Lezak acknowledges the interaction between these four categories, even though they are implicitly presented in the form of a hierarchy, similar in concept to the model of behaviour as a hierarchy of function presented by Stuss and Benson (1986). In their model, self-awareness is regarded as the highest attribute of frontal function, which is why Lezak's category of quality control is so important to social behaviour.

Several authorities have referred to this as a major problem underlying what we now refer to as executive dysfunction. Luria (1973) refers to a series of studies carried out in conjunction with his Russian colleagues showing that frontal injury results in the loss of ability to check the results of actions against the original intention. Ironically, this defect can be present even when a person is able to recognise errors in other people's performance. Konow and Pribram (1970) pointed to the fact that even when a person is able to recognise errors he or she cannot always use the information to correct performance, a characteristic they refer to as a *loss of error utilisation*. Walsh (1985) also refers to the *uncritical attitude* which frontal patients show towards their own performance. Lezak (1989) sees this as a symptom of a more serious problem of self-awareness, indicating a lack of insight and social judgement.

Self-regulation is another important executive function which impinges on many forms of social and emotional behaviour. This is often associated with a garrulous speech pattern, reflecting a discursive, tangential thought process, making it difficult to conduct an interview because the person seems unable to give direct answers to simple questions, or responds in a circumstantial way, often on an unrelated and irrelevant theme, or jumps from one topic to another. When engaged on a task, performance is often rushed, either leading to errors or causing the rapid build-up of fatigue because people seem unable to pace themselves on a task. Too many jobs are taken on and usually not enough time is allowed to finish them. Consequently, the person becomes frustrated, demoralised and develops a sense of inadequacy from a lack of achievement in relation to the amount of effort expended.

Luria and Homskya (1964) refer to *anticipation* as an important frontal function involved in the regulation of behaviour. They refer to people with frontal damage being unable to regulate current actions in anticipation of their future consequences. This received experimental support from Tanaka (1973) studying frontal damage in monkeys, and Friedman, Bleiberg, and Freedland (1987), who studied human subjects. Both studies showed that frontal injury did not affect escape behaviour (a non-anticipatory reaction) but prevented avoidance learning, a response which does rely on anticipation. This may explain why many people with frontal injury "spontaneously" (impulsively) decide to do something (such as take a foreign holiday), yet are apparently incapable of addressing more routine social activities which involve planning and an anticipation of outcome.

SOCIAL HANDICAP

The social impact of neurobehavioural disability is evident from the way different characteristics of impairment and disability combine to compromise social roles. One of the most common combinations is diminished inhibitory control and labile mood. Mood shifts are associated with feelings of tension, tiredness, and irritability. In many cases, people become socially withdrawn and find the effort of mixing with others very stressful. Relatives often report that the injured family member retreats to a bedroom or some other quiet area in an attempt to become isolated from the family. Children and partners find this kind of social withdrawal difficult to understand and may feel rejected or unloved, beginning a process of alienation that can lead eventually to a breakdown of the relationship. Many relatives act in a resentful way to the socially aloof behaviour displayed by the brain injured person at such times. This can precipitate angry outbursts, placing further strains upon relationships. Friends find it difficult to relate to someone who may be unusually quiet and "edgy" at times, or who refuses to join in social activities, often pulling out at the last moment. They may gradually withdraw their friendship, preferring to relate to others who are more dependable and consistent in personal interactions.

At times of low mood, people are more vulnerable to the influence of noise, stress, frustration, fatigue, etc. The associated lack of inhibitory control means that a person is more likely to react impulsively under pressure, then lose control of the reaction, allowing it to escalate out of proportion to the incident precipitating it. Angry reactions associated with labile mood are characterised by their unpredictability. On a day when mood is at a good level a person may be relatively impervious to minor forms of frustration. The boisterous activity of a young child, for example, may be tolerated and even encouraged. Conversely, when in the grip of a "bad mood", the same event could lead to an outburst of temper which leaves the child feeling frightened and insecure because of the inconsistent parental response. If angry outbursts occur frequently and unpredictably they could have a serious impact on the parent–child relationship, leading to emotional maladjustment in the child, and contributing to discord in personal relationships, eventually undermining the viability of the family unit.

The cognitive dimension of social handicap is frequently linked to attention deficit. People find it difficult to focus and sustain attention. The effort of concentrating leads to fatigue, muscle tension, headaches, and irritability. When mixed with poor inhibitory control and labile mood one can appreciate how vulnerable such people can be in a work environment where they have to make an effort to concentrate, tolerate noise or other stresses, and maintain a pleasant and controlled social manner. In a person with little tolerance and limited inhibitory control, antagonistic and volatile behaviour is almost inevitable if, in the workplace for example, a supervisor makes a critical remark about poor performance. Emotional outbursts of this kind increase the risk of a worker being dismissed. This is one of the reasons why many brain injured people find it easier to get jobs than to keep them.

If we add to the above scenario the problems imposed by executive weakness, comprising problems of initiative, goal-directed behaviour, etc., another dimension is imposed which contributes to the development of socially unacceptable behaviour. Many people with executive disorders need prompting or other forms of guidance, supervision, feedback, etc. The brain injured person will not always recognise the relevance of such feedback and even if they do may resent what they perceive as constant criticism by others. Low tolerance, impulsiveness, and lack of regulatory control combine to produce an explosive mixture, especially in supported housing or other one-to-one care settings where close social proximity is inevitable. The frequent feedback and guidance required by brain injured people can become confrontational and lead to an antagonistic attitude on the part of the brain injured client to the family member or support worker charged with the client's day-to-day care. This can lead to a withdrawal of family support and the loss of paid support staff because of the challenging, often ungrateful and argumentative behaviour on the part of the brain injured client. Without support, many brain injured people live alone, confined to a very limited routine of activities, often not eating properly and neglecting personal hygiene. In some cases the social behaviour patterns of many brain injured people reflects the social drift patterns which characterised hebephrenic schizophrenics before the introduction of neuroleptic medication.

The net result of intrusive neurobehavioural problems is a significant reduction in the brain injured person's capacity to sustain family and social relationships or the social roles of parent and employee. There is also a significant risk of secondary emotional problems because of the insecurity experienced by many brain injured people as a result of unpredictable (and often unexplained) changes of mood and temperament. Their inability to maintain friendships leads to social isolation that can generate a hostile, even suspicious attitude which further alienates others. Social anxiety and a negative outlook can lead to reactive depression which becomes entrenched because executive deficits make it difficult for the individual to develop strategies to overcome social problems.

Unfortunately, many of those who sustain traumatic brain injury are in their late teens or early twenties, a time of life when immature thinking and impulsive, unconventional behaviour is the norm. Young people often reject parental values and stretch the tolerance of many in the community. If brain injury occurs at this time, or earlier in adolescence, the normal maturational process can be seriously affected. Many young people lack a maturational template to know what is required of them in various social situations, making their behaviour very difficult to tolerate or contain. When this is combined with diminished insight it leads to a serious lack of judgement and unwillingness to listen to the advice of others. The adverse consequences of this type of neurobehavioural disability is reflected in various social outcome studies. Brooks and McKinlay (1983) describe lack of insight as "a persistent problem and a significant predictor of poor social outcome". Thomsen (1989) makes a similar comment: "in young patients, immaturity and lack of insight have a negative influence on social outcome". In the author's experience, many young people drift into alcohol or drug subcultures and engage in petty offences of burglary, shoplifting or other "minor" crime. All too often, there is no external evidence of disability which could signal to police or other authorities that the individual is in need of special consideration.

As stated earlier in this chapter, neurobehavioural disability is often subtle but has a pervasive influence on human behaviour and an individual's capacity to maintain a reasonable quality of life. Many people with these patterns of disability have no neurological handicap and can appear as bright, eloquent, and physically fit, when in reality they are seriously disabled in a way that often does not fit into conventional medical or psychological categories of disability. As medical technology and standards of emergency care improve, many more people who would have died of brain injury will survive. The quality of their survival is questionable however, and will remain so until the full extent of neurobehavioural disability is understood because this will be a prerequisite for effective treatment at both the early stages of neurological recovery as well as later stages when complex neuropsychological problems predominate.

REFERENCES

Adolphs, R. (1999). Social cognition and the human brain. *Trends in Cognitive Science, 3,* 469–479.

Baddeley, A.D. (1986). *Working memory.* Oxford: Oxford University Press.

Blumer, D., & Benson, D.F. (1975). Personality changes with frontal and temporal lobe lesions. In D.F. Benson & D. Blumer (Eds.), *Psychiatric aspects of neurologic disease* (pp. 151–170). New York: Grune and Stratton.

Bond, M.R. (1984). The psychiatry of closed head injury. In D.N. Brooks (Ed.), *Closed head injury: Psychological, social and family consequences* (pp. 148–178). Oxford: Oxford University Press.

Brooks, D.N., & McKinlay, W. (1983). Personality and behavioural change after severe blunt head injury: A relative's view. *Journal of Neurology, Neurosurgery and Psychiatry, 46,* 336–344.

Burgess, P.W., & Wood, R.Ll. (1990). Neuropsychology of behaviour disorders following brain injury. In R.Ll. Wood (Ed.), *Neurobehavioural sequelae of traumatic brain injury.* London: Taylor and Francis.

Charcot, J.M. (1889). *Clinical lectures on diseases of the nervous system,* Vol III. London: New Sydenham Society.

Cummings, J.L. (1985). *Clinical neuropsychiatry.* London: Grune and Stratton.

Damasio, A.R. (1994) *Descartes' error: Emotion, reason and the human brain.* New York: Grosswell/Putnam.

Damasio, A.R., Tranel, D., & Damasio, H. (1990). Individuals with sociopathic behaviour caused by frontal damage. *Behavioural Brain Research, 41,* 81–94.

Davidson, R.J., & Irwin, W. (1999) The functional neuroanatomy of emotion and affective style. *Trends in Cognitive Science, 3,* 11–21.

Dimitrov, M., Phipps, T., Zahn, T.P., & Grafman, J. (1999). A thoroughly modern Gage. *Neurocase, 5,* 345–355.

Eames, P.G. (1990). Organic bases of behaviour disorders after traumatic brain injury. In R.Ll. Wood (Ed.), *Neurobehavioural sequelae of traumatic brain injury.* London: Taylor & Francis.

Eames, P.G. (1992). Hysteria following brain injury. *Journal of Neurology, Neurosurgery and Psychiatry, 55,* 1046–1053.

Eames, P.G., & Wood, R.Ll. (1984). Consciousness in the brain damaged adult. In R. Stevens (Ed.), *Aspects of consciousness.* London: Academic Press.

Eames, P.G., Cotterill, G., & Kneale, T.A. (1995). Outcome of intensive rehabilitation after severe brain injury: a long term follow-up study. *Brain Injury, 10,* 631–650.

Eslinger P.J. (1999). Orbitofrontal cortex: Historical and contemporary views about its behavioural and physiological significance. *Neurocase, 5,* 225–229.

Eslinger, P.J., & Damasio, A.R. (1985). Severe disturbances in higher cognition following bilateral frontal lone ablation: Patient EVR. *Neurology, 35,* 1731–1741.

Friedman, P.E., Bleiberg, J., & Freedland, K. (1987). Anticipatory behaviour deficits in closed head injury. *Journal of Neurology, Neurosurgery and Psychiatry, 50*, 398–401.

Grafman, J., Vance, S.C., & Weingarter, H. (1986). The effects of lateralised frontal lesions on mood regulation. *Brain, 109*, 1127–1148.

Greenwood, R. (1999). The consequences of brain injury: Classification and assessment of outcome. *Neuropsychological Rehabilitation, 9*, 231–241.

Greenwood, R., Bhalla, A., Gordon, A., & Roberts, J. (1983). Behaviour disturbance during recovery from herpes simplex encephalitis. *Journal of Neurology, Neurosurgery and Psychiatry, 46*, 809-817.

Grimshaw, L. (1964). Obsessional disorder and psychological illness. *Journal of Neurology, Neurosurgery and Psychiatry*, *27*, 229–231.

Gualtieri, T., & Cox, D.R. (1991). The delayed neurobehavioural sequelae of traumatic brain injury. *Brain Injury, 5*, 219–233.

Humphreys, G.W., & Forde, E.M. (1998). Disorganised action schema and action disorganisation syndrome. *Cognitive Neuropsychology, 15*, 771–811.

James, W. (1890). *The principles of psychology.* New York: Holt.

Jahanshah, M., & Frith, C.D. (1998). Willed action and its impairments. *Cognitive Neuropsychology, 15*, 483–533.

Jastrowitz, M. (1888). Beitrage zur localisation im grosshirn und uber deren praktische verwerthung. *Deutsche Medizinische Wochenschrift, 14*, 81–83.

Kimble D.P. (1963). *Physiological psychology.* Reading, MA: Addison-Wesley.

Kleist, K. (1931). Die storungen der ichleistungen und ihre lokalisation im orbital-, innen und zwischenhirn. *Monatsschrift fur Psychiatrie und Neurologie, 79*, 338–350.

Konow, A., & Pribram, K.H. (1970). Error recognition and utilization produced by injury to the frontal cortex in man. *Neuropsychologica, 8*, 489–491.

Lezak, M.D. (1978). Living with a characterologically brain injured patient. *Journal Clinical Psychiatry, 39*, 592–598.

Lezak, M. (1989). *Assessment of the behavioural consequences of head trauma.* New York: Alan R. Liss.

Lezak, M.D. (1995). *Neuropsychological Assessment, Third Edition.* Oxford: Oxford University Press.

Lipsey J.R., Robinson, R.G., Pearson, G.D., Krishna, R., & Price, T. R. (1983). Mood change following bilateral hemisphere brain injury. *British Journal of Psychiatry, 143*, 266–273.

Lishman, W.A. (1968). Brain damage in relation to psychiatric disability after head injury. *British Journal of Psychiatry, 116*, 373–410.

Lishman, W.A. (1978). *Organic psychiatry: The psychological consequences of cerebral disorders.* Boston: Blackwell Scientific.

Lishman, W.A. (1997). *Organic psychiatry (Third Edition): The psychological consequences of cerebral disorders.* Boston: Blackwell Scientific.

Luria, A.R. (1973). *The working brain: An introduction to neuropsychology* (B. Haigh, transl.). New York: Basic Books.

Luria, A.R., & Homskya, E.D. (1964). Disturbances in the regulative role of speech with frontal lobe lesions. In J.M. Warren & K.A. Ahert (Eds.), *The frontal granular cortex and behaviour.* New York: McGraw-Hill.

Mark, V.H., & Ervin, F.R. (1970). *Violence and the brain.* New York: Harper and Row.

Mathews, C., Shaw, D., & Klove, H. (1966). Psychological test performance in neurologic and pseudo-neurologic subjects. *Cortex, 2*, 244–253.

McKeon, J., McGuffin, P., & Robinson, P. (1984). Obsessive–compulsive neurosis following head injury: A report of four cases. *British Journal of Psychiatry, 144*, 190–192.

Meir, M.J., Benton, A.L., & Diller, L. (1987). *Neuropsychological rehabilitation*. London: Churchill Livingstone.

Milner, B. (1963). Effects of different brain lesions on card sorting. *Archives of Neurology, 9,* 90–100.

Milner, B., & Petrides, M. (1984). Behavioural effects of frontal lobe lesions in man. *Trends in Neuroscience, 7,* 403–407.

Newson, E. (1989). *Pathological demand avoidance syndrome: Diagnostic criteria and relationship to autism and other developmental coding disorders*. Nottingham: Child Development Research Unit, University of Nottingham.

Paget, J. (1873). Nervous mimicry of organic diseases. *Lancet, ii,* 511–513.

Pang, D. (1989). Physics and pathophysiology of closed head injury. In M. Lezak (Ed.), *Assessment of the behavioural consequences of head trauma* (pp. 1–17). New York: Alan Liss.

Post, R.M., Denicoff, K.D., Frye, M.A., & Leverich, G. (1997). Re-evaluating carbemazepine prophylaxis in bipolar disorder. *British Journal of Psychiatry, 170,* 202–204.

Raine, A., Meloy, J.R., Bihrle, S., & Stoddard, M.A. (1998). Reduced prefrontal and increased subcortical brain functioning, assessed using PET in predatory and affective murderers. *Behaviour, Science, Law, 16,* 319–332.

Reason, J.T. (1979). Actions not as planned. In G. Underwood & R. Stevens (Eds.), *Aspects of consciousness,* Vol. I. London: Academic Press.

Reason, J.T. (1984). Lapses of attention in everyday life. In R. Parasurman (Ed.), *Varieties of attention,* London: Academic Press.

Robertson, I.H. (1993). Rehabilitation of visuospatial, visuoperceptual and apraxic disorders. In R. Greenood, M. Barnes, T.M. McMillan, & T.Ward (Eds.), *Neurological rehabilitation* (pp. 179–189) London: Churchill Livingstone.

Rolls, E.T. (1975). *The brain and reward*. Oxford: Pergamon Press.

Rolls, E.T. (1999). *The brain and emotion*. Oxford: Oxford University Press.

Schefft, B.K., Malec, J.F., Lehr, B.K., & Kanfer, F.H. (1991). The role of self-regulation therapy with the brain injured patient. In M.E. Maruish & J.A. Moses (Eds.), *Clinical neuropsychology: Theoretical foundations for practitioners*. Hillsdale, NJ: Erlbaum.

Shallice, T. (1982). Specific impairments of planning. In D.E. Broadbent & L. Weiskrantz (Eds.), *The neuropsychology of cognitive function*. London: The Royal Society.

Shallice, T., & Burgess, P.W. (1991). Deficits in strategy application following frontal lobe damage in man. *Brain, 144,* 727–741.

Starkstein, S.E., & Robinson, R.G. (1989). Affective disorders and cerebrovascular disease. *British Journal of Psychiatry, 154,* 170–182.

Starkstein, S.E., & Robinson, R.G. (1991). The role of the frontal lobes in affective disorder following stroke. In H.S. Levin, H.M. Eisenberg & A.L. Benton (Eds.), *Frontal lobe function and dysfunction*. Oxford: Oxford University Press.

Stuss, D.T., & Benson, D.F. (1986). *The frontal lobes*. New York: Raven Press.

Tanaka, D. (1973). Effects of selective prefrontal decortication on escape behaviour in the monkey. *Brain Research, 53,* 161–173.

Thomsen, I.V. (1989). Do young patients have worse outcomes after severe blunt head trauma? *Brain Injury, 3,* 157–162.

Trimble, M.R., & Cummings, J.L. (1981). Neuropsychiatric disturbances following brain stem lesions. *British Journal of Psychiatry, 138,* 56–59.

van Zomeren, A.H., & Brouwer, W.H. (1994). *Clinical neuropsychology of attention*. New York: Oxford University Press.

Walsh, K.W. (1985). *Understanding brain damage: A primer of neuropsychological evaluation.* London: Churchill Livingstone.

Welt, L. (1888). Ueber charakterveranderungen des menschen infolge von lasionen des stirnhirns. *Deutsche Archiv fur Klinische Medizine, 42,* 339–390.

Whitlock, F.A. (1967). The aetiology of hysteria. *Acta Psychiatrica Scandinavia, 43,* 144–162.

WHO (1980). ICIDH: *International classification of impairment, disabilities and handicap.* A manual of classification relating to the consequences of disease. Geneva: WHO.

WHO (1997). *ICIDH-2: International classification of impairment, activities and participation.* A manual of disablement and functioning. Beta-1 draft for field trials. Geneva: WHO.

Wood, R.Ll. (1987). *Brain injury rehabilitation: A neurobehavioural approach,* London: Croom Helm.

Wood, R.Ll. (1992). Disorders of attention: Their effect on behaviour, cognition and rehabilitation. In B.A. Wilson & N. Moffat (Eds.), *Clinical management of memory problems.* London: Chapman and Hall.

Wood, R.Ll., & Eames, P.G. (1981). Applications of behaviour modification in the rehabilitation of traumatically brain injured patients. In G. Davey (Ed.), *Applications of conditioning theory.* London: Croom Helm.

Wood, R.Ll., & Yurdakul, L.K. (1997). Change in relationship status following traumatic brain injury. *Brain Injury, 11,* 491–502.

Wood R.Ll., McCrea, J., Wood, L.M., & Merriman, R.M. (1999). Clinical and cost effectiveness of post acute neurobehavioural rehabilitation. *Brain Injury, 13,* 69–88.

CHAPTER TWO

Distinguishing the neuropsychiatric, psychiatric, and psychological consequences of acquired brain injury

P.G. Eames
Grafton Manor Brain Injury Rehabilitation Unit,
Northants, UK

INTRODUCTION

Any injury to the brain inevitably disturbs the normal functioning of brain systems. In trying to understand the effects of injury on the person it is appropriate therefore to ask, "What does the brain do?" The simplest and ultimately the most accurate answer is "Everything". There is nothing that we sense, perceive, judge, do, think, recall, learn, feel, imagine, or create that is not done through the medium of brain mechanisms. Since most forms of injury have diffuse impacts, they are likely to interfere directly, to at least some extent, with a wide range of brain systems and therefore with a wide variety of brain functions. There are, of course, factors other than the brain injury that can cause disorders. These include the circumstances in which the injury occurred, its consequences for the individual's personal, social, and economic independence, as well as the rebound effects of the impacts it has on family, friends, and society at large. All of these may lead to secondary or reactive disorders, although their appearances may well be atypical because of distortion of the mechanisms through which they are expressed or indeed perceived, as a result of direct damage from the trauma to the brain.

In the treatment, management, and rehabilitation of the disorders that appear in the wake of an acquired brain injury, it is clearly of the greatest importance to distinguish between disorders that are primarily organic from those that are primarily reactive, or indeed unrelated to the injury but coincidental in time, since it is likely that understanding the true nature of a problem will lead to its best management. In other words, accurate diagnosis is essential to efficient treatment. The process of medical diagnosis basically involves the recognition of patterns of symptoms and signs and of their development over time. Patterns are made up of

29

individual elements and it is essential that each individual element in a perceived pattern be as accurately identified as the pattern itself. Thus the process of diagnosis must seek to identify the elements present in a disorder, and then to recognise some pattern that matches a "template" in the knowledge base of the observer. Each step requires the same degree of accuracy. In addition, the knowledge base must contain the right templates. These requirements present some difficulties for practitioners of all kinds in the context of acquired brain injury; but since so many of its consequences affect emotional and behavioural aspects of the injured person's life, the difficulties are of special importance to the psychiatrist and the psychologist, whose usual stores of templates tend mainly to match disorders that arise from primary mental illnesses or that are reactive to stresses of various kinds, rather than matching those that result directly from traumatic disturbances of brain mechanisms.

First, it is important to distinguish between *symptoms* and *diagnoses* (or *elements* and *patterns*). For example, "headache" is not a diagnosis, it is simply a broad description of a symptom. There are standard *classifications* of the different kinds of headaches, based on the detailed analysis of particular features, that allow a full diagnosis of the nature and cause of the headache to be reached, thus facilitating treatment and management. In the same way, "behaviour disorder" and "emotional disturbance" are not diagnoses. There are extensive classifications of emotional ("psychiatric") disorders; there is no doubt that the successful management of disorders of social behaviour also requires some kind of classification. Although there is no universally agreed taxonomy at present, Eames (1988) has suggested a framework that has proved useful in practice. It attempts to classify both behaviours (elements) and some "syndromes" (patterns) and is therefore somewhat cumbersome, but probably no more so than the prevailing attempts at the taxonomy of general psychiatric disorders (DSM-IV and ICD10).

For practical and classificatory purposes "behaviours" can be thought of as complexes or sequences of actions that may show evidence of purpose, affect, perception, or cognition; they can be identified only through observation and objective description; they can be quantified only through measurement. (It is essential to avoid the temptation to "interpret" them in terms of motive or explanation, rather than describe them in objective terms; the misunderstandings that can result from nurses' and carers' "identification" of seizures, rather than description of the events, are well known to epileptologists in much the same way.) The necessary parameters for measurement depend to some extent on the specific behaviour, but usually include location, occasion, frequency, amplitude, duration, content, and consequences (see Wood & Worthington, 1999). "Syndromes" are by definition clusters (patterns) of behaviours that are usually seen together. They can be identified by inspection, or by statistical analysis of the findings of behavioural observations across individuals and over time.

IDENTIFYING ABNORMAL FEATURES

In trying to identify individual features (symptoms, "elements", or items of disordered behaviour) it is important to remember that the descriptive details must be correct and therefore the terminology must be exact. For example, brief nocturnal wakings and early morning waking could both be described loosely as "poor sleep", but they have quite different implications for diagnosis. Similarly, shouting abuse and homicide are both "aggression", but their social impact is very different.

"Headache" provides a particularly useful example of misidentifications that can arise. Pounding unilateral headache and "a tight band round the head" are both "headache", but they have very different causes. After head injury the commonest kind is *post-concussional* headache: It is present from the start, it affects the vertex or the whole head, has a steady persistent quality, is usually described as "tight" or "a pressure", has no regular accompaniments apart from an unpleasant feeling of arousal or non-specific dizziness, and in the majority of patients tends to improve progressively as time goes by. On the other hand *post-traumatic migraine* tends to appear after an initial delay, is either unilateral, localised or sometimes global, is episodic, has a throbbing quality, is usually accompanied by photophobia and nausea (and sometimes vomiting), may be associated with drowsiness or even syncope, and shows little tendency to reduced frequency over long periods of time. Clearly these kinds of headaches are quintessentially distinct and need to be distinguished in the identification of post-traumatic syndromes. If one merely identifies "headache", one cannot reach an accurate diagnosis or achieve the appropriate treatment.

Confusion

A feature that often causes difficulty within the range of acknowledged traumatic disorders is "confusion". Disorientation in time and place, and initially sometimes even in person, is consistently present in the early stages of the emergence from coma. Post-traumatic confusional states of this kind involve all aspects of cognition, are continuous although usually fluctuating in degree, resolve gradually but progressively, and are associated with amnesia for the period of duration of the state. Quite distinct, but easily confused with "confusion" unless attention is paid to the detail of the mental state, are a number of specific "misidentification disorders", of which by far the most common is Reduplicative Paramnesia (Benson, Gardner, & Meadows, 1976) affecting place or time orientation (or both). In this disorder the "confusions" are restricted to those domains, are pervasive, and resolve by becoming episodic with progressive reductions in frequency, duration, and intensity. Most commonly, this disorder resolves spontaneously within just a week or two after the end of the post-traumatic confusional state, but in some people it may continue for many months, despite positive evidence of the restoration of ongoing day-to-day memory. Probably the most useful distinguishing feature is that reduplicative symptoms usually outlast the period of post-traumatic confusion, so that the reduplicative "false beliefs" are later remembered, often with embarrassment. During this early stage of recovery it is also possible for dysphasia to be misinterpreted as "confusion", because the person's verbal output seems bizarre or incomprehensible, but this error can be avoided by careful attention to the detail of the mental state examination.

Depression

In later stages of recovery the identification of "depression" is particularly difficult, but important. This is a topic that has been considerably muddied by the application of rating scales, most notably the Beck and Hamilton scales. The latter was explicitly designed for the purpose of measuring the *severity* of states of depressed mood and its changes over time in response to treatment: Hamilton himself made it abundantly clear that it was not intended to be a diagnostic instrument. Close examination of the Beck scale shows that it answers the same kind of need, rather than diagnosis. Unfortunately both have been used for just that purpose in numerous studies of affective disorders after brain injury, leading to claims that anything from 10 to 77% of individuals suffering acquired brain injury suffer from "major affective disorder" (Fedoroff et al., 1992; Gualtieri and Cox, 1991; Jorge, Robinson, Starkstein, & Arndt, 1994; Linn, Allen, & Willer, 1994; Robinson, 1997; Rosenthal, Christensen, & Ross, 1998). The inference has often been that injury to particular areas of the brain "causes" affective disorder. However, the fact that studies comparing those with acquired brain injury with those suffering non-cerebral forms of chronic disease have shown little difference in the incidence of affective disorders measured in this way (Pincus et al., 1986) suggests that loss of autonomy and independence is depressing in itself and is probably the major cause of this kind of "affective disorder".

It is clear that self-rating scales are inadequate when it comes to making a distinction between primary affective disorders and understandable reactive states. Given the losses of independence and of family and social "power" experienced by those who suffer severe brain injury, the fact that many feel miserable, powerless, and unsatisfied with their lives is hardly surprising. It seems overwhelmingly likely that the apparently very large increase in the incidence of "affective disorders" comes from reactive states easily understood in terms of the adverse effects on life situation. It is common experience in head injury follow-up clinics (personal observation) that such states usually appear late and gradually after injury, as the person becomes self-aware and begins to perceive the changes in his or her life: This is an essentially normal, indeed healthy development, although it demands a great deal of support and understanding from both professional and family contacts. (It is important to understand that almost always the last higher cognitive function to return after traumatic brain injury is self-awareness, a topic that has been discussed particularly by Prigatano, e.g., 1990.) Later in recovery, when the injured individual begins to confront the effects of the changes in social and economic terms, there is often a depressive reaction, again demanding support (for both individual and family), backed up by information about what may be expected and what might be done to begin to establish a new way of life, together with understanding and implicit acceptance. What such developments do not need, however, is antidepressant drug treatment. (An exception to this principle is that individuals with marked pre-morbid obsessional traits may find it particularly difficult to deal with such disappointments by "leaving them behind" and may be helped by the anti-obsessional effects of specific serotonin reuptake inhibitors [SSRIs] [personal observation and Amit, Smith, & Gill, 1991; DeVeaugh-Geiss, 1994; Murphy et al., 1989].

Nevertheless among the references cited above there does appear to be evidence of an increase in the incidence of *typical* depressive and indeed hypomanic illnesses in those who have suffered severe acquired brain injury, probably about 5–10%, compared with 2% in the general population (see Lishman, 1998). However, neither published descriptions nor clinical experience suggests that these illnesses differ in any clinically identifiable way from "spontaneous" or primary illnesses of the same kinds, supporting the possibility that at least some kinds of injury to the brain can cause them. The clinical picture of depressive illnesses is quite different from that seen in reactive states, regardless of the kinds of life stresses that produce them. As in ordinary psychiatric practice, important distinguishing features of depressive illness (as distinct from reactive states) are the prominence of "biological" features (early morning waking, loss of appetite and weight, diurnal variation with mornings the worst and evenings the best, constipation, psychomotor retardation), lack of responsiveness to happy events and circumstances, and the presence of feelings of guilt and unworthiness.

There are two specific traumatic disorders that may be confused with depressive illness ("Major Depressive Disorder"). The first usually results from high midbrain lesions, but sometimes bilateral cortical lesions, and is traditionally known by names like "pseudobulbar palsy", "pathological laughing and crying", "emotional lability" or "emotionality". The problem with such terms is that they tend to suggest that it is a disorder of emotion, whereas it is in reality a disorder of the midbrain mechanisms concerned with the *outward expression* of emotion. It was in order to focus on this fact that Eames and Papakostopoulos (1990) suggested the term "dysprosopeia", derived from the Greek word for the smiling and crying masks of the ancient theatre. (It is a term that has the additional advantage of being able to be turned easily into an adjective!) The depressed mood of a primary depressive illness is pervasive, usually shows a consistent diurnal pattern, and is expressed in facial and bodily appearances that overtly match the described mood. Dysprosopeia, on the other hand, presents with clear-cut brief episodes of a depressed appearance (usually rather grotesque weeping), set against otherwise normal affective behaviour, and during which the individual is aware of behaving in a way that does not match his or her inner feelings. The crucial diagnostic procedure is simply to ask the person about his or her inner feelings at the time, because these do not match the outer appearances. Often the person is embarrassed by this and is aware of the misconstruction put upon the behaviour by observers.

The second confusing disorder is distinguished from depressive syndromes in much the same way. It consists of the driveless, inert state that can be produced by lesions of the medial frontal (particularly the cingulate) cortex, especially if this is bilateral (see Chapter 1). It is characterised by almost complete lack of initiative and activity in the absence of definite external stimuli, and by an overall appearance and demeanour of depressed mood. When the individual is questioned, however, lowered mood is consistently denied; there is little variation except when others initiate interactions, when the individual briefly seems quite normal (within the limitations imposed by any other deficits, of course).

IDENTIFYING SYNDROMES

When trying to recognise clusters of symptoms or disordered behaviours it is helpful to recognise that there are four different kinds of "syndromes". There are those that (1) simply consist of a stereotyped cluster of core features that regularly appear together (e.g., the episodic dyscontrol syndrome), (2) have a unifying patho-physiological cause (e.g., depressive illness or major affective disorder, or the abulic syndrome) and (3) consist of a chance concatenation through either (3a) shared anatomy (e.g., frontal lobe or Gerstmann's syndromes), or (3b) the mechanism of injury (e.g., the "triad" of normal pressure hydrocephalus, Adams et al., 1965). Table 2.1 gives a simple classification of post-traumatic syndromes affecting behaviour and mood.

Major mental illness

Pure "psychiatric" syndromes (forms of schizophrenia, paranoid states, hypomania, manic-depressive disorders) are readily recognisable through the criteria specified in various taxonomic systems, specifically DSM-IV and ICD10. There are insuperable difficulties in distinguishing between truly primary disorders and those that result directly from brain injury, especially with psychotic and major affective disorders, since the features are usually identical: At a purely clinical level it is not possible to identify such illnesses one way or the other. Nevertheless there is solid evidence that such illnesses occur with increased frequency after brain injury, particularly when this is severe (Davison, 1983; Davison & Bagley, 1969). This has more medico-legal than clinical importance, because the treatment approach is basically the same. Primary disorders are more likely to occur in people with a family or previous history of similar illnesses, although this cannot be used as a basis for diagnosis in any one individual, since the associations are only probabilistic. The writer's personal clinical experience suggests that psychotic illnesses are characterised principally by paranoid ideation and reduced initiative.

TABLE 2.1

Classification of post-traumatic behavioural syndromes

Psychiatric syndromes
  Phobic anxiety disorder
  Affective disorders
    Manic-depressive illness
    Depressive illness
    Hypomania
  Schizophreniform disorders

Post-concussional syndrome

Frontal lobe syndromes
  Orbitofrontal (disinhibited, egocentric)
  Lateral frontal (dysexecutive)
  Medial frontal/cingulate (aspontaneous)

Temporo-limbic syndromes
  Episodic dyscontrol syndrome
  Temporo-limbic affective disorders
    Dysphoric
    Manic-depressive
    Anxiety/panic
    Psychotic

Syndromes of the very diffuse brain insults
  Abulia (especially from raised intracranial pressure)
  The "hysteria" syndrome (especially from hypoxic insults)

Sometimes auditory hallucinations are reported. These occur with or without the "first rank" feature of being in the third person, and without any degree of "thought disorder" or passivity features. This description is more frequent after brain injury than "typical" schizophrenic pictures, but there have been no formal studies to examine this question. From a practical point of view, the most important consideration is that, because the injured brain is more susceptible to a variety of adverse drug effects, including dopaminergic and cholinergic blockade and the risk of precipitating epilepsy, it is necessary to be especially thoughtful and cautious in selecting drug treatments, choosing those with the least probability of adverse effects.

A possible confusion can occur between the orbitofrontal syndrome and hypomanic states, because both tend to present with euphoria and relative overactivity, but the combination of appropriate expectation (some forms of injury can be expected to cause frontal problems) with attention to the detail of the abnormalities of mood and behaviour should avoid this.

There are several so-called "encapsulated" psychotic syndromes. Some of these have strong associations with brain disorder, for example some of the "misidentification syndromes" such as the Capgras syndrome, in which the individual believes that he or close relatives or friends have been replaced by false but identical doubles. Others are probably unconnected with brain injury, but can occur by coincidence or as a secondary result of perceptual or cognitive disorder: an example is the syndrome of Pathological Jealousy. Like the other major mental illnesses, these require antipsychotic treatment, so that the same care in the choice of medications is essential to avoid adverse effects as far as is possible.

Post-concussional syndrome

The post-concussional syndrome (PCS), best characterised by its core symptoms of post-concussional headache (see earlier), dizziness and noise intolerance, but often associated with fatigue, irritability, depressed mood, and poor concentration and memory, is complex because it most often follows minor injuries (indeed it is rare after more severe ones). Traditionally the "proper" diagnosis (as characterised by the core features listed above) has been reserved for patients who still have their symptoms beyond the period expected on the basis of the duration of post-traumatic amnesia. Lishman (1988) has argued persuasively that, whereas the acute self-limiting version of the syndrome has clear organic causes, the chronic version is determined mainly by factors related to personality, life events, and the features of the causative circumstances. This view receives considerable support from neurophysiological studies (Fenton, 1996), which have shown a strong correlation between abnormalities of brainstem evoked responses and symptoms that persist from the beginning, but poor correlations between the responses and symptoms in those who experience a delayed exacerbation, who also have a much higher incidence of adverse social and personality factors. There is also a small subset of individuals who develop the typical symptoms of PCS after very mild or even no concussive injury and whose brainstem evoked responses are normal from the outset. Not surprisingly, these individuals are likely to have the highest contribution from adverse personality features, although for the time being they represent the most puzzling group as far as an overall understanding of the syndrome is concerned. (They should not, however, be confused with those who suffer PCS after clear-cut "whiplash injury" without apparent injury to the head: The mechanics of such injuries are capable of causing concussion, especially if the person's head is turned even slightly to one side at the moment of impact, because the forces involved readily induce the oscillatory movements of the brain within the skull that are responsible for concussive injury.)

PCS tends to be over-diagnosed (Lishman, 1998). Sometimes this is because of a failure to identify the symptoms with sufficient accuracy (see section on identifying abnormal features earlier). Table 2.2 illustrates this by contrasting the typical symptoms of PCS with those of a patient who appeared superficially to have the same cluster of symptoms, but in whom each of the individual symptoms had features that were qualitatively different from the classical ones, had alternative origins and were amenable to individual specific treatments in a way that was much more effective than the usual treatment strategies advocated for PCS. For example, his headaches were of migraine type rather than post-concussional (see section on identifying abnormal features), his "dizziness" was in fact of the benign positional vertigo type rather than non-specific postural dizziness, his "irritability" was not pervasive but consisted in occasional dramatic outbursts of episodic dyscontrol, and so on. Not one of his symptoms said to be a part of PCS had the qualities of the typical components of the syndrome. A more common cause of over-diagnosis is that the term tends to be used loosely to indicate a variety of symptoms typically experienced (usually briefly) after *any* concussional brain injury, rather than restricting it to those who present the established core features that do not resolve in the usual way. As with any complex disorder, accurate diagnosis is essential for adequate treatment. If each individual element has an individual cause (as in Table 2.2), then each deserves specific treatment. If not, then the treatment of the "proper" syndrome is likely to be difficult and protracted, increasingly as the time since injury increases.

TABLE 2.2
Syndromes of disordered behaviour: Post-concussional syndrome (PCS)

PCS	Mr M's symptoms
Post-consussional headache	Cervical migraine and spondylosis
Postural dizziness	Benign positional vertigo
Noise intolerance	Reduced, distorted hearing in one ear
Irritability	Episodic dyscontrol syndrome
Attentional deficit	Persisting cognitive deficits (PTA 6 days)

PTA; post-traumatic amnesia

"Personality disorder"

"Personality disorder" is a difficult concept, because it is all too easy to confuse it with "behaviour disorder". The difference between personality and behaviour is the same as the difference between climate and weather or between temperament and mood: The first describes a general tendency, the latter a temporary, current state. The most "typical" frontal lobe disorder, which results from orbitofrontal injury and consists of a mixture of social disinhibition, childishness, egocentricity, and a lack of awareness of the needs and "rights" of others, certainly qualifies as a disorder or change of personality. Unlike *primary* personality disorders, however, this kind of frontal lobe disorder tends to improve over time. Sometimes, when the frontal lobe injury is not particularly severe, the improvement occurs progressively during the first months or years after injury. But even in more severe cases, there is likely to be gradual recovery over many years. Planned and sometimes chance follow-up often reveals remarkable improvements in the person's ability to develop more normal social interactions, and even increased ability to take responsibility and to manage everyday aspects of personal, domestic and even community and financial management (personal observations). The importance of this phenomenon is that in general and forensic psychiatric practice there is an understandable tendency to assume that disorders of personality are untreatable and unchangeable, whereas traumatic *changes* of personality may well resolve, even if only gradually over many years.

Of the changes in the person that are most easily mislabelled "personality disorder", the dysexecutive syndrome can be especially elusive, because it is not possible to identify it simply on examination. Relatives' descriptions of difficulties with everyday "complex tasks" and of changes from pre-injury abilities need to be taken seriously, and problems should not lightly be dismissed as evidence of mere fecklessness or primary "personality disorder". It is worth remembering that Eslinger and Damasio (1985) described their dysexecutive patient as suffering from "acquired sociopathy". Wood expands on the social impacts of the dysexecutive syndrome in Chapter 1 of this volume.

Post-traumatic temporo-limbic disorders

The commonest confusions between "primary" psychiatric illnesses and those that stem specifically from brain injury arise in relation to disorders of behavioural control and mood, the so-called "temporo-limbic disorders" (Monroe, 1970, 1986). Because these latter are relatively poorly known, they will be described and considered in some detail.

The commonest is the episodic dyscontrol syndrome (EDS), characterised by core features identified in the two large series that first clarified the disorder (Bach-y-Rita, Lion, Climent, & Ervin, 1971; Elliott, 1982) and shown in Table 2.3.

TABLE 2.3
Classification of post-traumatic behavioural syndromes

Core features	Explosive aggression:
	Sudden and short-lived
	Agitated, abusive, destructive
	"Out of character" for the individual
	Discrete episodes
	Trivial or no trigger
	Often (1/3 episodes) patchy amnesia
	Followed by remorse, depression, tiredness
	Victims usually emotionally closest (rarely children)
Associated features	Impulsivity
	Using a vehicle as a weapon
	Anomalous sexual behaviour
Clinical associations	Developmental disorder ("minimal brain dysfunction" or "multiple neuro-developmental anomalies")
	Traumatic brain injury
	Haemorrhagic brain injury (subarachnoid or intracerebral)
	Temporal lobe tumours
	Temporal lobe epilepsy
	Sex: male–female ratio 3–4:1
	(Socioeconomic status appears not to be important)

Commonly but not universally associated features are general impulsivity, the use of a car (or other vehicle) as a weapon, and various anomalies of sexual behaviour, mainly of an aggressive but unpredictable kind. There is a male:female ratio of about 3–4:1; very similar features were found both by Bach-y-Rita in an inner-city emergency department and by Elliott in private practice, so that socioeconomic status does not appear to be an important determinant. The most common clinical associations are with developmental disorders (once known as "minimal brain damage", and later as "minimal brain dysfunction", terms that are no longer used) and with previous brain injury from trauma or subarachnoid haemorrhage. Occasionally it is seen in a context of temporal lobe epilepsy or even temporal lobe tumour (Elliott, 1982).

Traumatic brain injury can cause shallow irritability and outburst behaviours in other ways and can of course happen to individuals with pre-existing aggressive personality disorders. It is therefore important to make the diagnosis of EDS only if the core features are unequivocally present, because it has become clear that there are specific treatments that are very effective, but that have little impact on other causes of "aggressiveness". Post-traumatic and frontal irritability are both characterised by pervasive "snappiness" which is present from immediately after the recovery of consciousness; they follow almost any frustration or other stress, gradually improve over time, and are usually apparent to the sufferer, who tends to see them as justified by the circumstances. Outbursts of EDS, in contrast, usually first appear after a delay of weeks, months, or sometimes years, occur in brief, clear-cut episodes usually seen as "out of character" for the individual, are unpredictably provoked by trivial triggers, tend to persist or worsen over time, and are almost always followed by remorse, despite amnesia for the events in many cases. Despite the clarity and specificity of the published descriptions, EDS does not yet find a proper place in the major classifications of psychiatric disorders. In ICD it appears as "impulse control disorders not elsewhere classified". In DSM-IV it exists as "intermittent explosive disorder", with criteria that closely match those described by Bach-y-Rita and Elliott, but additional criteria exclude the diagnosis if there is evidence of impulsivity or sociopathy.

What has been less clear in the literature, because descriptions, despite being sufficiently detailed in themselves, have not been collected together, is that there are other definable syndromes that are likely to be closely related to EDS because they are also characterised by paroxysmal changes. These may be changes of mood (including anxiety), episodes of confusion, or rarely even paranoid states.

By far the most common paroxysmal disorder of mood is non-specific dysphoria. However, "classical" depressed and hypomanic clinical pictures can be seen, often distinguishable from typical "major affective disorders" only by their temporal pattern and short duration (Monroe, 1986; Hellekson, Buckland, & Price, 1979): episodes usually last for hours or a day or two, occasionally as long as a week, but never longer than two weeks. These are particularly likely to cause diagnostic confusion in outpatient settings, if antidepressant drugs are prescribed before the true temporal pattern has been identified: When seen after two or three weeks the patient may well be normal, fulfilling the expectation of a treatment response thus seeming to confirm the original (incorrect) diagnosis. It may be some time before a subsequent appointment happens to coincide with another episode of altered mood, at which point it becomes clear that the appearance of a treatment response was illusory.

Episodes of acute anxiety, of either diffuse or panic types, without clear precipitants or adequate psychogenesis, have been reported (Brodsky & Zuniga, 1978; Harper & Roth, 1962): These tend to be very short, lasting from minutes to an hour or two. Of similar duration to the affective disorders are episodes of frank confusion (which have to be distinguished from partial status epilepticus) (Bacon & Haslam, 1982; Pond, 1957), milder disorders amounting to clumsiness and "incompetence" (personal observation), or paranoid states, sometimes with auditory hallucinations (Bacon and Haslam, 1982; Monroe, 1982; Pond, 1957). In almost all of these various disorders the onset and offset of individual episodes are usually abrupt and are often described by the patient and by relatives or friends as happening "like a switch", although sometimes the change occurs after sleep. Explosive outbursts of the episodic dyscontrol kind can be associated with any of these paroxysmal disorders, in which case they are more likely to occur during the altered state than at other times (personal observations).

As with EDS, there seems to be no proper place for these affective disorders in the ICD or DSM classifications, although both of these do include "brief affective disorder", with criteria that are only partially restrictive by requiring "at least one episode a month for one year". This excludes individuals with less regular frequencies, for example, with several episodes in a week, but periods of freedom of more than a month. In the author's clinical experience, these various episodic disorders, like EDS itself, have a high probability of being prevented by treatment with carbamazepine (Lewin & Sumners, 1992; Maletzky, 1973; Monroe, 1989; Stein, 1992; Stone, McDaniel, Hughes, & Hermann, 1986).

Disorders of drive and motivation

"Motivation" is a complex and difficult issue, since it represents the "final common path" of the interaction of a wide range of brain functions (see Chapter 1). These include drive, arousal, perceptions and memories of incentive and reward, the ability to initiate movements (initiation) or activities (initiative), and the whole range of cognitive abilities that allow the analysis of the environmental, emotional, and existential characteristics of situations.

Drive disorder

"Drive" is an individual characteristic that in the general population varies considerably and is recognised in lay terms. After brain injury it may be significantly diminished; in the author's experience this occurs most typically after severe brainstem injuries, whether from direct impacts (as in low blows to the side of the head, for example) or from compression secondary to sustained raised intracranial pressure as a result of intracranial haematoma or reactive brain swelling. Typically such individuals show a "brainstem syndrome" characterised by both spasticity and rigidity of the limbs, dysarthria (or even anarthria), and swallowing difficulties, often in a context of relatively well-preserved cognitive abilities. They have low arousal, excessive sleepiness, and marked fatiguability, but can be provoked by increased general and perceptual stimulation into increased activity which persists for as long as the stimulation lasts (within the limitations imposed by fatiguability). They usually show normal facial and bodily expressiveness, as far as their neurological disorder allows. There is some evidence to suggest that this kind of disorder may improve with treatment with stimulant drugs (Glenn, 1998) or with regular vestibular stimulation (Goodman-Smith & Turnbull, 1983).

Abulia

Lesions that destroy cells or axons of the dopaminergic meso-cingulate system produce the syndrome of abulia (Fisher, 1983). The individual is usually alert and has normal sleep duration, but shows little or no initiative and is slow to initiate movements in response to command, whether from within or without. As a result the picture, in repose, resembles a "butter sculpture", and the individual can be stimulated into activity only briefly, usually only by a good deal of "razamatazz" or by unexpected stimuli. Fisher described the specific energising effect of the telephone. Invariably there are associated static and dynamic disorders of extrapyramidal motor function, such as cogwheel rigidity at rest or on contralateral effort ("activated rigidity"), impassive facies except when specifically stimulated, and sometimes more gross manifestations such as chorea. Abulia predictably responds to treatment with direct dopamine agonists like bromocriptine, with the curious feature that a fairly short period of treatment usually results in prolonged if not permanent improvement (Eames, 1989; Powell, al-Adawi, Morgan, & Greenwood, 1996).

Anergia, aspontaneity, "apathy", "inertia"

As mentioned earlier in the section on depression, a somewhat similar clinical picture occurs in those who have suffered destructive lesions of the cingulate gyrus itself, commonly, for example, after anterior cerebral artery infarction. The main differences from the abulic syndrome are that such individuals usually appear quite normal in repose (without the "butter sculpture" feature) and do not show extrapyramidal motor disorders. The result is usually an overall appearance of retarded depression, although they typically deny any depression of mood if asked. They describe or admit to interest in doing things, though even when apparently chosen activities are made immediately available, they do not pursue them. This disorder does not have an agreed name, though expressions used to describe it in standard neurological texts include "aspontaneity" and "anergia"; it has much in common with classical descriptions of "apathy" in psychiatric texts. It is important to distinguish it from abulia, because it results from damage to the target neurones of the dopaminergic meso-cingulate system and therefore does not respond to treatment with dopamine agonists.

"Hysteria" following brain injury

After any of the "very diffuse" insults (hypoxia from any cause, or hypoglycaemia) a proportion of victims begin, often after an initial delay, to show evidence of disordered behaviour with characteristics that resemble the gross hysterical disorders described in the last century by Charcot (Eames, 1992), although with some features that are more akin to the pathological demand avoidance syndrome of Newson (1989). The feature that is most obvious, although often not noticed for some time because of the apparent implications, is a manipulative kind of playfulness; very frequent are variations on the theme of the so-called Ganser symptom ("approximate answers"); both neurological and psychological dissociative symptoms are usual; there is a general lack of hedonic responsiveness that probably underlies the universal feature of failure to change behaviour despite consistent positive reinforcement. More often than not, the individual seems quite unable to change behaviour in ways that would increase social acceptability, despite apparently being aware that this would enhance his or her quality of life. The incidence of this disorder is about equal between the sexes and across age groups; there is no greater vulnerability in terms of family or personal psychiatric history in those that develop it than in those with similar degrees of severity of other kinds of insult who do not, except that a parental history of psychopathic disorder is probably more common. Thus it seems possible that the very diffuse brain insults are capable of producing hysterical disorder *de novo*. No specific treatment has so far proved effective, but the best outcomes have been achieved (Eames et al., 1996) with an approach that avoids direct confrontation or "demand", but attempts to set up situations so that the most "normal" responses are implicit. For example, a person who claimed to know or remember nothing about anything, and to be incapable of even the most simple task whenever he was asked directly, managed on a pub visit to go to the bar, buy the requested drinks for four companions and bring them back to the right people, when simply asked "Is it your round?"

"Reactive" emotional disorders

Although many of the disturbances of affect and behaviour seen after acquired brain injury are generated specifically by direct effects of the injury itself, there certainly are many problems and emotional difficulties that result from the individual's reaction to increasing awareness of changes in both person and life situation. In principle these should be dealt with through the same techniques as are used in any other group of people with "life-reactive" disorders. It is important to remember, however, and therefore to attempt to assess, the cognitive deficits that are more or less the rule after brain injury, because they may well be sufficient to prevent adequate use of many standard psychotherapeutic techniques. (Prigatano, 1989 disputes this.) It is important always to keep in mind the particular vulnerability of the injured brain to most of the predictable adverse effects of psychotropic medications.

CONCLUSION

A number of disorders of emotion or behaviour following acquired brain injury superficially resemble primary or reactive psychiatric disorders, yet are based in specific aspects of injury to brain systems. Learning to distinguish them can suggest treatment approaches that are more likely to be successful, and less likely to be harmful, than the treatments presupposed by an assumption that the disorders are of primary psychiatric types.

REFERENCES

Adams, R.D., Fisher, C.M., Hakim, S., Ojemann, R.G., & Sweet, W.H. (1965). Symptomatic hydrocephalus with "normal" cerebrospinal fluid pressure: A treatable syndrome. *New England Journal of Medicine, 273*, 117–126.

Amit, Z., Smith, B.R., & Gill, K. (1991). Serotonin uptake inhibitors: Effects on motivated consummatory behaviors. *Journal of Clinical Psychiatry, 52* (Suppl.), 55–60.

Bach-y-Rita, G., Lion, J.R., Climent, C.E., & Ervin, F.R. (1971). Episodic dyscontrol: A study of 130 violent patients. *American Journal of Psychiatry, 127*, 1473–8.

Bacon C., & Haslam M. (1982). Psychiatric presentation of psychomotor epilepsy. *British Journal of Clinical Social Psychiatry, 2*, 16–17.

Benson, D.F., Gardner H., & Meadows, J.C. (1976). Reduplicative paramnesia. *Neurology, 26*, 147–151.

Brodsky, L., & Zuniga, J. (1978). *Refractory anxiety: A masked epileptiform disorder*. Paper presented to the IInd World Congress of Biological Psychiatry.

Davison, K. (1983). Schizophrenia-like psychoses associated with organic cerebral disorder: A review. *Psychiatry and Development, 1*, 1–33.

Davison, K., & Bagley, C.R. (1969). Schizophrenia-like psychoses associated with organic disorders of the central nervous system: A review of the literature. In R.N. Herrington (Ed.), *Current problems in neuropsychiatry, British Journal of Psychiatry,* Special Publication No. 4, 113–184.

DeVeaugh-Geiss, J. (1994). Pharmacologic therapy of obsessive compulsive disorder. *Advances in Pharmacology, 30*, 35–52.

Eames, P. (1988). Behavior disorders after severe brain injury: Their nature, causes and strategies for management. *Journal of Head Trauma Rehabilitation, 3*, 1–6.

Eames, P. (1989). The use of sinemet and bromocriptine [Letter]. *Brain Injury, 3*, 319–322.

Eames, P. (1992). Hysteria following brain injury. *Journal of Neurology, Neurosurgery and Psychiatry, 55*, 1046–1053.

Eames, P., & Papakostopoulos, D. (1990). Crying and laughing after brain damage [Letter]. *Journal of Neurology, Neurosurgery and Psychiatry, 53*, 1111.

Eames, P., Cotterill, G., Kneale, T.A., Storrar, A.L., & Yeomans, P. (1996). Outcome of intensive rehabilitation after severe brain injury: A long-term follow-up study. *Brain Injury 10*, 631-650.

Elliott, F.A. (1982). Neurological findings in adult minimal brain dysfunction and the dyscontrol syndrome. *Journal of Nervous and Mental Disease, 170*, 680–687.

Eslinger, P.J., & Damasio, A.R. (1985). Severe disturbance of higher cognition after bilateral frontal lobe ablation: Patient EVR. *Neurology, 35*, 1731–1740.

Fedoroff, J.P., Starkstein, S.E., Forrester, A.W., Geisler, F.H., Jorge R.E., Arndt, S.V., & Robinson, R.G. (1992). Depression in patients with acute traumatic brain injury. *American Journal of Psychiatry, 7*, 918–923.

Fenton, G.W. (1996). The postcussional syndrome reappraised. *Clinical Electroencephalography, 27*, 174–182.

Fisher, C.M. (1983). Abulia minor vs. agitated behavior. *Clinical Neurosurgery, 31*, 9–31.

Glenn, M.B. (1998). Methylphenidate for cognitive and behavioral dysfunction after traumatic brain injury. *Journal of Head Trauma Rehabilitation, 13*, 87–90.

Goodman-Smith, A., & Turnbull, J. (1983). A behavioural approach to the rehabilitation of severely brain-injured adults. *Physiotherapy, 69*, 393–396.

Gualtieri, T., & Cox, D.R. (1991). The delayed neurobehavioural sequelae of traumatic brain injury. *Brain Injury, 5*, 219–232.

Harper, M., & Roth, M. (1962). Temporal lobe epilepsy and the phobic anxiety-depersonalisation syndrome. *Comprehensive Psychiatry, 3*, 129–151; 215–226.

Hellekson, C., Buckland, R., & Price, T. (1979). Organic personality disturbance: A case of apparent atypical cyclic affective disorder. *American Journal of Psychiatry, 136*, 833–835.

Jorge, R.E., Robinson, R.G., Starkstein, S.E., & Arndt, S.V. (1994). Depression and anxiety following traumatic brain injury. *Journal of Neuropsychiatry and Clinical Neuroscience, 5*, 369–374.

Lewin, J., & Sumners, D. (1992). Successful treatment of episodic dyscontrol with carbamazepine. *British Journal of Psychiatry, 161*, 261–262.

Linn, R.T., Allen, K., & Willer, B.S. (1994). Affective symptoms in the chronic stage of traumatic brain injury: A study of married couples. *Brain Injury, 8*, 135–147.

Lishman, W.A. (1988). Physiogenesis and psychogenesis in the "post-concussional syndrome". *British Journal of Psychiatry, 153*, 460–469.

Lishman, W.A. (1998). Organic psychiatry: The psychological consequences of cerebral disorder (3rd Ed.). Oxford: Blackwell.

Maletzky, B.M. (1973). The episodic dyscontrol syndrome. *Diseases of the Nervous System, 34*, 178–185.

Monroe, R.R. (1970). *Episodic behavioral disorders.* Cambridge, MA: Harvard University Press.

Monroe, R.R. (1982). Limbic ictus and atypical psychoses. *Journal of Nervous and Mental Disorders, 170*, 711–716.

Monroe, R.R. (1986). Episodic behavioral disorders and limbic ictus. In B.K. Doane & K.E. Livingston (Eds.), *The limbic system: Functional organization and clinical disorders* (pp. 251–266). New York, Raven Press.

Monroe, R.R. (1989). Dyscontrol syndrome: Long-term follow-up. *Comprehensive Psychiatry, 30*, 489–497.

Murphy, D.L., Zohar, J., Benkelfat, C., Pato, M.T., Pigott, T.A., & Insel, T.R. (1989). Obsessive-compulsive disorder as a 5-HT subsystem-related behavioural disorder. *British Journal of Psychiatry* (Suppl.), *8*, 15–24.

Newson, E. (1989). *Pathological demand avoidance syndrome: Diagnostic criteria and relationship to autism and other developmental coding disorders.* Nottingham: Child Development Research Unit, University of Nottingham.

Pincus, T., Callahan, L.F., Bradley, L.A., Vaughn, W.K., & Wolfe, F. (1986). Elevated MMPI scores for hypochondriasis, depression, and hysteria in patients with rheumatoid arthritis. *Arthritis Rheumatology, 29,* 1456–1466.

Pond, D.A. (1957). Psychiatric aspects of epilepsy. *Journal of the Indian Medical Profession, 3,* 1441–1451.

Powell, J.H., al-Adawi, S., Morgan, J., & Greenwood, R.J. (1996). Motivational deficits after brain injury: Effects of bromocriptine in 11 patients. *Journal of Neurology, Neurosurgery and Psychiatry, 60,* 416–421.

Prigatano, G.P. (1989). Work, love and play after brain injury. *Bulletin of the Meninger Clinic, 53,* 414–431.

Prigatano, G.P. (1990). Impaired awareness of behavioral limitations after traumatic brain injury. *Archives of Physical Medicine and Rehabilitation, 71,* 1058–1064.

Robinson, R.G. (1997). Neuropsychiatric consequences of stroke. *Annual Review of Medicine, 48, 217–229.*

Rosenthal, M., Christensen, B.K., & Ross, T.P. (1998). Depression following traumatic brain injury. *Archives of Physical Medicine Rehabilitation, 79,* 90–103.

Stein, G. (1992). Drug treatment of the personality disorders. *British Journal of Psychiatry, 161,* 167–184.

Stone, J.L., McDaniel, K.D., Hughes, J.R., & Hermann, B.P. (1986). Episodic dyscontrol disorder and paroxysmal EEG abnormalities: Successful treatment with carbamazepine. *Biological Psychiatry, 21,* 208-212.

Wood, R.Ll. (1987). *Brain injury rehabilitation: A neurobehavioural approach.* London: Croom Helm.

Wood, R.Ll., & Worthington, A.D. (1999). Outcome in community rehabilitation: Measuring the social impact of disability. *Neuropsychological Rehabilitation, 9,* 505–516.

CHAPTER THREE

Families living with the effects of acquired brain injury

B. Willer
State University of New York at Buffalo, NY, USA

P.M. Flaherty
G.F. Strong Rehabilitation Centre, Vancouver, Canada

S. Coallier
Charles LeMoyne Hospital, Montreal, Canada

INTRODUCTION

When an individual suffers a serious trauma leading to brain injury, family members are affected in a significant fashion. The ability of the family to cope with the trauma is important in the rehabilitation of the individual with the injury. In this chapter, we review the extensive literature that exists on families living with the effects of acquired brain injury. The majority of this literature documents the level and type of stress experienced by families. It is recognised that the type of stress experienced varies somewhat with the relationship of the family to the individual with the injury. Most of the early research on families focused on parents of adults with brain injury; thus, we organised the literature reviews to focus on spouses whose partner has brain injury and parents of children with brain injury. We also look at the specific sequelae of brain injury and their impact on the family. Finally, we review the research on the specific needs of families and the interventions that could be provided.

The issue of family stress after brain injury was first brought to our attention by pioneers in the brain injury rehabilitation field (Bond, Brooks, & McKinlay, 1979; Brooks et al., 1986; Lezak, 1988; Oddy, Humphrey, & Uttley, 1978; Panting & Merry, 1972; Romano, 1974; Rosenbaum & Najenson, 1976). These early presentations of family burden described the family response as critical to the success of rehabilitation and adjustment of the individual. Panting and Merry (1972) suggested that the family should be viewed as a patient that requires medical and social support. Romano (1974) described the family response to the trauma in pathological terms indicating that the injury to the family member leads to various unhealthy reactions in the family such as denial. The various studies by Brooks and colleagues (Bond et al., 1979; Brooks & Aughton, 1979; Brooks et al., 1986; Livingston, Brooks, & Bond, 1985a,b; McKinlay, Brooks, & Bond, 1983; McKinlay et al., 1981) indicated one or more family members can be expected to experience symptoms of depression as much as seven years post-injury. The Brooks studies suggest that family burden may actually increase with time.

Allen, Linn, Guttierez, and Willer (1994) not only specified the types of stress families experience, but also compared families living with the effects of brain injury to families living with effects of other disabilities. The study employed a measure of burden that was multi-dimensional, assessing the following areas of stress:

1. Dependency: Stress associated with the actual demands of caring for an individual with disabilities. This includes the stress of dealing with an individual who may become very demanding.
2. Personal burden: Stress associated with the feeling that all of the responsibility for care falls on one person. This stress includes the perception that no one will be there to care for the individual in the future. High personal burden is also associated with a perception that one's efforts are not appreciated. Personal burden is often associated with a preference for institutional care.
3. Family problems: Stress associated with the effects of care on the family. Prime examples of family costs include opportunity loss for the primary caretaker, financial costs of care, and the presence of anger or resentment among family members.

The Allen et al. (1994) study found that families living with an individual with brain injury were generally experiencing more stress than families living with individuals who have physical disabilities (e.g., spinal cord injury) or debilitating illness (e.g., cystic fibrosis). The care providers of individuals with brain injury were more likely to experience dependency and perceived lack of personal reward. In addition, families living with brain injury were more likely to experience disharmony. The study by Allen et al. (1994) included mothers and spouses of adults with brain injury. It showed that the overall burden was similar between spouses and parents but that important qualitative differences existed. This points to the need to examine family stress and burden from the perspective of the relationships between the individual with the brain injury and his or her family.

STRESS OF BRAIN INJURY ON SPOUSES

The research of Rosenbaum and Najenson (1976) was critical in identifying the particularly stressful situation of wives of men with brain injuries from war. There has since been a host of studies on spouses that indicate minor differences in the level of stress experienced when compared to parents, but important differences in the type of stress experienced (Allen et al., 1994; Gervasio & Kreutzer, 1997; Hall et al., 1994; Kravetz et al., 1995; Kreutzer, Gervasio, & Camplair, 1994a,b; Leathem, Heath, & Woolley, 1996; Linn, Allen, & Willer, 1994; Liss & Willer, 1990; Moore, Stambrook, & Peters, 1993; Moore, Stambrook, Peters, & Lubosko, 1991; Peters, Stambrook, Moore, & Esses, 1990; Peters et al., 1992a; Resnick, 1993; Rosenbaum & Najenson, 1976; Santos, Castro-Caldas, & De Sousa, 1998; Wood & Yurdakul, 1997). For example, Hall et al. (1994) found that spouses report consistently greater behaviour problems in the individual with brain injury than parents. Kreutzer and his colleagues (Kreutzer et al., 1994a,b), and Allen et al. (1994) reported that spouses had greater family dysfunction and increased likelihood of depression when compared to parents of adults with brain injury. Moore and colleagues (Moore et al., 1991, 1993; Peters et al., 1990, 1992a) indicated that spouses are likely to assume the role of both spouses with the added burden of caring for the injured spouse. Moore and colleagues (Moore et al., 1991; Moore & Stambrook, 1992; Moore, Stambrook, & Peters, 1989) also point out that financial pressures are more evident when a spouse is injured and such pressures amplify the level of distress.

Another major stress factor in families where a spouse is injured is the effect of brain injury on marital relations. Kravetz et al. (1995) describe a general loss of self-esteem for both partners and, ultimately, a loss of marital cohesion. Wood and Yurdakul (1997) suggest that a divorce or separation rate of 49% in a 5–8-year range post-injury is abnormal and likely the result of living with the effects of brain injury. One of the common characteristics of brain injury is a loss of the ability to empathise with others. Certainly, loss of empathy of a partner has to serve as an important source of marital difficulty.

Having young children in the home has also been found to add to the stress experienced by couples when one spouse has a brain injury (Moore et al., 1991, 1993; Romano, 1974; Urbach & Culbert, 1991; Urbach, Sonenklar, & Culbert, 1994). The uninjured spouse, in this instance, has the stress of caring for an injured spouse on top of the stress associated with raising small children. In addition, the research on parents with brain injury has demonstrated significant effects on the behaviour and well-being of their children. Pessar, Coad, Linn, and Willer (1993) reported that where one parent was injured 10 of 24 families reported significant behavioural difficulties in children at school and at home. Children were at greater risk of developing behavioural difficulties if the father was injured. Often this was due to the father being less tolerant, more egocentric, and less motivated to play or interact with the children in a manner which is normally seen as fulfilling the parental role. Another major risk factor was the presence of depression in the uninjured parent. They concluded that behaviour difficulties in children were more evident when the uninjured parent was unable to compensate for the lack of parenting ability of the injured parent. It appeared that depression in the uninjured spouse is the most significant factor in predicting behavioural difficulties in the children.

Uysal et al. (1998) compared families with an injured parent to families where neither parent was injured. These authors found few differences in the behaviour of the children, implying that brain injury in one parent was not a significant risk factor for the children. On the other hand, injured parents were described as less able to fulfil the parenting role. Parents with brain injury were less capable of assisting the children to set meaningful goals, were less nurturing, and provided less discipline. The uninjured parent in the family also reported decreased effectiveness as a parent and described themselves as being less actively involved in the parenting role. Despite the obvious impact of brain injury on parenting skills and children, there are no studies on interventions to assist families with these important issues.

STRESS ON FAMILIES WHEN A CHILD IS INJURED

There is a separate and distinct body of research on the effects of paediatric brain injury on family functioning (Conoley & Sheridan, 1996; Coster, Haley, & Baryza, 1994; Guerriere & McKeever, 1997; Max et al., 1998; McDonald & Jaffe, 1992; Menezes & Shinebourne, 1998; Osberg et al., 1997; Patterson, 1998; Rivara, 1994; Rivara et al., 1992, 1993, 1994, 1996; Sokol et al., 1996; Waaland, Burns, & Cockrell, 1993; Wade, Drotar, Taylor, & Stancin, 1995; Wade et al., 1996, 1998; Yeates et al., 1997). While it is safe to assume that brain injury has a demonstrable effect on all families, there are no studies that compare families of young children with brain injury to families where the injured person is an adult. Thus, it is impossible to determine whether the stress of having a child injured is greater than having an adult son or daughter injured.

It is possible to speculate on the specific problems of young families living with the effects of paediatric brain injury. First, the literature on paediatric brain injury consistently points out the lack of resources for these families. Financial problems, for example, are much more likely to be a source of stress for the young family versus a more established family (Osberg et al., 1997; Sokol et al., 1996). Pre-injury family functioning is a significant predictor of family functioning after injury as well as a significant predictor of functional outcome for the injured child (Max et al., 1998; Rivara, 1994; Rivara et al., 1992, 1993, 1994, 1996). The assumption is that the young family has not established the strong social network or core values and beliefs that help to sustain the more established family. Unfortunately, the vast majority of research on these families focuses on the first few years post-injury. There is little known about the long-term impact of paediatric brain injury on the family.

There is little research on the impact of brain injury on siblings. However, research on siblings of young people with psychiatric disorders shows that it is more likely for them to have episodes of aggressiveness or of withdrawal and depression (Breslau & Prabucki, 1987). However, one has to take account of genetic and environmental factors when relying on data from psychiatric sources because these may precipitate psychiatric problems in siblings.

RELATIONSHIP BETWEEN FAMILY STRESS AND NEUROBEHAVIOURAL SEQUELAE

High levels of family stress are associated with alterations to personality, interpersonal behaviour, and cognition that occur as a result of brain injury. Lezak (1978, 1988) was one of the first to highlight the relationship between neurobehavioural sequelae of brain injury and family burden. She described the effects of increased dependence and decreased cognitive efficiency on family function. Although she based her observations on clinical experience, these observations have since been borne out by the research of others (Groswasser & Stern, 1998; Hall et al., 1994; Kinsella, Packer, & Olver, 1991; Knight, Devereux, & Godfrey, 1998; Lezak, 1978, 1988; Marsh, Kersel, Havill, & Sleigh, 1998a, b; Max et al., 1998; Peters et al., 1990; Peters, Gluck, & McCormick, 1992b; Sokol et al., 1996; Thomsen, 1992; Uomoto & Brockway, 1992).

Whilst a broad range of behaviour problems lead to family stress, the presence of aggressive behaviour is a major contributor (Hall et al., 1994; Kinsella et al., 1991; Knight et al., 1998; Marsh et al., 1998a, b; Peters et al., 1990), even when the injured person displaying the aggression is a child (Max et al., 1998). The presence of aggressive, antisocial behaviour also appears to pose the greatest threat to marriage (Peters et al., 1990) and seems to lead to an increase in aggressive behaviour in other members of the family (Hall et al., 1994). However, aggression rarely occurs in isolation and is often accompanied by other behaviour or personality problems. These are often linked to cognitive deficits which, when combined with behaviour disturbance, increases the likelihood of family stress (Dywan & Segalowitz, 1996; Godfrey, Knight, & Bishara, 1991; Hillier & Metzer, 1997; Linn et al., 1994; Malec, Machulda, & Moessner, 1997; Phipps, Dipasquale, Blitz, & Whyte, 1997; Thomsen, 1992).

Of greatest significance are deficits attributed to frontal lobe function. For example, Dywan and Segalowitz (1996) point out the frustrations for the family when the individual exhibits deficits in planning, initiation, and social monitoring. Anosognosia is especially problematic for families (Hillier & Metzer, 1997). The study of couples living with the effects of brain injury by Linn et al. (1994) found a high correlation between depression of the uninjured spouse and lack of awareness of behavioural and emotional disabilities on the part of the injured spouse. Other studies point to other executive dysfunction as sources of stress. For example, the inability to express empathy (Bond & Godfrey, 1997; Eslinger, 1998) and difficulty with problem solving (Godfrey et al., 1991) has also been associated with increased stress among families.

There are a number of sequelae of acquired brain injury that relate to the expression of sexuality, such as impulsiveness and changes in sexual drive. A review of the literature by Elliott and Biever (1996) suggests that problems in the expression of sexuality are likely to be a major source of stress for family members, especially spouses, but there has been little in the way of research on the topic.

Research on long-term outcome for individuals with acquired brain injury and their families consistently points to the reduced social network that results (Finset, Dyrnes, Krogstad, & Berstad, 1995; Kinsella, Ford, & Moran, 1989; Kozloff, 1987; Marsh et al., 1998a; Morton & Wehman, 1995; Wallace et al., 1998; Weddell, Oddy, & Jenkins, 1980). Immediately after the injury, members of the extended family and friends tend to be very supportive, but within a year the network of support is greatly reduced. The individual with the injury becomes increasingly dependent on family members for friendship that previously was provided by non-family members. The role of all family members is therefore significantly altered but immediate family members tend to take a more supportive role whilst extended family members tend to drift away.

It appears that most individuals with brain injury either lose their role or have significant changes in role (Hallett et al., 1994; Schmidt et al., 1995). For example, the man who was previously a provider may no longer be a provider. As one member of the family is unable to fulfil a role another member of the family must take over that role. Even if the role change is only necessary on a temporary basis, it is often difficult for the individual with disabilities to re-acquire the role.

NEEDS OF FAMILIES

Reviews of the literature on families and brain injury conclude that families experience considerable stress and burden (Florian, Katz, & Lahav, 1991; Kreutzer, Marwitz, & Kepler, 1992; Liss & Willer, 1990; Livingston & Brooks, 1988; Mauss-Clum & Ryan, 1981; Rosenthal & Young, 1988; Wade et al., 1995). However, while there is considerable research and discussion of the burden in families, relatively little is written about the needs of families and how to meet them. Serio, Kreutzer, and Witol (1997) are the exception, in that their survey provided a comprehensive breakdown of family needs. These are as follows:

Information.   The highest rated need was the need for information. Families need information on brain injury, and often information that is specific to the brain injury of their relative. There is some question in the literature as to whether the need for information can be equated with a need for education (Johnson, 1995; McMordie, Rogers, & Barker, 1991; Resnick, 1993). Education implies that families will be offered a fuller understanding of brain injury than can be obtained by reading a brochure or a book about brain injury. There is also some debate about the best time to provide education. Many families are unable to benefit from education if it is provided too soon after the injury. This education can be provided by rehabilitation staff or by booklets on brain injury and its consequences, written in a form that the average lay person will understand. However, families are much more receptive to information after the early recovery period is over and a more realistic attitude about the injured person's ability has been established.

Emotional support.   It has been suggested that families need to have the opportunity to grieve for the losses associated with brain injury (Testani-Dufour, Chappel-Aiken, & Gueldner, 1992). There is some question as to whether emotional support is something that can come from professionals or should come from family, friends and others with more personal experiences living with the effects of brain injury. Generally, family members and friends provide a great deal of emotional support but this support may not extend over a long period of time. In addition, the emotional support of family and friends is usually provided during the period of time when professionals have the most contact with the family. Ironically, years after the injury when families appear to have a greater need for support contact with professionals is usually quite limited.

Families also report that hope is one aspect of emotional support that they rarely receive from professionals (Linge, 1990; Ridley, 1989; Testani-Dufour et al., 1992). Family and friends may attempt to provide hope but professionals are in a position to make a more objective prognosis based on experience of recovery patterns in a number of people with different types of brain injury. Many professionals are judged to be too pessimistic when asked to predict future outcomes, particularly during the acute care stage, thus discouraging "hope". Families are often in denial and expect their family member will recover fully and professionals know that this is impossible. Whether to reduce denial or just express the obvious, professionals are often viewed by families as pessimistic and discouraging (Johnson & Roberts, 1996).

Instrumental support.   Instrumental support refers to the kind of practical support that, again, is generally provided by extended family members and friends. Instrumental support can include anything from looking after small children to assisting with financial and other aspects of maintaining the home life during the long periods spent at the hospital. Long after the injury, families appear to have continuing need for assistance of an instrumental nature. For example, families who have assumed the responsibility for caring for an individual who is severely disabled often need a break from the continuing demands of care. Respite care would be extremely helpful but is only rarely made available to families.

Professional support.   At the acute care stage, professional support includes good medical care for the injured family member (Merritt & Evans, 1990), which, according to families, is not always received. During the rehabilitation phase there is a supposed need for staff to include the family as part of the rehabilitation team. McLaughlin and Carey (1993) point out that there is an inherent conflict between the rehabilitation goals of staff and the expectation for cure on the part of families. This conflict interferes with the development of a therapeutic alliance. After discharge from in-patient services the family needs professional assistance with planning for the future and accessing available services (Tennant, Macdermott, & Neary, 1995). This type of assistance is generally referred to as case management

(Resnick, 1993), and represents a service which is becoming less available to families in North America because of restrictions in funding.

Social support.   Research on family coping strategies consistently points to the perceived value of social support (Douglas & Spellacy, 1996; Sander, High, Hannay, & Sherer, 1997; Stansfield, 1991; Wallace et al., 1998; Willer, Allen, Liss, & Zicht, 1991). While social support is clearly important there may be little that the professional caregivers can do to assist families in maintaining a social support system or developing a social support system once isolation has been established.

Care support.   Family involvement in rehabilitation is an important topic that has not necessarily received adequate attention in the literature. There are advantages to family involvement in care and rehabilitation. Families know their family member and impart that knowledge in the rehabilitation setting. Families need to learn how to provide appropriate care because in most instances they will assume responsibility for care once rehabilitation is finished. However, families may not understand rehabilitation principles and may let their own goals and emotional needs override the needs of the family member. In addition, family members that assume a rehabilitation role may have difficulty fulfilling other roles such as parent or spouse. The extent and type of family involvement in care and rehabilitation that is most appropriate for the family and the individual with brain injury is something that must be negotiated on an individual basis. However, research into interventions and other strategies to assist families is not readily available.

A FAMILY EDUCATION PROGRAMME

Few will disagree with the need to provide educational opportunities for families. The assumption is that families will be able to provide greater assistance to their family member with a brain injury if educated and/or trained. However, experience with the development of education and training for families has taught us that there are many unanswered questions about what works best. Family education based within the medical model is problematic because of a tendency to focus on impairment and disabilities rather than the community integration (handicap) aspects. There is also a tendency to partition such educational programmes into discipline-specific topics rather than presenting a holistic approach to issues and their resolution.

A family thinks about their loved one as a whole person, whether or not he or she is healthy, injured, or ill. In theory, this holds true for families of people with an acquired brain injury but there is a primary need for these families to learn and understand about brain injury and the problems of their loved one (Junque, Bruna, & Mataro, 1997). Other relevant family concerns, especially during the initial stages following brain injury, may include how the roles of family members have been altered and how permanent these alterations may be (Serio et al., 1997). Families struggle with how to cope with the imposed role changes and uncertainties. In addition they often face the uncertainty of how best to seek financial and emotional support, resources, and other information. During this time families often feel isolated, alone, sad, and frightened (Acorn, 1993). Bearing all of this in mind, a family's first priority is to find and provide the most appropriate treatment and best care for their loved one. No doubt, this is an overwhelming and terrifying experience given the constraints of the traditional medical model. People who have been catastrophically injured often find themselves in a very complicated and controlling medical system with an overwhelming number of different specialists and caregivers providing assessment, treatment, and care, primarily only to the person with the brain injury. Family members are often left on their own to learn about the medical interventions and problems their loved one is experiencing. In addition they must learn to cope with their own losses, as well as to seek understanding of the medical system, which is confusing to many. Due to the hierarchical structure of the medical system, clients and their families often tend to have the least power within the system. As a result they often feel unempowered, unprepared, and thus less able to cope with the changes that result from a family member's brain injury.

Flaherty (1997) experimented with an educational programme that was non-traditional and aimed to overcome some weaknesses in the medical model approach. The programme assumed that the primary needs of the family were: (1) a need to be informed, (2) a need to have hope, and (3) a need to be confident that staff in the hospital or rehabilitation centre are caring for their family member in an appropriate and professional manner. The programme assumed that successful and productive education for families would also allow exploration of personal experiences and personal identification with the topic of discussion (Dell Orto & Power, 1994). The provision of integrated information about acquired brain injury, emotional support, and the sharing of personal experiences and feelings was the foundation for this holistic approach to family education. One of the most effective approaches to education for the group of families was to provide a loosely defined structure within which discussion could occur. This structure was open and flexible in order to provide an avenue to address questions from participants. It also encouraged the sharing of feelings and experiences. Families placed greater value on information that was functional and relevant to their experiences. In order to ensure relevance and utility, the education material was often presented in a question and answer format rather than a didactic format. It was felt that a discussion following participants' questions allowed families to feel in control, and encouraged them to help each other. This non-directive approach contrasts with the traditional medical model where families are given information that professionals think is important. Of course, the informal approach has the risk of overlooking information that families fail to recognise as important. Professionals participating in this collaborative process have the opportunity to share their expertise while at the same time learning from the families. Thus the professionals ultimately gain an understanding of the issues and fears that families and survivors live with (McMordie et al., 1991; Williams, 1991).

In order to foster a comprehensive, collaborative, and supportive environment for the education session, facilitators of the educational programme found it essential to focus on the family living with acquired brain injury as a whole system. In other words, facilitators had to forgo the tendency to focus on their specific discipline, in favour of a focus on the individuals with brain injury and their families. Facilitators also found they must be receptive about learning from families and about sharing knowledge in a respectful, forthright, and optimistic manner. The facilitators' attitude, philosophy, and skills were evident throughout the educational programme and variance from the philosophical expectations of families impeded the success of the education session. Of course, the facilitators' knowledge of acquired brain injury, the health care system, and community service is a necessity and also helps to establish the credibility of professionals (Venzie, Felicetti, & Cerratyl, 1996). The foundation of the education session was built on the facilitators' humanistic approach and respect for clients and their families.

Theoretically, a range of professions has the ability to facilitate education sessions. Although they may possess different skills and expertise, an empathic and compassionate approach to families and individuals is critical to success. The facilitators should also have an in-depth level of knowledge and understanding of acquired brain injury and the role that rehabilitation professionals and community support plays in the ongoing rehabilitation process. They should also have an understanding of and be open to learning about the issues and fears individual families must live with. These common skills and qualities help to nurture a comprehensive, collaborative, and supportive environment.

FAMILY TRAINING

Training is distinguished from education in the way families are educated but also taught specific skills for management of issues such as behavioural or cognitive difficulties. Coallier (1997) conducted a training programme with nine families where brain injury ranged between mild and severe. The purpose of the training programme was to assist families in their coping strategies and to improve their ability to solve specific problems posed by their family member with brain injury. Attention was also paid to resources and the process for accessing resources in the formal system of health and social services and the informal system offered by friends and relatives.

The programme was considerably more structured than the education programme described earlier. There were educational sessions and discussion of specific topics but the primary emphasis was on providing training in behaviour management techniques. An important characteristic of this training programme was timing. It was offered to families at approximately the same time as their family member was returning home from hospital. Formal evaluation of the programme did not reveal any particular improvement in the behaviour patterns of brain injured individuals from families who received training but family members indicated that they felt more confident in their ability to manage outbursts and other behavioural issues. Families also indicated a high level of satisfaction with practical aspects of the training. Learning "how to" intervene was perceived as far more valuable than learning "why" an intervention strategy was proposed.

A major issue in providing training to families is the fact that the training alters the nature of the relationship between family members. For example, when professional staff apply a strict behaviour management programme to an individual with acquired brain injury the professional staff must have control over consequences. A management programme necessarily involves rewards for appropriate behaviour and punishment, or the removal of rewards for inappropriate behaviour. Family members do not necessarily have control over consequences, especially if the family member with brain injury is considered an equal, such as a parent or spouse. Thus, control over consequences places the non-injured family member in a position of greater power or control than was the norm pre-injury.

CONCLUSIONS

Professionals argue strongly that families are greatly affected by severe injury to one family member and therefore various psychological interventions or other forms of social support and training are warranted to meet their needs. Education, training, or counselling of families could be justified if it was clearly demonstrated that these services would have a marked influence on outcomes for the individual. To date, there is little concrete evidence that individuals with brain injury have improved outcomes as a result of family interventions. In fact, there is little research evidence that families benefit from these interventions. An important issue is the timing of family interventions in order to have the maximum benefit. Soon after the injury, families are distraught and may not be in the best state to take in information. While the injured family member is in in-patient rehabilitation, families are generally described as unrealistic in their expectations and therefore in conflict with the rehabilitation treatment staff. Families are more likely to complain about the inadequacies of the rehabilitation programme than they are to request information on how to cope once rehabilitation has ended. During the hospital stay in acute care or rehabilitation, families probably benefit more from specific information about their family member than from a general education programme devoted to the effects of brain injury. However, whilst one-to-one meetings with professional staff are probably of more value than group discussions, the Flaherty (1997) project found that families benefit greatly from the wisdom of other families whose relative had been through rehabilitation and who had learned to cope with their injured family member at home. This project also pointed out the communication difficulties experienced by many professional staff during family interactions. Thus, even the one-to-one discussions between professionals and families can probably be improved. Hence, training and education of professionals on how best to relate to families may have more value than education and training of families at this stage.

The literature on families, as discussed, indicates that families experience considerable burden once their injured family member returns home. At the same time, research on the effectiveness of home-based services indicates that families provide a reasonable environment for improvement and are very effective at assisting the injured family member to re-integrate within the community (Willer, Button, & Rempel, 1999). Families continue to require professional services when the brain injury is severe and at this juncture may also have the greatest benefit of practical education and training. Education and training are likely to have the greatest benefit when the family caregivers are most aware of their *long-term* needs. The non-directive approach to education, as described by Flaherty (1997), may be particularly useful since it aims to answer the specific questions raised by families. In addition, training in specific techniques for managing behaviour as described by Coallier (1997) is recommended since behavioural issues are one of the primary sources of stress.

There are, of course, many other considerations in determining the timing, approach, and providers of interventions for families that have not been addressed in any research to date. It is clear from this review of the literature that we know considerably more about the stress and burden experienced by families than about how to assist families to overcome this stress. Further evaluation of family intervention strategies remains a high priority in the long-term community support of people with brain injury.

REFERENCES

Acorn, S. (1993). An education/support program for families of survivors of head injury. *Canadian Journal of Rehabilitation, 7*, 149–151.

Allen, K., Linn, R., Gutierrez, H., & Willer, B. (1994). Family burden following traumatic brain injury. *Rehabilitation Psychology, 39*, 29-48.

Bond, F., & Godfrey, H.P. (1997). Conversation with traumatically brain-injured individuals: A controlled study of behavioural changes and their impact. *Brain Injury, 11*, 319–329.

Bond, M.R., Brooks, D.N., & McKinlay, W. (1979). Burdens imposed on the relatives of those with severe brain damage due to injury. *Acta Neurochirurgica Supplement, 28*, 124–125.

Breslau, N., & Prabucki, K. (1987). Siblings of disabled children: Effects of chronic stress in the family. *Archives of General Psychiatry, 44*, 1040–1046.

Brooks, D.N., & Aughton, M.E. (1979). Psychological consequences of blunt head injury. *International Rehabilitation Medicine, 1*, 160–165.

Brooks, N., Campsie, L., Symington, C., Beattie, A., & McKinlay, W. (1986). The five year outcome of severe blunt head injury: A relative's view. *Journal of Neurology, Neurosurgery and Psychiatry, 49*, 764–70.

3. FAMILIES LIVING WITH ABI **59**

Coallier, S. (1997). *An exploratory study of a psychological support group for families with a traumatic brain injury.* Unpublished Doctoral Thesis, University of Quebec at Montreal, Montreal.

Conoley, J.C., & Sheridan, S.M. (1996). Pediatric traumatic brain injury: Challenges and interventions for families. *Journal of Learning Disability, 29*, 662–629.

Coster, W.J., Haley, S., & Baryza, M.J. (1994). Functional performance of young children after traumatic brain injury: A 6-month follow-up study. *American Journal of Occupational Therapy, 48*, 211–218.

Dell Orto, A., & Power, P. (1994). *Head injury and the family: A life and living perspective.* Winter Park, FL: PMD Publishers.

Douglas, J.M., & Spellacy, F.J. (1996). Indicators of long-term family functioning following severe traumatic brain injury in adults. *Brain Injury, 10*, 819–839.

Dywan, J., & Segalowitz, S.J. (1996). Self- and family ratings of adaptive behavior after traumatic brain injury—psychometric scores and frontally generated erps. *Journal of Head Trauma Rehabilitation, 11*, 79–95.

Elliott, M.L., & Biever, L.S. (1996). Head injury and sexual dysfunction. *Brain Injury, 10*, 703–717.

Eslinger, P.J. (1998). Neurological and neuropsychological bases of empathy. *European Neurology, 39*, 193–199.

Finset, A., Dyrnes, S., Krogstad, J.M., & Berstad, J. (1995). Self-reported social networks and interpersonal support 2 years after severe traumatic brain injury. *Brain Injury, 9*, 141–150.

Flaherty, P.M. (1997). *A non-traditional approach to family education for people living with acquired brain injury.* Unpublished Masters of Education Thesis, Brock University, S. Catharines, Canada.

Florian, V., Katz, S., & Lahav, V. (1991). Impact of traumatic brain damage on family dynamics and functioning: A review. *International Disability Studies, 13*, 150–157.

Gervasio, A.H., & Kreutzer, J.S. (1997). Kinship and family members' psychological distress after traumatic brain injury—a large sample study. *Journal of Head Trauma Rehabilitation, 12*, 14–26.

Godfrey, H.P., Knight, R.G., & Bishara, S.N. (1991). The relationship between social skill and family problem-solving following very severe closed head injury. *Brain Injury, 5*, 207–211.

Groswasser, Z., & Stern, M.J. (1998). A psychodynamic model of behavior after acute central nervous system damage. *Journal of Head Trauma Rehabilitation, 13*, 69–79.

Guerriere, D., & McKeever, P. (1997). Mothering children who survive brain injuries: Playing the hand you're dealt. *Journal of the Society of Pediatric Nursing, 2*, 105–115.

Hall, K.M., Karzmark, P., Stevens, M., Englander, J., O'Hare, P., & Wright, J. (1994). Family stressors in traumatic brain injury: A two-year follow-up. *Archives of Physical Medicine and Rehabilitation, 75*, 876–884.

Hallett, J.D., Zasler, N D., Maurer, P., & Cash, S. (1994). Role change after traumatic brain injury in adults. *American Journal of Occupational Therapy, 48*, 241–246.

Hillier, S.L., & Metzer, J. (1997). Awareness and perceptions of outcomes after traumatic brain injury. *Brain Injury, 11*, 525–536.

Johnson, B.P. (1995). One family's experience with head injury: A phenomenological study. *Journal of Neuroscience Nursing, 27*, 113–118.

Johnson, L.H., & Roberts, S.L. (1996). Hope facilitating strategies for the family of the head injury patient. *Journal of Neuroscience Nursing, 28*, 259–266.

Junque, C., Bruna, O., & Mataro, M. (1997). Information needs of the traumatic brain injury patient's family members regarding the consequences of the injury and associated perception of physical, cognitive, emotional and quality of life changes. *Brain Injury, 11*, 251–258.

Kinsella, G., Ford, B., & Moran, C. (1989). Survival of social relationships following head injury. *International Disability Studies, 11*, 9–14.

Kinsella, G., Packer, S., & Olver, J. (1991). Maternal reporting of behaviour following very severe blunt head injury. *Journal of Neurology, Neurosurgery and Psychiatry, 54*, 422–426.

Knight, R.G., Devereux, R., & Godfrey, H.P. (1998). Caring for a family member with a traumatic brain injury. *Brain Injury, 12*, 467–481.

Kozloff, R. (1987). Networks of social support and the outcome from severe head injury. *Journal of Head Trauma and Rehabilitation, 2*, 14–23.

Kravetz, S., Gross, Y., Weiler, B., Ben-Yakar, M., Tadir, M., & Stern, M.J. (1995). Self-concept, marital vulnerability and brain damage. *Brain Injury, 9*, 131–139.

Kreutzer, J.S., Gervasio, A.H., & Camplair, P.S. (1994a). Patient correlates of caregivers' distress and family functioning after traumatic brain injury. *Brain Injury, 8*, 211–230.

Kreutzer, J.S., Gervasio, A.H., & Camplair, P.S. (1994b). Primary caregivers' psychological status and family functioning after traumatic brain injury. *Brain Injury, 8*, 197–210.

Kreutzer, J.S., Marwitz, J.H., & Kepler, K. (1992). Traumatic brain injury: Family response and outcome. *Archives of Physical Medicine and Rehabilitation, 73*, 771–778.

Leathem, J., Heath, E., & Woolley, C. (1996). Relatives' perceptions of role change, social support and stress after traumatic brain injury. *Brain Injury, 10*, 27–38.

Lezak, M.D. (1978). Living with the characterologically altered brain injured patient. *Journal of Clinical Psychiatry, 39*, 592–598.

Lezak, M.D. (1988). Brain damage is a family affair. *Journal of Clinical Experimental Neuropsychology, 10*, 111–123.

Linge, F.R. (1990). Faith, hope, and love: Nontraditional therapy in recovery from serious head injury, a personal account. *Canadian Journal of Psychology, 44*, 116–129.

Linn, R.T., Allen, K., & Willer, B.S. (1994). Affective symptoms in the chronic stage of traumatic brain injury: A study of married couples. *Brain Injury, 8*, 135–147.

Liss, M., & Willer, B. (1990). Traumatic brain injury and marital relationships: A literature review. *International Journal of Rehabilitation Research, 13*, 309–320.

Livingston, M., & Brooks, D. (1988). The burden on families of the brain injured: A review. *Journal of Head Trauma and Rehabilitation, 3*, 6–15.

Livingston, M.G., Brooks, D.N., & Bond, M.R. (1985a). Patient outcome in the year following severe head injury and relatives' psychiatric and social functioning. *Journal of Neurology, Neurosurgery and Psychiatry, 48*, 876–881.

Livingston, M.G., Brooks, D.N., & Bond, M.R. (1985b). Three months after severe head injury: Psychiatric and social impact on relatives. *Journal of Neurology, Neurosurgery, and Psychiatry, 48*, 870–875.

Malec, J.F., Machulda, M.M., & Moessner, A.M. (1997). Differing problem perceptions of staff, survivors, and significant others after brain injury. *Journal of Head Trauma Rehabilitation, 12*, 1–13.

Marsh, N.V., Kersel, D.A., Havill, J.H., & Sleigh, J.W. (1998a). Caregiver burden at 1 year following severe traumatic brain injury. *Brain Injury, 12*, 1045–1059.

Marsh, N.V., Kersel, D.A., Havill, J.H., & Sleigh, J.W. (1998b). Caregiver burden at 6 months following severe traumatic brain injury. *Brain Injury, 12*, 225–238.

Mauss-Clum, N., & Ryan, M. (1981). Brain injury and the family. *Journal of Neurosurgical Nursing, 13*, 165–169.

Max, J.E., Castillo, C.S., Robin, D.A., Lindgren, S.D., Smith, W.L., Jr., Sato, Y., Mattheis, P.J., & Stierwalt, J.A. (1998). Predictors of family functioning after traumatic brain injury in children and adolescents. *Journal of the American Academy of Child Adolescent Psychiatry, 37*, 83–90.

McDonald, C.M., & Jaffe, K.M. (1992). Neurobehavioral and family functioning following traumatic brain injury in children. *Western Journal of Medicine, 157*, 664.

McKinlay, W.W., Brooks, D.N., & Bond, M.R. (1983). Post-concussional symptoms, financial compensation and outcome of severe blunt head injury. *Journal of Neurology, Neurosurgery and Psychiatry, 46*, 1084–1091.

McKinlay, W.W., Brooks, D.N., Bond, M.R., Martinage, D.P., & Marshall, M.M. (1981). The short-term outcome of severe blunt head injury as reported by relatives of the injured persons. *Journal of Neurology, Neurosurgery and Psychiatry, 44*, 527–533.

McLaughlin, A.M., & Carey, J.L. (1993). The adversarial alliance: Developing therapeutic relationships between families and the team in brain injury rehabilitation. *Brain Injury, 7*, 45–51.

McMordie, W.R., Rogers, K.F., & Barker, S.L. (1991). Consumer satisfaction with services provided to head-injured patients and their families. *Brain Injury, 5*, 43–51.

Menezes, A.M., & Shinebourne, E.A. (1998). Severe brain injury after cardiac surgery in children: Consequences for the family and the need for assistance. *Heart, 80*, 286–291.

Merritt, K.L., & Evans, R.L. (1990). Family satisfaction with medical care after traumatic brain injury. *Psychological Reports, 67*, 129–130.

Moore, A.D., & Stambrook, M. (1992). Coping strategies and locus of control following traumatic brain injury: Relationship to long-term outcome. *Brain Injury, 6*, 89–94.

Moore, A.D., Stambrook, M., & Peters, L.C. (1989). Coping strategies and adjustment after closed-head injury: A cluster analytical approach. *Brain Injury, 3*, 171–175.

Moore, A., Stambrook, M., & Peters, L. (1993). Centripetal and centrifugal family life cycle factors in long-term outcome following traumatic brain injury. *Brain Injury, 7*, 247–255.

Moore, A., Stambrook, M., Peters, L., & Lubosko, A. (1991). Family coping and marital adjustment after traumatic brain injury. *Journal of Head Trauma and Rehabilitation, 6*, 83–89.

Morton, M.V., & Wehman, P. (1995). Psychosocial and emotional sequelae of individuals with traumatic brain injury: A literature review and recommendations. *Brain Injury, 9*, 81–92.

Oddy, M., Humphrey, M., & Uttley, D. (1978). Stresses upon the relatives of head-injured patients. *British Journal of Psychiatry, 133*, 507–513.

Osberg, J.S., Brooke, M.M., Baryza, M.J., Rowe, K., Lash, M., & Kahn, P. (1997). Impact of childhood brain injury on work and family finances. *Brain Injury, 11*, 11–24.

Panting, A., & Merry, P. (1972). The long term rehabilitation of severe head injuries with particular reference to the need for social and medical support for the patient's family. *Rehabilitation, 38*, 33–37.

Patterson, C.M. (1998). The role of the primary care physician in maximizing cognitive and behavioral recovery from moderate to severe pediatric traumatic brain injury. *Journal Ark Med Soc, 95*, 109–113.

Pessar, L.F., Coad, M.L., Linn, R.T., & Willer, B S. (1993). The effects of parental traumatic brain injury on the behaviour of parents and children. *Brain Injury, 7*, 231–240.

Peters, L.C., Stambrook, M., Moore, A.D., & Esses, L. (1990). Psychosocial sequelae of closed head injury: Effects on the marital relationship. *Brain Injury, 4*, 39–47.

Peters, L.C., Stambrook, M., Moore, A.D., Zubek, E., Dubo, H., & Blumenschein, S. (1992a). Differential effects of spinal cord injury and head injury on marital adjustment. *Brain Injury, 6*, 461–467.

Peters, M.D., Gluck, M., & McCormick, M. (1992b). Behaviour rehabilitation of the challenging client in less restrictive settings. *Brain Injury, 6*, 299–314.

Phipps, E.J., Dipasquale, M., Blitz, C.L., & Whyte, J. (1997). Interpreting responsiveness in persons with severe traumatic brain injury—beliefs in families and quantitative evaluations. *Journal of Head Trauma Rehabilitation, 12*, 52–69.

Resnick, C. (1993). The effect of head injury on family and marital stability. *Social Work and Health Care, 18*, 49–62.

Ridley, B. (1989). Family response in head injury: denial ... or hope for the future? *Social Sciences Medicine, 29*, 555–561.

Rivara, J.B. (1994). Family functioning following pediatric traumatic brain injury. *Pediatric Analysis, 23*, 38–44.

Rivara, J.B., Fay, G.C., Jaffe, K.M., Polissar, N.L., Shurtleff, H.A., & Martin, K.M. (1992). Predictors of family functioning one year following traumatic brain injury in children. *Archives of Physical Medicine and Rehabilitation, 73*, 899–910.

Rivara, J.B., Jaffe, K.M., Fay, G.C., Polissar, N.L., Martin, K.M., Shurtleff, H.A., & Liao, S. (1993). Family functioning and injury severity as predictors of child functioning one year following traumatic brain injury. *Archives of Physical Medicine and Rehabilitation, 74*, 1047–1055.

Rivara, J.B., Jaffe, K.M., Polissar, N.L., Fay, G.C., Martin, K.M., Shurtleff, H.A., & Liao, S. (1994). Family functioning and children's academic performance and behavior problems in the year following traumatic brain injury. *Archives of Physical Medicine and Rehabilitation, 75*, 369–379.

Rivara, J.M., Jaffe, K.M., Polissar, N.L., Fay, G.C., Liao, S., & Martin, K.M. (1996). Predictors of family functioning and change 3 years after traumatic brain injury in children. *Archives of Physical Medicine and Rehabilitation, 77*, 754–764.

Romano, M.D. (1974). Family response to traumatic head injury. *Scandinavian Journal of Rehabilitation Medicine, 6*, 1–4.

Rosenbaum, M., & Najenson, T. (1976). Changes in life patterns and symptoms of low mood as reported by wives of severely brain-injured soldiers. *Journal of Consulting Clinical Psychology, 44*, 881–888.

Rosenthal, M., & Young, T. (1988). Effective family intervention after traumatic brain injury: Theory and practice. *Journal of Head Trauma and Rehabilitation, 3*, 42–50.

Sander, A.M., High, W.M., Jr., Hannay, H.J., & Sherer, M. (1997). Predictors of psychological health in caregivers of patients with closed head injury. *Brain Injury, 11*, 235–249.

Santos, M.E., Castro-Caldas, A., & De Sousa, L. (1998). Spontaneous complaints of long-term traumatic brain injured subjects and their close relatives. *Brain Injury, 12*, 759–767.

Schmidt, M.F., Garvin, L.J., Heinemann, A.W., & Kelly, J.P. (1995). Gender- and age-related role changes following brain injury. *Journal of Head Trauma Rehabilitation, 10*, 14–27.

Serio, C.D., Kreutzer, J.S., & Witol, A.D. (1997). Family needs after traumatic brain injury: A factor analytic study of the Family Needs Questionnaire. *Brain Injury, 11*, 1–9.

Sokol, D.K., Ferguson, C.F., Pitcher, G.A., Huster, G.A., Fitzhugh-Bell, K., & Luerssen, T.G. (1996). Behavioural adjustment and parental stress associated with closed head injury in children. *Brain Injury, 10*, 439–451.

Stansfield, K. (1991). Adaptation of family members of brain-injured patients: Perceptions of the hospitalization event. *Axone, 12*, 71–76.

Tennant, A., Macdermott, N., & Neary, D. (1995). The long-term outcome of head injury: Implications for service planning. *Brain Injury, 9*, 595–605.

Testani-Dufour, L., Chappel-Aiken, L., & Gueldner, S. (1992). Traumatic brain injury: A family experience. *Journal of Neuroscience Nursing, 24*, 317–323.

Thomsen, I.V. (1992). Late psychosocial outcome in severe traumatic brain injury: Preliminary results of a third follow-up study after 20 years. *Scandinavian Journal of Rehabilitation Medicine, 26*, 142–152.

Uomoto, J.M., & Brockway, J.A. (1992). Anger management training for brain injured patients and their family members. *Archives of Physical Medicine and Rehabilitatin, 73*, 674–649.

Urbach, J.R., & Culbert, J.P. (1991). Head-injured parents and their children: Psychosocial consequences of a traumatic syndrome. *Psychosomatics, 32*, 24–33.

Urbach, J.R., Sonenklar, N.A., & Culbert, J.P. (1994). Risk factors and assessment in children of brain-injured parents. *Journal of Neuropsychiatry and Clinical Neuroscience, 6*, 289–295.

Uysal, S., Hibbard, M.R., Robillard, D., Pappadopulos, E., & Jaffe, M. (1998). The effect of parental traumatic brain injury on parenting and child behavior. *Journal of Head Trauma Rehabilitation, 13*, 57–71.

Venzie, D.R., Felicetti, T., & Cerratyl, D. (1996). Planning considerations for community integrative brain injury programs. *Journal of Head Trauma Rehabilitation, 11*, 51–64.

Waaland, P.K., Burns, C., & Cockrell, J. (1993). Evaluation of needs of high- and low-income families following paediatric traumatic brain injury. *Brain Injury, 7*, 135–146.

Wade, S., Drotar, D., Taylor, H.G., & Stancin, T. (1995). Assessing the effects of traumatic brain injury on family functioning: Conceptual and methodological issues. *Journal of Pediatric Psychology, 20*, 737–752.

Wade, S.L., Taylor, H.G., Drotar, D., Stancin, T., & Yeates, K.O. (1996). Childhood traumatic brain injury: Initial impact on the family. *Journal of Learning Disability, 29*, 652–661.

Wade, S.L., Taylor, H.G., Drotar, D., Stancin, T., & Yeates, K.O. (1998). Family burden and adaptation during the initial year after traumatic brain injury in children. *Pediatrics, 102*, 110–116.

Wallace, C.A., Bogner, J., Corrigan, J.D., Clinchot, D., Mysiw, W.J., & Fugate, L.P. (1998). Primary caregivers of persons with brain injury: Life change 1 year after injury. *Brain Injury, 12*, 483–493.

Weddell, R., Oddy, M., & Jenkins, D. (1980). Social adjustment after rehabilitation: A two year follow-up of patients with severe head injury. *Psychological Medicine, 10*, 257–263.

Willer, B., Button, J., & Rempel, R. (1999). Residential and home-based postacute rehabilitation of individuals with traumatic brain injury: A case control study. *Archives of Physical Medicine and Rehabilitation, 80*, 399–406.

Willer, B.S., Allen, K.M., Liss, M., & Zicht, M.S. (1991). Problems and coping strategies of individuals with traumatic brain injury and their spouses. *Archives of Physical Medicine and Rehabilitation, 72*, 460–464.

Williams, J. (1991). Family support. In J. Williams & T. Kay (Eds.), *Head injury: A family matter* (pp. 299–312). Baltimore, MD: Paul H. Brooks.

Wood, R.Ll., & Yurdakul, L.K. (1997). Change in relationship status following traumatic brain injury. *Brain Injury, 11*, 491–501.

Yeates, K.O., Taylor, H.G., Drotar, D., Wade, S.L., Klein, S., Stancin, T., & Schatschneider, C. (1997). Preinjury family environment as a determinant of recovery from traumatic brain injuries in school-age children. *Journal of International Neuropsychological Society, 3*, 617–630.

CHAPTER FOUR

Assessing the nature and extent of neurobehavioural disability

G.E. Powell
Chartered Clinical Psychologist, London, UK

R.Ll. Wood
Brain Injury Rehabilitation Trust, Birmingham, UK

INTRODUCTION

Neurobehavioural disability is not associated with impairment of any particular cognitive function but reflects a breakdown in the integrity of those cerebral systems that regulate and co-ordinate behaviour. Inevitably, this involves a variety of cognitive functions, some of which are more circumscribed and easier to measure than others. However, the description of neurobehavioural disability given by Wood (Chapter 1, this volume) makes it clear that the predominant system associated with such disability is the frontal system. Adams (1975) has described the frontal system as being particularly susceptible to decelerative closed head injury. This means that disorders of behaviour and cognition encountered in a post-acute brain injury rehabilitation setting are especially associated with impairment of frontal function because closed head injuries comprise the largest group of referrals to such services (Wood, McCrea, Wood, & Merriman, 1999).

Unfortunately, satisfactory assessment of cognitive functions associated with the frontal system has historically proved to be rather elusive. Newcombe (1993) comments that people with frontal lesions are more difficult to assess than those with posterior lesions, especially by routine clinical examination, using the conventional tests typically employed in a consulting room setting. For example, both Stuss (1987) and Wood (1987) point to the discrepancy between cognitive performance obtained when testing is carried out in a quiet, structured environment (such as an office) compared to real-life situations in which the same cognitive abilities are required.

This dislocation between measured abilities and real-life application of abilities has also been considered by Kay and Silver (1989, p.157):

When placed in situations in which they should (based on their measured skill or cognitive level) be able to function, such clients often make numerous errors that they do not detect, fail to adapt their strategy to the task at hand, cannot adjust their performance or behaviour as the situation changes or in the presence of negative feedback, cannot anticipate or plan ahead, and generally fail to execute tasks appropriately, for procedural, not task content reasons.

A good single case example of the dislocation between cognitive performance on standardised tasks and real-life situations is that of EVR, described by Eslinger and Damasio (1985). This 35-year-old accountant had a large left orbitofrontal meningioma removed, following which he performed normally on a series of standardised tests measuring intelligence, memory, language, and visuospatial ability. He also performed normally on tests assumed to be sensitive to frontal damage, such as the Wisconsin Card Sorting Test, and on other measures designed to assess problem solving in hypothetical social situations. In real life, however, he presented a very different picture. He was unable to use his intelligence and other abilities to carry out his work properly. He made poor decisions and not only lost his job but failed to meet performance standards in less demanding jobs. His marriage broke down, he re-married but that relationship also failed and he eventually proved unable to manage his life at anything other than the most basic level of self-care.

Newcombe (1993) points to the difficulties such cases present in the context of personal injury litigation: "It is difficult for lawyers ... to understand that a plaintiff with a superior verbal and performance IQ and intact language and memory skills can nevertheless fail to earn a living or get on with other human beings as a consequence of frontal lobe injury rather than as a contrived decision to opt out" (p. 337). She points out that the court expects neuroscientists to provide convincing explanations based on systematic and repeatable measures. In cases of "high level" dysfunction, associated with subtle forms of neurobehavioural disability, this is not yet something which neuropsychologists have succeeded in doing with any reliability.

One of the main aims of this chapter is therefore to examine some of the principles upon which assessment of neurobehavioural disability relies. We consider, in general terms, whether the various tests and procedures used to examine people in a consulting room or other setting are reasonably reliable psychometric measures, capable of use as indices of social handicap. It is not our intention to examine the statistical properties of tests in any detail, nor to recommend individual tests because this is largely a matter of clinical judgement determined by the type of injury sustained, the problems displayed by the person being examined, and the nature of the circumstances at the time of referral. Those readers wishing to obtain such information on recent neuropsychological tests are referred to such texts as Lezak (1995), Spreen and Strauss (1998), and Powell (2000).

PURPOSE OF ASSESSMENT

The first step in any assessment procedure is to determine its purpose. This, in turn, will determine the context in which the assessment will take place, the reasonable time parameters, and the type of tests that can reasonably be employed. For example, most legal assessments are carried out in a consulting room setting, which usually means that the person being assessed will be sitting in a comfortable chair, in a quiet room, helped to relax and feel at ease, given some refreshment, and so on. Time parameters vary from one clinician to another, but in cases where the assessment takes longer than 2–3 hours rest breaks are allowed so that the client does not tire and is able to produce his or her best performance. In cases with very severe disabilities the assessment may take place in a nursing home or the patient's own home, but even then attempts are made to recreate a quiet, comfortable, uninterrupted "consulting room" environment. An assessment carried out in a rehabilitation centre could follow similar lines. For example, it may include the same conditions but testing may be spread over many days, with only one or two tests administered at any session. This further avoids problems of fatigue, maintains co-operation, and ensures motivation, again allowing the client to perform to the best possible level of ability.

This approach is valid if one is deliberately seeking to establish a person's best level of *ability*. However, in most individuals there is a difference between *ability* and *performance*, the latter defined as how well or consistently a person is able to apply their abilities day by day. This is particularly evident after brain injury of any kind and is often reflected in variations in how well a client does on cognitive tests, especially those demanding mental effort, speed, and accuracy of information processing.

Consequently, an assessment for rehabilitation purposes should *not* simply spread the administration of tests over several days or weeks, but vary the time of day when measures of ability are obtained, vary the environment in which data are collected, and use appropriate re-testing procedures where possible. This allows staff to determine, for example, the influence of mood or state of mind, or the influence of fatigue on task performance at different times of day or after different mental or physical activities. The context in which the assessment is carried out can be varied to expose the client to different levels of background noise and other distractions. In a neurobehavioural rehabilitation unit, tests of functional and social skills will be carried out more often in the community than in the unit itself and will use systematic behavioural observations of structured tasks, rather than standardised measures of ability. This approach is more likely to yield information about the client's weaknesses rather than strengths, but these weaknesses can then be clinically interpreted in terms of a client's neurobehavioural disability and become the target of rehabilitation interventions.

There is an implicit purpose to the assessment, which is that it is undertaken with due regard to the psychometric or scientific framework of measurement. In brief, there are two key concepts, both of which have already been intrinsically referred to in the preceding few paragraphs. The first is *reliability*, which is the notion that the results of the test procedure are replicable. At a simple level this means that an IQ test score will be broadly stable over time. At a more complex level, one more relevant to the concept of neurobehavioural disability, the procedure may be designed to demonstrate that behaviour is variable, i.e., that there are abnormal variations in performance, such as from one setting to another. In this case, it is the conclusion "This client's performance is unreliable", that must be reliable—if the same assessment procedure were carried out again, the responses from the client would again be variable.

The second concept is *validity*; that the test measures what it is meant to measure. This might mean, for example, showing that a new IQ test correlated with academic achievement. Again at a more complex level, more applicable to neurobehavioural disability, the assessment might aim to measure how intellectual or cognitive performance deteriorates excessively under conditions of distraction or uncertainty or pressure.

As can be seen, assessing the reliability and validity of measures of neurobehavioural disability can pose a particular, even unique, degree of difficulty. This must be taken as a long-term challenge, and does not excuse the failure to provide any reliability or validity data whatsoever. All of the procedures cited in this chapter do have at least some information on validity (e.g., whether they discriminate between certain key groups), and they have all taken steps to help achieve reliability (e.g., specified procedures, defined scoring method, training of test administrator). The need for information on reliability and validity applies to assessment procedures that yield both quantitative and qualitative information. Quantitative data is a normal test score, e.g. raw score, scaled score, *t*-score, percentile. Qualitative data is categorical in nature, e.g., diagnosis, assignment to a category, the presence or absence of a pattern of behaviour or performance. The only difference between quantitative and qualitative data, as far as reliability and validity is concerned, is the type of statistical test used.

DIFFERENT APPROACHES TO ASSESSMENT

The obvious debate in neuropsychological measurement of neurobehavioural disability is about the relative merits of a quantitative versus qualitative approach. Neuropsychological assessment attempts to identify the presence and nature of cognitive dysfunction associated with different forms of brain injury and to measure its severity, either on some normative scale, or by reference to the effects of the dysfunction upon the person's psychosocial functioning (e.g., as determined by reports from family, friends, and other clinicians). Historically, typical functions such as reasoning, literacy skills, perception, and visuospatial abilities have been broken down into discrete functional systems that can be measured in terms of hypothetical constructs or cognitive models. However, the primary interest in relation to neurobehavioural disability is the qualitative change to the cognitive process and how knowledge of this cognitive dysfunction helps us interpret and understand the various forms of social or functional behaviour problem. This point has been made by Lezak (1995): "For many brain damaged patients, test scores alone give relatively little information about the patient's functioning. The meat of the matter is often how a patient solves a problem or approaches a task, than what the score is." Lezak further cautions on a reliance of standardised test scores to interpret neuropsychological functions: "Some examiners come to equate a score with the behaviour it is supposed to represent... Reification of test scores can lead the examiner to overlook or discount direct observations. A test score approach to psychological assessment that minimizes the importance of qualitative data can result in serious distortions in the interpretations, conclusions and recommendations drawn from such a one sided data base" (p. 148). However, many neuropsychologists seem to ignore this advice and focus on the numeric component of the assessment process.

Typically, test procedures are employed in which some aspect of neuropsychological functioning is broken down into a series of subtests reflecting different facets of that function, for example, testing memory using the Wechsler Memory Scales, intelligence by the Wechsler Intelligence Scales, or language by any of the aphasia batteries. The assessment results are interpreted by comparing statistically an individual to a "normal" population, providing a quantitative measure of cognitive impairment. This approach is based on the following arguments:

1. There are usually large standardisation samples (versus a series of individual case studies or a series of small-scale, tightly controlled experimental studies in which no attempt is made to normalise the sample).
2. Full details are published in their entirety (so that the test can be given immediately and the tester does not have to design any aspect of the assessment).
3. The test is easily obtainable through mainstream publishers (avoids writing to authors of papers for copies of procedures or materials).
4. The tests are easily carried out in a consulting room setting (no laboratory equipment needed; no technical advice needed; portable materials).
5. The materials are supplied in a convenient box (no putting together one's own kit).
6. Performance is easy to compare with other people's (using Z-scores or t-scores for example) or with other tests (using statistics relating to the reliability and abnormality of difference scores).
7. Performance is easy to compare over time, drawing upon statistical knowledge of the tests, including test–retest reliability data.
8. Validity is relatively easily established by correlating test scores with those on tests of known validity, or by comparing the scores of various criterion groups.

These advantages and the underlying statistical bases of this approach are conveniently summarised in Powell (2000). However, in the assessment of neurobehavioural disability, if the current tests do not measure what we want to know, then the value of this albeit stringent approach is highly questionable. This has been recognised for a long time. For example, Newcombe and Artiola i Fortuny state in 1979 that "conventional psychometric testing has inevitable shortcomings. In particular, intelligence tests (with or without a risky juggling of test scores) are flagrantly inadequate as measures of intellectual handicap following brain injury" (p. 185). In similar vein, Diller and Gordon (1981) state that "test scores in and of themselves are lacking, since they provide little insight into the mechanisms and processes of impaired performance" (p. 826). Wood (1987) comments that a return to an estimated pre-morbid level of performance on psychometric tests is no guarantee that a person will be able to function at that level in daily life. Ponsford (1995) presents a similar argument, commenting that "cognitive impairments are however, not always readily apparent on standardised psychometric assessment. Moreover, it is frequently difficult to predict how those problems that are apparent will affect the individual's daily life and roles in society" (p. 65).

Sbordone (1996) has cogently made various points about how advantages of the current psychometric model in neuropsychology can be overstated and its disadvantages overlooked:

1. Numbers can usurp the importance of the clinical history in formulating the nature of the problem.
2. Deficits can be for a variety of reasons, not explained by the test data themselves.
3. The emphasis may be too much on "reliable" findings whereas a person's problem might be intrinsic unreliability.
4. Large generalisations have to be made from test results to the sort of problem the person complains of.
5. The relationship between norms and clinical significance is usually obscure.
6. The person is tested under optimum conditions, whereas their complaints might be of poor performance under challenging conditions.
7. Details of responses are often lost in favour of a few summary numbers.
8. The person is only seen in one "standard" setting, usually involving a desk, whereas in reality this is an unusual setting in everyday life, or only one specific setting.
9. The breadth of functions measured is not as great as at first sight.
10. The breadth of functions measured is usually determined by how easy it is to make that measurement.

ASSESSING NEUROBEHAVIOURAL DISABILITY

Neuropsychological assessment of neurobehavioural disability requires that three general principles are addressed:

1. There needs to be a clear focus on those neuropsychological systems that are specifically felt to underpin certain important cognitive functions, behaviour patterns, and personality traits.
2. That test performance will predict performance in real-life settings relevant to the individual.
3. That behaviours or traits known to reflect organic deficit can (or will be) directly measured.

The principles we have proposed present a significant challenge to neuropsychologists. Tests will need to be designed to enhance both *face* validity and *ecological* validity. These are not statistical concepts. The former indicates how tests mirror real life, which can be an important factor determining the co-operation and motivation of the client, whilst the latter reflects how *criterion variables*, those factors which the test must predict validly, are chosen to represent important functions in everyday life. The cognitive tasks must, by their nature, be structured yet not too structured because this could compensate for the executive weaknesses the task is trying to identify, reducing the assessment to a self-defeating exercise. The tasks need to stretch the attentional capabilities of the client without being too difficult or too intellectual, thereby limiting their application to those above a certain level of intelligence. Finally, the test must comply with basic demands implicit to psychometric measurement. As neuropsychologists move away from reasonably stable and circumscribed cognitive skills (memory, IQ, specific perceptual and language abilities), in order to measure weakness in cognitive *systems* that have a controlling influence on human behaviour (the so-called frontal tests), the reliability of tests has become increasingly less certain. It is very difficult to construct a test that measures not only ability but also the performance of that ability in different situations.

This can be illustrated by reference to a well-known ecological measure of human performance—the driving test. Many brain injured people lose their driving licences for a time but then have their driving ability re-examined by a driving expert in real-life conditions. However, this type of test only measures technical driving ability, at relatively low driving speed, in day time. Many people who display obvious executive dysfunction in a variety of real-life situations are able to satisfy the examiners regarding their competence to drive according to the criterion variables established for this test. However, the ability of such individuals to drive safely at night, in rain, in heavy traffic, and at speed, possibly when at the extreme of their attentional capability, does not form part of the criterion variables of the driving test, yet are vital to most people's understanding of good driving behaviour. Good driving skill in a test situation cannot be equated to good driving behaviour when subject to fatigue, irritation, when judgement is required, or when anticipation is needed to make a split second decision and response to avoid a collision.

The basic problem underlying the psychometric assessment of neurobehavioural disability is that psychological tests are most reliable when assessing relatively circumscribed cognitive skills, such as those comprising subtests of the WAIS-III, WMS-III (Wechsler, 1997a, b), or other specific tests of memory, perception, language, etc. Human behaviour, however, is not based on any one cognitive ability but upon combinations of ability, the nature and composition of which vary from one task or situation to another. It is also the case that people with different types of brain damage may perform similarly (badly) on the same test but for different reasons. On memory tests for example, a person who has suffered herpes simplex encephalitis may perform as badly as one who has suffered head trauma. In the first case, the poor performance can be attributed to memory impairment *per se* because amnesic syndromes are frequent legacies of the herpes simplex virus. After head injury, however, the most probable cause of poor memory is an attention deficit (amnesia after head trauma is rare), making it difficult for the person to absorb information with the result that there is poor recovery of information. Simply relying on test performance, without an understanding of the impact of different types of cerebral pathology, could lead an inexperienced clinician into drawing erroneous conclusions.

The cognitive constructs that underlie neurobehavioural disability present problems for quantitative analysis and consulting room assessments. They require expert clinical analysis as well as psychometric interpretation. Some of these cognitive constructs are considered below in the context of tests used to examine them.

ASSESSING "FRONTAL SYSTEMS"

There are a limited number of cognitive systems underpinning social and functional behaviour. For example, we must be able to grasp rules so that we can interpret events and solve novel tasks; we must be able to recognise errors in our performance in order to make corrections or adjustments to ongoing behaviour; we must plan our actions in order to have strategies for living; we must develop accurate social judgement; we must be able to attend to the right cues and to rapidly understand their significance. Few traditional neuropsychological tests are able to measure these often elusive cognitive properties. Clinicians have relied heavily on such tests as the Wisconsin Card Sorting Test (Berg, 1948) to examine rule attainment, flexibility of thinking, response competition and so on, but recently there has been an effort to design tests which elucidate the nature of executive dysfunction more precisely. Whilst accepting that the clinical value of these newer tests has often yet to be determined, the progress made in various areas is as follows.

Rule attainment and response competition.   The Brixton Test (Burgess & Shallice, 1997) is designed to measure rule attainment in a more straightforward way than the Wisconsin test. The test comprises 10 circles on each page of a booklet and one is coloured blue. As the pages of the booklet are turned, so the blue circle moves according to a rule (e.g., moving across the page left to right) and this rule is periodically changed (e.g., right to left). The test requires the subject to learn the rule determining the movement of the circle and to recognise when a new rule needs to be applied. The authors found that frontal patients make more errors than either posterior or normal controls; often making bizarre responses because they simply guess the answer.

The Hayling test (Burgess & Shallice, 1997) measures response competition, which reflects the ability to suppress inappropriate responses needed to combat thoughtlessness and impulsivity. In the first part of the test, sentences have to be completed as rapidly as possible, e.g., "The job was easy most of the ———", "The baby cried and upset her ———". The second part is exactly the same but this time the tester must supply a word that is *not* related to the sentence. This time there are two scores, obviously the total time again but also the errors, i.e., when a connected word rather than an unconnected word was supplied. There were 64 frontal cases, who scored worse than either the posterior or normal controls. Of the frontal cases, the bi-frontal subjects did especially poorly. For example, in terms of scaled scores, the normals did three times as well as the bi-frontals on error score.

Planning and organisation.   The Behavioural Assessment of the Dysexecutive Syndrome (BADS, Wilson et al., 1996) is designed to measure planning and related abilities. It is not simply a "frontal" test and does not claim to measure the site of any lesion. It has been standardised on a group of 78 patients of mixed diagnosis, over half of whom had suffered closed head injury. Unfortunately the severity of head injury is not mentioned in the manual. Seven subtests comprise the main battery. To give a flavour of them two examples will be given. The first is the *Action Programme Test* in which the patient is presented with a rectangular stand, a beaker set into it, a lid for the beaker with a small central hole in it, and a thin transparent tube with a piece of cork in the bottom, also set into the stand. There is also an L-shaped metal rod (too short to reach the cork) and a screw top container (lid off). Patients have to get the cork out of the tube without lifting the stand, tube or beaker, and without touching the lid of the beaker with their fingers. To solve the task the person has to work out a five-step procedure that requires a combination of judgement, planning, sequencing, and anticipation, all of which are sensitive to frontal dysfunction. Patients with difficulty in this task often persevere with an inappropriate strategy, such as repeatedly trying to hook the cork out with wire that is too short.

A second example of subtests from the BADS is the Zoo Map Test, in which patients show how they would visit a series of designated locations on a map of a zoo. Various rules have to be followed when planning the route. They have to start and finish at a designated place, going from the entrance to a picnic area, seeing various sights *en route*, using paths just once. The first trial emphasises planning ability, especially the efficient sequencing of events. On the second trial the patient is simply required to follow the plan without making any errors. The authors propose that comparison of performance across the two trials will permit quantitative evaluation of a person's planning ability and help clinicians decide how well check-list procedures may help patients ameliorate difficulties in executive functioning. Unfortunately, this procedure has poor test–retest reliability, which may indicate the variability in the performance of "frontal" patients, rather than a weakness in test construction.

To test for validity of the BADS test, patients were given three tests of frontal lobe functioning: the Cognition Estimates Test (Shallice & Evans, 1978); Wisconsin Card Sorting Test (Berg, 1948), and Benton's Word Fluency Test (FAS; Benton & Hamsher, 1989). Unfortunately, correlations between test scores on these and the BADS tests are not given. Rather, BADS is validated by correlating scores with a questionnaire covering 20 of the features felt to be most commonly associated with the dysexecutive syndrome, e.g., abstract thinking, impulsivity, confabulation, planning problems, apathy and lack of drive, disinhibition, and so on. This is known as the Dysexecutive Questionnaire (DEX). This strategy of validating the BADS is far from ideal because the DEX itself has not been validated as far as one can tell from the manual. However, the BADS did predict DEX scores better than did the traditional frontal tests. There are, of course, other groups who will perform poorly on the BADS other than those who have sustained traumatic brain injury. One such group is patients with schizophrenia. Evans, Chua, McKenna, and Wilson (1997) gave the BADS to 31 schizophrenics matched to brain injured and healthy controls, schizophrenics being felt to have a disturbance of the supervisory attentional system, giving rise to some of the core symptoms of dysexecutive syndrome. The schizophrenics scored as badly as the brain injured patients on both the BADS and the DEX.

Estimation.   The ability to make estimates is required for successful planning because different hypothetical outcomes need to be weighed up. Estimation tasks have quite a long history and seem to be invested with a degree of ecological validity. A good example is Smith and Milner (1984), who looked at the ability of people with frontal and temporal lobe lesions to estimate the prices of objects such as a pair of scissors, a house, a car, a sewing machine, tennis racquet, and so on. The frontal group (7 left and 12 right frontal) made the most pricing errors. They did not just overestimate or underestimate, but got it wrong in both directions, and it was the right frontal group that was worst of all. The problem with using this approach as a test of ability is that prices change over time and so if it were to be used clinically it would have to be re-normed regularly to remain valid. The most commonly used estimation task is the "Cognitive Estimates Test" (Shallice & Evans, 1978) in which the person estimates the size, number, or weight of various things, such as the weight of a bottle of milk, but this test suffers from similar problems in that it was developed in pre-metric days (and most milk is now in cartons), so it may not be appropriate for younger people.

Strategy tasks.   The way someone goes about a task provides important information about how they approach real-life situations. The Route-Finding Task is an example of an ecological test of adaptation and task solution (Boyd & Sautter, 1993). Thirty-one traumatic brain injury cases, at Rancho levels VI–VIII, followed a protocol whereby they had to start at a designated point on the campus and find an office also on the campus, with which they were not familiar. Performance on this unstructured and open-ended task requires patients to use their initiative by asking for directions, and requires that they realise when they have got lost. Their performance is rated along various dimensions, such as information-seeking, retaining directions, error detection (self-monitoring), and error correction. Performance correlated with scores on a frontal test (the Category Test, Reitan & Wolfson, 1993) and also with verbal comprehension. The most prominent feature of their performance was the need for cues about what needed to be done once they had lost their way.

Another environmental measure of strategic thinking is the Multiple Errands Test devised by Shallice and Burgess (1991). The test is undertaken in a pedestrian precinct, preferably one which is unfamiliar to the patient. The patient is given eight instructions which essentially comprise three task sets, each of which has slightly different requirements. One task involves a simple five-item shopping list, such as: buy a loaf of bread, throat pastilles, pound of tomatoes, etc. Another task involves working memory and requires the subject to be at a certain place 15 minutes after starting the shopping task. The final task requires the subject to obtain certain information available in the precinct, such as the exchange rate of the French franc, or the lowest temperature in the UK the previous day. The subject is not presented with three different sets of tasks but with a general set of instructions which comprise all the task requirements. In addition to task instructions the subject is also presented with a list of rules to observe during test performance, such as only to enter shops within the prescribed area, not to enter a shop unless it is to purchase something, etc. The examiner must ensure that the subject understands the task requirements but leaves it up to the subject to give some structure to the general instructions.

The three frontal lobe patients in this study all had superior scores on WAIS-R verbal tests and high average to superior scores on performance tests. Memory function was in the average range on most tests and a normal performance was obtained on "frontal" tasks, such as the Wisconsin test, Verbal Fluency, and Cognitive Estimates. Their performance on the Multiple Errands Test was compared to nine normal controls. The patients' performance were characterised by rule breaks—going out of bounds, interpretation failure—misunderstanding the task, inefficiencies—failure to check the time, looking in irrelevant shops, and stopping before all the errands had been completed. Their performance was both qualitatively and quantitatively inferior to the controls. Clinical experience has shown that this procedure, whilst time-consuming for staff, provides very useful information on a range of executive weaknesses. However, it is more suitable for assessments which take place in rehabilitation units than in the consulting room. The test is impossible to standardise because it has to be adapted to suit the layout of local shopping precincts.

A similar approach, that of observing how an open-ended task is carried out, is to be found in the Structured Observational Test of Function (SOTOF) (Laver & Powell, 1995). This was developed to provide a detailed description of functional status and associated neuropsychological deficits in the performance of personal activities of daily living. There are four tasks: eating from a bowl, washing hands, pouring and drinking from a cup, and putting on a shirt. As can be seen from the simplicity of the tasks, the test is most useful in the early stages of recovery. The patient carries out the tasks while an observer completes a detailed schedule of observation of the component skills required, and these observations are then used to identify various cognitive problems. Norms are provided for 86 healthy elderly controls and data is reported from 151 stroke patients.

Speed and accuracy of attention and information processing. Mental speed is necessary to deal with complex real-time situations. One measure of performance in the Hayling Test is speed, and speed of processing can be the prime focus of other tests. An example with ecological relevance is Godfrey et al. (1989). They investigated speed of information processing and social interaction in 18 adults who had suffered very severe head injury with a PTA longer than 7 days. Speed of processing was assessed on lexical and visual tasks and by measuring speed of speech. Social interaction was measured by directly observing the person talking, "chatting" to a research worker over a coffee break from tests. A second measure was a role-played situation of a job interview. Both speed of information processing and speech were slowed, and speech seemed less spontaneous. Speech speed and spontaneity correlated strongly with ratings of how interesting, likeable, and socially skilled the people were.

Another recently published test of speed and accuracy of attention is the Test of Everyday Attention (Robertson, Ward, Ridgeway, & Nimmo-Smith, 1994). This uses tasks which are ecologically relevant, such as searching for restaurants on a map, or for plumbers in a telephone directory. There are also tasks which assess divided attention by asking the patient to do two things at once, such as searching the telephone directory whilst counting. The reliability data is good but the test may be more sensitive in discriminating attentional weaknesses in people with higher levels of intelligence. Speed and accuracy of information processing are also measured by the Speed of Comprehension Test (Baddeley, Emslie, & Nimmo-Smith, 1992). Patients have to indicate as fast as possible whether quite simple sentences are true or false, e.g., "Nuns are made in factories". The test has good reliability and comes in four forms, which allows for retesting.

Memory. We must retrieve relevant information so as to be in a position to make decisions wisely. Unfortunately, good performance on clinical tests of memory does not necessarily mean good performance of everyday memory. This is because of the different attentional demands required in each setting (in a clinical test of memory one is able to focus all of one's attention on a task but in real life attention is divided over several ideas or activities). One of the first tests explicitly aiming for higher ecological validity is the Rivermead Behavioural Memory Test (Wilson, Cockburn, & Baddeley, 1985). The nature of different subtests reflects an interest in what the patient has to do on a daily basis: e.g., remember a name, remember a hidden object, remember an appointment, remember a newspaper article, recognise a face, learn a new route, deliver a message, remember the day and date, and recall things that have been shown to them. This is as far from the learning of nonsense syllable or meaningless word lists as it is possible to get in the context of a consulting room assessment. Furthermore, the authors recognise the need for repeat testing to monitor change, and so there are four different versions. The test can lack sensitivity (and hence validity) in cases of milder head injury and more subtle memory deficits, because it takes quite gross impairment for the patient to fail many items, but it is a very useful test early on in the recovery phase, and as Spreen and Strauss (1998) say, "failure on most of the tests in this battery is unequivocal evidence of a socially crippling memory disorder" (p. 512).

Making social judgements.   People in the community are confronted with a wide range of interpersonal tasks, the satisfactory handling of which requires accurate perception of the other person. Pettersen (1991) looked at social behaviour in 20 head injured children, who had been in a coma for a median of 7.5 days, to see if they were sensitive to emotional cues and whether such cues were used to help determine appropriate social behaviour. The 20 patients (and 20 controls) undertook several tasks: recognising the emotional content of pictures of events, identifying the emotion of characters in a story that is read out, and labelling facial expression. The children with head injury were, for example, less able to reason out why a person in a vignette should feel a particular way, and made errors of emotional recognition. On a parents' questionnaire of appropriate and mature social behaviour, the head injured children were less able to respond to hints or indirect cues in conversation, more likely to try and monopolise conversation, less likely to apologise for hurting other peoples' feelings, and more likely to have trouble understanding the point of others' jokes or humorous remarks. Overall, children who had been in longer coma were at greater risk for some of the deficits described in this study. For example, they tended to "fuse" positive and negative emotions, i.e., treat them as the same on the grounds that they were both emotional states, ignoring their opposite polarity.

SELF- AND OTHER REPORTS

Instead of a formal assessment, either patients themselves or someone who knows them can complete a rating scale, the latter often acting as a measure of validity of the former. A range of relevant measures have been used in relation to neurobehavioural disability. A brief outline of some of them follows.

Everyday memory questionnaires.   Hickox and Sunderland (1992) have reviewed questionnaire and check-list approaches in the assessment of everyday memory problems. There appears to be a difference in the way such problems are perceived by the brain injured person and relatives or friends who are in daily contact with the injured person. The perceptions of the former are unreliable, either over- or underestimating the intrusive impact of poor memory, with a poor relationship between self-reports and memory test performance. Lezak (1995) comments on the value of self-report methods to help distinguish the often exaggerated reports of memory deficits in depressives compared to the underestimates after certain types of brain injury.

Cognitive failure.   Ahead of its time and underused, the Cognitive Failures Questionnaire (Broadbent, Cooper, Fitzgerald, & Parkes, 1982) systematically probes for those inexplicable lapses that we all have, but which become a resident feature of dysexecutive syndrome and neurobehavioural problems. The questionnaires, one for the person with brain damage and one for someone who knows them well, cover absent-mindedness and slips of action, such as failing to see what you want in a supermarket although you know it is there; accidentally throwing away the thing you want and keeping what you meant to throw away; starting to do one thing and finding yourself doing another; and experiencing the tip of the tongue phenomenon. Norms are provided for a wide range of normal groups, totalling over 600 people. There is a small but significant correlation with neuroticism and anxiety (about 10% of variance shared), and it is not often significantly related to IQ or scores on various objective memory tests.

Executive functions.   The Dysexecutive Questionnaire from the BADS has already been described, but there are alternatives available, such as the Executive Functions Scale (Coolidge & Griego, 1995). The scale specifically sets out to test "the executive function of the frontal lobes" and draws items from the Coolidge Axis II inventory, which assesses personality and neuropsychological change in accordance with DSM-IV. There are three subscales: Decision-Making Difficulty, Task Incompletion, and Poor Planning. Seventeen patients in a cognitive rehabilitation programme were particularly poor on the decision-making scale (e.g., letting other people make decisions, difficulty starting projects, avoiding or postponing making decisions).

Ways of coping.   The Revised Ways of Coping Scale (Folkman et al., 1986) is widely used and is clearly relevant to people with neurobehavioural problems who struggle to cope with everyday demands. The various ways of coping are confrontive, problem solving, averting responsibility, distancing, self-controlling, escape avoidance, position reappraisal, and seek social support. Moore and Stambrook (1992) used the scale in 53 cases of traumatic brain injury, the majority in the moderate to severe category, and all men. The subjects formed two clusters, distinguished by the ability to exert self-control and to appraise things in a more positive light. Those who could exert self-control had a better quality of life with less mood disturbance and psychosocial difficulties (they were also older and had more physical injuries). This work has been extended by Malia, Powell, and Torode (1995a), who compared 74 brain injured cases with 46 controls—the brain injured cases being mainly in the very severe category, with an average post-traumatic amnesia (PTA) of 26 days. Factor analysis showed four broad patterns of coping—problem focused, emotion focused, wishful thinking and avoidance. Better psychosocial outcome was found in those who used problem rather than emotion focused coping and who did not use wishful thinking or avoidance strategies.

Adjustment.   The product of the coping process is of course the degree of adjustment shown by the individual. The Katz Adjustment Scale has been modified for use with victims of traumatic brain injury by Jackson et al. (1992), and it is filled in by a relative or someone who knows the patient well. There are three first order factors: emotional or psychosocial (e.g., argues, temper, no control of emotions), physical/intellectual (e.g., concentration, repetition, decision making, clumsy, slow movement, slow speech), and psychiatric (e.g., fears, bizarreness, depression). Those with more severe head injuries were especially high on poor social judgement, incongruent emotional behaviour, and apathetic or amotivational behaviour. Alternatively, the original version of the Katz can be used. For example, Newton and Johnson (1985) reported poor social performance, high social anxiety, and low self-esteem in severely head injured patients.

Personality.   There are various ways that personality has been assessed following head injury. Tyerman and Humphrey (1984) use semantic differential-type bipolar ratings of Present Self, Past Self and Future Self (e.g., worried–relaxed, despondent–hopeful, inactive–active). Patients typically see major detrimental changes in themselves but hope to get back to their normal, past self at some stage in the future. Herbert and Powell (1989a, b) use the Eysenck Personality Questionnaire and various measures of insight. Those patients who were extraverted and optimistic about themselves and their recovery were better motivated and did best in rehabilitation. Lanoo et al. (1997) used the Neuroticism–Extraversion–Openness Five-Factor Inventory (NEO-FFI) with 68 cases of moderate to severe head injury. Both the patients and the relatives filled it in, with respect to both pre-injury and current personality. After the head injury, patients were more neurotic and less extraverted, and patients tended to underestimate the degree of change in comparison with the changes observed by the relatives.

Agitation.   A key factor in adjustment is overt behavioural disturbance, and this is assessed in the Agitated Behaviour Scale (Corrigan & Bogner, 1994), a 14-item scale for use primarily in the acute or early phase, standardised on 212 patients with acquired brain injury. The scale covers impulsiveness, uncooperativeness, violence or threat of violence, self-stimulation behaviour, wandering, restlessness, sudden changes of mood, and so forth. There are three factors—disinhibition, aggression, and lability—but straightforward use of the total score is recommended by the authors.

Aggression. Later on in the recovery phase, agitation may evolve into aggression. In such cases the Overt Aggression Scale can be useful (Alderman, Knight, & Morgan, 1997), covering verbal aggression, aggression against objects, aggression against self, and aggression against others. Data is provided on 18 cases of very severe head injury. The scale gives not just a description of the aggressive act itself, but also codes the antecedent events and the consequences. For example, most aggression took place during structured sessions, and very often in response to a verbal prompt or other patients' verbal behaviour or attempts at verbal interaction. The most frequent response of the rehabilitation staff was to ignore the behaviour or withdraw reinforcement.

Sexuality. Changes in sexual behaviour and feelings after head injury are very common and frequently give rise to sexual dysfunction. This can be assessed by the Golombok–Rust Inventory of Sexual Satisfaction (GRISS) (Rust & Golombok, 1986). It is a 28-item self-report scale coming in both male and female versions, covering the main specific dysfunction and general aspects such as dissatisfaction and non-communication. O'Carroll, Woodrow, and Maroun (1991) present data on 36 cases of closed head injury, two thirds in the moderate or severe categories. Of these cases, half fell into the dysfunctional range.

Kreuter et al. (1998) provide similar information in a rather larger sample of 92 traumatic brain injury cases, the great majority of whom were in the severe category, with a mean PTA of four weeks. A structured questionnaire was used and it was found that head injury alters sexual functioning as well as desire. For example, 30% of the men reported decreased or absent ability to achieve an erection. *Hyper*-sexuality was rare—only 5% reported an increase in libido.

Interpersonal relationship. Interpersonal relationships in a more general sense have been assessed by Elsass and Kinsella (1987) and Kinsella, Ford, and Moran (1989). The first study individually matched 15 severely head injured patients with 15 controls, and employed the Interview Schedule for Social Interaction, which measures the availability and adequacy of attachment and social integration, tolerance to not having attachments, and the number of attachments. The head injury group had significantly less opportunity for attachment and integration, and relied significantly more upon their family as the source of attachments. The second study was larger scale, comprising 38 severe closed head injury patients, and confirmed reduced availability of attachments, especially in men rather than women.

Response bias. Finally comes a reminder of possible biases in self-report. Lees-Haley et al. (1997) compared the self-report of 131 litigants seeing forensic neuropsychologists with 315 non-litigants. Litigants and non-litigants did not differ on any demographic variable. The litigants recalled prior functioning as more superior or less problematic than did non-forensic patients, e.g., better concentration, better memory, less depression and anxiety, less headache, less confusion, less fatigue, and so forth. In effect, litigants over-idealise their state prior to the accident or injury. As a second example of response bias, Mittenberg et al. (1992) found that patients with brain injury underestimated the frequency of symptoms before their injury compared with a group of matched controls, significant on 21 of the 30 specific symptoms studied.

Overall, as can be seen from these papers, there are a range of questionnaire and report measures available to help gauge neurobehavioural disability, but their focus is narrow and normative data is often sparse, so their use should be to inform clinical interviewing and decision making rather than supplant them.

COMMUNICATION AND INTERPERSONAL BEHAVIOUR

Communication, as a measure of social competence, was assessed by Marsh and Knight (1991) in a study of 18 very severely head injured patients, living in the community with rehabilitation support, compared with 27 matched controls. Three social interactions were videotaped of each patient, twice with someone they knew and once with an opposite-sex stranger. With their friends, they discussed solving a problem or making a decision, and with the stranger it was in the guise of a social break from doing questionnaires. Using rating schedules, various barriers to successful reintegration were noted: Patients were less appropriate in their use of language and speech delivery, and had developed a speech style that lacked fluency, continuity, and clarity. They also showed less interest in the other person, not reinforcing others or stimulating them to converse.

Even finer detail of conversation after head injury has been considered by Bond and Godfrey (1997). They compared the conversation of 62 traumatic brain injury patients (PTA in excess of 24 hours) with 25 orthopaedic controls. The patients were videotaped spending 15 minutes just getting to know someone they had met for the first time. There was a particular interest in prompts that initiated or maintained conversations. The brain injured patients used fewer cues to prompt conversation from the other person, and once they were speaking they spoke longer before giving the other person a turn. This meant that talking to a brain injured person was rated more of an effort and less rewarding and interesting. This will relate also to why head injured patients can create a poor first impression, as found by Spence, Godfrey, Knight, and Bishara (1993). Each of 14 patients was videotaped while engaged in an informal chat, during which time seven standard prompts were used to elicit a response, and a 2-minute segment of speech was analysed in fine detail. The head injury patients were rated as less skilful than controls, with a tendency to over-respond to prompts; i.e., to perseverate on topics.

Deficits in conversation and interpersonal behaviour could be construed as a problem of social cognition (see Chapter 1). This has intuitive appeal because of the way that patients with frontal lobe or executive disorders appear as immature and gauche (Thomsen, 1989). Coelho, Lites, and Duffy (1995) showed how aspects of narrative discourse correlated with a standard measure of frontal involvement, the Wisconsin Card Sorting Test. They found that patients were able to describe episodes within stories, but the episodes were more likely to be incomplete in those scoring badly on the card sorting task, i.e., they might miss out what precipitated an episode, what was actually done in that episode, or what the direct consequences were. In other words, they failed to give the listener all the information necessary to understand an episode. Problems negotiating and communicating properly are also described, amongst other problems, in a unique study by Goel et al. (1997). Ten patients with frontal lobe damage and 10 matched controls had to advise a young couple how to balance their budget, purchase a house in the next 2 years, send their children to college in 15–20 years, and have sufficient funds to retire in 35 years. All of the patients prior to the accident had worked, rented or bought a house, raised children and sent them to school, so they could identify with the task. Each patient did the task individually by examining balance sheets and income statements, and by asking for further information. The authors did not volunteer information or initiate discussion or help directly in any way, but did encourage them to ask questions as necessary. The patients were videotaped as they analysed the task and went about solving it. The tape was then subjected to protocol analysis. The frontal lobe patients had trouble deciding how much time and effort to devote to each problem-solving phase. They had difficulty dealing with the fact that there were no right or wrong answers; they found it problematic to generate their own feedback; they could not take full advantage of the fact that constraints on real-world problems are negotiable; and they invariably terminated the session before the details were fleshed out and all the goals satisfied.

Disorders of social communication following brain damage have been thoroughly reviewed in a recent textbook (McDonald, Togher, & Code, 1999). This book addresses the different aims and procedures of *discourse analysis*, exploring the relationships between structure and function of language; *pragmatic analysis*, which evaluates the relationship between conversational language and the context in which it occurs; and *conversational analysis*, to determine how brain injured people manage spontaneous conversation. Deficits in these aspects of communication are then considered in respect of their impact on decision making and social interaction. This is a specialist area which has considerable relevance to neurobehavioural rehabilitation and those working in this area are advised to become conversant with the concepts and methods described by McDonald et al.

FAMILY RELATIONSHIPS

Living with socially de-skilled people who have undergone major personality change can be a considerable burden, straining marriages and relationships (Brooks, 1991; Lezak, 1988; Liss & Willer, 1990; Chapter 3, this volume). Therefore, the full assessment of neurobehavioural disorder requires an assessment of marital and family functioning. The scale of the problem is set out by Wood and Yurdakul (1997), who looked at the relationship histories of 131 adults with head injury, three quarters of whom had severe head injuries with a PTA longer than one day. All of these patients prior to the accident had been married or with long-term partners, but afterwards 49% had divorced or separated by eight years post-accident. The divorce rate in the general population is not cited, but this does seem a very high figure. It did not matter whether the patient was male or female, nor whether they had children, nor their age. However, the longer the couple had been together before the accident, the better chance of their relationship surviving. Wood's study took marital breakdown as the index of relationship breakdown. Another index is the emergence of battering, and here Rosenbaum et al. (1994) looked at the history of head injury in men who battered their wives, to find that a significantly higher percentage of batterers than non-batterers had a history of significant head injury; indeed, 53% had had a mild head injury (typically rendered unconscious but with a PTA less than one hour) and 21% had had at least a moderate head injury (PTA more than one hour).

One of the most straightforward ways of assessing strains in the marriage is to evaluate the level of symptomatology in each of the partners. A typical example is Linn, Allen, and Willer (1994), who gave a symptom check-list (the SCL-90) to 60 brain injured people and their spouses, about 6 years post-injury. Depression was shown by 70% of the patients and 73% of spouses, with similar figures for anxiety: 50% and 55% respectively. Bearing in mind the findings of Rosenbaum et al. about battering, Linn et al. also used the Social Aggression Scale, which assesses anger, verbal and physical outbursts, aggressive behaviour, and the tendency to make obscene gestures. Aggression in the head injured person proved to be a key factor in predicting depression in the partner.

Rather than use standard scales of symptoms, some studies use measures that more directly tap the nature of the interaction. For example, Peters, Stambrook, Moore, and Esses (1990) used the Dyadic Adjustment Scale (DAS) and the Personal Assessment of Intimacy in Relations (PAIR). Scores on these interaction variables related to severity of head injury; those with more severe injuries emitted fewer overt acts of physical or verbal affection, and it was more difficult to achieve dyadic consensus with them. Peters et al. (1992) also used the DAS, this time comparing head injury with spinal cases as well as looking at the effects of severity of head injury. Partners of the more severely head injured again reported less expressed affection, reduced cohesiveness, and lower overall marital adjustment.

The effects on the relationship were more pronounced for the severe head injury group than for the spinal cord group.

Another measure more directly tapping the nature of interactions is the Family Assessment Device (FAD). This assesses general functioning but also has subscales concerning Behaviour Control, Affective Involvement, Affective Responsiveness, Roles, Communication, and Problem Solving. Kreutzer, Gervasio, and Camplair (1994a, b) administered the FAD in 62 cases of traumatic brain injury, of whom the majority were in the moderate or severe category. It was found that family functioning was worse than in 627 normals but not as bad as in 1138 psychiatric cases. The worst aspect of function was the communication between family members; 56% were above the cut-off point for unhealthy functioning. The special problem with communication is understandable in the light of the earlier studies cited to do with social skill deficiencies and reduced developmental level of reasoning.

Hall et al. (1994) followed up the caregivers of 51 traumatic brain injury patients at 6, 12 and 24 months post-injury. An important feature of such a design is to show how certain problems *increase* over time. Normally, one thinks of functions such as memory, language, apraxia, and so on improving quite rapidly early on and then tailing off to gentle long-term improvement. However, a distinctive feature of neuro*behavioural* problems is that they are determined by situational and behavioural principles, and do not simply echo the organic recovery process. The behaviour of the individual over time may deteriorate as a result of, for example:

1. Increasing frustration at handicaps.
2. Increasing awareness of type of deficits.
3. Increasing awareness of permanency of deficits.
4. Increasing tensions in previously stable relationships.
5. Decreasing attention from the environment.
6. Decreasing demands made by the environment.
7. Fewer cues to correct behaviour emitted by the environment once removed from the rehabilitation setting.
8. Increasing loss of status.
9. Gradual estrangement from normal environments and relationships.
10. Increasing habit strength of abnormal behaviours.

In Hall and colleagues' study, temper outbursts and aggressiveness were problems in 30% and 20% of cases at 6 months, but in 48% and 35% of cases at 2 years. In spite of this increase in difficult behaviours, the caregivers actually tended to report less subjective stress. This was because they were acquiring appropriate skills—caregivers became more confident at handling problems, were less likely to come up against difficulties they would not overcome, and felt more able to control important things. However, it will be recalled from the previously described research on divorce that just because the caregiver feels more capable does not mean the relationship becomes more rewarding and hence sustainable. Essentially, the role of wife can change to that of caregiver, allowing the marital relationship to wither.

The process of coping with such role changes was investigated by Willer, Liss, and Zicht (1991). The able-bodied wives of traumatically brain injured patients placed high priority on the use of support groups. This study used structured, small group discussion to elicit a prioritised list of coping strategies. Use of support groups apparently helped them develop a realistic outlook; become more assertive with their disabled husbands, care providers, in-laws, and insurance representatives; helped them to allow their husband to become more independent; and reinforced the need for them to take time for themselves. Again, though, it needs to be stated that just because someone copes better with change, does not mean that family relations are more rewarding or more normal. So, for example, Brown and Nell (1992) found family relationships *worsening* from 6 to 12 to 24 months, in a large-scale longitudinal study of 143 cases, more than half of whom had moderate to severe head injuries. Brown and Nell conclude, along with all clinicians who work in this field, that rehabilitation programmes must include caregivers, and that the focus must be on the adjustment of both parties to their new circumstances and roles.

CONCLUSIONS

In reviewing measures relating to neurobehavioural disability, various questions should be borne in mind:

1. To what extent do traditional tests address cognitive processes underpinning neurobehavioural disability?
2. Do more recently developed tests actually replicate real life and achieve ecological validity?
3. Is there a role for self-reports, and significant-other reports of behaviour and cognition?
4. Should we be employing methods of direct observation of behaviour?
5. Should we seek to determine how neurobehavioural disability may reflect complex personality problems that may be generated or reinforced by the individual's family relationships?

These questions need to be addressed to help shape future trends in neurobehavioural assessment.

Whilst not necessarily statistically robust at present, many of the observational and self-report measures described in this chapter help to elucidate the characteristics of frontal dysfunction and neurobehavioural disability in a more objective, structured, and reproducible manner. Having reviewed developments in the assessment of neurobehavioural disability and considered the purpose and requirements of such tests and assessment procedures, it is possible to identify various crucial trends. These are:

1. To focus on key psychometric tests thought to relate to key behavioural domains.
2. To choose behavioural domains that are predictive of rehabilitation needs and progress.
3. To modify the format of tests better to reflect real-life tasks.
4. To modify the assessment to better reflect real-life settings and conditions,
5. To use and develop questionnaires, interviews, and small groups to elicit clearer accounts of behaviour.
6. To incorporate the measurement of well-being and frank mental health.
7. To extend the assessment to partners and families and to the nature of interactions.

In short, the assessment of neurobehavioural problems involves the use of the full armoury of assessment techniques available to psychology today. Any one test, any one approach, at any one point in time, in any one setting is likely, at best, to give partial information and, at worst, miss the disability and handicap altogether. Reports and questionnaires may show various response biases due, for example, to lack of insight, wishful thinking, memory failures, and even intentional manipulation. Another strategy therefore is to try and observe the behaviour itself, in as near a real-life setting as possible (see Wood & Worthington, 1999). Assessments that take place in rehabilitation centres should be capable of going beyond straightforward, descriptive, frequency accounts of behaviour. It is possible to analyse real-time behaviour, i.e., recording, transcribing, and coding behaviour and language to reflect the processes in behaviour that might underpin the many psychosocial problems that are known to reflect neurobehavioural disability. This could provide a more substantial basis for developing treatment interventions and measuring social recovery.

Structured and systematic observations of brain injured people attempting to execute routine activities of daily living have helped rehabilitation practitioners distinguish between intelligence as a psychological construct, and applied intelligence, as a form of socially adaptive behaviour. One important observation has been to differentiate between a person's ability to express knowledge (the idea of how a task is performed) from the actual ability itself (successfully implementing the task). Walsh (1985) commented on the dislocation between being able to verbalise how one should proceed with a task, yet not being able to act on that knowledge, what Teuber (1964) referred to as "the curious dissociation between knowing and doing". This legacy of frontal injury is easily overlooked if one restricts oneself to testing a person's verbal intelligence (IQ) rather than attempting to measure knowledge by observations of cognitive performance in real-life activities.

REFERENCES

Adams, J.H. (1995). The neuropathology of head injury. In P.J. Vinken & G.W. Bruyn (Eds.), Handbook of clinical neurology (Vol. 23, pp. 55–65). Amsterdam: North Holland Publishing.

Alderman, N., Knight, C., & Morgan, C. (1997). Use of a modified version of the Overt Aggression Scale in the measurement and assessment of aggressive behaviour following brain injury. *Brain Injury, 11*, 503–523.

Baddeley, A., Emslie, H., & Nimmo-Smith, I. (1992). *The speed and capacity of language-processing test.* Bury St. Edmunds: Thames Valley Test Company.

Benton, A.L., & Hamsher, K. de S. (1989). *Multilingual Aphasia Examination.* Iowa City, IA: AJA Associates.

Berg, E.A. (1948). A simple objective treatment for measuring flexibility in thinking. *Journal of General Psychology, 39*, 15–22.

Bond, F., & Godfrey, H.P.D. (1997). Conversation with traumatically brain-injured individuals: A controlled study of behavioural changes and their impact. *Brain Injury, 11*, 319–329.

Boyd, T.M., & Sautter, S.W. (1993). Route-finding: A measure of everyday executive functioning in the head-injured adult. *Applied Cognitive Psychology, 7*, 171–181.

Broadbent, D.E., Cooper, P., FitzGerald, P., & Parkes, K.R. (1982). The Cognitive Failures Questionnaire (CFQ) and its correlates. *British Journal of Clinical Psychology, 21*, 1–16.

Brooks, D.N. (1991). The head-injured family. *Journal of Clinical and Experimental Neuropsychology, 13*, 155–188.

Brown, D.S., & Nell, V. (1992). Recovery from diffuse traumatic brain injury in Johannesburg: A concurrent prospective study. *Archives of Physical Medicine Rehabilitation, 73*, 758–770.

Burgess, P.W., & Shallice, T. (1997). *The Hayling and Brixton Tests; manual.* Bury St Edmunds: Thames Valley Test Company Ltd.

Coelho, C.A., Lites, B.Z., & Duffy, R.J. (1995). Impairments of discourse abilities and executive functions in traumatically brain-injured adults. *Brain Injury, 9*, 471–477.

Coolidge, F.L., & Griego, J. A. (1995). Executive function of the frontal lobes: Psychometric properties of a self-rating scale. *Psychological Reports, 77*, 24–26.

Corrigan, J.D. & Bogner, J.A. (1994). Factor structure of the Agitated Behaviour Scale. *Journal of Clinical and Experimental Neuropsychology, 16*, 386–392.

Diller, L., & Gordon, W.A. (1981). Criteria for cognitive deficits in brain injured adults. *Journal of Consulting and Clinical Psychology, 49*, 822–834.

Elsass, L., & Kinsella, G. (1987). Social interaction following severe closed head injury. *Psychological Medicine, 17*, 67–78.

Eslinger, P.J., & Damasio, A.R., (1985) Severe disturbance of higher cognitive function after bilateral frontal lobe ablation: Patient EVR. *Neurology, 35*, 1731–1741.

Evans, J.J., Chua, S.E., McKenna, P.J., & Wilson, B.A. (1997). Assessment of the dysexecutive syndrome in schizophrenia. *Psychological Medicine, 27*, 635–646.

Folkman, S., Lazarus, R.S., Dunkel-Schetter, C., Grunen, R.J., & DeLongis, A. (1986). Appraisal, coping, health status and psychological symptoms. *Journal of Personality and Social Psychology, 50*, 571–579.

Godfrey, H.P.D., Knight, R.G., Marsh, N.V., Moroney, B., & Bishara, S.N. (1989). Social interaction and speed of information processing following severe closed head injury. *Psychological Medicine, 19*, 175–182.

Goel, V., Grafman, J., Tajik, J., Gana, S., & Danto, D. (1997). A study of the performance of patients with frontal lobe lesions in a financial planning task. *Brain, 120*, 1805–1822.

Hall, K.M., Karzmark, P., Stevens, M., Englander, J., O'Hare, P., & Wright, J. (1994). Family stressors in traumatic brain injury: A two-year follow-up. *Archives of Physical Medicine and Rehabilitation, 75*, 876–884.

Herbert, C.M., & Powell, G.E. (1989a). The role of personality factors in rehabilitation. *Personality and individual Differences, 10*, 969–973.

Herbert, C.M., & Powell, G.E. (1989b). Insight and progress in rehabilitation, *Clinical Rehabilitation, 3*, 125–130.

Hickox, A., & Sunderland, A. (1992). Questionnaire and checklist approaches to assessment of everyday memory problems. In J.R. Crawford, D.M. Parker, & W.W. Mckinley (Eds.), *A handbook of neuropsychological assessment.* Hove, UK: Lawrence Erlbaum.

Jackson, H.F., Hopewell, C.A., Glass, C.A., Warburgh, R., Dewey, M., & Ghadiali, E. (1992). The Katz Adjustment Scale: Modification for use with victims of traumatic brain and spinal injury. *Brain Injury, 6*, 109–127.

Kay, T., & Silver, S.M. (1989). Closed head injury trauma: Assessment for rehabilitation. In M.D. Lezak (Ed.), *Assessment of behavioural consequences of head trauma.* (pp. 145–170). New York: Liss Inc.

Kinsella, G., Ford, B., & Moran, C. (1989). Survival of social relationships following head injury. *International Disability Studies, 11*, 9–14.

Kreuter, M., Dahllöf, A.-G., Gudjonsson, G., Sullivan, M., & Siösteen, A. (1998). Sexual adjustment and its predictors after traumatic brain injury. *Brain Injury, 12*, 349–368.

Kreutzer, J.S., Gervasio, A.H., & Camplair, P.S. (1994a). Patient correlates of caregivers' distress and family functioning after traumatic brain injury. *Brain Injury, 8*, 211–230.

Kreutzer, J.S., Gervasio, A.H., & Camplair, P.S. (1994b). Primary caregivers' psychological status and family functioning after traumatic brain injury. *Brain Injury, 8*, 197–210.

Lanoo, E., DeDeyne, C., Colardyn, F., De Soete, G., & Jannes, C. (1997). Personality change following head injury: Assessment with the NEO five-factor inventory. *Journal of Psychosomatic Research, 43*, 505–511.

Laver, A.J., & Powell, G.E. (1995). *The Structured Observational Test of Function; manual.* Windsor, UK: NFER-Nelson.

Lees-Haley, P.R., Williams, C.W., Zasler, N.D., Marguites, S., English, L., & Stevens, K. (1997). Response bias in plaintiffs' histories. *Brain Injury, 11*, 791–799.

Lezak, M.D. (1988). Brain damage is a family affair. *Journal of Clinical and Experimental Neuropsychology, 10*, 111–123.

Lezak, M.D. (1995). *Neuropsychological assessment* (Third Edition). Oxford: Oxford University Press.

Linn, R.T., Allen, K., & Willer, B.S. (1994). Affective symptoms in the chronic stage of traumatic brain injury: A study of married couples. *Brain Injury, 8*, 135–147.

Liss, M., & Willer, B. (1990). Traumatic brain injury and marital relationships: A literature review. *International Journal of Rehabilitation Research, 13*, 309–320.

Malia, K., Powell, G.E., & Torode, S. (1995a). Coping as psychosocial function after brain injury. *Brain Injury, 9*, 607–618.

Malia, K., Powell, G.E., & Torode, S. (1995b). Personality and psychosocial function after brain injury. *Brain Injury, 9*, 697–712.

Marsh, N.V., & Knight, R.G. (1991). Behavioural assessment of social competence following severe head injury. *Journal of Clinical and Experimental Neuropsychology, 13*, 729–740.

McDonald, S., Togher, L., & Code, C. (1999). *Communication disorders following traumatic brain injury.* Hove, UK: Psychology Press.

Mittenberg, W., DiGiulio, D.V., & Perrin, S. (1992). Symptoms following mild head injury: Expectation as aetiology. *Journal of Neurology, Neurosurgery, and Psychiatry, 55*, 200–204.

Moore, A.D., & Stambrook, M. (1992). Coping strategies and locus of control following traumatic brain injury: Relationship to long-term outcome. *Brain Injury*, 6, 89–94.

Newcombe, F. (1993). Frontal lobe disorders. In R. Greenwood, M. Barnes, T.M. McMillan, & C.D. Ward (Eds.), *Neurological rehabilitation* (pp. 377–389). London: Churchill Livingstone.

Newcombe, F., & Artiola i Fortuny, L.A. (1979). Problems and perspectives in the evaluation of psychological deficits after cerebral lesions. *International Journal of Rehabilitation Medicine, 1*, 182–192.

Newton, A., & Johnson, D.A. (1985). Social adjustment and interaction after severe head injury. *British Journal of Clinical Psychology, 24*, 225–234.

O'Carroll, R.E., Woodrow, J., & Maroun, F. (1991). Psychosexual and psychosocial sequelae of closed head injury. *Brain Injury, 5*, 303–313.

Peters, L.C., Stambrook, M., Moore, A.D., & Esses, L. (1990). Psychosocial sequelae of clonal head injury: Effects on the marital relationship. *Brain Injury, 4*, 39–47.

Peters, L.C., Stambrook, M., Moore, A.D., Zubek, E., & Dubo, H. (1992). Differential effects of spinal cord injury and head injury on marital adjustment. *Brain Injury, 6*, 461–467.

Pettersen, L. (1991). Sensitivity to emotional cues and social behaviour in children and adolescents after head injury. *Perceptual and Motor Skills, 73*, 1139–1150.

Ponsford, J. (1995). *Traumatic brain injury*. Hove, UK: Lawrence Erlbaum.

Powell, G.E. (2000). Cognitive assessment. In M.G. Gelder, J.J. Lopez-Ibor, & N.C. Anderson (Eds.), *New Oxford textbook of psychiatry*. Oxford: Oxford University Press.

Reitan, R.M., & Wolfson, D. (1993). *The Halstead–Reitan Neuropsychological Test Battery: Theory and clinical interpretation*. Tuscon, AZ: Neuropsychology Press.

Robertson, I.H., Ward, T., Ridgeway, W., & Nimmo-Smith, I. (1994). *The Test of Everyday Attention*. Bury St Edmunds: Thames Valley Test Company.

Rosenbaum, A., Hoge, S.K., Adelman, S A., Warnken, W.J., Fletcher, K.E., & Kane, R. L. (1994). Head injury in partner-abusive men. *Journal of Consulting and Clinical Psychology, 62*, 1187–1193.

Rust, J., & Golombok, S. (1986). *Manual of the Golombok–Rust Inventory of Sexual Satisfaction*. Windsor: NFER-Nelson.

Sbordone, R.J. (1966). Ecological validity. In R.J. Sbordone & C.J. Long (Eds.), *Ecological validity of neuropsychological testing*. Florida: G R Press / St Lucia Press.

Shallice, T., & Burgess, P. W. (1991). Deficits in strategy application following frontal lobe damage in man. *Brain, 114*, 727–741.

Shallice, T., & Evans, M.E. (1978). The involvement of the frontal lobes in cognitive estimation. *Cortex, 14*, 294–303.

Smith, M.L., & Milner, B. (1984). Differential effects of frontal-lobe lesions on cognitive estimation and spatial memory. *Neuropsychologia, 22*, 697–705.

Spence, S.E., Godfrey, H.P.D., Knight, R.G., & Bishara, S.N. (1993). First impressions count: A controlled investigation of social skill following closed head injury. *British Journal of Clinical Psychology, 32*, 309–318.

Spreen, O., & Strauss, E. (1998). *A compendium of neuropsychological tests: Administration, norms and commentary* (2nd edn.). New York: Oxford University Press.

Stuss, D.T. (1987). Contribution of frontal lobe injury to cognitive impairment after closed head injury. In H.S. Levin, J. Grafman, & H.M. Eisenberg (Eds.), *Neurobehavioural recovery from head injury* (pp. 16–177). New York: Oxford University Press.

Teuber, H.L. (1964). The riddle of frontal lobe functioning in man. In J.M. Warren & K.A. Albert (Eds.), *The frontal granular cortex and behaviour*. New York: McGraw-Hill.

Thomsen, I.V. (1989). Do young patients have worse outcomes after blunt head trauma? *Brain Injury, 3*, 157–162.

Tyerman, A., & Humphrey, M. (1984). Changes in self-concept following severe head injury. *International Journal of Rehabilitation Research, 7*, 11–23.

Walsh, K.W. (1985). *Understanding brain damage: A primer for neuropsychological examination*. London: Churchill Livingstone.

Wechsler, D. (1997a). *Wechsler Adult Intelligence Scale—Third Edition*. San Antonio, TX: The Psychological Corporation.

Wechsler, D. (1997b). *Wechsler Memory Scale—Third Edition*. San Antonia, TX: The Psychological Corporation.

Willer, B.S., Allen, K.M., Liss, M., & Zicht, M.S. (1991). Problems and coping strategies of individuals with traumatic brain injury and their spouses. *Archives of Physical Medicine Rehabilitation, 72*, 460–464.

Wilson, B.A., Alderman, N., Burgess, P.W., Emslie, H., & Evans, J.J. (1996). *Behavioural Assessment of the Dysexecutive Syndrome; manual*. Bury St Edmunds, Thames Valley Test Company.

Wilson, B.A., Cockburn, J., & Baddeley, A.D. (1985). *Rivermead Behavioural Memory Test; manual*. Bury St Edmunds, Thames Valley Test Company.

Wood, R.Ll. (1987). Neuropsychological assessment in brain injury. In M.G. Eisenburgh, & R.C. Greziak (Eds.), *Advances in clinical rehabilitation* (Vol. 1, pp. 47–92), Springer. New York.

Wood, R.Ll., & Worthington, A.D. (1999). Outcome in community rehabilitation: Measuring the social impact of disability. *Neuropsychological Rehabilitation, 9*, 505–517.

Wood, R.Ll., & Yurdakul, L.K. (1997). Change in relationship status following traumatic brain injury. *Brain Injury, 11*, 491–501.

Wood, R.Ll., McCrae, J., Wood, L.M., & Merriman, R.M. (1999). Clinical and cost effectiveness of post acute neurobehavioural rehabilitation. *Brain injury, 13*, 69–89.

CHAPTER FIVE

Understanding and assessing capacity

D. Lush
Court of Protection, London, UK

INTRODUCTION

Capacity is synonymous with competence and simply means the ability to do something. In a legal context it means the ability to make a decision, to enter into a transaction, to engage in an activity, or to exercise rights which may have legal implications not only for the individual concerned but also for others. For example: the capacity to make a will, a gift, or a contract; the capacity to consent to medical treatment or the capacity, generally, to manage one's property and affairs.

From the incapacitated individual's perspective, there is a tension between, on the one hand, maximising his or her freedom and autonomy, and, on the other, ensuring that he or she is adequately safeguarded against exploitation and abuse. There may also be a need to ensure that the interests of third parties, and even society at large, are protected from the possibly adverse consequences of any action taken or decision made by an individual who may lack the capacity to take such action or make such a decision.

CAPACITY IS FUNCTION-SPECIFIC

There are three different ways of approaching capacity (Law Commision, 1991). These can be described as:

1. The outcome approach.
2. The status approach.
3. The function approach.

The *outcome approach* looks at the result of a decision, rather than the processes involved in making it. A person who makes the "right" decision, or a "reasonable" or "responsible" decision, is deemed to have been competent, whereas a decision which rejects conventional wisdom or is inconsistent with the views and values of the assessor or society at large is deemed to have been made incompetently. The difficulty with this approach is that it is always retrospective and it promotes societal goals and values at the expense of personal autonomy.

The *status approach* is almost a form of social segregation. For policy reasons members of a specified class or category are deemed to be incapable of making a decision or engaging in an activity. This approach applies particularly nowadays to children, although historically it also applied to women, convicted felons, and enemies of the state. For example, children aged under 18 are unable to vote; children under 17 are unable to drive a car, and children under 16 are unable to marry. The problem with this approach, especially when it is applied to adults, is that it fails to take account of any individual skills and competencies. For example, an assertion that "anyone who has suffered an acquired head injury in a road traffic accident is incapable of driving or making a valid will" would be a grossly misleading and unjust oversimplification.

Although, no doubt, the outcome and status approaches are applied frequently in day-to-day practice, the *function* or *understanding approach* is, in theory at least, the one generally favoured by English law and most other legal systems based on English law. Using this approach, decision making need not be rational either in process or in outcome. Unwise choices are permitted. Nevertheless, at the very minimum, an individual must be able to understand a simple explanation of the information relevant to the decision, including information about the reasonably foreseeable consequences of deciding one way or another or of failing to make the decision. How the individual actually weighs that information, evalutes it, and reaches a decision is not important.

Because capacity is usually function- or decision-specific, an individual may be capable of making some decisions but incapable of making others. Accordingly, the law has laid down discrete criteria for making particular decisions. The main exception to this rule is the capacity to manage and administer one's property and affairs generally.

CAPACITY AND EVIDENCE

Whether an individual has the capacity to make a decision or enter into a transaction is ultimately a decision for the court, rather than a doctor or clinical psychologist. Doctors and psychologists are expert witnesses whose function is to provide the court with material on which it can reach its own conclusions. Mr Justice Neville expressed this particularly bluntly in the case of Richmond v Richmond (1914).

> With regard to the question of whether in any, or what degree, she is capable of managing her own affairs, and being bound by her own contracts and by her own acts, that, in my opinion is always a question for the court to decide. I say that, because ... it is obvious that an idea obtained that this was a question for the doctors to decide,

and that the question was whether the doctors thought that she was capable of managing her own affairs or whether they did not. In my opinion that is not so. It is for the court to decide, although the court must have the evidence of experts in the medical profession who can indicate the meaning of symptoms and give some general ideas of the mental deterioration which takes place in cases of this kind.

Issues involving capacity rarely ever get as far as court. When they do, the judge makes his or her determination on the basis of evidence from the patient's doctors or psychologists and others with first-hand knowledge. Accordingly, assessing capacity is closely linked to the law of evidence.

Proof of incapacity depends on the operation of two rebuttable presumptions. The first is the *presumption of capacity*, traditionally known as the *presumption of sanity*. This says that a person is presumed to be capable until the contrary is proved. However, there may come a time when, from a medical or psychological point of view, a person with a particular disability must be presumed to be incapable unless the contrary is shown (Simpson v Simpson, 1989). The second presumption is known as the *presumption of continuance*. Once it has been proved by acceptable evidence that someone is mentally incapable of doing something, that incapacity is presumed to continue until the contrary is proved.

The *standard of proof* is the usual standard in civil proceedings, namely *the balance of probabilities*. In other words, the question to be decided is whether, on balance, a person is more likely to be capable or incapable of making a decision, entering into a transaction or engaging in an activity. The assessor does not need to be satisfied *beyond reasonable doubt*, which is the standard of proof required in criminal proceedings.

CREATING THE RIGHT ENVIRONMENT FOR ASSESSING CAPACITY

Ideally, people should be assessed when they are at their highest level of functioning as this is the only realistic way of gauging their maximum potential (Applebaum & Grisso, 1988; Law Commision, 1991). Various measures can be taken to optimise the conditions for assessing someone's capacity. These mainly involve getting the setting right and putting the subject at ease (see Chapter 3). For example:

1. Try to minimise anxiety or stress by making the client feel at ease.
2. Be aware of any medication which could affect capacity.
3. Be sensitive towards other disabilities, such as impaired hearing or eyesight, which could mislead you into assuming that a person lacks capacity.
4. If there are communication or linguistic problems, consider enlisting the services of a speech therapist or a translator.

5. Choose the best time of day for the examination. Some people are better in the morning, others are more alert and attentive in the afternoon or early evening.
6. Be thorough, but keep the assessment within manageable bounds timewise to avoid tiring or confusing the patient.
7. Avoid obtrusive time-checking. It should be possible, without too much discernible eye-movement, to keep a check on the time.
8. If more than one test of capacity has to be applied (for example, if you need to establish whether someone is capable of managing his or her property and affairs generally, and you also need to establish whether he or she is capable of making a will), try to do each assessment on a different day, if possible.
9. Choose the best location. Usually, someone will feel more comfortable in his or her own home than in, say, a surgery or office.
10. Try and ensure that there are no obstructions between you and the person who is being assessed which could hinder the development of a relationship of equals, for example, the height and positioning of the chairs.
11. So far as it is within your control, make sure that the temperature in the room is comfortable and that the lighting is soft and indirect, but sufficiently bright for easy eye contact and interpretation of expression and to study any relevant documentation.
12. Consider whether or not a third party should be present. In some cases, the presence of a relative or friend could reduce anxiety. In others, their presence might actually increase anxiety. In some cases a third party might be a useful interpreter. In others, they could be intrusive.
13. Where the assessment relates to a confidential matter (such as making a will), or if there is any suspicion of undue influence or pressure, the client or patient must be seen alone.
14. Try and eliminate any background noise or distractions, such as the television or radio, or people talking.
15. If possible, make sure that other people cannot overhear you and that others will not interrupt you either from outside or within the room, for example, by telephone.
16. Speak at the right volume and speed. Try to use short sentences with familiar words. If necessary, accompany your speech with slightly exaggerated gestures or facial expressions and other means of non-verbal communication.
17. If necessary, provide verbal or visual aids to stimulate and improve the person's memory.
18. When carrying out various tests of cognitive functioning allow a reasonable time for general relaxed conversation between each test so as to avoid any sense of disappointment at failing a particular test.
19. If possible, try to avoid subjecting the patient to an increasingly demoralising sequence of "I don't know" answers.

HOW TO ASSESS CAPACITY

1. If you are assessing someone's capacity, make sure that you personally understand fully the nature and effect of the particular transaction in respect of which you are making the assessment. Among other things, this means making sure you have all the relevant documentation and background information you need.
2. Be aware of the legal test (if there is one) for assessing this type of capacity.
3. Although medical tests (such as the Mini-Mental State Examination) and psychometric tests (such as the Wechsler Adult Intelligence Scale—Revised) may be valuable tools for diagnostic purposes and for assessing an individual's cognitive skills and ability to reason generally, they must never be allowed to usurp the actual legal test.
4. The information relevant to making the decision or the nature and effect of the transaction should be explained to the subject in broad terms and simple language.
5. After a reasonable timespan the subject should be able to para-phrase roughly the explanation he or she was given a few minutes earlier.
6. Avoid asking questions which are susceptible to "yes" or "no" answer, for example, "Do you understand this?" Generally speaking, they are insufficient for the purpose of assessing whether or not a person has capacity. However, if there are major communication difficulties, it is conceded that there may be no practical alternative to "yes" or "no" responses.
7. Do not be misled by a person's preserved social skills into believing that he or she has the requisite capacity to enter into a transaction or to make a particular decision.
8. Consider repeating the assessment on another occasion to allow for the possibility of fluctuating capacity.
9. An individual should not be regarded as lacking capacity merely because he or she makes a decision which would not be made by someone of ordinary prudence. Although the law requires an individual to be capable of understanding the nature and effect of a transaction or decision, it does not require him or her to behave "in such a manner as to deserve approbation from the prudent, the wise, or the good" (Bird v Luckie, 1850).
10. You should be satisfied as to the subject's capacity or incapacity on the *balance of probabilities*. It is not necessary to be satisfied *beyond reasonable doubt*.
11. Immediately make a comprehensive record of the examination and your findings (Kenward v Adams, 1975; Simpson, deceased; Schaniel v Simpson, 1977).

LEGAL TESTS OF CAPACITY

The test for capacity generally favoured in England and Wales and most other Common Law countries is the ability to understand the nature and effect of a decision or transaction. In Gibbons v Wright (1954), Sir Owen Dixon, the Chief Justice of Australia, held that:

> The law does *not* prescribe any fixed standard of sanity as requisite for the validity of all transactions. It requires, in relation to each particular matter or piece of business transacted, that each party shall have such soundness of mind as to be capable of understanding the general nature of what he is doing by his participation…The mental capacity required by the law in respect of any instrument is relative to the particular transaction which is being effected by means of the instrument, and may be described as the capacity to understand the nature of that transaction when it is explained.

In other words, mental capacity is usually "function-specific" or "decision-specific'—the main exception being the capacity to manage and administer one's property and financial affairs generally. Discrete tests apply to different transactions or decisions, and these tests are usually to be found in the common law (judge-made law) rather than in statutes. Several of these tests which are relevant to decision making by persons with a neurological disability are summarised below.

Capacity to make a will

The legal test for testamentary capacity, or the capacity to make a will, was described by Mr Justice Cockburn in the case of Banks v Goodfellow (1870). He said:

> it is essential … that a testator shall understand the nature of the act and its effects; shall understand the extent of the property of which he is disposing; shall be able to comprehend and appreciate the claims to which he ought to give effect; and, with a view to the latter object, that no disorder of the mind shall poison his affections, pervert his sense of right, or prevent the exercise of his natural faculties—that no insane delusion shall influence his will in disposing of his property and bring about a disposal of it which, if the mind had been sound, would not have been made.

Where a patient of the Court of Protection expresses a wish to make a will, the court will require his or her testamentary capacity to be assessed by a doctor or other specialist assessor. An assessment by a clinical psychologist is acceptable for this purpose: the court is not compelled by the legislation to accept purely "medical" evidence, but it does need to be satisfied that the patient is capable of making a valid will for him or herself (see Mental Health Act, 1983, s 96 (4)b). If the patient has testamentary capacity, he or she will be authorised to go ahead and instruct a solicitor to draw up the will. If the patient is incapable of making a valid will for him or herself, an application may be made to the court by any interested party for an order authorising the execution of a what is commonly known as a "statutory will" on the patient's behalf (Mental Health Act, 1983).

Capacity to make a gift

The leading case on capacity to make a gift is Re Beaney deceased (1978). In this case an elderly woman suffering from dementia purported to sign a deed transferring her house to one of her three children. She died shortly afterwards and her other two children applied successfully to the court for an order setting the transfer aside. The judge held that:

> The degree or extent of understanding required in respect of any instrument is relative to the particular transaction which it is to effect. In the case of a will the degree required is always high. In the case of a contract, a deed made for consideration or a gift *inter vivos*, whether by deed or otherwise, the degree required varies with the circumstances of the transaction. Thus, at one extreme, if the subject-matter and value of a gift are trivial in relation to the donor's other assets a low degree of understanding will suffice. But, at the other, if its effect is to dispose of the donor's only asset of value and thus for practical purposes to pre-empt the devolution of his estate under his will or on his intestacy, then the degree of understanding required is as high as that required for a will, and the donor must understand the claims of all potential donees and the extent of the property to be disposed of.

Capacity to make an enduring power of attorney

An enduring power of attorney is a document, which must be in a prescribed form, in which a person (known as "*the donor*") appoints one or more people to be attorneys with general authority to manage his or her property and financial affairs. The power comes into effect immediately and will endure, or remain in force, if the donor subsequently becomes incapable by reason of mental disorder of managing his or her property and affairs.

When the attorney has reason to believe that the donor is, or is becoming, mentally incapable, he or she has a duty to register the power with the Public Trust Office. The donor, and at least three of his or her closest relatives, must be notified of the attorney's intention to register the power, and they can object to the registration on various grounds. Once the power has been registered, the attorney can carry on managing the donor's affairs as before, and the power cannot be revoked by the donor unless the revocation is confirmed by the Court of Protection.

The capacity required to create an enduring power of attorney was described by Mr Justice Hoffmann in the case of Re K, Re F (1988). He said:

> Finally I should say something about what is meant by understanding the nature and effect of the power. What degree of understanding is involved? Plainly one cannot

expect that the donor should have been able to pass an examination on the provisions of the 1985 Act. At the other extreme, I do not think that it would be sufficient if he realised only that it gave cousin William power to look after his property.

Counsel as *amicus curiae* helpfully summarised the matters which the donor should have understood in order that he can be said to have understood the nature and effect of the power:

- first, if such be the terms of the power, that the attorney will be able to assume complete authority over the donor's affairs;
- second, if such be the terms of the power, that the attorney will in general be able to do anything with the donor's property which the donor could have done;
- third, that the authority will continue if the donor should be or become mentally incapable;
- fourth, that if he should be or become mentally incapable, the power will be irrevocable without confirmation by the court.

I do not wish to prescribe another form of words in competition with the explanatory notes prescribed by the Lord Chancellor, but I accept the summary of counsel as *amicus curiae* as a statement of the matters which should ordinarily be explained to the donor whatever the precise language which may be used and which the evidence should show he has understood.

Enduring powers of attorney are particularly useful for older people who are still competent and wish to plan for possible future incapacitation as a result of, say, Alzheimer's disease or multi-infarct dementia. However, they are not really suitable for people who have an acquired head injury or brain damage and are likely to be awarded damages, even though the donor may have the capacity to create such a power. This is because enduring powers are particularly susceptible to abuse (Lush, 1998). Unlike a receiver appointed by the court, the attorney is a free agent with unrestricted access to the donor's capital and income. The attorney is not generally required to present accounts to anyone, is not required to pursue any particular strategy for the investment of a damages award, and is unable to give security for his or her defaults because no insurance company is willing to underwrite such a risk.

Capacity to manage one's property and affairs

There is a remarkable dearth of information about the criteria for assessing whether someone is mentally capable of managing and administering his or her property and affairs. This is particularly surprising since it is the cornerstone of the Court of Protection's jurisdiction under both the Mental Health Act, 1983 and the Enduring Powers of Attorney Act, 1985.

The definition of mental incapacity in both Acts is "incapable, by reason of mental disorder, of managing and administering his property and affairs". This contains three prerequisites. A person must:

1. be suffering from *mental disorder*;
2. have *property and affairs* that need to be managed and administered; and
3. *be incapable* (or, in the case of the donor of an enduring power of attorney, *be becoming incapable*) by reason of mental disorder, of managing and administering his or her property and affairs.

Mental disorder is defined in the Mental Health Act, 1983, s 1(2) and means "mental illness, arrested or incomplete development of mind, psychopathic disorder; and any other disorder or disability of mind". However, the conditions falling within this residual category depend to some extent on how broadly mental illness is defined, but are likely to include disabilities resulting from head injuries, brain tumours, and toxic confusional states. The expression "incapable of managing and administering his property and affairs" is neither defined in the Act, nor is there any reported decision in English law to shed light on its meaning. The leading textbook on Court of Protection practice, Heywood and Massey (1991), cites the unreported decision of Mr Justice Wilberforce (as he then was) in Re CAF on 23 March 1962 as the authority for the following principle:

> The question of the degree of incapacity of managing and administering a patient's property and affairs must be related to the circumstances including the state in which the patient lives and the complexity and importance of the property and affairs which he has to manage and administer.

Despite the fact that Re CAF has never been reported, it has been the subject of an extensive debate in the Australian courts. The fundamental question is whether an individual's capacity to manage his or her affairs is subjective (as was decided in Re CAF) or objective. In New South Wales, in PY v RJS (1982), Mr Justice Powell introduced an objective test. He said:

> It is my view that a person is not shown to be incapable of managing his or her own affairs unless, at the least, it appears:
>
> (a) that he or she is incapable of dealing, in a reasonably competent fashion, with the ordinary routine affairs of man; and
> (b) that by reason of that lack of competence there is shown to be a real risk that either:
>   (i) he or she may be disadvantaged in the conduct of such affairs; or
>   (ii) that such moneys or property which he or she may possess may be dissipated or lost; it is not sufficient, in my view, merely to demonstrate that the person lacks the high level of ability needed to deal with complicated transactions or that he or she does not deal with even simple or routine transactions in the most efficient manner.

However, in Victoria, in Re MacGregor (1985), Mr Justice Starke followed Re CAF and approved the subjective test.

The Act itself appears to me to lay down the test. It speaks of "managing his affairs", not the "ordinary routine affairs of man". The Court under the Act is exercising its protective jurisdiction in respect of individuals, not a class of persons, albeit before the jurisdiction is exercised it must be shown that the person is an infirm person for the purposes of the Act. In my opinion the decision in *Re an Alleged Incapable Person* and the passage in Heywood and Massey which I have quoted seem to support the proposition that the subjective test is the appropriate test.

As was mentioned above, this is the major exception to the general rule that capacity is function-specific or decision-specific.

WHEN TO APPLY TO THE COURT OF PROTECTION

To become a patient of the Court of Protection a person must be incapable, by reason of mental disorder, of managing his or her property and affairs. Accordingly, he or she must have property and finances that need to be managed and administered. If he or she has no capital, and no income other than Department of Social Security benefits, the Secretary of State for Social Security will consider appointing an appointee to handle those benefits on the person's behalf (see Social Security [Claims and Payments] Regulations, 1987).

In many personal injury and medical negligence claims there is no need to apply for the appointment of a receiver until an award, whether interim or final, is imminent. If the claimant is mentally incapacitated, nobody has authority to deal with capital on his or her behalf until a receiver has been appointed by the Court of Protection. A litigation friend does not have that right, nor does the solicitor in the action (Leather v Kirby, 1965; M v Lester, 1966).

MEDICAL CERTIFICATION

When an application is made to the Court of Protection for the appointment of a receiver, the court has to be satisfied, after considering "medical" evidence, that a person is incapable, by reason of mental disorder, of managing and administering his or her property and affairs (Mental Health Act, 1983). For this purpose the Court of Protection Rules 1994 specifically require the applicant to file a medical certificate (form CP3) completed by a registered medical practitioner (Court of Protection Rules, 1994). There is no particular requirement that the form should be completed by a consultant, or by a neurologist or psychiatrist. Any registered medical practitioner will suffice: Usually it is the patient's general practitioner. This has occasionally caused difficulties where the medical certificate has been completed by a clinical psychologist. A clinical psychologist may be better qualified than anyone else to assess a patient's capacity, but unfortunately the court is bound to reject such evidence because it is not "medical".

Although the court will consider "medical" evidence other than in form CP3, the prescribed certificate, which was prepared in consultation with the Royal College of Psychiatrists and the British Medical Association, contains some useful additional information which assists the court in making decisions on investment policy and whether a patient needs to be visited periodically.

The section in form CP3 which appears to cause the most difficulty is section 4, "My opinion is based on the following diagnosis and the following evidence of incapacity". In this section a diagnosis and a simple statement are required giving clear evidence of incapacity which an ordinary intelligent lay person could understand. For example, references to a defect of short-term memory, or of spatial and temporal orientation, or of reasoning ability, or of reckless spending without regard for the future, or evidence of vulnerability to exploitation.

In many cases of senile dementia, severe brain damage, acute or chronic psychiatric disorder, and severe mental impairment, the assessment of incapacity should present little difficulty. Cases of functional and personality disorders may give more problems and assessment may depend on the individual doctor's interpretation of mental disorder. The court tends towards the view that these conditions render a person liable to come within its jurisdiction if there is a real danger that they will lead to dissipation of considerable capital assets.

CHILDREN WHO ARE ALSO "PATIENTS"

Children who are claimants in personal injury and medical negligence actions present a particular difficulty in terms of jurisdiction. Indeed, the High Court and the Court of Protection have concurrent jurisdiction over children who are also patients. It is not always clear whether they are incapable of managing their affairs by reason of mental disorder (even if they are mentally disordered) or whether their incapacity is the result of their age. There was a time when the Court of Protection was reluctant to assume jurisdiction in the case of children, but in recent years there has been a change in policy.

Where the injury is such that it is unlikely that the claimant will be able to manage his or her own affairs on reaching the age of 18, the Court of Protection will agree to become involved because it is usually in the claimant's best interests that a long-term, long-lasting regime of investment and management should be put in place at an early stage. In any event, the court can always ask for a patient's capacity to manage their affairs to be re-assessed when they reach 18.

PROPOSED REFORM

In 1989 the Law Commission, the body charged with promoting law reform in England and Wales, embarked on a project to investigate the adequacy of legal and other procedures for making decisions on behalf of mentally incapacitated adults. After issuing four consultation papers, it published a final report, Mental Incapacity

Law Commission (1995). In clause 2 of its draft Mental Incapacity Bill, which appears as an appendix to its report, the Law Commission has proposed the following definition of "persons without capacity":

2. (1) For the purposes of this Part of this Act a person is without capacity if at the material time (a) he is unable by reason of mental disability to make a decision for himself on the matter in question; or

    (b) he is unable to communicate his decision on that matter because he is unconscious or for any other reason.

2. (2) For the purposes of this Part of this Act a person is at the material time unable to make a decision by reason of mental disability if the disability is such that at the time when the decision needs to be made

    (a) he is unable to understand or retain the information relevant to the decision, including information about the reasonably foreseeable consequences of deciding one way or another or of failing to make the decision; or

    (b) he is unable to make a decision based on that information,

and in this Act "mental disability" means a disability or disorder of the mind or brain, whether permanent or temporary, which results in an impairment or disturbance of mental functioning.

2. (3) A person shall not be regarded as unable to understand the information referred to in subsection 2(a) above if he is able to understand an explanation of that information in broad terms and in simple language.

2. (4) A person shall not be regarded as unable to make a decision by reason of mental disability merely because he makes a decision which would not be made by a person of ordinary prudence.

2. (5) A person shall not be regarded as unable to communicate his decision unless all practicable steps to enable him to do so have been taken without success.

2. (6) There shall be a presumption against lack of capacity and any question whether a person lacks capacity shall be decided on the balance of probabilities.

This proposed definition of capacity essentially consolidates the existing common law on the subject. The Law Commission's report was considered in a consultation paper, *Who Decides?*, published by the Lord Chancellor's Department in December 1997, and a policy statement *Making Decisions*, published in October 1999. In the policy statement the Government has pledged that it will introduce the Mental Incapacity Bill when sufficient time is available in its legislation schedule.

CONCLUSIONS

Assessing capacity means establishing whether a specific individual is capable of entering into a specific transaction. This requires a careful analysis of not only the individual but also the transaction. One traumatic brain injury patient may be capable of making a will but incapable of managing his or her finances. Another person may be incapable of entering into a consumer credit agreement, but capable of getting married. Each case differs from the next and some present entirely unique problems.

Deciding whether someone has capacity involves a determination of that person's civil rights and obligations. It is, therefore, a legal issue which may ultimately need to be decided by a judge. Cases of this kind rarely ever get as far as a court and decisions on capacity are made day-in-day-out by doctors, psychologists, and other expert professionals. By making such a decision, the expert is, in effect, acting as a judge in the first instance.

Accordingly, it is imperative that the expert assessor acts fairly and impartially; keeps a meticulous record of the questions asked and answers given; considers all the material facts; knows the relevant statute and case law; applies the law to the facts, and provides a fully reasoned written decision which is capable of withstanding close scrutiny on appeal, if the matter does finally come before a judge.

REFERENCES

Applebaum, P.S., & Grisso, T. (1988). Assessing patients' capacities to consent to treatment. *New England Journal of Medicine*, *319*, 635–638.

Banks v Goodfellow (1870). *LR, 5, QB, 549*, p. 565.

Bird v Luckie (1850). *8, Hare, 301.*

Court of Protection Rules (1994). SI, *3046, rule 20*.

Gibbons v Wright (1954). 91, CLR 423, 437–438.

Heywood, N.A., & Massey, A.S. (1991). *Court of Protection Practice* (12th Edition), London: Sweet & Maxwell.

Kenward v Adams (1975). *The Times*, 29 November.

Law Commission Consultation Paper (1991). *Mentally incapacitated adults and decision-making: An overview* (No 119, pp. 50–53). London: HMSO.

Law Commission Report (1995). Mental incapacity (No. 231). London: HMSO.

Leather v Kirby (1965). 1 WLR 1489.

Lord Chancellor's Department (1997). *Who decides?* (Cm 3803).

Lush, D. (1998). Taking liberties: enduring powers of attorney and financial abuse. *Solicitors Journal,* 11, September, 808–809.

Mental Health Act (1983). s 96(4)(b).

Mental Health Act (1983), s 96(1)(e).

M v Lester (1966). 1 WLR 134.

PY v RJS (1982). 2, NSWLR, 700–702.

Re K, Re F. (1988). 1, All ER, 358, 363c-f.

Re Beaney (deceased). (1978). 2, All ER, 595, p. 601f-h.

Re MacGregor (1985). VR 861.

Richmond v Richmond (1914). LT, 273.

Simpson v. Simpson (1989). 1, Fam Law, 20, p2l, *per* Morritt J.

Simpson, Deceased: Schaniel v Simpson (1977). 121, SJ , 224.

PART TWO

Rehabilitating neurobehavioural disability

CHAPTER SIX

Neurobehavioural rehabilitation: A conceptual paradigm

R.Ll. Wood and A.D. Worthington
Brain Injury Rehabilitation Trust, Birmingham, UK

INTRODUCTION

This chapter discusses the conceptual basis for neurobehavioural rehabilitation in terms of its historical influences and implications for treatment. The principles underlying assessment and treatment of disability within the neurobehavioural paradigm are summarised, and the core features of the organisation of a neurobehavioural service are outlined. A description of how principles of neurobehavioural rehabilitation are translated into practice will be found in Chapter 7.

Recovery from serious brain injury has been defined in a variety of ways by different experts over the past 20 years. Initially, the emphasis was on physical recovery (Lewin, 1968) then, largely as a result of psychological follow-up studies, cognitive recovery became the dominant theme (Brooks & Aughton, 1979; Miller, 1984). Increasing realisation of the impact of psychosocial problems after head injury (Bond, 1976; Oddy & Humphrey, 1980) shifted the emphasis to specific behavioural legacies (Bond, 1984; Wood, 1987). More recently, the complex and integrated nature of brain injury sequelae has been appreciated and recovery is now largely construed in terms of *neurobehavioural disability* (see Chapter 1).

Before 1980, brain injury rehabilitation was essentially "stroke rehabilitation". Treatment interventions were construed primarily within a medical frame of reference and administered in a medical context (a rehabilitation hospital), under the direction of medical specialists. This approach to rehabilitation focused mainly on a patient's impairments. Therapeutic input was structured around the provision of treatment *sessions,* using specific therapy disciplines and/or medical interventions. Prognostic indicators of outcome were based on a reduction of impairment or disability (Zasler, 1995) and then mapped onto indices of social outcome by a process of extrapolation.

By the end of the 1980s, efforts were made to distinguish traditional stroke-orientated brain injury rehabilitation from head injury rehabilitation (McGrath & Davis, 1992; McMillan & Greenwood, 1993; Oddy et al., 1989; Soryal, Sloan, Skelton, & Pentland, 1992), giving the latter the status of a subspecialty within the ambit of services covered by rehabilitation medicine. To a large extent, this development reflected a growing awareness of the impact of cognitive and behavioural sequelae common to traumatic brain injury, setting it apart (to some extent at least) from other aspects of neurological rehabilitation (see Barnes, 1993; Ward & McIntosh, 1993). This awareness probably developed because of the increasing number of people surviving serious head trauma as the result of improvements in neurotrauma management. Unfortunately, many survivors had to face a lifetime of serious social handicap because of the complex pattern of cognitive, emotional, and behavioural disability such injuries produced. Practitioners of brain injury rehabilitation began to realise that many of the persisting problems following head trauma, and other forms of acquired brain injury, were far more psychological than medical in character. Such problems required a different approach to treatment than that offered by traditional rehabilitation services which were orientated primarily to physical disability. Rehabilitation programmes subsequently focused upon what is sometimes referred to as "social health" (Donald et al.,1978) employing criteria reflecting social competence as measured by a person's capacity for social independence. Consequently, rehabilitation services began to incorporate methods and systems which addressed the impact of cerebral dysfunction on the person's ability to pursue important social roles. A social perspective to rehabilitation starts from an examination of what the person can and cannot do for themselves, by asking the question, "Why can this person not live an independent fulfilling life in society?" This leads to an identification of constraints (disabilities) to independent living, which form the basis of treatment goals. The nature of a person's impairments is not directly related to these constraints, and therefore (although important to identify clinically) they will not exert the same degree of influence over the rehabilitation process.

These conceptual changes were reflected in the development of rehabilitation services, which moved away from their initial preoccupation with physical impairment and began to embrace circumscribed cognitive deficits. A neuropsychological approach was taken to ameliorate the cognitive legacies of brain injury (e.g., Meier, Benton, & Diller, 1987). Other authorities, most prominently Ben Yishay and Gold (1990) and Prigatano (1986), recommended addressing combinations of cognitive and emotional problems in the context of a therapeutic milieu, employing psychotherapeutic techniques. Unfortunately, these approaches did not address the complex interaction of cognitive and behaviour disorders that play such a prominent part in the rehabilitation of more severe brain injuries, and

therefore, did not accommodate people who had severe physical, cognitive, or *integral*
behavioural adjustment problems. Neuropsychological rehabilitation largely
focused on the more articulate patients who had less debilitating handicaps, usually
following mild or moderate head trauma. What such approaches to rehabilitation
lacked was a system that addressed cognitive, behavioural, *and* physical sequelae,
in severe as well as minor and moderate disability, at both early and late stages of
recovery, and with potential application on an inpatient or day patient basis. This
has been the goal of neurobehavioural rehabilitation: to provide a conceptually
driven approach of how to improve psychosocial functioning (Goll & Hawley, 1989;
Groswasser, 1994; Johnston & Lewis, 1991; Kendall & Terry, 1996; Schalen,
Hansson, Nordstrom, & Nordstrom, 1994; Vilkki et al., 1994; Willer et al., 1993).

WHAT IS NEUROBEHAVIOURAL REHABILITATION?

Neurobehavioural rehabilitation is an approach to brain injury rehabilitation that
originated in behavioural rather than cognitive psychology (see Wood & Eames,
1981) and which has evolved to incorporate those aspects of cognitive theory which
are seen as fundamental to human behavioural learning (Davy, 1988).
Neurobehavioural rehabilitation is not promoted as a *model* of rehabilitation but
as a conceptual scheme or *paradigm*, incorporating cognitive and behavioural
theories relating, on the one hand, to the *acquisition* of functional and social skills,
and on the other, the spontaneous and adaptive *performance* of such skills in the
context of social behaviour (see Wood, 1990a). It is based on the premise that
rehabilitation is essentially a *learning process* facilitating the recovery of functional
skills, cognitive abilities, and social behaviours that have been lost or rendered
ineffective as a result of damage to cerebral mechanisms which control higher level *Executive*
activities. Another central construct of a neurobehavioural paradigm is that once
skills which promote functional independence are *acquired* they are capable of
being *applied* spontaneously and adaptively. It is the spontaneous application of
skills that allows the injured person to achieve the highest level of social
independence possible, within the constraints imposed by physical disability or
damaged cognitive functions. Consequently, a neurobehavioural paradigm
incorporates constructs, theories, and procedures from cognitive, behavioural, and
social psychology to promote the acquisition and spontaneous use of functional
and social skills that will ameliorate the social handicap produced by permanent
forms of neurobehavioural disability.

Certain elements such as programme structure and a team approach are core
features of many rehabilitation services (Ponsford, 1995) and are not unique to the
neurobehavioural paradigm. What is unique is the combination of procedural and
practical applications linked to an explicit conceptual framework. Some aspects
of the approach could also be incorporated into hospital-based rehabilitation, but
experience has shown that the long-term nature of neurobehavioural problems and
the need for persistent and systematic application of treatment interventions and a

truly interdisciplinary team structure are not easily assimilated into an acute rehabilitation setting, especially when this is based within statutory health services (Eames, Turnbull, & Goodman-Smith, 1989).

THE ORGANISATION OF A NEUROBEHAVIOURAL REHABILITATION SERVICE

Neurobehavioural rehabilitation differs from the traditional approach of clinical rehabilitation in several important ways. It focuses on social handicap caused by disability, rather than the relationship between impairment and disability. It is primarily a form of post-acute rehabilitation (although the underlying principles and procedures can be applied in any context and at any stage of recovery). Rehabilitation is carried out in the community, not in a hospital setting. The team structure is inter- or transdisciplinary, and it is driven by concepts that are essentially psychological, not medical. It is helpful to examine each of these issues in more detail.

Neurobehavioural rehabilitation happens post-acutely

Early in recovery, treatment may involve restorative pharmacological efforts (Stein, Glasier, & Hoffman, 1994) aimed at enhancing neurochemical substrates of behaviour. At this stage, the focus of nursing and therapy staff is often on such problems as skin breakdown, contractures, swallowing integrity, continence, and balance (Frieden, 1993; Murdoch, 1996). Inevitably, deficiencies in these basic functions need to be ameliorated as soon as possible to prevent secondary complications. At this stage, the social consequences of brain injury are not uppermost in mind because the long-term outcome is uncertain and because more immediate (often life-threatening) problems have to be tackled. A hospital setting is the obvious place to focus on these basic aspects of brain injury because the eventual degree of handicap can be reduced by successful treatment of specific problems (Neumann, 1995). Long after leaving hospital the treatment of physical impairments may continue, but essentially it is in the post-acute phase that a person's impairments become more stable and work can begin on assessing the long-term functional and social impact of residual disabilities. This forms the starting point for the evaluation and amelioration of handicap in a community setting which constitutes the focus of neurobehavioural rehabilitation (e.g., Allen & Beattie, 1987).

Neurobehavioural rehabilitation therefore continues beyond the period when medical rehabilitation finishes. Often, people are referred when they have completed a period of rehabilitation in hospital but have not recovered the functional abilities or social behaviours that make discharge home possible. Other people are referred for neurobehavioural rehabilitation when they fail to make a successful adaptation to community living after they have returned home from hospital. This is usually due to the intrusive impact of neurobehavioural problems which were not evident whilst the patient was in hospital, often because such problems are masked by the structure and support implicit in such a setting.

Many neurobehavioural sequelae of brain injury evolve late in recovery. Such a delayed onset needs to be recognised (Gualtieri & Cox, 1991) so that appropriate treatment can be devised. This is particularly true of mood and personality disorders, which often take several months to appear (Eames, 1990) yet have a profound impact on the person's capacity to maintain personal relationships or cope with routine pressures, such as those intrinsic to most working environments. Given the persistent, seemingly intractable nature of many psychosocial sequelae (Anderson et al., 1996), the duration of neurobehavioural rehabilitation is also much longer than one usually associates with hospital-based medical rehabilitation; measured in months, rather than weeks. Such treatment is not therefore best carried out in a hospital but in a post-acute community setting, incorporating a social milieu that is a more acceptable environment for long-term, less intensive psychosocial interventions.

Neurobehavioural rehabilitation is community based

Neurobehavioural rehabilitation is directed towards achieving social outcomes. An essential difference therefore between such an approach to rehabilitation and more traditional models of service delivery is that neurobehavioural rehabilitation takes place in community-based centres, rather than in hospitals. This contrasts with the traditional dichotomy of service delivery, organised either on the basis of domiciliary teams (Evans & Skidmore, 1989; Palat & Palat, 1995) for persons already settled at home, or inpatient hospital rehabilitation for those not ready for discharge (Barnes,1995). The advantage of residential community-based units is that social and behavioural training procedures, initially acquired in the rehabilitation centre itself, are refined and consolidated through regular (daily) exposure to real-life events in the community, using a broad range of social training opportunities.

As such, a neurobehavioural rehabilitation service employs a psychological model of rehabilitation and is not at all *medical* in its structure or approach. Consequently, in a neurobehavioural service, the leadership of the rehabilitation team is usually undertaken by a clinical psychologist, reflecting the cognitive and psychosocial nature of the training programme. Also the people receiving rehabilitation are variously referred to as clients, residents, participants, etc., to distinguish their active learning role from the more passive role traditionally associated with being a *patient*.

Neurobehavioural rehabilitation is transdisciplinary

The nature of the rehabilitation programme, concentrating as it does on behaviours rather than disabilities, makes it necessary to employ an *inter-* or, more appropriately, a *trans*disciplinary method of working. This means that whilst an occupational therapist or physiotherapist might be responsible for assessing a particular social handicap and preparing a training procedure to overcome the problem, the person carrying out the procedure would depend upon the type of staff employed and the way the staff team were organised on that particular day. This will largely depend on the nature of the client's social training programme. A physiotherapist may be responsible for a client's morning washing, dressing, and personal care routine, for example, whilst the speech therapist may accompany a physically disabled client using public transport to get to and from town. The person carrying out the training procedure may not even be a professionally trained therapist. Social rehabilitation relies heavily on the use of therapy support workers to carry out social and functional skill training procedures. As a result of in-service training and careful supervision, these skilled staff can become highly competent and much valued general therapists in this type of rehabilitation programme (see Wood, 1996).

The transdisciplinary nature of the work also discourages different attitudes to disability that beset caring and therapy professions (Strasser, Falconer, & Martino-Saltzmann, 1994; White & Olson, 1998). A transdisciplinary team structure places an emphasis on good communication and effective leadership. This is important in any type of clinical environment, but in neurobehavioural rehabilitation the goals are designated to address social and functional behaviours which, by their nature, are less circumscribed than disabilities *per se* and therefore less easily monitored.

Assessments are functionally oriented, focusing on what clients actually do. For example, a physiotherapist might assess a client's competence to transfer independently, but the assessment does not stop there. In terms of evaluating handicap, possession of the requisite physical capabilities is no guarantee that the person will use them optimally. Information from a specialist assessment provides a background for other staff members to assess how effectively this skill is undertaken in different functional contexts. Treatment objectives are therefore client-centred and are not the responsibility of any single therapy profession (Worthington, 1996). An intervention to promote walking, for example, may involve contributions from a physiotherapist, occupational therapist, and psychologist as well as therapy care staff charged with the responsibility of carrying out the training procedure (see Worthington, Williams, Young, & Pownall, 1997).

Several members of staff may be simultaneously involved in one aspect of a client's training programme, and several different but complementary procedures may be employed simultaneously. The logistics of running a social training programme for a group of individuals with different combinations of neurobehavioural disability and patterns of social handicap can therefore be complicated and stressful. Effective communication between different members of the team is vital to ensure the fluent running of the programme generally, keeping the level of staff stress to a minimum and client motivation to a maximum. In practice, there is often a degree of "creative tension" within the team as individual members contribute to the melting pot of clinical thinking from which a consensus of formulation and intervention planning arises.

Neurobehavioural rehabilitation demands a structured environment

The notion of a structured environment is central to many forms of rehabilitation (Burke, 1995; Eames et al., 1989) and is no less important for neurobehavioural rehabilitation. Social atmosphere and the physical environment contribute greatly to a person's sense of well-being, motivation, and social awareness. Within such a "prosthetic environment" (Wood, 1990b) a person's awareness and capacity for social learning are optimised. The following are the main characteristics of a structured environment in neurobehavioural rehabilitation.

Operates by a clearly identifiable system of rules.   Social learning occurs in response to society's rules. These rules shape the social awareness of children and are an important part of maturational development. Some regulations (such as the laws governing society) are more obvious and applied more strictly than others, or have greater impact. Other rules, such as those based on family values or social conventions, are often less evident and may be applied inconsistently, depending on the social setting. The rules therefore vary in their salience, significance, impact, consistency, and social value but they still shape the development of most members of society. They teach us self-restraint, make us aware of (and respect) other people's needs and values, and create a framework for our social interactions. The rules, learned over 10–15 years of adolescent development, often need to be relearned after brain injury, especially when this involves damage to the frontal lobes, which comprise our "social brain". However, people with brain injury lack self-awareness and fail to note the impact of their actions on others. Consequently, the rules they need to re-learn form a framework for adult behaviour and must be clearly identified and consistently applied. The consequences of breaking such rules must be clearly conveyed, to make the individual more aware of his or her behaviour in relation to the rule.

Systematic application of rehabilitation procedures.   The goals of neuro-behavioural rehabilitation involve a reduction in social handicap. They are aimed at different aspects of social and functional behaviour and rely on associational learning for their acquisition. A number of staff will be involved in the application of treatment interventions, usually over several weeks or months. This means that a system is needed to ensure the regular and consistent application of "rules" and staff expectations. If different types of staff or staff on different shifts introduce variations of training methods, or employ different expectations in respect of how behaviours are "performed", the learning will be compromised. The client may therefore be confused and frustrated by inconsistency and become angry, unmotivated, and withdraw co-operation.

Regular and frequent practice of functional and social skills. The acquisition of skills relies largely on procedural, rather than conceptual learning (see later). This means that social behaviours are learned and consolidated most efficiently if the client has the chance to practise them regularly in the context where the skill or behaviour will eventually be applied. When teaching social skills, for example, not much is gained if all the client group does is sit and talk about what they *should* do in a certain situation. Much more is achieved if the skill is practised frequently in a variety of social settings, allowing the skill to consolidate and become a habit, capable of being generalised and employed in different activities.

Systematic exposure to community activities. Skills learned in a rehabilitation unit must be applied in/generalised to a social context. This means that a significant part of rehabilitative training is carried out in a community, rather than a clinical setting. This creates problems for many rehabilitation therapists. Some do not like to work with clients in shopping centres, possibly because of the risk of inappropriate and embarrassing behaviours being displayed. Others find it difficult to move away from the comfortable timetable, often built upon 45 or 60-minute therapy sessions, that provides structure and predictability to the therapist's day. Related to this is the logistical difficulty of trying to organise a therapy programme for an interdisciplinary team when some members of the team may spend several hours in the local shopping precinct with one or more clients. Allowing for these difficulties, rehabilitation professionals must recognise the importance of gradually and systematically exposing clients to community settings so that they can practise the skills they are in the process of acquiring. The advantages of community training include: greater realism; making clients more aware of their problems and what they must do to overcome them; increasing motivation to participate in therapy; and the opportunity to practise the same social or functional skill in a variety of settings, thereby reducing the monotony of training and maintaining the client's involvement and effort.

Frequent feedback opportunities. People learn best if they are made aware of the results of their efforts. Feedback is used to explain the nature and level of performance expected from clients, thereby helping them maintain their awareness of the goals of therapy whilst minimising the impact of memory impairment on learning. Feedback also serves to reinforce and shape behaviour and is often more effective than a straightforward token economy (Kazdin, 1989). Means of giving feedback are discussed in the following chapter.

An effective communication system. Few people would deny that communication in a clinical environment is important. In brain injury rehabilitation the quality and consistency of communication are at a premium because of the diverse nature of treatment interventions, often applied over long periods of time. It is not realistic to rely on the notion that one's colleagues will always inform others of their observations of clients. They may not remember to do so, or may not consider the observation to be particularly relevant. They may not *see* something that is relevant because they are not looking for it. Consequently, it is necessary to have documents in which staff record their observations on clients according to prescribed criteria, or which inform staff how to respond to certain behaviours or situations, so that interventions are made in a consistent manner.

A process to evaluate and (if necessary) adapt rehabilitation procedures. Social handicap is judged on the basis of a person's behaviour; therefore a person's readiness for community re-entry needs to be measured in terms of personal and social awareness, judgement, self-control, ability to adapt, and so on. These social skills are not amenable to psychometric measurement (see Chapter 4) and require structured observational analysis, either by employing functional rating scales, such as the Functional Activities Questionnaire (Pfeffer et al., 1982), or behavioural observation methods which record the frequency, duration, or intensity of behaviours (see Wood & Worthington, 1999). It is important to remember that rehabilitation plans address a number of skills, abilities, and behaviours. Change occurs slowly, often over months, making it almost impossible to accurately recall the details of a person's disability after an interval of 2–3 months, especially on a unit in which upwards of 15 clients may be receiving treatment. Only by regularly sampling different abilities and behaviour can staff determine whether treatment interventions are working or need to be adjusted in some way. Also, regular behavioural recording allows staff to determine the presence of a *trend* which can be used to predict outcome and allow those funding rehabilitation to appreciate the probable length of treatment required to achieve a designated goal.

Opportunities for vocational training.   Some form of work placement is vital for those with lifelong neurobehavioural disability. Many individuals will never achieve more than part-time sheltered or supervised employment but this still provides them with a purpose and gives some structure to their lives which, over time, can ameliorate problems of planning and organisation, and reduce the impact of drive disorders. A work placement demands that a person be ready and presentable by a certain time to go to work. It often motivates brain injured people to get out of bed, shower and dress appropriately, something they do not do willingly on non-working days. A community work placement allows them to interact with "*normal*" people and exhibit the social and functional skills learned in a rehabilitation setting, but which are often not spontaneously evident in a home environment or on a residential unit. They have to exhibit tolerance and self-control in the face of frustration, and learn to be flexible in order to accommodate changing procedures and demands in the workplace.

Constructive use of leisure time.   Many brain injured people are not able to settle into work placements because they lack motivation, suffer from fatigue, have difficulty relating to others, or display personality characteristics that are inappropriate for a community work setting. For these individuals, an activities programme that helps them use leisure time constructively is very important. Without such structure such individuals may simply sit in front of a television all day or develop habit patterns that involve excessive smoking or drinking. Some resort to hoarding behaviour and their living areas become filled with useless clutter (old magazines, empty egg boxes, and other paraphernalia). Without a structured leisure programme the lives of many brain injured people take on an aimless character. They drift from one activity to another, often with bursts of enthusiasm for something which is short lived. Many young people with brain injury drift into alcohol or drug cultures and engage in socially deviant behaviours (theft, public nuisance, assault) which often leads to police involvement. Finding activities that will engage a brain injured person for any length of time is difficult and can involve care workers, case managers, and families in many hours of searching for suitable occupation.

Who is it for?

Having outlined the conceptual basis of a neurobehavioural paradigm of rehabilitation, it is appropriate to consider the people who are likely to benefit most from such an approach. Neurobehavioural rehabilitation is primarily for those who, after serious acquired brain injury, have persisting neurobehavioural disability which makes them heavily dependent upon others for their social and functional needs. This type of disability may take various forms, including:

1. Antisocial forms of behaviour or unpleasant personality characteristics which put an individual at risk in a community setting.
2. A lack of drive, initiative, or motivation, which prevents brain injured people looking after themselves properly.
3. Executive weakness or other cognitive deficits that reduce a person's self-care capabilities and prevent the use of social judgement or limit a person's ability to make decisions important to the management of his or her affairs.

Serious physical disability is not in itself a reason for social rehabilitation. A referral for this type of treatment would be for one of three reasons:

1. The person is unable to learn compensatory strategies to minimise the handicap produced by physical disability.
2. Compensatory strategies have been learned but are not applied spontaneously, being only implemented if prompted.
3. Behaviour or motivational problems make it difficult or impossible to work with such clients.

The pattern of disability varies enormously from person to person. Some have significant physical disability; others have serious cognitive impairment that may or may not be associated with behaviour problems. Often, the most complex rehabilitation problems are those presented by individuals with no measurable mental/cognitive impairment, or disability of a physical kind, yet are crippled by the inability to organise their thinking to plan and execute actions which are fundamental to daily life and which lie at the heart of social independence (Dimitrov, Grafman, & Hollnagel, 1996; Shallice & Burgess, 1991a; Varney & Menefee, 1993). If one had to categorise the different groups of clients who, at any time, represent the population of a neurobehavioural rehabilitation centre it would comprise those with:

1. Challenging behaviour.
2. Challenging behaviour with cognitive impairment.
3. Challenging behaviour with physical disability.
4. Challenging behaviour, cognitive impairment, and physical disability.
5. Cognitive impairment and physical disability.
6. "High-level" executive disorder with or without physical disability.

It is clear that the majority of people who present with persisting neurobehavioural disability have suffered injuries to the frontal structures of the brain or present a constellation of problems associated with some form of frontal dysfunction (Burgess & Wood, 1990; Cummings, 1999; Jasper, Riggio, & Goldman-Rakic, 1995). Most rehabilitation centres deal mainly with victims of traumatic brain damage, usually as a result of road traffic accidents. However, neurobehavioural disorders are also common after cerebral hypoxic injuries (Matthey, 1996), and encephalitis (Alderman & Burgess, 1994; Brazzelli, Colombo, Della Sala, & Spinnler, 1994). In contrast, they are not a common legacy of stroke. Some of the most frequent and devastating neurobehavioural disabilities follow injury to the orbitomedial regions of the frontal lobes (Malloy, Bihrle, Duffy, & Cimino, 1993; Shallice & Burgess, 1991a). Occasionally these result from surgical interventions, for example, to excise tumours (Eslinger & Damasio, 1985; Worthington, 1999) or to relieve epilepsy (Goldstein et al., 1993) but are most common after traumatic brain injury.

OPERATIONAL PRINCIPLES

Since the early 1980s many diverse sequelae of brain injury have been described under the rubric of neurobehavioural, with the result that there is now widespread inconsistency in how the term is used. The designation of a service as *neurobehavioural* implies that the rehabilitation process is based on certain characteristics and operational principles that need to be elaborated in an attempt to illustrate the utilitarian value of a neurobehavioural paradigm in brain injury rehabilitation. This section addresses some of the more obvious principles.

Recognising organic underpinnings of neurobehavioural disability

The organic underpinnings of cognitive–behavioural problems must be fully understood in order to understand the nature of neurobehavioural disability. Neurological and neuropsychological disabilities reflect cerebral dysfunctioning which imposes constraints on a person's capacity to learn new skills or apply skills spontaneously and adaptively in a social setting (see Chapter 1). Understanding the nature and mechanism of brain injury can provide clues about how cerebral dysfunction leads to neurobehavioural disability. For example, decelerative concussional injuries often compromise functions of the frontal structures. This results in a loss of specific inhibiting functions or modulatory controls. Herpes encephalitis attacks frontal, temporal, and limbic structures in a more selective, and usually more destructive manner, leading to a different clinical presentation and prognosis (Damasio & Van Hoesen, 1984). Knowledge of the mechanisms involved in brain injury allows us to understand the nature of cerebral constraints which, in turn, helps predict patterns of cognitive–behavioural dysfunction emerging later in recovery which could affect learning and compromise progress in rehabilitation. This type of information contributes significantly towards a more accurate assessment of a patient's rehabilitation potential.

The broad aim of rehabilitation is to help individuals recover social and functional skills necessary for life in the community. The successful outcome of brain injury rehabilitation depends not only upon how well a patient learns skills commensurate with functional independence, but how well those skills are employed to minimise social handicap. Brain injury can interfere with the acquisition of skills and coping strategies in a number of ways:

1. Cognitive deficits interfere with the ability to process information about the environment in terms of the meaning and relevance of events. In particular, attentional weaknesses, memory problems, comprehension difficulties, and problems with reasoning and problem solving may undermine the learning process itself.
2. More specifically, executive weaknesses may prevent a person recognising the need to adopt a particular strategy (failure of analogical reasoning) or impede the execution of a skill in the right situation (failure of initiation). The effect in both cases is a reduction in the spontaneous use of a skill after it has been acquired; in other words, the skill is not transferred from the training environment.
3. The brain injury may change personality in such a way that the need to learn strategies is not recognised, either because the person lacks insight into the nature and extent of his or her disability or denies the significance of an impediment (Prigatano, 1991).

4. The capacity to co-operate in therapy may be compromised by damage to the inhibitory and regulatory mechanisms of the brain, leading to reduced tolerance, labile mood, and disinhibition.

The presence of such cognitive–behaviour problems can delay or prevent the acquisition of coping strategies. It can therefore be argued with some authority that cognitive–behavioural patterns of disability after brain injury are potentially of greater significance than physical disability as a cause of social handicap. This perspective on rehabilitation does not deny the significance of physical disability after brain injury, but makes explicit the notion that whilst physical legacies of brain injury, such as hemiplegia, may be a major *disability,* they do not have to become a major *social handicap.* This is because people can learn strategies to minimise the social obstacles caused by physical disability (something which is clearly evident following rehabilitation for spinal cord injury). However, a failure to learn, or to employ spontaneously what one learns, or the inability to participate meaningfully in rehabilitation because of personality or behaviour problems, means that physical disabilities become obstacles to social independence, not because of the physical disability itself, but because of a failure to learn or employ compensatory skills.

Understanding the organic underpinnings of cognitive–behavioural disorders allows us to select realistic goals for rehabilitation and employ procedures appropriate for people whose ability to benefit from rehabilitation has been limited by organic constraints on how they learn, or deploy what they learn, to promote adaptive social behaviour. Damage to the lateral convexity of the frontal lobes, for example, is likely to be associated with deficits in high-level planning and organising skills, even in a motivated individual, which is in contrast to the reduction in drive and spontaneity typically associated with more medial frontal damage. Alternatively, damage to the medial regions of the frontal lobes (or anterior cingulate) would lead the practitioner to expect problems of motivation, initiative, and mood control. This can help distinguish organically mediated disorders of drive and motivation from those which have a purely psychiatric or psychological (emotional) basis and avoid the mistaken diagnosis of reactive depression. Similarly, knowing that a person has a very poor memory following encephalitis should immediately alert one to the probability of anterograde amnesia, rather than the attentional memory deficit that usually follows head trauma. As such, employing memory training procedures would be far less effective with the former than with the latter.

Another behaviour problem often (mis)construed entirely within a psychological framework is the markedly exaggerated and often contextually inappropriate change in apparent mood that characterises emotional lability. Mood disorders are a common legacy of head trauma but the idea that cerebral factors may directly precipitate changes of mood is often overlooked. Indeed, emotional lability may not reflect a mood disorder but merely the expression of mood. It is, however, common for low moods or volatile emotional outbursts to be attributed to adjustment difficulties, relationship problems, frustration, etc., when in fact organic factors, linked directly to the brain injury itself, may be responsible for emotional instability (e.g., Elliot, 1982). Failure to identify the correct cause of a problem may result in the wrong or less effective treatment approach being used. This can lead to patients spending fruitless hours in psychological therapy or being prescribed antidepressant medication, when a more effective method of treatment (often carbamazepine—see Chapter 2) could produce more beneficial (and probably more immediate) results.

Unfortunately, the multidisciplinary structure of brain injury rehabilitation teams is not always conducive to a systematic analysis of disability. Often, staff formulate ideas about treatment of a person's disabilities and handicaps without carefully considering their organic basis in relation to the treatment method being employed. The neurobehavioural paradigm therefore uses the assessment stage of rehabilitation, which is integral to treatment planning, as a period of systematic observation. The aim of this period is to identify the specific constraints that constitute a person's pattern of neurobehavioural disability. This information is then related to what is known of the person's brain injury in an attempt to identify the neurological, neuropsychiatric, and/or neuropsychological basis of cognitive–behaviour problems that underpin an individual's social handicap and likely act as impediments to learning.

Behavioural goals of rehabilitation

The term "neurobehavioural" should not be construed simply as an approach to rehabilitation that focuses on organically caused behaviour disturbance, without recourse to the impact of the behaviour on the person's functioning in society (which constitutes the dimension of *social handicap*). An approach that sees the description "neurobehavioural" as implying simply an organic, as opposed to a psychological orientation, or as merely a collective term for a set of therapeutic procedures, is unduly restrictive. It fails to encompass the real objectives of rehabilitation, namely amelioration of the handicaps that result from disorders of social behaviour.

As a result of the studies of Oddy and Humphrey (1978), Oddy et al. (1989), and Thomsen (1984) recovery from brain injury has increasingly been defined by criteria that characterise *social outcome*. Social recovery focuses more upon how a person thinks and behaves than on physical parameters of recovery. In the eyes of society, therefore, cognitive and behavioural legacies of brain injury represent a far greater handicap to community reintegration and social independence than physical disability. The implications of this are obvious. It is what a person does, in respect of self-care ability, or behaves in society, that represents recovery in this broader social context. In contrast, improvements in terms of neuropsychological test scores have minimal direct bearing on outcome (Teasdale, Skovdal, Gade, & Christensen, 1997). The principal goals of brain injury rehabilitation must therefore be behavioural, reflecting a person's capacity to think and act in a purposeful manner, conducive to social reintegration at a level commensurate with the constraints imposed by physical disability. This point is emphasised by the behavioural suffix of the term neurobehavioural.

The end product of rehabilitation is social and functional *behaviour,* defined broadly to represent abilities compatible with independent living. This goal is sometimes overlooked at the early stages of rehabilitation. Acute neurological rehabilitation understandably construes recovery in terms of a reduction in some aspect of disability. This is often defined in ways specific to the discipline of particular therapists and can lead to a short-sighted and rather narrow interpretation of what constitutes the ultimate goal of rehabilitation. For example, reducing muscle tone in a person with a left hemiplegia allows a person to walk and use their right hand more effectively. Whether or not this can be construed as a successful rehabilitation outcome largely depends upon where the person walks to, and what they do when they get there. Increased mobility and motor co-ordination, for example, may allow a person to walk to a public house then use the improved control of their right hand to drink several pints of beer. As a result they become drunk, and may lash out aggressively with the right hand when others try to intervene. In such circumstances, it might be felt that the reduction in physical disability has been achieved at the expense of creating a problem of social behaviour, the implications of which far exceed those associated with the original hemiplegia. The lesson from this example is that whilst rehabilitation goals which target disability are appropriate during the early stages of recovery from brain injury, they may be unsuitable for post-acute rehabilitation where social handicap is the focus of attention.

The ultimate objective of neurobehavioural rehabilitation therefore is to eliminate or ameliorate the social handicap produced by complex patterns of disability that follow brain injury. One might reasonably expect this to be the aim of any form of brain injury rehabilitation. However, Ponsford (1995) makes the point that simply training people to carry out self-care activities does not guarantee successful social adaptation. The purpose of neurobehavioural rehabilitation is to ensure not only that the procedures and goals of treatment emphasise socially relevant methods of training, but also involve the frequent application of skills to develop habit patterns that promote a person's capacity for community living at the highest level of independence possible, given the nature of their disability.

The role of learning

Rehabilitation is fundamentally a process of re-acquiring old skills or learning new ones to compensate for lost abilities. This emphasises the role of learning in rehabilitation, something which is frequently acknowledged by practitioners but not always reflected in the way training programmes are designed and applied. Paradigms of learning theory and, in particular, operant or instrumental conditioning are central to neurobehavioural rehabilitation. The role of associational learning in shaping or changing behaviour has a long history (de Silva, 1984). This century, the insights of Thorndike (1911) that behaviour is influenced by its effects and of Tolman (1925) that behaviour can be seen as goal-directed are well known. Later, Hull's (1943) influential theory of learning emphasised the development of *habit* as the basis for strengthening associations between events—a concept that retains a central place in the neurobehavioural approach. Hull also introduced the notion of *organic drive* as setting some limits on the learning process. Although his views about the role of drive in learning are no longer held, states of arousal and drive remain significant factors in determining rates of learning, especially after brain injury. For example, apparent inconsistency in learning ability can often be attributed to fluctuations in a person's arousal. From these early theoretical contributions there developed many empirically proven therapeutic techniques based on principles of learning (Wood, 1987) which could be applied in residential (Page, Luce, & Willis, 1992) and community settings (Hogan, 1988).

The focus of neurobehavioural rehabilitation is not simply about learning to reduce the less savoury aspects of a person's behaviour but also about equipping people with the skills that underlie effective social adaptation. It incorporates many psychological techniques, both behavioural (Hogan, 1988; McGlynn, 1990) and cognitive (Gianutsos, 1991; Szekeres et al., 1987) that have previously been applied in brain injury rehabilitation, recognising that there are significant weaknesses in traditional approaches to learning in rehabilitation. The most obvious is that a skill may be learned but never spontaneously employed (Keeley, Shemberg, & Carbonell, 1976). The reason for this lies in the difference between the acquisition of a skill and its application. Unless the process of acquiring a skill is associated with its application, what is learned may never be spontaneously implemented.

Failure to appreciate this important aspect of learning has been a criticism levelled at cognitive approaches to brain injury rehabilitation (Baddeley, 1993). Neurobehavioural rehabilitation addresses this dilemma by employing a procedural approach to learning (see later), in which the practice of a skill in real-life situations forms the basis of how the skill is acquired. This promotes the development of habit patterns that act as a platform for all activities of daily living upon which the client will rely to promote independence (McNeny, 1990). Given that the broad goal of rehabilitation is the acquisition of skills that will promote independence, the methods employed in neurobehavioural rehabilitation are derived directly from an appreciation of the characteristics of skilled behaviour and skill acquisition. From a clinical perspective the important characteristics of skilled performance are that it is:

1. Planned.
2. Well-timed.
3. Executed smoothly.
4. "Effortless" yet controlled.

5. Learned through experience.
6. Consolidated through repeated practice.

Procedures are employed that will promote the learning of adaptive skills possessing such properties, by repetitive practice in real-life situations. The neurobehavioural approach to skills learning in brain injury rehabilitation thus avoids the common dislocation between thinking and practice that bedevils therapists who are aware that brain injury weakens cognitive functions important for learning yet overlook this fact when working with clients.

Awareness training

The emphasis on skilled behaviour arises from an appreciation of how skills are acquired. As Dickinson (1980) observed, one can consider human conditioning either in terms of behavioural changes observed during the conditioning process itself or in terms of the learning process underlying the changes. The emphasis in neurobehavioural rehabilitation is very much on the latter; understanding how learning takes place allows us to improve the speed and effectiveness of learning. To take one example of this important principle, persons who have impairments of selective attention tend to have difficulty in discriminating relevant aspects of the environment, and are slower to learn as a result (Baron, Myerson, & Hale, 1988). In order to compensate for this, and facilitate learning, the associative links between events in the environment must be strengthened and made more salient. It should be recalled that the capacity to learn associations between stimulus events and their consequences fundamentally underpins the neurobehavioural approach to treatment.

The assumption is made that people must be aware of their environment in order to respond appropriately to changing social conditions. In any given situation a person must be able to discriminate between aspects that are relevant to their behaviour, such as the reaction of other people in the room, from irrelevant aspects, such as the telephone ringing. It is no use responding to a specific instance of "inappropriate behaviour" with a recognised strategy such as "time-out-on-the-spot" if the recipient has no idea that your behaviour has anything at all to do with their own actions. In order for that person to learn, they may have to be made aware that a problem exists and why they need to behave differently. This means that self-awareness and awareness of others has to be developed, a process that involves the training of selective or *discriminative attention.*

As the capacity for sustained and selective attention is associated with frontal lobe functioning it should not be unexpected that decrements in attention are common after severe brain injury (Azouvi et al., 1996; Brouwer, Ponds, Van Wolffelaar, & Van Zomeren, 1989). The right hemisphere especially seems to be important in maintaining a focus of attention (see review by Foster, Eskes, & Stuss, 1994), lesions of which result in resource-limited performance under situations of high demand and poor attentional control under low or intermittent demand (Manly & Robertson, 1997). Alderman (1996) reported that poor responders to behavioural management procedures had difficulty monitoring concurrent tasks, which suggests an impairment in allocation of attention. Significantly, these persons' monitoring abilities improved when given verbal feedback on their performance. An important aspect of neurobehavioural rehabilitation therefore is training in self-awareness and discriminative attention through feedback methods (see Chapters 7 and 8).

Verbal mediation

Impaired awareness directly affects a person's behaviour and results in difficulties in social perception and social judgement. A key notion in this respect is that of self-regulation, people's ability to monitor their own behaviour and alter their actions in response to changes in the environment (Lunzer, 1968; Meichenbaum, 1977). Luria (1973) identified the capacity for "programming, regulation, and verification" of behaviour as the highest order of cognitive functions—functions that are crucial to maintaining socially acceptable behaviour. This concept of behavioural regulation underlies much of the present-day understanding about the role of the frontal lobes in modulating behaviour (Shallice & Burgess, 1991b). It follows that disorders of social behaviour may be amenable to attempts to restore a degree of self-control. In Luria's influential approach to neuropsychology, such control is mediated by language (Vocate, 1987). This point was also made by Stuss and Benson (1986), who emphasise the regulating power of language. The major influence of Luria's contribution to rehabilitation was his emphasis on using verbal prompts or scripts to guide behaviour, and on clear and consistent feedback on performance (Christensen & Caetano, 1996; Horton & Miller, 1985). These tenets are embodied in the verbal mediation programmes for skill learning that lie at the heart of neurobehavioural rehabilitation. Verbal regulation provides a means of raising a person's awareness of maladaptive or inappropriate behaviour, whilst also providing cognitive strategies that both inhibit inappropriate behaviours and provide more socially acceptable alternatives.

Procedural learning and the development of habit patterns

Procedural learning methods are the most effective means of promoting the acquisition of habitual behaviours, skills with which a person may be equipped to function, not only more independently, but more acceptably in society. The techniques can be traced to the influence of early theorists like Hull (1943) for whom the development of habits was crucial to learning. Recent interest has focused on the neural basis of purposeful action (Jeannerod, 1997) and its everyday naturalistic occurrence (Schwartz & Buxbaum, 1997). It is now recognised that learning to demonstrate knowledge (e.g., how to get up and dressed in the morning) as an *activity* makes use of aspects of the brain involved in co-ordinating movement such as the cerebellum (Bracha et al., 1999; Molinari et al.,1997), basal ganglia (Jueptner & Weiller,1998), and motor parts of the frontal lobes (Passingham, 1993). This introduces the role of crucial attention systems of the cingulate and frontal regions (Posner & Dehaene, 1994), which are initially involved in awareness training. In fact, recent research has indicated that the more automatic or habitual a task becomes, the less it involves the attention functions of the frontal lobes (Passingham, 1998), thereby freeing up attention for other matters. Consequently, helping people establish self-care activities as habit patterns means that neurobehavioural constraints imposed by attentional or other executive weaknesses are minimised, increasing the chances of the behaviour pattern surviving the change of environment from clinic to community.

Habit formation is therefore central to neurobehavioural rehabilitation. Learning through experience rather than learning by instruction is the essence of *procedural learning*. This means that the rehabilitation process must allow individuals the opportunity to repeatedly practise the execution of socially adaptive skills in real-life contexts (McNeny, 1990). This allows brain damaged individuals with limited insight and social judgement to develop better awareness of their social capabilities. This in turn can enhance motivation and speed up learning.

CONCLUDING COMMENTS

Improvements in neurotrauma management mean that many people who previously would have died as a result of brain injury now survive. Therefore it is imperative that rehabilitation techniques improve to address complex patterns of neurobehavioural disability so that the quality of life for those who survive serious brain injury makes the whole process worth while. Whatever the cause of the brain injury, it is usually the neurobehavioural legacies that render people incapable of returning to the community, resuming family life, or engaging in some form of employment or constructive leisure activity. These legacies are responsible for antisocial behaviours that often break up family relationships and lead to young people drifting into lifestyles characterised by drug or alcohol abuse or criminal activity. Many become friendless, socially isolated, and vulnerable to exploitation. It is vital that rehabilitation methods are developed to directly address these problems. This has been the aim of neurobehavioural rehabilitation. It is usually employed with those who have a poor prognosis and who display a pattern of disability that is difficult to manage. Even so, the few outcome studies undertaken have provided encouraging results, both in respect of the ability to improve the care and social reintegration of those with serious problems of behaviour (Eames & Wood, 1985; Eames et al., 1995) and in terms of the cost-effectiveness of such rehabilitation methods (Wood et al., 1999).

REFERENCES

Alderman, N. (1996). Central executive deficit and response to operant conditioning methods. *Neuropsychological Rehabilitation, 6,* 161–186.

Alderman, N., & Burgess, P.W. (1994). A comparison of treatment methods for behaviour disorder following herpes simplex encephalitis. *Neuropsychological Rehabilitation, 4,* 1–96.

Allen, L.R., & Beattie, R.J. (1987) The role of leisure as an indicator of overall satisfaction with community life. *Journal of Leisure Research, 16,* 99–109.

Anderson, S.I., Wilson, C.L., McDowell, I.P., Pentland, B., Gray, J.M., & Robertson, I.H. (1996). Late rehabilitation for closed head injury: A follow-up study of patients 1 year from time of discharge. *Brain Injury, 10,* 115–124.

Azouvi, P., Jokic, C., Van der Linden, M., Marlier, N., & Bussel, B. (1996). Working memory and supervisory control after severe closed head injury: A study of dual-task performance and random generation. *Journal of Clinical and Experimental Neuropsychology, 18,* 317–337.

Baddeley, A.D. (1993). A theory of rehabilitation without a model of learning is a vehicle without an engine. A comment on Caramazza & Hills. *Neuropsychological Rehabilitation, 3,* 235–244.

Barnes, M. (1993). Organisation of neurological rehabilitation services. In R. Greenwood, M.P. Barnes, T.M. McMillan, & C.D. Ward (Eds.), *Neurological rehabilitation.* London: Churchill Livingstone.

Barnes, M. (1995). A regional service: Developing a head injury service. In M.A. Chamberlain, V. Neumann, & A. Tennant (Eds.), *Traumatic brain injury rehabilitation: Services, treatments and outcomes* (pp. 37–50). London: Chapman & Hall.

Baron, A., Myerson, J., & Hale, S. (1988). An integrated analysis of the structure and function of behavior: Aging and the cost of dividing attention. In G. Davey & C. Cullen (Eds.), *Human operant conditioning and behavior modification* (pp. 139–166). Chichester: Wiley.

Ben-Yishay, Y., & Gold, J. (1990). A theraputic milieu approach to neuropsychological rehabilitation. In R.Ll. Wood (Ed.), *Neurobehavioural sequelae of traumatic brain injury.* London: Taylor Francis.

Bond, M. (1976). Assessment of psychosocial outcome after traumatic brain injury. *Acta Neurochirgica, 34,* 57–70.

Bond, M. (1984). Psychiatry of closed head injury. In D.N. Brooks (Ed.), *Closed head injury: Psychological, social, and family consequences.* Oxford: Oxford University Press.

Bracha, V., Zhao, L., Wonderlich, D.A., Morrissy, S.J., & Bloedel, J.R. (1999). Patients with cerebellar lesions cannot acquire but are able to retain conditioned eyeblink reflexes. *Brain, 120,* 1401–1413.

Brazzelli, M., Colombo, N., Della Sala, S., & Spinnler, H. (1994). Spared and impaired cognitive abilities after bilateral frontal damage. *Cortex, 30,* 27–51.

Brooks, D.N., & Aughton, M.E. (1979). Psychological consequences of blunt head injury. *International Journal of Rehabilitation Medicine, 1,* 160–165.

Brouwer, W.H., Ponds, R.W.H.M., Van Wolffelaar, P.C., & Van Zomeren, A.H. (1989). Divided attention 5 to 10 years after severe closed head injury. *Cortex, 25,* 219–230.

Burgess, P.W., & Wood, R.Ll. (1990). Neuropsychology of behaviour disorders following brain injury. In R.Ll. Wood (Ed.), *Neurobehavioural sequelae of traumatic brain injury* (pp. 110–133). London: Taylor & Francis.

Burke, D.C. (1995). Models of brain injury rehabilitation. *Brain Injury, 9,* 735–743.

Christensen, A.-L., & Caetano, C. (1996). Alexandr Romanovic Luria (1902–1977): Contributions to Neuropsychological Rehabilitation. *Neuropsychological Rehabilitation, 6*, 241–360.

Cummings, J. (1999). Towards a neuropsychiatric epistemology. *Neurocase, 5*, 181–188.

Damasio, A.R., & Van Hoesen, G.W. (1984). The limbic system and the localisation of herpes simplex encephalitis. *British Journal of Psychiatry, 18*, 297–301.

Davy, G. (1988). Trends in operant human theory. In G. Davy & C. Cullen (Eds.), *Human operant conditioning and behavioural learning*. Chichester: Wiley.

deSilva, P. (1984). Buddism and behaviour modification. *Behaviour Research and Therapy, 22*, 661–678.

Dickinson, A. (1980). *Contemporary animal learning theory*. Cambridge: Cambridge University Press.

Dimitrov, M., Grafman, J., & Hollnagel, C. (1996). The effects of frontal lobe damage on everyday problem solving. *Cortex, 32*, 357–366.

Donald, C.A., Ware, J.E., & Brook, R.H. (1978). *Conceptualization and measurement of health for adults in the health insurance study. Vol. IV: Social health*. Santa Monica, CA: Rand Corporation.

Eames, P. (1990). Organic bases of behaviour disorder after traumatic brain injury. In R.Ll. Wood (Ed.), *Neurobehavioural sequelae of traumatic brain injury*. London: Taylor & Francis.

Eames, P., & Wood, R.Ll. (1985). Rehabilitation after severe head injury: A follow-up study of a behaviour modification approach. *Journal of Neurology, Neurosurgery and Psychiatry, 48*, 613–619.

Eames, P., Turnbull, J., & Goodman-Smith, A. (1989). Service delivery and assessment of programs. In M.D. Lezak (Ed.), *Assessment of the behavioural consequences of head trauma* (pp. 195–214). New York: Alan Liss.

Eames, P., Cotterill, G., & Kneale, T.A. (1995). Outcome of intensive rehabilitation after severe brain injury: A long term follow-up study. *Brain Injury, 10*, 631–650.

Elliott, F.A. (1982). Neurological findings in adult minimal brain dysfunction and the dyscontrol syndrome. *Journal of Nervous and Mental Diseases, 170*, 680–687.

Eslinger, P.J., & Damasio, A.R. (1985). Severe disturbance of higher cognition after bilateral frontal ablation: Patient EVR. *Neurology, 35*, 1731–1741.

Evans C., & Skidmore, B. (1989). Rehabilitation in the community. In R.Ll. Wood & P. Eames (Eds.), *Models of brain injury rehabilitation* (pp. 59–72). London: Chapman & Hall.

Foster, J.K., Eskes, G.A., & Stuss, D.T. (1994). The cognitive neuropsychology of attention: A frontal lobe perspective. *Cognitive Neuropsychology, 11*, 133–147.

Frieden, R.A. (1993). Early rehabilitation after stroke. In W.A. Gordon (Ed.), *Advances in stroke rehabilitation* (pp. 18–34). Stoneham, MA: Andover.

Gianutsos, R. (1991). Cognitive rehabilitation: A neuropsychological speciality comes of age. *Brain Injury, 5*, 353–368.

Goldstein, L.H., Bernard, S., Fenwick, P., Burgess, P.W., & McNeil, J. (1993). Unilateral frontal lobectomy can produce strategy application disorder. *Journal of Neurology, Neurosurgery and Psychiatry, 56*, 271–276.

Goll, S., & Hawley, K. (1989). Social rehabilitation: The role of the transitional living centre. In R.Ll. Wood & P. Eames (Eds.), *Models of brain injury rehabilitation* (pp. 142–163). London: Chapman & Hall.

Groswasser, Z. (1994). Rehabilitating psychosocial functioning. In A.-L. Christensen & B.P. Uzzell (Eds.), *Brain injury and neuropsychological rehabilitation* (pp. 187–199). Hillsdale, NJ: Lawrence Erlbaum.

Gualtieri T., & Cox, D.R. (1991). The delayed neurobehavioural sequelae of traumatic brain injury. *Brain Injury, 5*, 219–233.

Hogan, R.T. (1988). Behavior management for community integration. *Journal of Head Trauma Rehabilitation, 3*, 62–71.

Horton, A.M., & Miller, W.G. (1985). Neuropsychology and behaviour therapy. In M. Hersen, R.M. Eisler, & P.M. Miller (Eds.), *Progress in behavior modification, Vol. 19* (pp. 1–5). San Diego: Academic Press.

Hull, C.L. (1943). *Principles of behavior.* New York: Appleton-Century-Crofts.

Jasper, H.H., Riggio, S., & Goldman-Rakic, P. (1995). *Epilepsy and the functional anatomy of the frontal lobe. Advances in Neurology, Vol. 66.* New York: Raven Press.

Jeannerod, M. (1997). *The cognitive neuroscience of action.* Oxford: Blackwell.

Johnston, M.V., & Lewis, F.D. (1991). Outcomes of community re-entry programmes for brain injury survivors. Part 1: Independent living and productive activities. *Brain Injury, 5,* 141–154.

Jueptner, M., & Weiller, C. (1998). A review of differences between basal ganglia and cerebellar control of movements as revealed by functional imaging studies. *Brain, 121,* 1437–1449.

Kazdin, A.E. (1989). *Behaviour modification in applied settings.* Pacific Grove, CA: Brooks/Cole Publishing.

Keeley, S., Shemberg, K., & Carbonell, J. (1976). Operant clinical intervention: Behaviour management or beyond. Where are the data? *Behavior Therapy, 7,* 292–305.

Kendall, E., & Terry, D.J. (1996). Psychosocial adjustment following closed head injury: A model for understanding individual differences and predicting outcome. *Neuropsychological Rehabilitation, 6*, 101–1.

Lasure, L.C., & Mikulas, W.L. (1996). Biblical behavioural modification. *Behaviour Research and Therapy, 34*, 563–566.

Lewin, W. (1968). Rehabilitation after head injury. *British Medical Journal, 1*, 456–470.

Lunzer, E.A. (1968). *The regulation of behaviour.* London: Staples Press.

Luria, A.R. (1973). *The working brain: An introduction to neuropsychology.* Harmondsworth: Penguin.

Malloy, P., Bihrle, A., Duffy, J., & Cimino C. (1993). The orbitomedial frontal syndrome. *Archives of Clinical Neuropsychology, 8*, 185–201.

Manly, T., & Robertson, I. (1997). Sustained attention and the frontal lobes. In P. Rabbitt (Ed.), *Methodology of frontal and executive function* (pp. 135–153). Hove: Psychology Press.

Matthey, S. (1996). Modification of perseverative behaviour in an adult with anoxic brain damage. *Brain Injury, 10*, 219–227.

McGlynn, S.M. (1990). Behavioral approaches to neuropsychological rehabilitation. *Psychological Bulletin, 108*, 420–441.

McGrath, J.R., & Davis, A.M. (1992). Rehabilitation: Where are we going; how do we get there. *Clinical Rehabilitation, 6,* 225–235.

McMillan, T.M., & Greenwood, R. (1993). Models of rehabilitation programmes for the brain injured adult. II: Model services and suggestions for change in the UK. *Clinical Rehabilitation, 7*, 346–355.

McNeny, R. (1990). Daily living skills. The foundation of community living. In J.S. Kreutzer & P. Wehman (Eds.), *Community integration following traumatic brain injury* (pp. 105–113). York, PA: Paul H. Brookes.

Meichenbaum, D. (1977). *Cognitive–behavior modification.* New York: Plenum Press.

Meier, M.J., Benton, A.L., & Diller, L. (1987). *Neuropsychological rehabilitation.* New York: Churchill Livingstone.

Miller, E. (1984). *Recovery and management of psychological impairment.* Chichester: Wiley.

Molinari, M., Leggio, M.G., Solida, A., Ciorra, R., Misciagna, S., Silveri, M.C., & Petrosini, L. (1997). Cerebellum and procedural learning: Evidence from focal cerebellar lesions. *Brain, 120,* 1753–1762.

Murdoch, B.E. (1996). Physiological rehabilitation of disordered speech following closed head injury. In B.P. Uzzell & H.H. Stonnington (Eds.), *Recovery after traumatic brain injury* (pp. 163–184). Mahwah, NJ: Lawrence Erlbaum.

Neumann, V. (1995). Principles and practice of treatment. In M.A. Chamberlain, V. Neumann, & A. Tennant (Eds.), *Traumatic brain injury rehabilitation: Services, treatments and outcomes* (pp. 101–118). London: Chapman & Hall.

Oddy, M., & Humphrey, M. (1980). Social recovery during the year following head injury. *Journal of Neurology, Neurosurgery and Psychiatry, 43,* 798–802.

Oddy, M., Bonham, E., McMillan, T.M., Stroud, A., & Rickard, S. (1989). A comprehensive service for rehabilitation and long term care of head injury survivors. *Clinical rehabilitation, 3,* 253–259.

Page, T.J., Luce, S.C., & Willis, K. (1992). Rehabilitation of adults with acquired brain injury. *Behavioral Residential Treatment, 7,* 169–179

Palat, M., & Palat, M. Jr. (1995). A home-based service: A community rehabilitation programme. In M.A. Chamberlain, V. Neumann, & A. Tennant (Eds.), *Traumatic brain injury rehabilitation: Services, treatments and outcomes* (pp. 84–87). London: Chapman & Hall.

Passingham, R. (1993). *The frontal lobes and voluntary action.* Oxford: Oxford University Press.

Passingham, R. (1998). Attention to action. In A.C. Roberts, T.W. Robbins, & L. Weiskrantz (Eds.), *The prefrontal cortex: Executive and cognitive functions* (pp. 131–143). Oxford: Oxford University Press.

Pfeffer, R.I., Kurosaki, T.T., Harrah, C.H., Chance, J.M., & Filos, S. (1982). Measurement of functional activities in older adults in the community. *Journal of Gerontology, 37,* 323–329.

Ponsford, J. (1995). *Traumatic brain injury: Rehabilitation for everyday adaptive living,* Hove, UK: Lawrence Erlbaum Associates Ltd.

Posner, M.I., & Dehaene, S. (1994). Attentional networks. *Trends in Neurosciences, 17,* 75–79.

Prigatano, G. (1986). *Neuropsychological rehabilitation after brain injury.* Baltimore: Johns Hopkins Press.

Prigatano, G.P. (1991). Disturbances of self-awareness of deficit after traumatic brain injury. In G.P. Prigatano & D.L. Schacter (Eds.), *Awareness of deficit after brain injury. Clinical and theoretical perspectives* (pp. 111–126). New York: Oxford University Press.

Schalen, W., Hansson, L., Nordstrom, G., & Nordstrom, C.-H. (1994). Psychosocial outcomes 5–8 years after severe traumatic brain lesions and the impact of rehabilitation services. *Brain Injury, 8,* 49–64.

Schwartz, M.F., & Buxbaum, L.J. (1997). Naturalistic action. In L.J.G. Rothi & K.M. Heilman (Eds.), *Apraxia: The neuropsychology of action* (pp. 269–289). Hove: Psychology Press.

Shallice, T., & Burgess, P.W. (1991a). Deficits in strategy application following frontal lobe lesions in man. *Brain, 114*, 727–741.

Shallice, T., & Burgess, P. (1991b). Higher-order cognitive impairments and frontal lobe lesions in man. In H.S. Levin, H.M. Eisenberg, & A.L. Benton (Eds.), *Frontal lobe function and dysfunction* (pp. 125–138). New York: Oxford University Press.

Soryal, I., Sloan, R.L., Skelton, C., & Pentland, B. (1992). Rehabilitation needs after haemorrhagic brain injury: Are they similar to those after traumatic brain injury? *Clinical rehabilitation, 6*, 103–110.

Stein, D.G., Glasier, M.M., & Hoffman, S.W. (1994). Pharmacological treatments for brain injury repair: Progress and prognosis. *Neuropsychological Rehabilitation, 4*, 337–357.

Strasser, D.C., Falconer, J.A., & Martino-Saltzmann, D. (1994). The rehabilitation team: Staff perceptions of the hospital environment, the interdisciplinary team environment, and inter-professional relations. *Archives of Physical Medicine and Rehabilitation, 75*, 177–182.

Stuss, D.T., & Benson, D.F. (1986). *The frontal lobes.* New York: Raven Press.

Szekeres, S.F., Ylvisaker, M., Henry, K., Sullivan, D.M., & Wheeler, P. (1987). Topics in cognitive rehabilitation therapy. In M. Ylvisaker & E.M.R. Gobble (Eds.), *Community re-entry for head injured adults* (pp. 237–215). Boston: Little Brown.

Teasdale, T.W., Skovdahl, H., Gade, A., & Chistensen, A.-L. (1997). Neuropsychological test scores before and after brain injury rehabilitation. *Neuropsychological Rehabilitation, 7*, 23–42.

Thomsen, I.V. (1984). Late outcome of very severe blunt head trauma: A 10–15 year follow-up. *Psychiatry, 47*, 260–268.

Thorndike, E.L. (1911). *Animal intelligence.* New York: Macmillan.

Tolman, E.C. (1925). Purpose and cognition: The determiners of animal learning. *Psychological Review, 32*, 285–297.

Varney, N.R., & Menefee, L. (1993). Psychosocial and executive defcitis following closed head injury: Implications for orbital frontal cortex. *Journal of Head Trauma Rehabilitation, 8*, 32–44.

Vilkki, J., Ahola, K., Holst, P., Ohman, J., Servo, A., & Heiskanen, O. (1994). Prediction of psychosocial recovery after head injury with cognitive tests and neurobehavioural ratings. *Journal of Clinical and Experimental Neuropsychology, 16*, 325–338.

Vocate, D.R. (1987). *The Theory of A.R. Luria: Functions of spoken language in the development of higher mental processes.* Hillsdale, NJ: Lawrence Erlbaum

Ward, C.D., & McIntosh, S. (1993). The rehabilitation process: A neurological perspective. In R. Greenwood, M.P. Barnes, T.M. McMillan, & C.D. Ward (Eds.), *Neurological rehabilitation.* London: Churchill Livingstone.

White, M.J., & Olson, R.S. (1998). Attitudes toward people with disabilities: A comparison of rehabilitation nurses, occupational therapists and physical therapists. *Rehabilitation Nursing, 23*, 126–130.

Willer, B., Rosenthal, M., Kreutzer, J.S., Gordon, W.A., & Rempel, R. (1993). Assessment of community integration following rehabilitation for traumatic brain injury. *Journal of Head Trauma Rehabilitation, 8*, 75–87.

Wood, R.Ll. (1987). *Brain injury rehabilitation: A neurobehavioural perspective.* London: Croom Helm.

Wood, R.Ll. (1990a). Towards a model of cognitive rehabilitation. In R.Ll. Wood & I. Fussey (Eds.), *Cognitive rehabilitation in perspective*. Hove, UK: Lawrence Erlbaum Associates Ltd.

Wood, R.Ll. (1990b). Neurobehavioural paradigm for brain injury rehabilitation. In R.Ll. Wood (Ed.), *Neurobehavioural sequelae of traumatic brain injury*, (pp.153–174), London: Taylor & Francis.

Wood, R.Ll. (1996). Ten years of post acute brain injury rehabilitation. *Personal Injury, 3*, 203–211.

Wood, R.Ll., & Eames, P. (1981). *Models of brain injury rehabilitation*. London: Chapman & Hall.

Wood, R.Ll., & Worthington, A.D. (1999). Outcome measurement in community rehabilitation: Measuring the social impact of disability. *Neuropsychological Rehabilitation, 9*, 505–516.

Wood, R.Ll., McCrea, J.D., Wood, L.M., & Merriman, R.N. (1999). Clinical and cost effectiveness of post-acute neurobehavioural rehabilitation. *Brian Injury, 13*, 69–88.

Worthington, A.D. (1996). Management of brain dysfunction. In V. Aitken, & H. Jellicoe (Eds.), *Behavioural sciences for healthcare professionals* (pp. 211–223). London: W.B. Saunders.

Worthington, A.D. (1999). Dysexecutive paramnesia: Retrospective and prospective remembering. *Neurocase, 5*, 47–57.

Worthington, A., Williams, C., Young, K., & Pownall, J. (1997). Re-training gait components for walking in the context of abulia. *Physiotherapy Theory and Practice, 13*, 247–256.

Zasler, N.D. (1995). Neurologic impairment and disability evaluation. In M. Rizzo & D. Tranel (Eds.), *Head injury and postconcussive syndrome* (pp. 351–374). New York: Churchill Livingstone.

CHAPTER SEVEN

Neurobehavioural rehabilitation in practice

R.Ll. Wood and A.D. Worthington
Brain Injury Rehabilitation Trust, Birmingham, UK

INTRODUCTION

This chapter addresses the practice of neurobehavioural rehabilitation as a paradigm for post-acute brain injury rehabilitation, in contrast to the previous chapter, which focused on the conceptual basis of the neurobehavioural paradigm.

It is well established that a significant proportion of brain injured people fail to make the kind of recovery that allows them to return to work or reintegrate into society in a meaningful way. Many are unable to drive (Brouwer & Witaar, 1997; Harjte et al., 1991; Priddy, Johnson & Lam, 1990), to regain competitive employment (Brooks et al.,1987; Johnson,1998), to live independently, or act in a socially acceptable manner in the community (Marsh et al., 1990; Newton & Johnson, 1985). This may occur irrespective of the person's exposure to rehabilitation, or the quality and intensity of treatment. Consequently, the prevalence of people whose lifestyle is affected by persisting neurobehavioural disability increases year by year, imposing an emotional and physical burden upon families and carers (Brooks et al., 1986; Kreutzer, Gervasio, & Camplair, 1994; Thomsen, 1984; Wallace et al., 1998), plus a substantial financial burden on the state and/or insurance companies who have to assume responsibility for the funding of such care (Bistany, 1994). Recently the National Institutes of Health in the US estimated that the prevalence of residual disability after traumatic brain injury could be as high as 6.5 million in the US (National Institutes of Health, 1999). In the UK too the strain upon families, carers, voluntary and charitable organisations, as well as the statutory health and social services, constitutes a major burden to society.

The persistent nature of neurobehavioural disability amongst brain injured people in the community necessitates a re-examination of the objectives and delivery of rehabilitation for such individuals. This, in turn, calls for a change of emphasis in the way the goals of rehabilitation are construed and designated. In 1980, the World Health Organisation introduced a classification scheme that characterised disability, occurring as a direct result of illness or injury, in bio-behavioural terms (World Health Organisation, 1980). This framework has been extremely influential in the development of hospital-based rehabilitation services and outcome evaluation (Chantraine & Berard, 1995) but so far (nothwithstanding recent efforts to revise the scheme) it has proved far less suitable for understanding the longer-term consequences of brain injury. Efforts to understand the genesis of disability and handicap in terms of this simplistic model (e.g., Fuher & Richards, 1996) are likely to produce distorted conclusions overplaying the importance of physical factors and the causal role of impairments (see Webb, Wrigley, Yoels, & Fine, 1995, for an example). Recent research suggests that disability is amenable to investigation and treatment in terms of psychological models of behaviour which are susceptible to social and environmental influences (Johnston, 1997). Consequently, we are now becoming less focused on disabilities in themselves and more upon the *behaviours* that represent such disabilities and the factors that shape them, including psychological and neuropsychological constraints to social adjustment (Kendall & Terry, 1996; Moore et al., 1990).

This is not to claim that focusing on behaviour is a new concept in rehabilitation. Nearly 20 years ago Stolov (1982) felt that because brain injury involved the loss of social, vocational, and psychological function, as well as physical function, disability should be described behaviourally. About the same time, Duckworth (1983) also recommended that disability following brain injury should be described in terms of behaviour and that the process of rehabilitation should be the correction of deviance from some social norm rather than simply the restoration of a functional skill. However, despite the articulation of such views, centres specialising in brain injury rehabilitation have been slow to accept the idea. Indeed, for many services, the notion that disabilities should not be treated in isolation from their functional context represents their last significant conceptual advance, again a view promoted some time ago (Eames & Wood, 1985).

The need for even hospital-based rehabilitation services to consider the broader social and societal parameters of disability has been slow to receive recognition amongst many practitioners. Wood (1989) referred to the dislocation in the thinking of rehabilitation professionals when setting down the goals of a person's rehabilitation programme. On one hand, staff are aware of the social problems and emotional burden on carers generated by serious brain injury, yet they often designate therapy goals that have little if anything to do with broader social or family issues that might have a positive, practical impact on psychosocial functioning. Although this has long been recognised as a problem, the paradox is still prevalent in the majority of rehabilitation services today. In contrast, the main thrust of neurobehavioural rehabilitation is to address those aspects of behaviour that are ineffective, counter-productive, antisocial, or otherwise act as obstacles to social reintegration. By eliminating or ameliorating the social handicap produced by neurobehavioural disability after brain injury it becomes possible to equip the injured person with skills that help him or her achieve the highest level of social independence possible, within the context of physical or other constraints imposed by the brain injury.

CHARACTERISTICS OF NEUROBEHAVIOURAL REHABILITATION

The designation of a service as *neurobehavioural* implies certain characteristics of the rehabilitation process.

Behaviour management capability

Many of those who are unable to resume life in the community after brain injury fail because they lack social skills or a sense of social propriety. They can be demanding, unreasonable, stubborn and obsessive, intemperate, reactive, embarrassing, threatening and, occasionally, dangerous to themselves or others because of impulsive and volatile reactions. The socially unacceptable behaviours most frequently reported after brain injury are (1) tirades of verbal abuse, (2) coarse sexual comments, (3) various forms of disinhibition, and (4) the kind of physical aggression that is impulsive and short-lived, rather than premeditated and sustained. Any or all of these behaviours are likely to emerge in a rehabilitation context because such individuals will be challenged to do certain things in certain ways and at certain times which will increase their sense of stress or frustration, leading to angry reactions. A brain injury rehabilitation unit is not necessarily the best place for the faint hearted or those sensitive to occasional insult. Few brain injured people actually want to become involved in months of rehabilitation and many fail to see that they have any problems that require rehabilitation. Motivation is a rare commodity and often all one receives is grudging co-operation from the client, which even then is unpredictable.

The aim is to create an atmosphere which is positive, rewarding, and happy; however, even the best social ambience can be disturbed by an outburst of angry swearing or sudden physical assault. Often, staff request that a stop is put to such behaviour. However, in a community-based unit there may not be any way to "stop" a reaction once it is under way and much depends on the confidence of staff and their ability to maintain a non-judgemental attitude in such situations. In these circumstances there are methods that can be employed to contain and control inappropriate and challenging behaviour, in order to create conditions in which it is possible to shape more effective social and functional skills.

The range of responses available to staff in such situations is reviewed in Chapter 8. Essentially, the guiding principle is to avoid responding to antisocial or otherwise inappropriate behaviour in a manner that is *positively reinforcing* for the individual client concerned. One of the most versatile means of achieving this is to adopt a time-out strategy, such as time-out-on-the-spot, (or "TOOTS"). This brief period of time out from positive reinforcement can be delivered as soon as the unwanted behaviour occurs. If used correctly, it can be a powerful social cue to learning more acceptable behaviour. More effective still is the selective use of social reinforcement (e.g., eye contact, conversation) when behaviour *other than* the target antisocial behaviour is demonstrated. This is the basis for the *differential reinforcement of other behaviour* (DRO). DRO strategies have general appeal for a wide range of inappropriate social acts. Another intervention within the same theme is the *differential reinforcement of incompatible behaviour* (DRI). This approach is adopted to reinforce a desired behaviour (e.g., polite conversation) which is *incompatible* with a target behaviour (e.g., abusive swearing). Kazdin (1989) provides a useful review of these methods which, over time, can promote socially adaptive behaviour. In contrast with tangible response–cost programmes, they offer more potential for application in the community and, thereby, for the generalisation of behaviour change.

Awareness training

Many people referred for social rehabilitation are disinhibited and impulsive. They are unable to regulate their behaviour in order to make a controlled or measured response to a social situation. If frustrated by something, or otherwise put under pressure, they may respond in a reflexive, stereotyped way, often reacting disproportionately to the eliciting stimulus, usually with no thought of the consequences (see Chapters 1 and 8). Most clinicians now recognise that brain injured people need to become aware of the consequences of their actions before they will accept the necessity to learn alternative strategies compatible with socially acceptable behaviour (Alderman, Fry, & Youngson, 1995). As stated above, many brain injured people are not aware they have problems in respect of life skills; alternatively they may be aware of a problem itself but fail to judge the impact of the problem on others. One of the first goals in a rehabilitation programme, therefore, is to help those with executive weaknesses, or behaviour and personality problems, recognise their nature and impact on personal relationships and other social activities (see Chapter 8).

The ability to learn new skills is considerably enhanced if a person understands what it is they are to learn and why. To overcome or ameliorate social handicap a person must first of all be able to recognise the nature and extent of his or her neurological disability and how the disability interferes with social or functional skills (Bergquist & Jacket, 1993). While very few brain injured people receiving rehabilitation show characteristics of denial or anosognosia, a significant number display diminished awareness (Malia, Torode, & Powell, 1993; Prigatano, 1991), sufficient to interfere with social judgement or the capacity to evaluate the impact of their behaviour on others (see Chapter 1). While some practitioners have raised concerns about the implications of raising awareness and possibly precipitating adjustment problems (Fleming & Strong, 1995), most accept that this is a nettle that has to be grasped.

Deficits of awareness are usually underpinned by attentional deficits. These deficits prevent the kind of self-monitoring of behaviour that makes it possible to adapt one's actions in the face of changing social circumstances. Attention is crucial on two accounts. First, learning processes involved in behavioural conditioning require the mediation of attention (Dickinson, 1980). Second, the satisfactory implementation of procedurally learned routine actions requires a degree of higher level attentional control (Shallice & Burgess, 1993) without which concrete stereotyped behaviours are likely to manifest inappropriately (Reason, 1990). Therefore, training attention is necessary to improve social awareness and should form an important element of a neurobehavioural rehabilitation programme. In accordance with the development of skilled behaviour, this is largely achieved by giving feedback clearly, frequently, and unambiguously throughout each client's working day (Wood, 1990).

Feedback

Feedback can be delivered in a variety of ways to promote awareness, understanding, and memory of events in an attempt to help clients recognise stimuli that elicit thoughts, feelings, and reactions that other people find unacceptable. Some of these methods are:

Incidental feedback.   This technique is similar to the process of operant reinforcement in learning theory as it involves praising or constructively criticising a specific behaviour whenever it is observed. It is usually carried out as a prescribed behavioural training procedure towards a designated goal. The effect of this kind of response is to modify the incidence and nature of the target behaviour. Staff need to be taught how to give this type of feedback in a manner that is neither autocratic nor patronising.

Structured feedback.   By contrast with incidental feedback, this is a non-contingent means of intervention that involves setting time aside several times each day to review with a client his or her progress in respect of designated behaviour goals. The content and structure of the short session (usually 10–15 minutes) vary according to the kind of feedback prescribed to meet the client's capabilities (Lewis, Nelson, Nelson, & Reusink, 1988), but essentially it begins by asking the client to make comments, based on their memory and interpretation of events, usually during the preceding three hours. This is followed by a more careful examination by the staff member, highlighting the positive and negative incidents during that period.

Points programmes.   These award a set number of points to clients at specified intervals throughout the day. Points are contingent upon a client's behaviour or performance in respect of designated rehabilitation goals. In this sense, such schemes are another means of operant reinforcement through a points system, as distinguished from a token economy (Blackerby, 1988), in that points are not linked to tangible reinforcement. They do, of course, have a powerful social reinforcement value when used as a means to praise effort, progress, etc., but their main value is to provide feedback systematically, in respect of quite specific behaviours or activities, at regular intervals throughout the day. The earning of points, or a failure to earn for some specified reason, approximates a response–cost procedure (Sullivan & O'Leary, 1990), which helps clients become more aware of those aspects of their behaviour or actions that influence their social environment. Consequently, the use of a points programme encourages self-monitoring in clients who have lost the ability to self-monitor automatically and who have to learn to make a conscious effort to engage in this attentional activity.

Cognitive behavioural techniques

Whilst awareness training is an important stage in the development of self-control, clients also have to learn how to inhibit inappropriate responses and replace them with socially acceptable forms of behaviour (Burke, Zencius, Wesolowski, & Doubleday, 1991). For those clients able to communicate meaningfully, a cognitive–behaviour therapy approach can be successfully employed to improve awareness and increase response options (Hollon & Kriss, 1984). Other psychotherapeutic approaches have been used with brain injured persons (Langer & Pardone, 1992). However, the more "directive" and problem-solving elements of a structured cognitive–behavioural therapy (CBT) approach are particularly suited to neurobehavioural rehabilitation, which emphasises changing behaviour from "disabled" to "enabled" (see Chapter 8). A CBT approach to behaviour change helps to focus on actions in functional or interpersonal situations that are currently ineffective. This can facilitate adjustment to disability and lead to greater objectivity on behalf of a client when he or she is trying to evaluate circumstances associated with failure of an action. This may, in turn, generate a less hostile and more positive attitude towards the nature and purpose of a rehabilitation programme, increasing the client's motivation and awareness of response options when faced with a particular problem.

The challenging behaviours encountered in social rehabilitation are rarely serious to life and limb but they are seen as threatening and unacceptable to the general public. Rehabilitation procedures therefore need to incorporate cognitive strategies capable of mediating thoughts that elicit responses of a socially appropriate character. The success of CBT with some brain injured people is a testimony to how such interventions can produce long-lasting behavioural improvements. However, not all clients are amenable to this approach and for some a more specific approach is warranted, based on the notion of verbal mediation.

Verbal mediation

As many seasoned rehabilitation practitioners know only too well, awareness of a problem is not in itself sufficient to ensure that behavioural change occurs. The problem for most brain injured persons goes beyond lack of awareness and includes, crucially, the inability to translate knowledge and intentions into action. In Chapter 1 it was argued that the reason for this can be found in a failure to use language to regulate behaviour (Luria, 1973; Stuss & Benson, 1986). Clinical experience has shown that a process of *verbal mediation* is the most effective means to promote effective or adaptive behaviour, whether formalised in a cognitive therapy intervention (Bandura, 1992) or structured in terms of a prompt schedule that directs a person's actions in respect of a specific activity. Thus, while disorders of complex behaviour can be viewed either as deficits in a system of working memory (Kimberg & Farah, 1993) or higher-level attentional control (Duncan, 1993; Shallice & Burgess, 1998), the crucial factor in remediation is whether language can be harnessed as a control mechanism.

Verbal mediation is the use of overt language to phrase statements that elicit thoughts and actions which initiate and shape behaviour. It is based on the notion of inner speech (Luria & Homskya, 1966; Luria & Yudovich, 1972) which, it is argued, is responsible for most forms of voluntary behaviour; directs attention to the most salient features of an activity; creates an internal plan; and helps monitor performance by comparing the outcome of an action with the original intention (Stuss & Benson, 1986). The aim is to help a client acquire sentences or phrases that identify a problem, offer a solution, initiate an action, guide the action to a goal, and finally, to recognise the outcome. Evidence from how people learn skills routinely suggests that this is indeed a plausible objective, and this forms the basis of the verbal mediation techniques at the core of neurobehavioural rehabilitation.

The structure of mediation procedures is based on a dialogue of questions and answers between the client and a member of staff. It is learned in exactly the same way as two actors would learn a script (by rote memory). The lines of the dialogue are then used to cue each other's response. The staff member asks a series of questions designed to elicit specific answers from the client relating to the nature of the problem and how to act in order to overcome it. A response to each question must be obtained before moving onto the next step of the question–response sequence. The responses one elicits from the client are worded so that they can be joined together to form a meaningful statement that will direct behaviour in a prescribed way to a specific problem or situation. For example, one client was so handicapped by executive problems that he was unable to sequence or regulate the actions involved in washing and dressing each morning. He used to take an inordinate time to get ready for breakfast and often missed the meal, which led to an angry outburst. He did not like being told to hurry, again responding angrily, nor did he like staff intervening when he was found not to have washed, shaved, or dressed properly. A verbal mediation programme was introduced in several stages, each stage dealing with a different component of the activity. The first stage, which involved initiating and guiding face washing, was as follows:

Q. Your face is dry, what should you do?
R. *I splash water on my face.*
Q. Your face is wet, the soap is dry, what should you do?
R. *Rub soap on my face.*
Q. There is soap on your face, what should you do?
R. *Splash water on my face.*
Q. Your face is wet, what should you do?
R. *Then I dry my face.*

This dialogue was rehearsed a number of times until the client could remember the mediational phrase, "*I splash water on my face, rub soap on my face, splash water on my face, then I dry my face*". This procedure, once it had been practised and employed subvocally during morning hygiene programmes, succeeded in reducing the time taken to carry out this step in a morning hygiene routine by 80% and also avoided aggression and associated behaviours which previously made his day-to-day management difficult.

The promotion of verbal regulation of behaviour is now an accepted therapeutic strategy (Christensen, 1986, 1996) and has been shown to be effective in training daily living skills. Consequently, verbal mediation is an important tool in neurobehavioural rehabilitation. It offers a means of raising both a person's awareness of dysfunctional and/or inappropriate behaviour, whilst simultaneously providing a cognitive strategy to inhibit inappropriate actions and generate alternative options for responding (Sohlberg, Sprunk, & Metzelaar, 1988). For example, a person becomes able to carry out tasks more effectively by repeating verbal prompts. These are initially given by others but, as a result of practice, become internalised as a sequence of cues that help initiate a response, link responses together to form complex action sequences, or redirect action when an obstacle is encountered.

In the mental health field the potential benefits of this kind of self-reinforcement were evident many years ago. For example, Weissberg (1977) reported that speech anxiety could be significantly reduced when people were taught a series of statements to repeat, which inhibited their anxiety. Thus self-statements were shown to be effective in reducing a problem even when the problem itself was speech-related. Successes like this, most celebrated in Meichenbaum's (1975) self-instructional training programme, were instrumental in the adoption of cognitive methods by behaviourally oriented clinicians. The self-regulation approach therefore pre-dates the development of cognitive behaviour therapy but unfortunately it has been slow to influence the treatment of people with severe brain injury (see, for example, Hux, Reid, & Lugert, 1994). However, methods to improve verbal mediation of behaviour, both in functional skills when dysexecutive weaknesses predominate, as well as in self-regulatory strategies for challenging behaviours, are being developed as a central strategy for neurobehavioural rehabilitation.

Executive skills training

Almost everything associated with social independence involves the ability to plan, sequence, organise, or co-ordinate actions. Whether one is making a cup of tea, a sandwich, or a four-course meal, one has to anticipate the order in which things are done, how much time each stage of the activity requires, what materials or components of the task need to be assembled, and so on. The most routine, commonplace social activities rely on executive skills. Most of the activities in which we engage daily become overlearned as social habit patterns (see later) and therefore their "executive" characteristics are less evident because the task is performed automatically. It is only when the cognitive skills mediating our actions become disrupted or impaired by brain injury that the need to consciously co-ordinate our actions becomes evident.

Every neurobehavioural rehabilitation programme must incorporate a range of social learning opportunities that address those activities of daily living essential to social independence and a purposeful, goal-orientated pattern of behaviour. These involve morning personal hygiene and dressing procedures, preparing weekly menus, shopping, cooking, managing a weekly budget, laundry, home care/cleaning, using public transport, and arranging leisure or work placement activities. Each of these activities requires some element of cognitive and executive control and therefore represent the "*stuff*" of brain injury rehabilitation. They are naturally occurring activities and therefore offer plenty of scope for practitioners in respect of treatment interventions of a behavioural or cognitive nature.

Procedural learning

The principal method of promoting functional socially adaptive skills is by developing knowledge or competence in the form of procedures, rather than as facts. In other words, information is learned and applied in a manner that is intimately related to the way a person uses it. This distinction is what underlies the difference between "knowing that" and the crucial "knowing how" in rehabilitation and is operationalised as procedural learning, a means of learning through doing rather than by being told. There may be an element of instruction (see verbal mediation above) but the critical point is that a person engages in the behaviour as part of the learning process. For complex actions comprising multiple components (subroutines) which need planning and organising in their execution, training involves practice in applying procedures on these subroutines in an open-ended way and to co-ordinate these with other procedurally based behaviours.

Procedural learning methods, with their emphasis on how to perform certain activities, also avoid the pitfalls of trying to teach people through declarative forms of learning, i.e., learning through understanding, employing concepts based on principles. By definition, this type of learning, which is employed in conventional rehabilitation, relies on information-processing ability, memory, flexible thinking, reasoning, and concept formation—all the things that brain injured people find difficult. Limited attentional capacity means that brain injured people are only able to process small amounts of information at any given time; instructions that exceed a certain level of complexity, or are delivered at too fast a rate, can lead to fragmented information processing, poor retention, and inefficient learning. The outcome is often fatigue (as a result of trying to concentrate) and frustration, possibly leading to angry outbursts and loss of motivation.

Procedural methods do not exploit these cognitive weaknesses to the same degree. Procedural learning takes place slowly; it is practical or applied in character, often with a strong motor co-ordination element. As competence increases, it becomes possible to withdraw or fade out extraneous assistance (Demchak, 1990). Most social and functional skills upon which we rely for social independence were originally acquired this way during maturational development. It therefore makes sense to replicate the original learning procedure in rehabilitation procedures aimed at restoring social competence.

Habit patterns

The aim of neurobehavioural rehabilitation is to help people re-acquire those *habit patterns* of behaviour which form the basis of many daily living skills. However, a common criticism of brain injury rehabilitation is that any improvement in behaviour and functional ability lasts only as long as the person remains in the rehabilitation unit. When such criticism is justified it is because the rehabilitation team failed to consolidate and generalise skills and behaviours acquired by the client before discharge. This almost inevitably leads to a breakdown in such newly acquired skills, largely because many people with frontal dysfunction are unable to adapt skills learned in one environment to another. Procedural learning, comprising repeated practice of a skill, small units of learning, and the consolidation of one element of a skill before moving on to another, is an ideal vehicle for redeveloping habit patterns of behaviour that will survive a change of environment (Vakil, Haffman, & Myzliek, 1998). Thus when, for example, individuals move from a structured routine which is a necessary feature of rehabilitation, back into a far less structured life in the community, they are better equipped to cope with their new surroundings. In neuropsychological terms, this process promotes the development and selection of preferential behaviours or "action schema" and the inhibition of incompatible, less socially acceptable acts (Burgess & Alderman, 1990).

NEUROBEHAVIOURAL REHABILITATION PLANNING

Behavioural assessment

The first stage of rehabilitation is an assessment, normally a process spread over several weeks or more. This establishes a person's potential for rehabilitation and also the goals towards which the rehabilitation team will be working. The overriding aim of neurobehavioural rehabilitation is to restore social and functional behaviours that promote independent living in the community. This focus on behaviour also underpins the assessment process. In other words, assessment of a person's abilities are carried out using a behavioural frame of reference, concentrating on how individuals present themselves in a social context, what they can and cannot do to help themselves, as well as what they won't do!

The essence of any behavioural assessment process is collation of information from diverse sources (e.g., family members, therapists) to establish the parameters of a person's behavioural repertoire (Touchette, MacDonald, & Langer, 1985; Treadwell & Page, 1996), through different means (direct behavioural observation, semi-structured interview, formal testing) in a multitude of contexts (in formal treatment sessions, during unstructured break times, on public transport, waiting in a check-out queue, etc.). The process of assessment therefore requires accumulation of evidence over a period of several weeks, during which time a person is exposed to many different real-life situations, and is monitored using a variety of recording measures. When evaluating a person's performance in a social context one also needs to consider how their behaviour is received by others, whether or not they alter a person's social or functional circumstances positively, and anything else that may have an impact on how one approaches a person's rehabilitation (Marsh & Knight, 1991).

In terms of behavioural observations, a variety of techniques are employed including time-sampling and partial interval techniques (Hartmann, 1984), rating scales, and video recordings. The key underlying principle is one of obtaining objective reliable information by a means that is sensitive to behavioural deficits after brain injury, including the so-called "negative" sequelae of apathy, aspontaneity, and anergia, which are poor prognostic indicators of social outcome (Gray et al., 1994). In practice this means having to tailor structured observations or recording schedules according to individual presentation. There are a number of well-established methods of recording frequency and duration of behaviours, and the importance of a functional analysis of behaviour cannot be overstated in the assessment phase.

The careful recording of behavioural observations is especially important for several reasons:

1. It helps staff maintain a focus on those aspects of a client's behaviour that are instrumental to his or her rehabilitation programme.

2. It provides a measure of a client's progress towards designated rehabilitation goals.
3. It also provides a feedback opportunity for the client, not only keeping a perspective on behaviours that need to be changed but also helping him or her evaluate progress in such a way that builds awareness (see later).

The emphasis on observational recording also permits a more responsive, hypothesis-testing approach to assessment. It rationalises the selection of observation targets and methods, and monitors interactions between environmental and interpersonal factors. Consider Figure 7.1 below. These data were obtained from a 51-year-old man who sustained bilateral frontal lobe damage following a road traffic accident two years previously. At mealtimes he would leave the dining room abruptly (with little chance of returning) if anyone joined his table. Further observation suggested that this happened less often if the person joining him was a member of staff, and it was speculated that this was because the staff member was more likely to engage him in conversation. A simple A-B-A-B approach (Sunderland, 1990; Worthington, 1995) was then taken towards monitoring the effect of engaging him in conversation. The graph clearly shows that the time he remained on task (eating his meal) could be significantly increased but only as long as he was being engaged in conversation at the dining table. When the intervention was withdrawn the time spent at the meal table decreased, but could be increased again on reinstatement of the intervention.

This example illustrates one of the most common neurobehavioural problems after traumatic brain injury—a disorder of attention. These can manifest in different ways depending on the context, and reflect the nature of the attention deficit, e.g.,

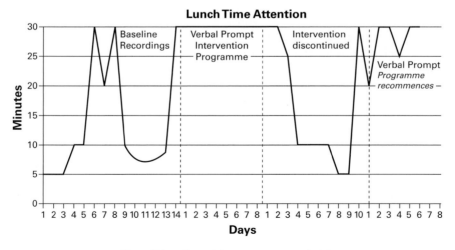

Figure 7.1.   Chart of time spent at the meal table.

whether it is primarily a disorder of sustained attention (attention span) or one of attentional control (distractibility). Rating scales therefore need to encompass the diversity of signs which may indicate an attentional problem (Ponsford & Kinsella, 1991).

For complex daily activities such as dressing, cooking, crossing the road, or managing finances, the task has to be broken down into stages. These stages are considered to be partially separable to the extent that they allow evaluation of each stage, rather than merely considering the task as a whole. The dependent variable being recorded may be the time taken to complete each stage, the number of errors made per stage, or the degree of initial prompting or assistance to complete each stage. For example, in order to record the amount of verbal prompting required, a dressing task might separate stages of wearing upper-body clothing, from lower body clothing (see Table 7.1). Another version of a dressing task might only distinguish whether a client could select clean suitable clothes, from their ability to dress themselves, whereas a more fine-grained analysis of the dressing task might discriminate between each item of clothing.

The extent to which a task is componentialised in this manner depends on the kinds of difficulties a person manifests. Someone who has the basic dressing skills may only need initial prompts to engage in collecting their clothes and then putting them on. Another person may not have the sequencing or organisational skills to perform this feat, in which case they would require prompts regularly throughout the task in order to see it through to completion. From a theoretical perspective the rationale is the same for each of these conditions. It is generally accepted that after a brain injury component actions of a complex activity, which are tightly integrated in smooth, skilled performance, become dislocated and fragmented. The frequency of prompting required to ensure task completion reflects the level at which this automatic process has broken down (Arnadottir, 1990).

Semi-structured rating scales of this nature offer the best means of assessing the impact of executive dysfunction on daily life (see Chapter 4). Performance on

TABLE 7.1

Three hypothetical task analyses of a dressing task

Dressing check-list					
(1a)	Take clothes from wardrobe	(1)	Take clothes from wardrobe	(1)	Get underclothes
(1b)	Select clean shirt			(2)	Select shirt
(1c)	Select clean underclothes			(3)	Select trousers
(1d)	Select clean socks			(4)	Select socks
(1e)	Check trousers not dirty			(5)	Select sweater
				(6)	Select shoes
(2)	Put on clothes	(2)	Put on shirt and trousers	(7)	Put on underclothes
		(3)	Put on trousers	(8)	Put on shirt
				(9)	Put on trousers
		(4)	Put on socks and shoes	(10)	Put on socks
				(11)	Put on shoes
				(12)	Put on sweater

these tasks is not simply judged in terms of overall task completion, but is also rated with respect to *how* a person completes the task. Typically the following aspects of performance are scored: the degree of planning involved; the efficiency of the strategy used; any omissions of task components; any breaking of rules or constraints; any impulsive or perseverative behaviours; instances of error correction or self-monitoring.

An example of this kind of assessment is shown in Figure 7.2. In this figure three individuals, who all sustained severe brain injuries in road traffic accidents, were evaluated on their ability to complete a semi-structured cooking task. Although each person had difficulty completing the task, there were marked differences in the nature of their problems and, in terms of amelioration, different strategies were clearly called for. It is interesting to note that even the most recent neuropsychological assessments of executive skills do not necessarily reveal these kinds of problem. Thus on the Hayling task of verbal suppression (Burgess & Shallice, 1997) client 2 was average; on the Brixton spatial anticipation task (Burgess & Shallice, 1997) client 3 was average; while client 1 was broadly within the average range on both these tasks and on the Behavioural Assessment of the Dysexecutive Syndrome (BADS) battery (Wilson et al.,1996).

As Figure 7.2 demonstrates, the data collated by check-lists and rating scales can be easily displayed graphically and subjected to visual analysis (Parenson & Baer, 1992) or statistical evaluation such as time series (Skinner, 1991) or non-parametric methods (Edginton, 1992). This makes it possible to examine patterns of performance over time and the influence of extraneous influences, such as time

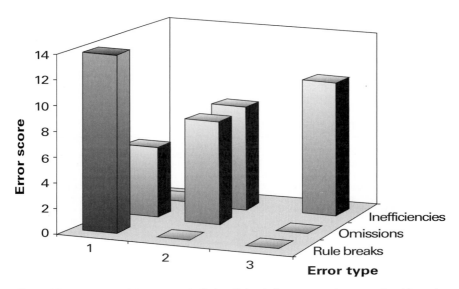

Figure 7.2   Error score of three traumatically head injured clients on a semi-structured cooking task.

of day or which particular staff were supervising the task. More detailed discussion of structured observational procedures can be found in Wood and Worthington (1999).

Neurobehavioural planning

The first step in planning a neurobehavioural rehabilitation programme is to formulate a concise summary of the person's presenting problems, couched in the context of their clinical history, with implications for treatment and prognosis. The formulation is based on the results of neurobehavioural assessment. It tries to establish a plausible (scientific) link between the nature of the brain injury, the pattern of cognitive and behavioural disability, the rehabilitation process, goals of treatment, and the overall length of time needed to carry out the rehabilitation plan. In essence, the formulation contains two parts; the first comprises the results of the assessment and includes:

1. A description of neurobehavioural disabilities and their probable neurological/neuropsychological/neuropsychiatric origin, linked to the known (or suspected) neuropathology.
2. A summary of the impact of those disabilities in respect of barriers to fulfilling desirable social roles—the extent of *social handicap*.
3. A summary of psychological and psychosocial factors that serve to maintain or "incubate" the disabilities and handicaps.

The second part of the formulation relates to the implications of such observations on discharge options and rehabilitation potential. Information obtained during the assessment period may indicate poor rehabilitation potential. For example, the client may lack insight into a range of cognitive and behaviour problems and refuse to participate in a rehabilitation programme. Others may lack the arousal or drive necessary to take any meaningful part in rehabilitation. The nature and severity of such neurobehavioural constraints must inevitably influence the selection of rehabilitation goals. If a person has significant constraints on learning or awareness then it may be unrealistic to propose goals associated with a more independent style of living. In such cases modest goals, directed at making a person's day-to-day social management easier for care workers, may be a more appropriate option.

The choice of rehabilitation goals will determine the activities of the treatment team and the development of a rehabilitation plan, usually comprising the following stages:

Stage 1. Setting discharge goals

The person's discharge options need to be explored with relatives, friends, funders, social workers, lawyers, etc. Once appropriate goals are determined the nature of the social and functional behaviours associated with them can be assessed. For example, if the family wants their relative to live at home, discharge goals will need to reflect the range of behaviours needed in family life (tolerence, empathy, good interpersonal skills, constructive use of leisure time, etc.). If, on the other hand, the client is destined to live apart from family, such as in sheltered accommodation, the type of social skills required may be different. For example, they may not need to show interest in the conversations or activities of others, but they may need to cook for themselves or attend a work placement.

Once appropriate discharge goals are agreed upon, it becomes possible to estimate the length of time needed to achieve those goals, giving the client, family, and those funding rehabilitation a frame of reference to determine cost of treatment in relation to probable outcome.

The discharge goals must relate to the performance of socially useful activities (e.g., being able to read a bus timetable, take a bus into town, purchase sufficient foodstuffs for three cooked meals for two, etc.). The patient's discharge goals are therefore defined *behaviourally*. They reflect the person's rehabilitation potential as well as what it is reasonable to achieve within the length of time allowed for rehabilitation.

Stage 2. Intermediate goals

Following the designation of discharge goals the rehabilitation team needs to determine intermediate treatment goals. These will direct the activities of the treatment team for several weeks at least. They will reflect the neurobehavioural constraints or disordered behaviours that currently prevent the client achieving their discharge goals and therefore act as obstacles to community integration (e.g., physical or cognitive disabilities that prevent a person taking a local bus into town to complete rudimentary shopping tasks). Barriers to successful performance of social and functional activities might include: inadequate motivation; topographical disorientation; reduced tolerance of waiting (at bus stops and shop queues); social or sexual disinhibition; or inefficient planning and organisation skills. These constraints on social independence become the focus of the rehabilitation programme and determine the activities of the intradisciplinary team.

Stage 3. Target behaviours

Target behaviours are specific social or functional behaviours that need to be immediately increased or decreased in frequency. They are of immediate concern to the rehabilitation team because they directly influence a client's co-operation or social performance. For example, rehabilitation of functional abilities cannot proceed if the client is antagonistic, uncooperative, or aggressive. The rehabilitation programme must therefore begin by targeting such behaviour, to decrease its frequency whilst simultaneously trying to change it to become more compliant and controllable. This would usually be achieved by removing anything that is reinforcing the behaviour whilst simultaneously raising the person's awareness of how such behaviour is perceived by members of society (in the sense that if they want to live an independent life in the community then this is not the best way to go about it). Target behaviours become the focus for observational analysis (behavioural recording) in order that a pre-treatment baseline can be established prior to the introduction of specific rehabilitation interventions. They are subject to weekly review by the treatment team and are directly linked to the more complex intermediate goals, to which they act as an obstacle.

A rehabilitation plan should be a working document for the evaluation and implementation of treatment. It should determine which rehabilitation interventions will be used, how and when they will be introduced, and who will administer them or record response characteristics. The behavioural goals should represent progress in cognitive, functional, physical, as well as self-regulatory aspects of emotional expression and social behaviour. They need to be ecologically valid, in the sense that the goals are meaningful to both the patient and his or her family or carers. The rehabilitation goals addressed by the treatment plan should reflect the type of performance or activity commensurate with improved social independence. This document summarises the goals for the period up to and including the next formal progress review. For each identified goal there are three elements:

1. A brief synopsis of the constraint upon community living, designated in behavioural terms.
2. A stated objective of intervention, again designated in objective measurable terms.
3. An action plan for intervention, often comprising several therapeutic strategies with clear indications of recording methods, and identifying key staff responsible for implementation and evaluation.

The rehabilitation plan thus provides an interdisciplinary synthesis of treatment objectives and intervention techniques. With the emphasis on the operationalisation of concepts and the designation of objective, quantifiable behaviours as goals, it is possible to measure progress towards socially adaptive skills in all aspects of community living. This, in turn, permits both at-a-glance monitoring of progress across multiple domains of independent living, and an empirical basis for predicting future progress. In our experience, not only can this kind of explicit visual statement benefit the brain injured person directly but it can also be particularly helpful to families and funders of rehabilitation. Most important, however, are the prescribed methods of treatment, which it is now appropriate to consider in more detail.

Evaluating outcome

Rehabilitation does not take place in a social or environmental vacuum. The aim is to help individuals re-acquire skills to ameliorate disability in order to minimise their socially handicapping nature. This means that every rehabilitation procedure should have a goal that is related to the reduction of social handicap, in one form or another. However, this immediately introduces a problem for the rehabilitation team because progress towards goals has to be monitored and measured as meaningfully and objectively as possible.

The need to measure progress has always been central to rehabilitation but traditionally such measures have been employed to record changes in some aspect of disability rather than handicap. Characteristics of disability are often more circumscribed and easier to measure than handicap but the measures themselves are often limited in their usefulness as indices of social recovery. For example, knowing that a person's range of movement has increased by several degrees illustrates a reduction in disability but it tells us nothing about what the person *does* with the additional range of movement to change social handicap. It is quite possible that restoring an active range of movement in a person's arm and hand will allow the arm to be used aggressively, lashing out at rehabilitation staff during periods of frustration. In this scenario, rehabilitation will have reduced disability but increased social handicap, because a person who might once have been manageable becomes unmanageable. Seen in this light, one could argue that rehabilitation has made the patient worse, not better.

Similar examples can be given across the rehabilitation spectrum to illustrate why measures showing a reduction in disability do not equate with an improvement in social handicap. It is also a reason to explain why reports of patients transferring from an acute rehabilitation unit to a post-acute setting often appear to give an inaccurate picture of their abilities. The explanation lies in the fact that acute and post-acute units often measure different things: the former reduction in disability, the latter improvements in social functioning. The "chalk and cheese" nature of these different measures reflects one of the areas of confusion in the continuum of brain injury rehabilitation.

The nature of outcome measurement in rehabilitation is largely determined by the presenting problems, the length of time needed for effective rehabilitation, and the frame of reference within which the problems are construed. For persons with complex neurobehavioural disability, where the emphasis is on amelioration of handicap, outcome can be measured over a period of months, an average being 12 months. Many rehabilitation teams deal with around 15 patients at any time, each of whom will present several neurobehavioural "problems" contributing to social handicap. Even if each team restricts itself to dealing concurrently with only three problem areas per client, then the total number of neurobehavioural problems being addressed by the team at any given time is notionally 45. With this number of potential rehabilitation targets or problem areas, it is virtually impossible to keep track of each person's progress, in a reliable way, over several months of rehabilitation, without an effective method of measurement.

Employing a neurobehavioural approach means that construing treatment goals in behavioural terms and carrying out observational assessments of behaviour become a central feature of the rehabilitation process—hence the emphasis on systematic data collection. Using behavioural baseline procedures to record the frequency or duration of behaviours, together with time sampling methods or rating scale procedures, allows information to be represented in as simple a form as possible. This is not only to provide information to the rehabilitation team, but can also be used as feedback for the patient and relatives. The behavioural measures that are employed from the outset during the assessment, and which guide the subsequent therapeutic process, also provide the means of evaluating rehabilitation outcome (see Wood & Worthington, 1999). In essence, social handicap is measured by what individuals do, i.e., how they act and what they say. It follows therefore that outcome is evaluated by how much a person demonstrates that he or she is integrated into society.

CONCLUSION

Rehabilitation of acquired brain injury has moved through a number of phases over the last 20 years, reflecting different traditions, perspectives, and interests. So far, there is no single "model" of rehabilitation that is appropriate to acute and post-acute rehabilitation services. However, the paradigm offered by neurobehavioural rehabilitation goes some way to addressing several key issues in the implementation of an empirically driven, conceptually based, pragmatically focused treatment. In particular the present chapter has outlined: (1) A rationale, linking the nature of the brain injury to probable cerebral pathology which, in turn, (2) provides a sound basis for understanding the nature of the disability displayed by a brain injured person, leading to (3) an explanation of social handicap stemming from such injury, and (4) giving a rationale for the type of treatment provided, in terms of how the goals of rehabilitation reflect the social and personal constraints imposed by the brain injury.

The principles underlying rehabilitation have been applied mainly in a post-acute setting but are also relevant to other stages of recovery and to disabilities other than those imposed by acquired brain injury. It does not offer a rehabilitation panacea but the neurobehavioural paradigm does provide a structure for the application and evaluation of treatment interventions used in brain injury rehabilitation. Neurobehavioural methods help staff appreciate whether or not specific interventions are effective and whether designated goals of treatment are reasonable, considering the nature of disability and the client's needs at discharge. Given the emphasis on developing self-awareness and the acquisition of socially adaptive habitual skills, this type of rehabilitation is not only cost-effective (Wood, McCrea,

Wood, & Merriman, 1999), but also offers considerable potential for successful long-term outcome.

REFERENCES

Alderman, N., Fry, R.K., & Youngson, H.A. (1995). Improvement of self-monitoring skills, reduction of behaviour disturbance and the dysexecutive syndrome: Comparison of response cost and a new programme of self-monitoring training. *Neuropsychological Rehabilitation, 5,* 193–221.

Arnadottir, G. (1990). *The brain and behavior: Assessing cortical dysfunction through activities of daily living.* St. Louis: C.V. Mosby.

Bandura, A. (1992). Exercise of personal agency through the self-efficacy mechanism. In R. Schwarzer (Ed.), *Self-efficacy: Thought control of action* (pp. 355–394). Washington, DC: Hemisphere.

Bergquist, T.F., & Jacket, M.P. (1993). Awareness and goal-setting with the traumatically brain injured. *Brain Injury, 7,* 275–282.

Bistany, D.V. (1994). Overview of the economics of rehabilitation in the United States. In A.-L. Christensen & B.P. Uzzell (Eds.), *Brain injury and neuropsychological rehabilitation: International perspectives* (pp. 245–267). Hillsdale, NJ: Lawrence Erlbaum Associates Inc.

Blackerby, W.F. (1988). Practical token economies. *Journal of Head Trauma Rehabilitation, 3,* 33–45.

Brooks, D.N., Campsie, L., Symington, C., Beattie, A., & McKinlay, W. (1986). The five year outcome of severe blunt head injury: A relative's view. *Journal of Neurology, Neurosurgery and Psychiatry, 49,* 764–770.

Brooks, D.N., McKinley, W., Symington, C., Beattie, A., & Campsie, L. (1987). Return to work within the first seven years of head injury. *Brain Injury, 1,* 5–19.

Brouwer, W.H., & Witaar, F.K. (1997). Fitness to drive after traumatic brain injury. *Neuropsychological Rehabilitation, 7,* 177–193.

Burgess, P.W., & Alderman, N. (1990). Rehabilitation of dyscontrol syndromes following frontal lobe damage. In R.L. Wood & I. Fussey (Eds.), *Cognitive rehabilitation in perspective.* Hove, UK: Lawrence Erlbaum Associates Ltd.

Burgess, P.W., & Shallice, T. (1997). *The Hayling and Brixton Test.* Bury St. Edmunds: Thames Valley Test Company.

Burke, W.H., Zencius, A.H., Wesolowski, M.D., & Doubleday, F. (1991). Improving executive function disorders in brain-injured clients. *Brain Injury, 5,* 241–252.

Chantraine, A., & Berard, E. (1995). Disability—the functional independence measure. In M.A. Chamberlain, V. Neumann, & A. Tennant (Eds.), *Traumatic brain injury rehabilitation: Services, treatments and outcomes* (pp. 213–224). London: Chapman & Hall.

Christensen. A.-L. (1986). Applying Luria's theory to the rehabilitation process of brain damage. In B.P. Uzzell & Y. Gross (Eds.), *Clinical neuropsychology of intervention* (pp. 169–177). Boston: Martinus Nijhoff.

Christensen, A.-L. (1996). Alexandr Romanovisch Luria (1902–1977). Contributions to neuropsychological rehabilitation. *Neuropsychological Rehabilitation, 6,* 279–303.

Demchak, M. (1990). Response prompting and fading methods: A review. *American Journal of Mental Retardation, 94,* 603–615.

Dickinson, A. (1980). *Contemporary animal learning theory.* Cambridge: Cambridge University Press.

Duckworth, D. (1983). The need for a standard terminology and classification of disablement. In C.V. Granger & G.E. Gresham (Eds.), *Functional assessment in rehabilitation medicine*. Baltimore: Williams and Wilkins.

Duncan, J. (1993). Selection of input and goal in the control of behaviour. In A.D. Baddeley & L. Weiskrantz (Eds.), *Attention: Selection, awareness and control* (pp. 53–71). New York: Oxford University Press.

Eames, P., & Wood, R.Ll. (1985). Rehabilitation after severe brain injury: A follow-up study of behaviour modification approach. *Journal of Neurology, Neurosurgery and Psychiatry, 48*, 613–619.

Eames, P., Turnbull, J., & Goodman-Smith, A. (1989). Service delivery and assessment of programs. In M.D. Lezak (Ed.), *Assessment of the behavioral consequences of head trauma* (pp. 195–214). New York: Alan R. Liss.

Edginton, E. (1992). Non-parametric tests for single-case experiments. In T.R. Kratochwill, & J.R. Levin (Eds.), *Single-case research design and analysis*, (pp.133–157), Hillsdale, NJ: Lawrence Erlbaum.

Fleming, J., & Strong, J. (1995). Self-awareness of deficits following acquired brain injury: Considerations for rehabilitation. *British Journal of Occupational Therapy, 58*, 55–60.

Fuher, M.J., & Richards, J.S. (1996). Medical rehabilitation outcomes with traumatic brain injury: Some recommended directions for research. In B.P. Uzzell & H.H. Stonnington (Eds.), *Recovery after traumatic brain injury* (pp. 247–255). Mahwah, NJ: Lawrence Erlbaum.

Gray, J.M., Shepherd, M., McKinlay, W.W., Robertson, I., & Pentland, B. (1994). Negative symptoms in the traumatically brain injured during their first year post-discharge, and their effect on rehabilitation status, work status, and family burden. *Clinical Rehabilitation, 8*, 188–197.

Hartje, W., Willmes, K., Pach, R., Hannen, P., & Weber, E. (1991). Driving ability of aphasic and non-aphasic brain-damaged patients. *Neuropsychological Rehabilitation, 1*, 161–174.

Hartman, D.P. (1984). In D.H. Barlow, & M. Hersen (Eds.), *Single case experimental designs* (pp. 107–139). New York: Pergamon Press.

Hollon, S.D., & Kriss, M.R. (1984). Cognitive factors in clinical research and practice. *Clinical Psychology Review, 4*, 35–76.

Hux, K., Reid, R., & Lugert, M. (1994). Self-instructional training following neurological injury. *Applied Cognitive Psychology, 8*, 259–271.

Johnson. R. (1998). How do people get back to work after severe head injury? A 10-year follow-up study. *Neuropsychological Rehabilitation, 8*, 61–79.

Johnston, M. (1997). Representations of disability. In K.J. Petrie & J.A. Weinman (Eds.), *Perceptions of health & illness* (pp. 189–212). Amsterdam: Harwood Academic.

Kazdin, A.E. (1989). *Behavior modification in applied settings, 4th edition.* Pacific Grove, CA: Brooks/Cole Publishing.

Kendall, E., & Terry, D.T. (1996). Psychosocial adjustment following closed head injury: A model for understanding individual differences and predicting outcome. *Neuropsychological Rehabilitation, 6*, 101–132.

Kimberg, D.Y., & Farah, M.J. (1993). A unified account of cognitive impairments following frontal lobe damage: The role of working memory in complex organised behaviour. *Journal of Experimental Psychology: General, 122*, 411–428.

Kreutzer, J.S., Gervasio, A.H., & Camplair, P.S. (1994). Primary caregivers' psychological status and family functioning after traumatic brain injury. *Brain Injury, 8*, 197–210.

Langer, K.G., & Pardone, F.J. (1992). Psychotherapeutic treatment of awareness in acute rehabilitation of traumatic brain injury. *Neuropsychological Rehabilitation, 2*, 59–70.

Lewis, F.D., Nelson, J., Nelson, C., & Reusink, P. (1988). Effects of three feedback contingencies on the socially inappropriate talk of a brain-injured adult. *Behavior Therapy, 19,* 203–211.

Luria, A.R. (1973). *The working brain.* London: Penguin.

Luria, A.R., & Homskya, E.D. (1966). Disturbances in the regulative role of speech with frontal lesions. In J.M. Warren & K.A. Ahert (Eds.), *The frontal granula cortex and behaviour.* New York: McGraw Hill.

Luria, A.R., & Yudovich, F. (1972). *Speech and the development of mental processes in the child.* London: Penguin.

Malia, K., Torode, S., & Powell, G. (1993). Insight and progress in rehabilitation after brain injury. *Clinical Rehabilitation, 7,* 23–29.

Marsh, N.V., & Knight, R.G. (1991). Behavioral assessment of social competence following severe head injury. *Journal of Clinical and Experimental Neuropsychology, 13,* 729–740.

Marsh, N.V., Knight, R.G., & Godfrey, H. (1990). Long term psychosocial adjustment following very severe closed head injury. *Neuropsychology, 4,* 13–27.

Meichenbaum, D.H. (1975). Self-instructional methods. In F.H. Kanfer & A.P. Goldstein (Eds.), *Helping people change: A textbook of methods* (pp. 357–391). New York: Pergamon.

Moore, A.D., Stambrook, M., Peters, L.C., Cardoso, E.R., & Kassum, D.A. (1990). Long term multidimensional outcome following traumatic brain injuries and traumatic brain injuries associated with multiple trauma. *Brain Injury, 4,* 379–389.

National Institutes of Health (1999). Rehabilitation of persons with traumatic brain injury. *Journal of the American Medical Association, 282,* 974–983.

Newton, A., & Johnson, D.A. (1985). Social adjustment and interaction after severe head injury. *British Journal of Clinical Psychology, 24,* 225–234.

Parsenson, B.S., & Baer, D.M. (1992). The visual analysis of data and current research into the stimuli controlling it. In T.R. Kratochwill & J.R. Levin (Eds.), *Single-case research design and analysis* (pp. 15–40). Hillsdale, NJ: Lawrence Erlbaum.

Ponsford, J., & Kinsella, G., (1991). The use of a rating scale of attentional behaviour. *Neuropsychological Rehabilitation, 1,* 241–257.

Priddy, D.A., Johnson, P., & Lam, C.S. (1990). Driving after a severe head injury. *Brain, 4,* 267–272.

Prigatano, G.P. (1991). Disturbances of self-awareness of deficit after traumatic brain injury. In G.P. Prigatano & D.L. Schacter (Eds.), *Awareness of deficit after brain injury: Clinical and theoretical issues* (pp. 111–126). New York: Oxford University Press.

Reason, J. (1990). *Human error.* New York: Cambridge University Press.

Shallice, T., & Burgess, P. (1993). Supervisory control of action and thought selection. In A. Baddeley, & L. Weiskrantz (Eds.), *Attention: Selection, awareness and control* (pp. 171–187). New York: Oxford University Press.

Shallice, T., & Burgess, P. (1998). The domain of supervisory processes and the temporal organisation of behaviour. In A.C. Roberts, T.W. Robbins, & L. Weiskrantz (Eds.), *The prefrontal cortex: Executive and cognitive functions* (pp. 22–35). New York: Oxford University Press.

Skinner, C. (1991). Time series. In P. Lovie, & A.D. Lovie, (Eds.), *New developments in statistics for psychology and the social sciences* (pp. 174–198). Leicester: British Psychological Society.

Stolov, W.C. (1982). Evaluation of the patient. In F.J. Kottke, G.K. Stillwell, & J.F. Lehmann (Eds.), *Handbook of physical medicine and rehabilitation.* Philadelphia: W.B. Saunders.

Stuss, D.T., & Benson, F. (1986). The frontal lobes. New York, Raven Press.

Sohlberg, M.M., Sprunk, H., & Metzelaar, K. (1988). Efficacy of external cueing system in an individual with severe frontal lobe damage. *Cognitive Rehabilitation, 6*, 36–41.

Sullivan, M.A., & O'Leary, S.G. (1990). Maintenance following reward and cost token programmes. *Behavior Therapy, 21*, 139–149.

Sunderland, A. (1990). Single-case experiments in neurological rehabilitation. *Clinical Rehabilitation, 4*, 181–192.

Thomsen, I.V. (1984). Late outcome of very severe blunt head trauma: A 10–15 year second follow-up. *Journal of Neurology, Neurosurgery and Psychiatry, 47*, 260–268.

Touchette, P.E., MacDonald, R.F., & Langer, S.N. (1985). A scatter plot for identifying stimulus control of problem behavior. *Journal of Applied Behavior Analysis, 18*, 343–351.

Treadwell, K., & Page, T.J. (1996). Functional analysis: Identifying the environmental determinants of severe behavior disorder. *Journal of Head Trauma Rehabilitation, 11*, 62–74.

Vakil, E., Haffman, Y., & Myzliek, D. (1998). Active versus passive procedural learning in older and younger adults. *Neuropsychological Rehabilitation, 8*, 31–41.

Wallace, C.A., Bogner, J., Corrigan, J.D., Clinchot, D., Mysiw, W.J., & Fugate, L.P. (1998). Primary caregivers of persons with brain injury: Life change 1 year after injury. *Brain Injury, 12*, 483–493.

Webb, C.R., Wrigley, M., Yoels, W., & Fine, P.R. (1995). Explaining quality of life for persons with traumatic brain injuries 2 years after injury. *Archives of Physical Medicine and Rehabilitation, 76*, 1113–1119.

Weissberg, M. (1977). A comparison of direct and vicarious treatments of speech anxiety: Desensitization, desensitization with coping imagery, and cognitive modification. *Behavior Therapy, 8*, 606–620.

Wilson, B.A., Alderman, N., Burgess, P.W., Emslie, H., & Evans, J.J. (1996). *BADS: Behavioural Assessment of the Dysexecutive Syndrome.* Bury St Edmunds: Thames Valley Test Company.

Wood, R.Ll. (1989). A salient factors approach to brain injury rehabilitation. In R.Ll. Wood & P.G. Eames (Eds.), *Models of brain injury rehabilitation.* London: Chapman and Hall.

Wood, R.Ll. (1990). Neurobehavioural paradigm for brain injury rehabilitation. In R.Ll. Wood (Ed.), *Neurobehavioural sequelae of traumatic brain injury* (pp. 153–174). London: Taylor & Francis.

Wood, R.Ll., & Worthington, A.D. (1999). Outcome in community rehabilitation: Measuring the social impact of disability. *Neuropsychological Rehabilitation, 9*, 505–516.

Wood, R.Ll., McCrea, J.D., Wood, L.M., & Merriman, R.N. (1999). Clinical and cost effectiveness of post-acute neurobehavioural rehabilitation. *Brain Injury, 13*(2), 69–88.

World Health Organisation (1980). *International classification of impairments, disabilities and handicaps.* Geneva: World Health Organisation.

Worthington, A.D. (1995). Single case design experimentation. *British Journal of Therapy and Rehabilitation, 2*, 536–538, 555–557.

CHAPTER EIGHT

Applying cognitive therapy in neurobehavioural rehabilitation

D. Manchester
Transitional Rehabilitation Unit, St. Helens, UK

R.Ll. Wood
Brain Injury Rehabilitation Trust, Birmingham, UK

INTRODUCTION

Many brain injured people who require post-acute social rehabilitation present changes in personality that alter their behaviour and affect their capacity for meaningful social relationships. This is particularly evident after traumatic brain injury because of the vulnerability of the frontal lobes and their role in self-awareness (see Chapter 1). Whilst usually only too apparent to relatives and friends, these changes often appear to remain beyond the client's own awareness (Oddy, Coughlan, Tyerman, & Jenkins, 1985; Prigatano, Altman, & O'Brien, 1990). Deficits in awareness can be as frustrating to carers and relatives as the original behavioural excesses themselves, not least because they can represent an impenetrable barrier to therapy. When clients do not acknowledge the existence of a problem they understandably see no need to alter their behaviour or their perception of life. Thus attempts at engagement in rehabilitation often lead to confrontation, resistance, and rejection. This chapter discusses cognitive therapy and its possible dual role with this client group; first, increasing clients' motivation to engage in the rehabilitation effort, and second, helping to establish enduring behaviour change.

Until recently, the rehabilitation of seriously brain injured people with disorders of personality and social behaviour relied largely on behaviour modification techniques to inhibit or extinguish unwanted behaviours and to "shape" responses that were socially acceptable. Although these methods met with a large degree of success (e.g. Eames & Wood, 1985; Wood, 1987) they ultimately proved to be limited, both in respect of the range of behaviours that could be effectively changed and the circumstances in which behavioural methods could be administered (Alderman & Burgess, 1990). In particular it was noted that some brain injured people did not respond to reinforcement contingencies because of drive or hedonistic weaknesses, whilst those individuals with predominantly frontal dysfunction often learned social or functional skills in a behaviourally oriented environment but failed to generalise those skills into the wider community (McGlynn, 1990). Another criticism made by many psychologists was that behaviour management's early emphasis on reinforcement contingencies and purely observable behaviour exposed it to the criticism of being unable to explain complex behaviour (Allen, 1998).

It is against this background that brain injury rehabilitation has begun to embrace cognitive therapy approaches derived from Meichenbaum's behaviourally oriented self-instructional training (Meichenbaum & Cameron, 1973), Bandura's (1977) efficacy model, and the more elaborate cognitive therapies of Beck (1976) and Ellis (1962). Cognitive psychological theory has emphasised the importance of what people think about their experience, i.e., how they attend to, interpret, store, and recall information. A fundamental tenet of this "information processing" approach is that few events are approached in a novel manner by adults (Nisbett & Ross, 1980), but are instead processed through pre-existing schemata, consisting of enduring prior beliefs, knowledge, and prepositions. In emotional disorders, key underlying schemata held by the individual are considered to guide information processing and to bias interpretation of experience in favour of schema maintenance. In this way thoughts of people with depression are seen to reflect schemata related to failure, hopelessness, and helplessness (Beck, 1976), in anxiety they reflect threat (Clark, 1989), whilst in anger they concern injustice and personal infringement (Novaco, 1979). Cognitive distortions allow even the most benign events to be interpreted as evidence supportive of the most sinister underlying schemata. For example, a person suffering depression may interpret a compliment as pity, an anxious person may interpret it as sarcasm, while an angry person may interpret the same compliment as ridicule. Although cognitive schemata tend to be thought of as being beyond conscious awareness they can be uncovered through careful investigation of their conscious product, i.e. the automatic thoughts triggered by events (e.g., Beck, Freeman, & colleagues, 1990; Young, 1994). Although research has failed to completely support Beck's original hypothesis (Power & Dalgleish, 1997; Teasdale & Barnard, 1993), there is strong evidence that biased information processing is a characteristic underpinning emotional disorders (e.g., Wells, 1997).

Employing this theoretical framework, cognitive therapy has focused on helping to change maladaptive thinking patterns. Thus by ameliorating cognitions it is contended that subsequent affect and behaviour are likewise altered. When applied in the context of social rehabilitation, cognitive therapy attempts to not only modify observable behaviour but also covert internal variables that mediate the way people think about and construe events. As such, a cognitive–behavioural approach attempts to change a person's perceptions (combining attitudes and emotions), as well as overt behaviour. Typically, therapists help clients to identify thinking distortions and to generate alternative (more rational) interpretations of events (e.g.,

Clark & Fairburn, 1997; Hawton, Salkovskis, Kirk, & Clark, 1989). Clients may also be asked to set up behavioural experiments to test the validity of their automatic thinking and to disconfirm beliefs. Overall, there is general support for the effectiveness of cognitive therapy when delivered by competent therapists, covering a broad range of disorders in both the short and longer term (King & Ollendick, 1998; Scott, 1997).

In brain injury rehabilitation the importance of integrating behavioural and cognitive approaches lies not only in helping brain injured people become more aware of those variables that drive behaviour but also in helping them learn more effective and socially acceptable responses that can be established as habit patterns. Generally, in those cases where cognitive therapy is used to treat psychological or psychiatric problems, awareness of the inappropriate or irrational behaviour might be sufficient to promote changes in the way a person both thinks about people or situations and behaves towards them. In brain injured people, however, whilst awareness *per se* is often a necessary condition for future behaviour change, it is not by itself sufficient. New responses have to be acquired procedurally, consolidated through practice, then employed spontaneously in the presence of stimuli that trigger a specific reaction. Therapy sessions have to be more structured, repetitive, frequent, and designed to deal with more specific behaviours—often in a more concrete way, compared to traditional forms of cognitive therapy. However, even when these therapeutic guidelines are employed, clients will rarely work on a problem unless (1) they are aware that it exists, and (2) they accept that what exists is indeed a problem.

The problem of awareness

Impaired awareness is a significant factor underpinning many neurobehavioural and neuropsychiatric disorders. When related to denial in psychiatry, it can lead to social alienation, delayed access to services, increased chance of compulsory detention, dropout from services, and increased morbidity, with impaired adaptation and higher relapse rates (Kemp & David, 1995; Kent & Yellowlees, 1994). Similarly, in traumatic brain injury insight is considered to be of primary importance to the success of the rehabilitation effort. Denial of cognitive and behavioural deficits can greatly impede social re-entry and re-employment (Prigatano, 1991) and contributes significantly to future relationship breakdown (Wood & Yurdakul, 1997). Unawareness of behavioural deficit in brain injury is not a transitory phenomenon, having been demonstrated to persist in the same individuals up to 30 months post-injury (Grosswasser et al., 1977). In patients with bilateral and deep brain lesions, denial of the severity of neuropsychological deficits may persist for years, whilst awareness of personality change is likely to be the last to alter over time (Prigatano, Altman, & O'Brien, 1990).

It is clear therefore that any psychological procedure employed in the rehabilitation of people with brain injury must be capable of addressing the significant problems that are imposed by diminished awareness. Traditionally, psychodynamic theorists viewed impaired awareness as reflecting the psychological defence mechanism of denial. The suggestion that people can protect themselves from unpleasant and anxiety-evoking truths by denying those truths, not only to themselves but also to others, is neither new (Freud, 1948) nor restricted to brain injury (e.g., Zervas, Augustine, & Fricchione, 1993). Certainly, in brain injury an increase in the incidence of depression has been associated with the development of more realistic self-awareness (e.g., Fordyce, Roueche, & Prigatano, 1983). Similarly, in psychiatry, Kemp and David (1995) found that poor insight was associated with fewer depressive symptoms, an association with affect found elsewhere (Dixon, King, & Steiger, 1998).

Denial of deficit may represent a defence mechanism in some brain injured clients but there are good reasons for not accepting this as the only explanation. Following brain injury, lack of awareness can be focal (such as in neglect) or general (related to awareness of self). Unawareness of a neurological deficit (anosognosia) is more commonly associated with non-dominant hemisphere damage than either left hemisphere or diffuse damage. It has also been found to correlate significantly with the degree of damage as measured by computed tomography (CT scan) (Hier, Mondlock, & Caplan, 1983). In addition, McGlynn and Schacter (1989) in their review of impaired awareness in neuropsychological syndromes have drawn attention to the large body of literature on patients who, in addition to impaired insight, also exhibit symptoms of frontal lobe damage, an area assumed critical for accurate self-monitoring and error correction.

At this stage it seems likely that organic and psychological factors play an interactive role in most cases of impaired social awareness. As Lewis (1991) in her review of the role of psychological factors in disordered awareness points out "… there is nothing about a brain lesion that ablates an individual's psyche or renders him or her free from reliance on mechanisms of defence" (p. 233). Similarly Malia (1995) has asserted how pre-existing personality styles of coping will inevitably affect adjustment, together with the explanations individuals generate to account for both external and internal experiences.

COGNITIVE THERAPY IN NEUROBEHAVIOURAL REHABILITATION

In clinical psychology clients who benefit from psychotherapy are typically expected to possess reasonable concentration, adequate memory, sufficient motivation, verbal intelligence, and insight. Given that traumatic brain injury can adversely affect any and all of these domains it is not surprising that people with organic brain syndromes have traditionally been considered unlikely candidates to benefit from standard cognitive therapy (e.g., Kanfer, 1997; Ludgate, Wright, Bowers, & Camp, 1993). Although therapy length and structure can be altered to accommodate changes in attention, concentration, and memory, it is the need to overcome alterations in awareness and motivation that often present the ultimate barrier to successful therapy engagement.

Self-awareness has been identified as an essential component in effective cognitive therapy (e.g., Crosson et al., 1989), whilst the importance of adequate motivation has been recognised across a range of psychotherapeutic modalities (Garfield, 1986; Tillett, 1996). Nevertheless, cognitive approaches have been utilised with considerable success in psychiatric populations where similar impediments to success exist (Chadwick, & Lowe, 1990; Drury, Birchwood, Cochrane, & MacMillan, 1996; Kemp et al., 1996; Kuipers et al., 1997; Tarrier et al., 1993). If cognitive therapy is to have a role to play in brain injury rehabilitation its aims must be twofold. First, it must help engage clients in the therapeutic process by establishing a therapeutic relationship aimed at increasing awareness and motivation. Second, it must ensure enduring behaviour change through repeated verbal mediation and behavioural practice. Those variables considered important to this endeavour are set about below.

Engagement

The therapeutic relationship.   No therapeutic relationship can succeed unless it is a supportive one, based on trust, respect, and understanding. The importance of the therapeutic relationship has long been recognised in psychotherapy, and more recently researchers have begun to acknowledge its importance in cognitive and behavioural psychotherapy (Castonguay et al., 1996; Follette, Naugle, & Callaghan, 1996; Saffron & Segal, 1990). In brain injury, therapist variables such as warmth, support, empathy, non-judgemental attitude, and expectancy for improvement have all been considered factors important to the therapeutic process (Leber & Jenkins, 1996). From a purely practical perspective if clients do not feel understood by the therapist they are likely to reject whatever the therapist says, irrespective of validity or merit as ultimately they reject the therapist (Miceli & Castelfranchi, 1998).

The need for understanding.   Although early cognitive models tended to concentrate on the perceived errors and illogical thinking in emotional disorder, there is ample evidence to suggest that people in general are prone to errors in reasoning (Evans, Newstead, & Byrne, 1983; Maher, 1992), and clinical psychologists are no exception (Ziskin & Faust, 1988). As Kunda (1990) has observed, human reasoning is guided by a desire for accuracy and consistency, and a motivation to arrive at personally desirable conclusions. In this endeavour we are all aided by the use of various heuristics, or "mental rules of thumb", which distort information in ways that are personally plausible and ultimately self-serving (e.g., Ross, 1977). Over time, our conclusions are supported by memory processes that are equally vulnerable to selection and distortion (Cohen, 1996; Loftus, 1993; Schacter, 1995). Despite the multifactorially determined nature of impaired awareness it is often the case in rehabilitation that clients consider their major interpersonal problem as simply the refusal of others to see the world as they do. The fact that this problem is often the same as that voiced by rehabilitation staff in relation to clients demonstrates clearly the importance of any individual's interpretation of "reality".

Errors in reasoning affect our attributions and explanations as to why things happen, both externally (Lazarus & Folkman, 1984) and, to some extent, internally (Schachter & Singer, 1962). This is especially important because our decision about *why* events occur often determines *how* we respond to them. In brain injury therapy it is important that the therapist learns why the client believes in the conclusions that he does. In other words, the therapist must ascertain those premises upon which conclusions are based. Only by doing this can the therapist really approach an understanding of why the client holds his or her beliefs. Individuals with a brain injury have reasons for thinking as they do. The therapist must try to understand these reasons rather than simply disagree with them.

The need for collaboration rather than confrontation.   Like most people, those with a brain injury are unlikely to want to solve something they do not see as a problem. Thus attempts to discuss areas of contention lead to rapid confrontation and denial. Although this is often viewed as further evidence of irritability, impulsiveness, and dyscontrol, it is equally likely to reflect understandable annoyance that has been shaped over hundreds of occasions. How many of us can remain calm when listening to unwelcome news we have received hundreds of times before, and with which we have consistently disagreed emphatically? In addition to confrontation not working, it may even contribute to a lack of awareness because it generates resistance to seeing another person's point of view, thereby strengthening forms of inappropriate behaviour.

We have previously mentioned how people arrive at conclusions that are personally desirable and how these may be maintained in the face of contrary evidence. If a brain injured person concludes his or her behaviour is justifiable and appropriate, anger will invariably be evoked if this attitude is disputed. Clients go on to marshal supportive evidence for their view in the same way anyone else might. They utilise various cognitive biases and recall events from the past in such a way (selectively, and distorted) that these are seen to support their initial conclusion. As this scenario is played out repeatedly with friends, families, and health care workers, justifications are continuously rehearsed and their affective and behavioural correlates strengthened.

Thus a supportive and empathic relationship is of primary importance in the rehabilitation of individuals with a brain injury. Not only does it contribute to the client feeling understood, it also ensures that rehearsal of unhelpful schemas and their related behaviours is circumvented. What follows below is a method of learning from the patient that at the same time allows both therapist and client to uncover discrepancies between what the client ultimately wants to achieve and what his or her current behaviour means the client will achieve. Similar to a more general emergent trend in cognitive therapy, motivational interviewing with the brain injured client is not about exposing irrational thinking and behaviour but rather questions the viability of current thinking and behaving. Therefore clients are not expected to accept they are wrong to think and behave as they do, but rather to consider that there may be more useful alternatives.

Motivation

In brain injury rehabilitation, clients can demonstrate high levels of motivation yet still be described by health professionals as "lacking motivation". However, what may actually be occurring in a number of cases is that clients are motivated, but they are motivated to reject rehabilitation (see Chapter 1). Miller (1993) has observed that after brain injury clients are often encouraged to receive therapy, e.g., as a result of court directives, or pressure from families (extrinsic reasons) and not because they themselves want to be there (intrinsic reasons). Because of this they are likely to be resistant from the outset. However, motivation to engage in rehabilitation need not be viewed as an all-or-none phenomenon. In their seminal work on motivational interviewing in the area of substance abuse, Miller and Rolnick (1991) have suggested viewing motivation as a state of readiness or eagerness to change which may fluctuate over time and across situations. It is a state they feel can be influenced by an approach drawn from Prochaska and DiClemente's (1982) six-stage model of change.

In this "wheel of change theory" the initial stage of *pre-contemplation* is one wherein the person is not yet considering the possibility of change, although others are aware that there is a problem. Following this is the *contemplative stage* which is marked by some awareness but also ambivalence. In the *determination stage* the client decides he or she should take action, and in the *action stage* the client engages in strategies intended to bring about such change. At the *maintenance stage* skills are learned (which may be very different to those required in previous stages) to avoid relapse, and in the final *relapse stage*, strategies are developed to help cope with relapse. By viewing motivation as existing along a continuum and tailoring intervention accordingly they propose that clients previously resistant to therapy become willing to engage in forms of counselling designed to alter their behaviour. This technique can be usefully employed in the initial stages of rehabilitation and may be an essential requirement for those who, because of a lack of awareness and judgement, may otherwise reject offers of treatment.

Increasing awareness

Pre-contemplation and contemplation.   In the initial stage of therapy it is the task of the therapist to engender a recognition of the discrepancy between the clients' present behaviour and their ultimate goal, and to increase their perception of risks associated with their current behaviour (Miller & Rolnick, 1991). In brain injury this is initially best done by the therapist simply exploring with the client why they behave as they do. As already stated, clients usually have well-rehearsed reasons to explain their behaviour, often based on feelings of frustration at being talked down to, or having their opinions dismissed, or being in a rehabilitation unit when they feel they do not need to be. The therapist must recognise the frustration evoked by such thoughts and perceptions. As Meichenbaum (1993) states, the cognitive therapist "not only helps to validate clients' reactions but indicates that such symptoms are normal". In fact, their emotional distress is viewed as a normal rehabilitative process. Once the client has explained why he or she engages in the behaviour, the therapist frames the behaviour in specific terms, agrees with the client the triggering stimulus, and reiterates the consequences as the client sees them.

Once the trigger, target behaviour, and perceived consequences have been elucidated the client is asked to suggest any negative consequences for the behaviour. As this usually involves taking a longer-term perspective, and also seeing the behaviour from the point of view of others, it is something the therapist typically has to help with initially. This is particularly important in cases of frontal brain injury because problems of organisation and planning make it difficult for the client to anticipate the immediate, as well as the long-term consequences of an action. Carberry and Burd (1986) have identified deficits in empathic response as a major therapeutic obstacle likely to be seen following frontal lobe brain damage (see also Chapter 1). One strategy they suggest is to consistently ask clients how their behaviour may make others feel. If the client is unable to generate negatives, the therapist may do so for him, but only in the form of tentative hypotheses for discussion, and prefacing his comments accordingly, e.g., "I can certainly see a lot of good reasons for you to engage in (specific behaviour), and hearing you describe why you do so makes good sense to me. But I do wonder if some people might see a possible disadvantage of (specific behaviour) as being ...".

In this manner, the client is encouraged to discuss disadvantages from a theoretical viewpoint without feeling directly challenged. This allows the therapist to summarise the specific trigger and the target response, along with the positive and negative consequences of the response that have been agreed with the client. Following this the client is asked to summarise the advantages and disadvantages himself. By this stage clients should begin to perceive a discrepancy between what they want to achieve behaviourally and what ultimately is being achieved, with the balance tipped firmly in the direction of disadvantages. Although this awareness is likely to induce discomfort initially it should also produce longer-term benefits.

Determination and action.   The next stages focus on goal setting and helping clients identify and commit to a more adaptive response, i.e., one that increases the likelihood of their attaining their long-term goal. This goal-setting stage is essential to the therapeutic process as it provides the incentive to participate. Whatever future desired events are generated it is up to the therapist to ensure that the final goals arrived at are specific, desirable to the client, and achievable

(Bandura, 1982). For a review of the importance in rehabilitation of setting specific behavioural goals, readers are directed to any general text on behaviour therapy.

Once goals are set, clients are asked to generate subgoals and an alternative response to the trigger that might achieve these. Again, if the client has difficulty with this, the therapist can suggest possible alternatives and guide discussion of their relative merits. Next, the client is asked to choose which strategy they feel is best and to state why. The reasons why the original target behaviour is not helpful in achieving this goal are then reviewed again, with the client encouraged to voice these disadvantages himself, and to compare the target behaviour with the new alternative behaviour. Finally the entire process is summarised in terms of the original trigger (be it an event, an automatic thought, or sudden physiological arousal), the alternative response, and its positive consequences. It is this summary that will form the verbal mediation script (see Chapter 7) that will be strengthened in later rehearsal. The therapist then acknowledges how difficult it is for any of us to change behaviours, and introduces the concept of verbal mediation and the need for repeated learning trials. Both agree on the number of practice sessions that will be conducted each day to help establish the alternative response. Exactly why practice is so important is discussed below.

Establishing durable change

It has already been noted that many forms of inappropriate behaviour following brain injury are demonstrated by individuals with pre-frontal brain damage (Chapter 1). It is generally accepted that the frontal lobes play a crucial role in the planning, organising, and controlling of action (Lezak, 1998; Luria, 1966). In their influential model of controlled action Norman and Shallice (1986) have proposed two frontal systems as being of primary importance in the control of action sequences. It is damage to a component of one of these systems, referred to as the supervisory attentional system (SAS), that is suggested to be responsible for many of the behaviours seen following anterior brain damage, including perseveration, disinhibition, concrete thinking, and distractibility.

According to this model, higher-level control (performed by the SAS) is required by those actions needing deliberate attentional resources. These include tasks that involve planning or decision making, are ill learned, contain novel sequences of action, or require the overcoming of a strong habitual response. It is in situations such as these that deficits in the SAS will be most apparent, as behaviour inappropriate to the overall situation is triggered by salient cues and continues unaltered despite changes in feedback. Conversely, well-learned skills and procedures do not require this higher level executive control. Thus, overlearned actions, once triggered, are capable of being performed with little or no conscious awareness and (unless interrupted by a more salient cue) run off automatically. The model has intuitive appeal. It is able to explain perseveration and increased distractibility in the same person and has demonstrated clinical utility (Burgess &

Alderman, 1990). Because executive problems such as these prevent application of knowledge, any therapeutic exchange has to be highly structured, repetitive, and linked to opportunities to practise ideas and strategies discussed in therapy. Finally, any new way of thinking must be repeatedly practised in social situations in order that it becomes consolidated and generalises.

Maintenance and the importance of practice

In light of the above it ought to be clear that simply increasing awareness is not sufficient for behaviour to alter. Similarly, verbal commitments to change habitual patterns of acting are unlikely to be effective. It is essential that alternative behaviours and related cognitions are taught in such a manner that the effects of attentional or awareness deficits are minimised. For those clients in whom the ability to monitor and inhibit behaviour is impaired it is paramount that any alternative cognitive–behavioural response is strengthened through practice to the point that it is more likely to be selected automatically over other competing responses in the future. Although initially any alternative action sequence requires conscious direction, it is expected that repetition will lead to its being established as a subroutine capable of being followed through with little concentration. As Kanfer (1997) has observed, with their reliance on procedural learning and implicit memory "well-established learned automatic behavioural sequences and the processes associated with them minimise clients' responsibility for planning actions" and "make fewer demands on clients' resources and run off with little effort" (p. 3).

As there is a known tendency for a stronger programme to take over from a weaker programme, particularly if some component tag is common to both (strong habit intrusion or capture error, Cohen, 1996), it is best if the alternative behaviour is as dissimilar to the original target behaviour as possible. Similarly, it is best if alternative sequences target behavioural change early in the behavioural chain. Finally, the nature of frontal deficits means that patients are less able to abstract from one situation to the other. Thus, behavioural gains are unlikely to generalise (Burgess & Alderman, 1990). This means that alternative action sequences will need to be generated and rehearsed for individual triggers or for a particular trigger that is common across different situations.

Structured practice

Verbal mediation practice sessions in brain injury are usually brief, highly structured, repetitive, occur initially when the client is calm, include role play, and require clients to do most of the talking. In the practice session the client is asked to:

1. Identify the trigger to the target behaviour.

2. State the alternative cognitive and behavioural response to the trigger that will be used on future occasions.
3. What are the positive consequences of the alternative response.
4. Role play the alternative response.
5. Repeat the entire verbal mediation sequence several times if necessary during each practice session.
6. Finally, clients are asked to anticipate any problems they may have implementing the alternative response *in vivo*, in particular, during periods of heightened physiological arousal.

Relapse

Because relapse is inevitable when trying to overcome a habitual response it is important that it is anticipated as part of the treatment plan. Clients are helped to think of relapse as normal, and as an opportunity for learning. Similarly, carers are encouraged to view behaviour change as a gradual process and not to become despondent when change is not rapid.

CASE EXAMPLES

Case 1

James is a 23-year-old man with severe residual cognitive and behavioural deficits. When given feedback by staff in the unit about his inappropriate sexual behaviour, he would become very agitated and protest vehemently. His anger would escalate rapidly to the point that he would abscond from the unit. Typically, he would make his way to the nearest public house where he would approach young female customers; behaviour that on occasion necessitated his being brought back by the police. Although the problem of absconding in brain injury has been approached successfully from a behavioural standpoint (Manchester, Hodgkinson, Pfaff, & Nguyen, 1997), a verbal mediation approach was adopted in place of significant environmental changes. The aims of intervention were twofold. First, to increase motivation to change his behaviour, and second, to help him establish any change as enduring. The stages are set out below in the order of the Prochaska and DiClemente model.

Pre-contemplation and contemplation.   Initially, and in a manner of curiosity rather than confrontation James was asked why he absconded from the unit. He explained that he felt others were always picking on him, and staying in the unit meant that people continued to criticise him. The therapist acknowledged how frustrating this must be for him and he was encouraged to talk about it. James was then asked what the consequences of his leaving the unit were. He explained that by leaving the unit, he escaped the criticism and also demonstrated his independence. The therapist reflected that given these perceived consequences the behaviour did indeed appear to make good sense.

James was then asked to consider any possible negative consequences to his behaviour. As already stated this often involves taking a longer-term perspective and encouraging empathy. In James's case he was not able to generate any negative consequences, so the therapist simply wondered what having to be brought back by the police had felt like. James acknowledged that this had been humiliating. The therapist then wondered what his relatives had felt about his being brought back by the police. Again James was able to acknowledge that they had been upset and angry with him. Finally the therapist wondered what he thought other people might think about his ability to live independently if it looked as though (rightly or wrongly) he could not control his temper, ran away from the unit, and needed to be brought back by the police. At this point James was able to say that others might think he could not control himself because of the brain injury. With guidance he also acknowledged that this made subsequent discharge less likely.

Determination and action.   The next stage involves generating longer-term goals and committing to an alternative response to achieve these. In James's case it was not difficult for him to generate the long-term goal of leaving the unit for good. He was therefore asked if not absconding from the unit would bring him closer to or further away from the goal. When it was agreed that not absconding from the unit brought him closer to discharge the therapist discussed with him a strategy for achieving this. The therapist agreed with James that he would probably continue to get feedback that he did not like, but that he could now view such occasions as an opportunity to prove to everyone he could control himself. To do this James suggested that he could tell the staff that he was going to complain to the clinical team leader, and go immediately to his room to calm down. James was then asked what the consequences of the alternative response were. It was agreed that consequences included his demonstrating to others that he can control himself, bringing himself closer to more independent living, getting away from people who were annoying him, and exercising his right to complain about staff.

Finally the whole process was reviewed, with James encouraged to state the trigger, the old response and its negative consequences, and the new response and its positive consequences. Rather than praising any subsequent commitment to change the therapist acknowledged his determination and also acknowledged how difficult it is for any of us to change our behaviour. This allowed the therapist to go on to suggest the need for practice to establish any new response as habit. Because clients with frontal deficits are unlikely to be able to plan or initiate practice themselves the therapist can suggest that staff help out by ensuring structured practice sessions throughout the day.

Maintenance and verbal mediation.   Once the alternative script and behavioural sequence were established James was encouraged in five sessions per day including role plays to go through it with guidance from a care worker. Following the introduction of the verbal mediation procedure absconding reduced to zero over the next three months, and there was no re-occurrence at three-month follow-up.

Relapse.   In both this case and the one that follows instances of relapse were used by therapists to help the client explore difficulties he had encountered in implementing the alternative behaviour sequence. These were incorporated as soon as possible into verbal mediation sessions and were always introduced as opportunities to learn from, rather than as examples of failure.

Case 2

Michael, a 19-year-old man admitted to the unit in a wheelchair, who left the unit repeatedly and refused to speak to staff, was approached in a similar fashion.

Pre-contemplation and contemplation.   When asked in a manner suggesting curiosity rather than blame why he wheeled himself out of the unit, and did not engage in therapy, Michael explained he was angry because he did not need to be in rehabilitation. The therapist acknowledged that thinking this must make him feel very angry on occasions. When asked what the consequences of his leaving the unit and refusing to talk appeared to be, Michael replied that if his behaviour deteriorated sufficiently he believed he would be discharged back to the family home. As with James previously, the therapist acknowledged that given these consequences his behaviour seemed reasonable.

Michael was then asked if his behaviour had any disadvantages. Like James he was initially unable to think of any, and so the therapist made tentative suggestions in the form of hypotheses for discussion. Disadvantages generated included his getting bored and feeling lonely, his behaviour appearing to others as childish, and the apparent fact that the worse his behaviour became the more reluctant his family were to have him home. The therapist then summarised the trigger (being asked to a rehabilitation exercise), his response (absconding and not talking), and the advantages and disadvantages of this response. These were all then discussed again collaboratively, with Michael asked to list the advantages and disadvantages himself, and with the therapist on occasion asking Michael to elucidate a point, e.g., "You've mentioned your family being less likely to take you back if you continue to leave the unit and stop talking. Why do you think this is so?"

Determination and action.   On admission Michael had talked about his ultimate goals of having a job and his own place to live. The therapist asked if his current response was more or less likely to help him achieve these goals. Michael acknowledged that it was less likely to, and again the therapist asked if he could explain the reasoning behind his answer.

With independent living and a job established as ultimate goals the therapist then helped Michael break these down into subgoals. Because Michael's rehabilitation programme was designed to address several skills deficits, improvements in each of these areas was related to his overall goal. For example, in order to work with others did he think he would need good social skills? When he answered yes he was asked if he thought attending social skills might be helpful. Did he think being able to walk would provide him with more possible job opportunities? When the answer was yes, he was asked if physiotherapy might therefore be helpful in securing his goal. Because people who live in their own place need to be able to cook, clean, shop, and handle money and bills he was asked if occupational therapy in each of these areas might help him achieve his goal. When Michael stated yes to any of these he was asked to explain why the answer was yes. Finally he was asked if any of the negative consequences to the "old" response (the word old is used specifically) were likely to be consequences of the new response, i.e., attending rehabilitation exercises.

The therapist then inquired what might be the alternative response to being asked into a rehabilitation exercise. It was agreed that he could think to himself, "I'll give it a go. It's getting me nearer my own job and my own place", and then go to the session. The therapist then conveys his appreciation of how important these goals are to Michael. He then offers to help by seeing that carers provide plenty of opportunities for him to learn to be able to adopt his new (alternative) response successfully over the next few weeks, if Michael is determined that this is what he wants. Following determination the client is ready for the maintenance stage.

Maintenance and verbal mediation.   Regular brief sessions throughout the day were devoted to verbal mediation and behavioural practice. Michael would be asked what were the triggers and negative consequences to the old behaviour. He was asked to describe the new response to the trigger. He was then encouraged to explain advantages of the new response. Staff were able to prompt the alternative response in role plays by wondering gently, "So if I asked you to come to a rehabilitation exercise now you'd think 'I'll give it a go.'—and what else? What would you do then? What are the advantages of you coming to the exercise? *What goals does it help you get nearer to?*"

To enhance maintenance, graphs were also placed on the wall in Michael's room with his agreement to reflect the number of times each day he attended a therapy session and the number of times he engaged in the "old" response. Each morning, when he was being helped with dressing, carers were asked to draw his attention to the graphs and to encourage Michael to explain what the graphs reflected. Carers were then asked to praise Michael for his efforts.

Over the next month Michael increasingly decided to attend rehabilitation groups. He appeared to take a pride in the change in his behaviour, and received considerable praise from his family. Eventually he was able to move on to a small supported group house where he remained for a further six months consolidating skills learnt in the unit before returning home.

CONCLUSION

We are aware that in writing this chapter we are prone to our own cognitive distortions in arriving at the conclusion that cognitive approaches have a role to play in social rehabilitation following brain injury. Of course, it is ultimately the place for controlled trials to determine whether motivational interviewing does increase engagement and whether or not verbal mediation establishes behaviour change that endures over time and across situations. Instead we do best to confine ourselves at this point to the observation that these approaches give access to a significant number of people in whom previous therapeutic attempts are rejected. It encourages listening and understanding on the part of all those involved in the care of those with traumatic brain injury and it discourages conflict. Finally it offers hope in a clinical area often devoid of it, and anything that does that deserves our fullest controlled attention.

REFERENCES

Alderman, N., & Burgess, P. (1990). Integrating cognition and behaviour. In R.Ll. Wood, & I. Fussey (Eds.), *Cognitive rehabilitation in perspective*. London: Taylor and Francis.

Allen, N.B. (1998). Cognitive psychotherapy. In S. Bloch (Ed.), *An introduction to the psychotherapies*. Oxford: Oxford Medical Publications.

Bandura, A. (1977). Self efficacy: Toward a unifying theory of behavioral change. *Psychological Review, 84*, 191–215.

Bandura, A. (1982). Self efficacy mechanism in human agency. *American Psychologist, 37*, 122–247.

Beck, A.T. (1976). *Cognitive therapy and the emotional disorders*. Madison, CT: International Universities Press.

Beck, A.T., Freeman, A., & colleagues (1990). *Cognitive therapy of personality disorders*. New York: Guilford Press.

Burgess, P.W., & Alderman, N. (1990). Rehabilitation of dyscontrol syndromes following frontal lobe damage: A cognitive neuropsychological approach. In R.Ll. Wood & I. Fussey (Eds.), *Cognitive rehabilitation in perspective*. London: Taylor and Francis.

Carberry, H., & Burd, B. (1986) Individual psychotherapy with the brain injured adult. *Cognitive Rehabilitation, 5*, 22–24.

Castonguay, L.G., Goldfried, M.R., Wiser, S., Raue, P.J., & Hayes, A.M. (1996). Predicting the effect of cognitive therapy for depression: A study of unique and common factors. *Journal of Consulting and Clinical Psychology, 64*, 497–504.

Chadwick, P.D., & Lowe, C.F. (1990). Measurement and modification of delusional beliefs. *Journal of Consulting and Clinical Psychology, 58*, 225–232.

Clark, D.M. (1989). Anxiety states: Panic and generalised anxiety. In K. Hawton, P.M. Salkovskis, J. Kirk, & D.M. Clark (Eds.), *Cognitive behaviour therapy for psychiatric problems: A practical guide*. Oxford: Oxford University Press.

Clark, D.A., & Beck, A.T. (1989). Cognitive theory and therapy of anxiety and depression. In P.C. Kendall & D. Watson (Eds.), *Anxiety and depression: Distinctive and overlapping features*. San Diego: Academic Press.

Clark, D.M., & Fairburn, C.G. (1997). *Science and practice of cognitive behaviour therapy*. Oxford: Oxford University Press.

Cohen, G. (1996). *Memory in the real world* (2nd ed.). Hove, UK: Psychology Press.

Crosson, B., Barco, P.P., Veloza, C.A., Bolesta, M.M., Cooper, P.V., Werts, D., & Brobeck, T.C. (1989). Awareness and compensation in post acute head injury rehabilitation. *Journal of Head Trauma Rehabilitation, 4,* 46–54.

Dixon, M., King, S., & Steiger, H. (1998). The contribution of depression and denial towards understanding the unawareness of symptoms in schizophrenic outpatients. *British Journal of Medical Psychology, 71,* 85–97.

Drury, V., Birchwood, M., Cochrane, R., & MacMillan, F. (1996). Cognitive therapy and recovery from acute psychosis: A controlled trial. II. Impact on recovery time. *British Journal of Psychiatry, 169,* 602–607.

Eames, P.G., & Wood, R.Ll. (1985). Rehabilitation after severe brain injury: A special unit approach to behaviour disorders. *International Rehabilitation Medicine, 7,* 130–133.

Ellis, A. (1962). *Reason and emotion in psychotherapy.* New York: Lyle Stuart.

Evans, J., St.B.T., Newstead, S.E., & Byrne, R.M.J. (1993). *Human reasoning: The psychology of deduction.* Hove, UK: Lawrence Erlbaum Associates Ltd.

Follette, W.C., Naugle, A.E., & Callaghan, G.M. (1996). A radical behavioural understanding of the therapeutic relationship in effecting change. *Behaviour Therapy, 27,* 623–641.

Fordyce, D., Roueche, J., & Prigatano, G. (1983). Enhanced emotional reactions in chronic head trauma patients. *Journal of Neurology, Neurosurgery and Psychiatry, 46,* 620–624.

Freud, A. (1948). *The ego and the mechanisms of defense.* London: Hogarth Press.

Garfield, S.L. (1986). An eclectic psychotherapy. In J.C. Norcross (Ed.), *Handbook of eclectic psychotherapy.* New York: Brunner/Mazel.

Groswasser, Z., Mendelson, L., Stern, M., Schecter, I., & Najenson, T. (1977). Re-evaluation of prognostic factors in rehabilitation after severe head injury: Assessment 30 months after trauma. *Scandinavian Journal of Rehabilitation Medicine, 9,* 147–149.

Hawton, K., Salkovskis, P.M., Kirk, J., & Clark, D.M. (1989). *Cognitive therapy for psychiatric problems: A practical guide.* Oxford: Oxford University Press.

Hier, D.B., Mondlock, J., & Caplan, L.R. (1983). Behavioural abnormalities after right hemisphere stroke. *Neurology, 33,* 337–344.

Kanfer, F.H. (1997). Motivation and emotion in behaviour therapy. In K.S. Dobson & K.D. Craig (Eds.), *Advances in cognitive behaviour therapy* (pp.1–30). Thousand Oaks, CA: Sage.

Kemp, R., & David, A. (1995). Psychosis: Insight and compliance. *Current Opinion in Psychiatry, 8,* 357–361.

Kemp, R., Hayward, P., Applewhaite, G., Everitt, B., & David, A. (1996). Compliance therapy in psychotic patients: Randomised controlled trial. *British Medical Journal, 312,* 345–349.

Kent, S., & Yellowlees, P. (1994). Psychiatric and social reasons for frequent rehospitalisation. *Hospital Community Psychiatry, 45,* 347–350.

King, N.J., & Ollendick, T.H. (1998). Empirically validated treatments in clinical psychology. *Australian Psychologist, 33,* 89–95.

Kuipers E., Garety, P., Fowler, D., Dunn, G., Bebbington, P., Freeman, D., & Hadley, C. (1997). London East Anglia randomised controlled trial of cognitive-behavioural therapy for psychosis. *British Journal of Psychiatry, 171,* 319–327.

Kunda, Z. (1990). The case for motivated reasoning. *Psychological Bulletin, 108,* 480–498.

Lazarus, R.S., & Folkman, S. (1984). S*tress, appraisal and coping.* New York: Springer.

Leber, W., & Jenkins, M.R. (1996). Psychotherapy with clients who have brain injuries and their families. In R.L. Adams., O.A. Parsons, J.L. Culbertson, & S.J. Nixon (Eds.), *Neuropsychology for clinical practice*. Washington, DC: American Psychological Association.

Lewis, L. (1991). Role of psychological factors in disordered awareness. In G. Prigatano & D. Schacter (Eds.), *Awareness of deficit after brain injury: Clinical and theoretical issues*. New York: Oxford University Press.

Lezak, M.D. (1998). *Neuropsychological assessment* (3rd ed.). New York: Oxford University Press.

Loftus, E.F. (1993). The reality of repressed memories. *American Psychologist, 48*, 518–537.

Ludgate, J.W., Wright, J.H., Bowers, W.A., & Camp, G.F. (1993). Individual cognitive therapy with inpatients. In J. H. Wright., M.E. Thase., T.A. Beck., & J.W. Ludgate (Eds.), *Cognitive therapy with inpatients*. New York: Guilford Press.

Luria, A.R. (1966). *Higher cortical functions in man*. London: Tavistock.

Maher, B.A. (1992). Delusions: Contemporary etiological hypotheses. *Psychiatric Annals, 22*, 260–268.

Malia, K. (1995). Insight after brain injury: What does it mean? *Journal of Cognitive Rehabilitation*, May/June, 10–15.

Manchester, D., Hodgkinson, A., Pfaff, A., & Nguyen, G. (1997). A non-aversive approach to hospital absconding in a head injured adolescent boy. *Brain Injury, 11*, 271–277.

McGlynn, S.M. (1990). Behavioural approaches to neuropsychological rehabilitation. *Psychological Bulletin, 108*, 420–441.

McGlynn, S.M., & Schacter, D.L. (1989). Unawareness of deficits in neuropsychological syndromes. *Journal of Clinical and Experimental Neuropsychology, 11*, 143–205.

Meichenbaum, D.H. (1993). Changing conceptions of cognitive behaviour modification. Retrospect and prospect. *Journal of Consulting and Clinical Psychology, 61*, 202–204.

Meichenbaum, D.H., & Cameron, R. (1973). Training schizophrenics to talk to themselves: A means of developing attentional controls. *Behaviour Therapy, 4*, 515–534.

Miceli, M., & Castelfranchi, C. (1998). Denial and its reasoning. *British Journal of Medical Psychology, 71*, 139–152.

Miller, L. (1993) *Psychotherapy of the brain injured patient*. New York: W.W. Norton.

Miller, W.R., & Rolnick, S. (1991). *Motivational interviewing*. New York: Guilford Press.

Nisbett, R., & Ross, L. (1980). *Human inference. Strategies and shortcomings of social judgement*. Englewood Cliffs, NJ: Prentice Hall.

Norman, D.A., & Shallice, T. (1986). Attention to action: Willed and automatic control of behaviour. In R.J. Davidson, G.E. Schwartz, & D. Shapiro (Eds.), *Consciousness and self regulation: Advances in research in theory* (Vol. 4, pp. 1–18). New York: Plenum Press.

Novaco R.W. (1979). The cognitive regulation of anger and stress. In P.C. Kendal & S.D. Hollon (Eds.), *Cognitive behavioural interventions*. New York: Academic Press.

Oddy, M., Coughlan, T., Tyerman, A., & Jenkins, D. (1985). Social adjustment after closed head injury: A further follow up seven years after injury. *Journal of Neurology, Neurosurgery, and Psychiatry, 48*, 564–568.

Power, M., & Dalgleish, T. (1997). *Cognition and emotion: From order to disorder*. Hove, UK: Psychology Press

Prigatano, G.P. (1991). Disturbances of self awareness of deficit after traumatic brain injury. In G.P. Prigatano & D.L. Schacter (Eds.), *Awareness of deficit after brain injury: Clinical and theoretical issues*. New York: Oxford University Press.

Prigatano, G.P., Altman, I.M., & O'Brien K.P. (1990). Behavioural limitations that brain injured patients tend to underestimate. *Clinical Neuropsychologist, 4,* 163–176.

Prochaska, J.O., & DiClemente, C.C. (1982). Transtheoretical Therapy: Towards a more integrative model of change. *Psychotherapy: Theory, research and practice, 19,* 276–288.

Ross, L. (1977). The intuitive psychologist and his shortcomings: Distortions in the attribution process. In L. Berkowitz (Ed.), *Advances in experimental social psychology, Vol 10.* New York: Academic Press.

Saffron, J., & Segal, Z.V. (1990). *Interpersonal processes in cognitive therapy.* New York: Basic Books.

Schacter, D. (1995). *Memory distortion: How minds brains and societies reconstruct the past.* Cambridge, MA: Harvard University Press.

Schachter, S., & Singer, J. (1962) Cognitive, social and physiological determinants of emotional psychological state. *Psychological Review, 69,* 379–99.

Scott, J. (1997). Advances in cognitive therapy. *Current Opinion in Psychiatry, 10,* 256–260.

Tarrier, N., Beckett, R., Harwood, S., Baker, A., Yusupoff, L., & Ugarteburu, I. (1993). A trial of two cognitive behavioural methods of treating drug resistant residual psychotic symptoms in schizophrenic patients: 1. Outcome. *British Journal of Psychiatry, 162,* 524–532.

Teasdale, J.D., & Barnard, P.J. (1993). *Affect cognition and change: Remodelling depressive thought.* Hove, UK: Lawrence Erlbaum Associates Ltd.

Tillett, R. (1996). Psychotherapy assessment and treatment selection. *British Journal of Psychiatry, 168,* 10–15.

Wells, A. (1997). *Cognitive therapy of anxiety disorders.* Chichester: Wiley.

Wood, R.Ll. (1987). *Brain injury rehabilitation: A neurobehavioural approach.* London: Croom Helm.

Wood, R, Ll., & Yurdakul, L.A. (1997). Change in relationship status following traumatic brain injury. *Brain Injury, 11,* 491–501.

Young, J.E. (1994). *Cognitive therapy for personality disorders: A schema focused approach* (rev. ed.). Sarasota, FL: Professional Resource Press.

Zervas, I.M., Augustine, A., & Fricchione, G.L. (1993) Patient delay in cancer. *General hospital psychiatry, 15,* 9–13.

Ziskin, J., & Faust, D. (1988). *Coping with psychiatric and psychological testimony* (4th ed., Vols. 1–3). Marina Del Rey, CA: Law and Psychology Press.

CHAPTER NINE

Managing challenging behaviour

N. Alderman
Kemsley Division, St. Andrews Hospital, Northampton, UK

INTRODUCTION—WHAT IS CHALLENGING BEHAVIOUR?

The notion of "challenging behaviour" is perhaps best described by Emerson et al. (1987) as:

> Behaviours of such intensity, frequency or duration that the physical safety of the person is likely to be placed in serious jeopardy, or behaviour which is likely to limit or delay access to or use of ordinary community facilities.

Whilst this definition was written to describe challenging behaviour exhibited by people with learning difficulties, it can be easily applied to those with acquired brain injury. It is clear that "challenging behaviour" does not only apply to physical aggression: instead, it may encompass many different, varied behavioural problems. For example, in the code of practice of one challenging behaviour team that works with people who have learning difficulties, it explicitly states that the concept is *not* limited to physical aggression, but includes all behaviour that restricts access to community facilities, such as extreme social withdrawal (Gentry, McDonnell, & Cory, 1991).

In effect, challenging behaviour may consist of the extremes of conduct that fall outside the normative boundaries of the community of which the person is a member: as such, and especially if it occurs regularly, it comprises behaviour that is unlikely to be tolerated by the local population with the result that the person who exhibits it will be rejected by that community.

CHALLENGING BEHAVIOUR AND BRAIN INJURY

Using this definition it becomes readily apparent that many brain injured people present with "challenging behaviour': we shall see later in this chapter evidence that neurobehavioural difficulties, comprising psychosocial problems and conduct disorders, often constitute long-term sequelae of acquired neurological damage. However, whilst there are similarities in many of the difficulties experienced by people with either learning difficulties or acquired brain injury, the nature of their onset may be very different. For example, the physical, cognitive, emotional, and psychosocial problems associated with traumatic brain injury are usually sudden, may be atypical of the individual's previous functioning, and catastrophic in their impact on the person, their family and the community of which they are a member. By contrast, many aspects of the person's previous personality and abilities may be left intact and it is this that clearly differentiates people with acquired brain injury from those with learning difficulties.

This difference in onset is important as it suggests the definition of challenging behaviour proffered by Emerson et al. (1987) should be expanded when applied to the brain injury population. Thus, whilst the presence of challenging behaviour amongst people with brain injuries may also "... limit or delay access to use of ordinary community facilities" it may also effectively constrain their ability to participate in post-acute neurological rehabilitation and therefore fail to exploit their potential for recovery, a point that has been made previously (for example, Eames & Wood, 1985; Wood, 1987).

Thus, there is a paradox in that whilst it would appear that brain injured people may benefit from exposure to rehabilitation (Cope, 1994), the presence of behaviour disorders may prevent this process. Such behaviours are therefore "challenging" because of the limitations they impose on rehabilitation and community reintegration. People admitted into rehabilitation programmes may be impulsive, disinhibited, and aggressive; alternatively, they may lack drive and motivation to participate because of lack of insight. People with traumatic brain injury (TBI) are not popular among rehabilitation professionals because of their often irritating, threatening, and embarrassing behaviour, as well as their general lack of motivation (Miller & Cruzat, 1981). As a result, they are often excluded from such programmes. This leads to a dilemma in that increased numbers of people with brain injury have a normal life expectancy thanks to better management in the immediate post-injury stage, but are subsequently denied access to rehabilitation because of their behaviour. As a result, the potential for maximising independence and increasing quality of life will not be fulfilled.

The presence of challenging behaviour may result in discharge home without the full rehabilitation potential of the person being exploited. It is at this point, in the words of Emerson et al. (1987), that the continued presence of challenging behaviour may "... limit or delay access to or use of ordinary community facilities". Challenging behaviour often renders the management of such people at home untenable and as a direct consequence they may gravitate to long-term placements that are clearly inappropriate for their needs, such as psychogeriatric, mental handicap, prison, and long-stay secure psychiatric units (Eames & Wood, 1985).

This phenomenon is illustrated by reference to data recently collated through a comprehensive review of case notes pertaining to people who had been admitted to a specialised neurobehavioural service for people with challenging behaviour undertaken by colleagues of the author, Keith Dawson and Cheryl Jones.[1]

Table 9.1 describes some of the placements from which people were admitted into the specialised service. It also presents the number of people resident in these placements and divides them into two groups: those who were admitted within three years of injury, and a second group who were more than three years post-injury by the time they had been admitted (this was used as a cut-off point as the median time elapsed between injury and admission in the total sample of 274 was three years).

TABLE 9.1

Placement immediately prior to admission to a specialised neurobehavioural programme for people with challenging behaviour up to and over three years after injury

	Placement up to three years after injury	Placement over three years after injury
Forensic	2	8
Psychiatric hospital	20	30
With parents as carers	17	44
Rehabilitation unit	17	4
Brain injury rehabilitation unit	10	5

The dotted line in Table 9.1 attempts to differentiate those placements that are less desirable from those that are more appropriate. Thus, individuals placed in forensic settings (prison, special hospital, regional secure unit), psychiatric hospitals, and with parents, the majority of whom have reverted to being carers for a group predominantly comprised of young men who had previously been living independently, lie above the line. Conversely, placement in a generic rehabilitation unit or, more desirably, a specialised brain injury rehabilitation unit, falls below the line.

Examination of Table 9.1 demonstrates that people gravitated to less suitable placements as time since injury increased. As the majority of people referred to the service had severe behavioural problems which excluded them from traditional neurorehabilitation programmes, it seems reasonable to suppose that one reason to account for this is the presence of challenging behaviour.

Thus, there is some evidence to support the idea that the presence of challenging behaviour is partly responsible for the tendency for people to gravitate to less appropriate placements as time since injury increases. Furthermore, challenging behaviour is likely to lead to an increased probability that an individual will make contact with the police and judicial system (for example, see Rarapta, Herrmann,

---

[1] Kemsley Division, St Andrew's Hospital, Northampton, UK (hereafter referred to as the Kemsley Unit).

Johnson, & Aycock, 1998). In Dawson and Jones' data set, 28 people had a forensic history prior to brain injury: however, this figure had nearly doubled to 49 following injury.

CHARACTERISTICS OF CHALLENGING BEHAVIOUR FOLLOWING BRAIN INJURY

What challenging behaviour occurs after brain injury to account for the above, and what evidence is there that it exists? To answer these questions let us briefly consider some outcome studies undertaken that have investigated traumatic brain injury.

A reasonable expectation held both by those unfortunate enough to acquire a brain injury, and especially by their relatives, is that the problems acquired will get better with the passage of time. Whilst some spontaneous improvement in cognitive and physical sequelae of brain injury is evident, the outcome literature paints a very different and pessimistic picture with regard to the behavioural and psychosocial problems that inevitably arise: There is general agreement that these constitute the greatest handicap that prevents social, family, and vocational reintegration (see, for example, Brooks et al., 1987; Thomsen, 1984).

Thus, instead of dissipating, the trend is for the number of such problems to endure or increase. Perhaps even more alarming is a tendency for the severity of these disorders to actually increase with the passage of time. Whilst much of this behaviour could be categorised as "challenging" in the light of the previous discussion regarding definition, the prevalence of actual or threatened aggressive behaviour, especially (but not exclusively) by people who have acquired severe and very severe brain injuries, is high. For example, Thomsen (1984) demonstrated that, 10–15 years after severe brain injury, behavioural disturbances were still evident. In addition she also found that the more severe the injury the greater the risk of such disturbance.

Other investigators have also highlighted the longevity and persistence of behaviour disorders and of their adverse impact on the family. Weddell, Oddy, and Jenkins (1980) found that behaviour disorders were not only a source of great stress within the family but that these persisted far longer than the severity of injury, as measured by the duration of post-traumatic amnesia (PTA), suggested. McKinlay et al. (1981) studied 55 individuals presenting with severe head injury and found an association between the incidence and severity of behavioural disturbance and the level of stress reported by the family.

What form do these behavioural and psychosocial changes take? The following description taken from Broe et al. (1981, p. 95) captures well the nature of the sudden and unexpected alteration in the conduct of those unfortunate enough to sustain brain injury.

> ... such patients may be impulsive, emotionally labile, disinhibited, aggressive, and
> as a consequence of their impairment have lost insight into their emotional response.
> So while physically and cognitively well recovered ... (these) patients experience

deficits which have adverse effects on their interpersonal relationships and return to employment.

More specific information on the nature of the behavioural and psychosocial problems observed after brain injury has been collected from relatives of survivors of brain injury living with their families in the community (Brooks et al., 1987). Two groups were investigated: first, those whose relatives had been injured one year previously, and second, another group whose relatives had been injured five years beforehand.

Five of the top 10 problems described by relatives reflect the presence of challenging behaviour (for example, "threats of violence"). It would be reasonable to expect that given the passage of time some improvement, commensurate with the expected partial recovery in physical and cognitive functioning, will take place. Unfortunately, data presented by Brooks and his colleagues suggests this is not the case, as relatives of people with brain injury also reported the presence of these problems after five years. What is more disturbing is that some appear to have even *increased* in prevalence over time. Perhaps the most alarming discovery was that the proportion of relatives reporting "threats of violence" increased from just 15% one year after injury to a very worrying 54% after five years.

Further evidence which substantiates the presence of challenging behaviour following brain injury is provided by another study investigating outcome reported by Johnson and Balleny (1996). These investigators followed a group of people with traumatic brain injuries over a three-year period. They had originally been admitted to a neurological rehabilitation unit following successful medical management during the immediate acute stage of their recovery. Each person was followed up on four separate occasions: Both relatives and professionals were asked to indicate the number of behavioural problems evident, and to rate their severity. Over three years, the average number of behaviour problems evident at each of the four follow-up points remained similar (about four). However, a very striking finding was that the average rating of the severity of these problems successively increased to the extent that on the last rating, made 30–36 months after injury, it was approximately double that found when first rated up to seven months afterwards. In addition, the types of behaviour disorder evident were those which had a high impact on the environment in that they were characterised by aggression.

The presence of aggression, particularly when this involves physical assaults on others, creates special problems for clinical teams in brain injury rehabilitation units. It compromises the safety of patients and staff, increases the vulnerability of the aggressor, and may prevent them achieving their full rehabilitation potential (Burke, Wesolowski, & Lane, 1988). Aggression may exclude an individual from some rehabilitation programmes altogether (Prigatano, 1987). When this happens, the probability of brain injured people gravitating to placements for management purposes that are entirely inappropriate for their needs increases significantly.

TABLE 9.2

Some examples of challenging behaviour exhibited by people with acquired brain injury encountered by professionals, relatives, and carers

Physical aggression against people	Sexual disinhibition
Physical aggression against objects	Disinhibition and impulsive behaviour
Self-injurious behaviour	Blunt social behaviour
Verbal aggression	Apathy and lack of drive
Active non-cooperation	Passivity
Screaming/shouting	Low arousal

The types of challenging behaviour exhibited by some brain injured people encountered by both professionals in a rehabilitation setting, and relatives or carers within the community, are more specifically characterised in Table 9.2.

Of course, this list does not pretend to be exhaustive, but simply reflects examples of challenging behaviour.

TREATMENT OF CHALLENGING BEHAVIOUR

Psychotherapy has been used with some success in the attempted remediation of behavioural and psychosocial problems following brain damage. Psychotherapy is in itself a broad and multiply defined concept (Jackson & Gouvier, 1992) which encompasses various therapies that have arisen from different models of psychopathology (Patterson, 1986). One of the earliest attempts in using psychotherapy with brain injured people was reported by Ben-Yishay and his colleagues during the early 1970s (for example, see Ben-Yishay et al., 1985). Faced with the task of attempting to rehabilitate soldiers injured in the Arab–Israeli wars they developed an intensive social milieu approach, the results of which suggested that the potential level of social recovery for patients with brain injury was greater than had previously been anticipated.

Another influential advocate of psychotherapy with this clinical population is George Prigatano, who has described successful outcomes using holistic neurobehavioural approaches (1986). He believes success is dependent on people with brain injury recognising the need for, and value of, therapeutic activity by becoming aware of their difficulties and learning to compensate for them. He has advocated the use of psychotherapy within a general rehabilitation programme to facilitate awareness and acceptance. Successful employment of various psychotherapeutic techniques, including individual and family counselling within a social milieu treatment programme, has been reported as leading to improvement of insight and psychosocial problems (Prigatano, 1986; Prigatano et al., 1984).

Successful outcomes have also been reported regarding the use of insight psychotherapy (Geva & Stern, 1985; Stern & Stern, 1985; Tadir and Stern, 1985), group psychotherapy conducted on both an inpatient and outpatient basis (Carberry & Burd, 1983; Corrigan, Arnett, Houck, & Jackson, 1985; Jackson & Gouvier,

1992; Leer, 1986; Leer & Sonday, 1986) and family therapy (Power & Dell Orto, 1980) in the treatment of psychosocial problems following brain injury.

Barriers to psychotherapy

Not all people with acquired brain injury will respond to these methods. Jackson and Gouvier (1992) pointed out that successful participation in group psychotherapy is usually dependent on the brain injured person having already made a "…moderately good cognitive and behavioural recovery" (p. 322). People who have sustained very severe brain injury are often not amenable to psychotherapy for a number of reasons. For example, Wood (1988) agrees that while methods such as counselling and group therapy can improve the behaviour and social adaptability of individuals with minor brain injury, they are generally not helpful in cases where damage is more severe.

One reason for this is that as a result of brain injury some individuals will have neuropsychological difficulties that may include lack of awareness, poor insight, inaccuracy in verbal self-report, and motivational problems. These will interfere with participation in psychotherapy (Burgess & Wood, 1990) and are extremely difficult to overcome (Sazbon & Groswasser, 1991). A second reason is that challenging behaviour exhibited by the brain injured person may be so severe that it excludes them from treatment (Wood, 1987).

Medication and challenging behaviour

Tables 9.1 and 9.2 suggest that many people with acquired brain injury who present with challenging behaviour will come into contact with medical services: for example, 82.2% of admissions to the Kemsley Unit came from hospital, rehabilitation, or forensic placements. It is also almost certain that the remaining 17.8% of admissions will have had some medical input regarding management, even if this was limited to contact with their general practitioner. It is therefore likely that attempts will be made at some point to help manage challenging behaviour using medication.

Medication undoubtedly has a role to play in the management of challenging behaviour: however, it has already been highlighted that people with TBI are not popular among rehabilitation professionals. In addition, there are few neuropsychiatrists in the UK. Exclusion from rehabilitation programmes that do not address neurobehavioural difficulties (indeed, their presence typically leads to exclusion), and lack of medical specialists who possess knowledge and skills relevant to the management of this clinical group, may result in medication being prescribed whose effects are antagonistic to rehabilitation aims. For example, psychiatrists who have not received specialised training regarding acquired brain injury may unwittingly attribute the presence of some neurobehavioural difficulties to an underlying functional illness, such as schizophrenia. Instead, behavioural "symptoms", including disinhibition, poor self-monitoring, and even delusions and hallucinations, may be attributable to underlying cognitive impairment. Similarly, problems with initiation that are secondary to impaired executive functioning may result in an inappropriate diagnosis of depression (see Halligan & Marshall, 1996). Of course, a functional illness may exist alongside neurobehavioural difficulties caused by brain injury: indeed, there is evidence to suggest that there is an increased likelihood of psychoses following head injury (McGuire & Sylvester, 1990). However, an attempt must be made to differentiate neurobehavioural difficulties from symptoms that reflect a functional illness by a skilled neuropsychiatrist (see Chapter 2).

One obvious problem that can arise if neurobehavioural difficulties are misdiagnosed is that inappropriate medication regimes may be implemented. Drugs such as haloperidol, lorazepam, and procyclidine may have little therapeutic value beyond sedation of behaviour. Whilst in extreme cases medication may be purposefully administered with this aim in mind, it will not purposefully target the underlying cause of challenging behaviour. Medication effects will also be unspecific: all behaviour, including that which is appropriate, may be suppressed. A further unwelcome effect of sedating medication is that it may depress impaired cognitive functioning further, thereby placing more obstacles to the learning of new inhibitory controls and the ability to benefit from wider rehabilitation. What is required instead are interventions whose purpose is to elicit aggressive behaviour, rather than suppress it, within an environment in which it can be properly assessed and effectively managed.

Indeed, expert assessment from a neuropsychiatrist may indicate an appropriate role for medication in the management of some aspects of challenging behaviour. For example, neuroleptics do have a role to play in the management of aggression when it can be demonstrated that variability in mood and behaviour may at least be partly attributable to an *episodic dyscontrol syndrome* (EDS). Here, disturbed behaviour, including aggression, is attributed to electrophysiological disturbance in the brain. It is beyond the purpose of this chapter to provide a detailed account of EDS: instead, it is suggested that the reader turns to sources such as Miller (1994) for a broader description of the syndrome.

The presentation of EDS may vary considerably. Aggression associated with EDS is typically thought of as being unprovoked and disorganised in nature. However, it may also take the form of a "short fuse" in which more organised aggressive behaviour is directed at the source of irritation in response to trivial frustration.

Whilst reduction of aggression using anticonvulsants has been successfully reported in the literature in the management of EDS (Hirsch, 1993; Mooney & Hass, 1993), use of carbamazepine would appear to have special relevance (Foster, Hillbrand, & Chi, 1989). Eames and Wood (Eames, 1988; Wood, 1987) recommend a combination of carbamazepine and behaviour modification methods (for example, see the description of patient MD provided by Alderman, Davies, Jones, &

McDonnel, 1999). Eames and Wood have argued that whilst medication controls underlying seizure activity, behaviour modification methods are used to teach adaptive forms of behaviour and new skills. Unfortunately, the extent of the contribution of anticonvulsant medication to the management of challenging behaviour remains poorly researched to date, and is an area that requires more detailed and vigorous clinical exploration.

Development of a neurobehavioural paradigm of rehabilitation

The use of behaviour modification methods in the management of challenging behaviour amongst people with acquired brain injury has many advantages. Behaviour modification techniques have been used within neurorehabilitation for at least three decades. Whilst Luria described earlier examples of such work (Luria, 1963; Luria, Naydin, Tsvetkova, & Vinarskaya, 1969), Goodkin (1966, 1969) was the first investigator to specifically refer to the use of behaviour modification methods with people who have acquired neurological disorders. This included improving functional skills such as handwriting, and wheelchair pushing with stroke patients and an individual with Parkinson's disease. Behaviour modification approaches have also been incorporated into interventions concerned with the rehabilitation of cognitive deficits (for example, Diller & Weinberg, 1977; Lincoln, 1979; Weinberg et al., 1979). However, these interventions have been paralleled by descriptions in the literature of the use of behaviour modification in the management of psychosocial, emotional, and behavioural problems amongst this clinical population, some of which could certainly be categorised as challenging (for example, Booream & Seacat, 1972; Ince, 1976; Taylor & Persons, 1970).

At first glance, behaviour modification models may appear over-simplistic. For example, operant conditioning is conceptualised as an active process of learning at the heart of which lies interaction with the environment. Behaviour acts upon the environment and results in consequences. The experience of these consequences (for example, whether they are pleasant or unpleasant) determines in part the likelihood of that behaviour that led to them being subsequently exhibited again. However, from these simple, objectively demonstrable principles, effective treatment techniques have evolved and been used with many diverse clinical populations (for example, see Kanfer & Goldstein, 1986).

There are considerable advantages in using behaviour modification with brain injured people which have been described by Powell (1981) and subsequently by Wilson (1989). These are summarised a follows:

1. There are many treatment techniques available to both decrease and increase behaviours of interest.
2. The underlying theoretical frameworks of behaviour modification are diverse (for example, learning theory, developmental psychology, information

processing, and social learning theory): this provides a richness and complexity to theory and treatments thereby benefiting many populations and differing problems.

3. Specific targets and goals for treatment are always clear and specified.
4. Behavioural assessment and subsequent treatment are inseparable, unlike some other forms of assessment and treatment.
5. Treatment is continuously evaluated through objective observation and recording, processes which Powell (1981) states are essential features of any applied science: the use of single-case experimental designs are particularly relevant in this respect (Hersen and Barlow,1984).
6. Behaviour modification programmes are individualised and take into account variables such as the biological condition of the person, antecedent causes, consequences, and social and environmental factors.
7. The behavioural approach provides a clear set of procedures to follow when designing and implementing a treatment programme (see Figure 9.1): This process ensures a consistent and objective approach is adopted by all who are involved in treatment.
8. Finally, objective measurement of change in behaviour further validates efficacy of the behavioural approach.

A key factor in the application of behaviour modification is the need for accurate, individualised assessments. The importance of ascertaining antecedents and consequences to behaviour, the state of the environment, and all other relevant variables has already been stressed. However, damage to the brain will, of course, be partly responsible for many behavioural and functional problems observed following injury. The nature of this damage will also have to be considered when deciding what form treatment will take. It is for this reason that the neuropsychological status of the individual must be investigated, as this will have implications for our understanding of the behaviour of the brain injured person. Knowledge of a person's general level of cognitive functioning, their ability to remember, plan and organise, comprehend spoken language, and so on, may be important factors that help explain why they are behaving in a certain way or why they cannot perform a given task. Knowledge of cognitive strengths and weaknesses will also help when choosing treatment goals and strategies employed to obtain them (Wilson, 1989).

The relationship between the damaged brain and behaviour is complex. Without knowledge of neuropsychological status, conclusions arrived at by observation of an individual's behaviour may lead to spurious assumptions being made concerning what factors underlie it. Without this knowledge, precise, functional descriptions of the aetiology of behaviour disorders are unlikely to be made. This may have contributed to the jaundiced attitude on the part of many medical doctors towards people with brain injury (for example, see Miller, 1966). Many behavioural control difficulties have been simplistically attributed to "personality change" or "lack of insight". There has also been an implicit assumption that behaviour disorders in

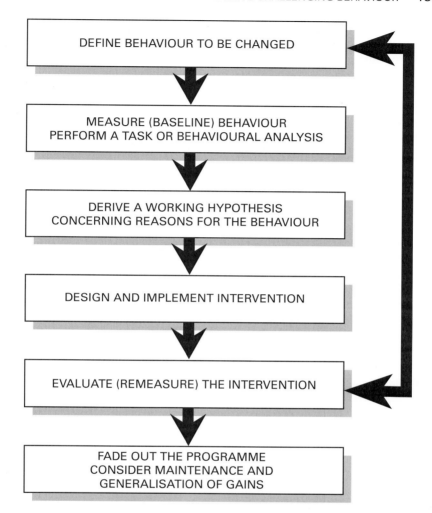

Figure 9.1.   Flowchart demonstrating one procedure that may be used to design, implement, and monitor behaviour modification interventions. The loop on the right should be followed if the evaluation (remeasurement) stage demonstrates the goal of the intervention is not being achieved.

this group are merely an extension of pre-morbid personality traits and are therefore irreversible (Symonds, 1937) despite the availability of evidence to the contrary (Oddy, 1984).

An additional consideration is that the use of vague terms like "personality change" do not provide the rehabilitation therapist with an adequate theoretical basis from which to understand the nature of behaviour problems and consequently plan effective treatment.

As a consequence, Wood (1987, 1990) and others (for example, Wood & Eames, 1981) have argued that behaviour problems observed following brain injury may be attributable to several factors, including organic, neuropsychological, and environmental variables. Often, observable behaviour is a function of complex brain–behaviour relationships involving one or all of these factors. To plan effective interventions that successfully inhibit negative aspects of behaviour and promote positive ones, an inductive approach that stresses objectivity needs to be adopted. To this end Wood and others have advocated that the principles of behaviour modification and those of neuropsychology should be combined to form what they have called a *neurobehavioural paradigm* (for example, see Wood, 1990, and also Chapters 6 and 7, this volume). This appears to lend itself perfectly to this role. The school of behaviour modification stresses that *all* behaviour needs to be analysed objectively and in a way that allows quantification of observations. This data-driven approach to analysing behaviour, together with detailed knowledge of an individual's neuropsychological status, facilitates the process of attributing the aetiology of any behaviour to predominantly organic or environmental factors.

There is a further reason as to why it is essential that neuropsychological factors are considered. Intuitively, it appears contradictory to use a rehabilitation approach based on new learning with people in whom the very ability to learn is characterised by cognitive deficits. Impairment of attention and memory are well known following traumatic brain injury and these play an obvious and key role in new learning. However, the process of learning may also be adversely influenced by other cognitive problems, including difficulties with communication, executive functioning, and monitoring. It may also be slow, variable and, especially in the early stage, a fragile process (Wood, 1987). Furthermore, poor ability to tolerate frustration and reduced insight may result in the learning of escape and avoidance behaviours, which further impairs rehabilitation (Alderman, 1991).

Cognitive impairment may also directly drive some behavioural problems. For example, impairment of executive skills which results in poor monitoring of the environment will reduce opportunities for learning, as the individual will be less likely to attend to relevant information directed at them by therapists. However, poor monitoring is also likely to result in social and other cues, whose presence informs people it is time to change behaviour, being missed. When this happens behaviour that was relevant and appropriate no longer remains so as social circumstances change: The result of this "behavioural perseveration" may be that such conduct becomes labelled as "problematic" (Alderman, 1996; Alderman, Fry, & Youngson, 1995).

Despite the deterring influence of cognitive impairment on learning, new skills and desirable behaviours may nevertheless still be acquired. Specialised neurobehavioural units are able to organise the service they provide to minimise the effect of cognitive impairment whilst maximising opportunities for new learning. It is beyond the scope of this chapter to provide a full account of the neurobehavioural paradigm: instead, the reader is referred to Wood (1987, 1990;

and Wood & Worthington, this volume, Chapters 6 & 7) regarding the assumptions underlying the model and examples of how these may be used in the rehabilitation of challenging behaviour, and to Fussey and Giles (1988) and Giles and Clark-Wilson (1999) with respect to discipline-specific approaches to wider therapy conducted within a neurobehavioural framework.

However, it is important that the reader is aware of the importance of *structure* when conducting rehabilitation using neurobehavioural principles (see Chapter 6), and how this is provided through the organisation of services. In a neurobehavioural rehabilitation unit, structure is sustained through the physical environment, the format of the day, strong interdisciplinary teamwork, appropriate levels of expectation regarding participation within rehabilitation, and the use of behaviour modification strategies. One important goal is for this structure to create an environment that encourages achievement and success, in which social approval and attention are routinely available, but withdrawn whenever inappropriate behaviour is exhibited. Consequently, individuals participate in personalised, needs-led treatment programmes that incorporate multiple interventions. The nature of structure will be expanded on later in this chapter.

When services are organised in this way, the net effect is the provision of a daily routine within which skills that aim to maximise independence and quality of life are practised repeatedly and acquired through procedural learning in the form of new habits. Good communication within the interdisciplinary team, together with a programme that is grounded in behavioural methods, helps ensure rehabilitation is established at the appropriate level for each individual, that goals are shared, and that management, including contingencies to behaviour, is consistent. The success of specialised neurobehavioural programmes has been well documented (for example, see Alderman & Knight, 1997; Alderman, Fry, & Youngson, 1995; Burgess & Alderman, 1990; Wood, 1987; Youngson & Alderman, 1994).

DIFFICULTIES MANAGING CHALLENGING BEHAVIOUR IN NON-SPECIALISED SERVICES

Despite the success of specialised neurobehavioural units, it remains the case that such services remain chronically underdeveloped and under-resourced for people with acquired brain injury and challenging behaviour (Medical Disability Society, 1988). It is possible to obtain good outcome using neurobehavioural methods within non-specialised services but there are few published case studies supporting this potential (for example, Davis, Turner, Rolinder, & Cartwright, 1994; Goll & Hawley, 1989; Johnston, Burgess, McMillan, & Greenwood, 1991; McMillan, Papadopoulas, Cornall, & Greenwood, 1990; Wood, 1988). Greenwood and McMillan (1993) point out that the extent of this problem in the UK is exacerbated further through the places that are available being restricted to people who happen to live within particular catchment areas, an observation that has international relevance. Furthermore, those services that do exist in the UK fall predominantly in the independent sector where the costs necessary to deliver effective neurobehavioural programmes may serve to further exclude people who should be in receipt of them. In other countries with different funding systems, access to more specialised services may be easier in principle, but often they do not exist, or sufficient funding is not available for the time needed.

Thus, there is a reasonable chance that many people reading this book will have encountered brain injured people within neurological rehabilitation services that are not organised to manage challenging behaviour. The reader will note that I will henceforth refer to such services as "non-specialised": of course, they *are* specialised in the sense that they are organised to meet the physical, functional, and care needs of people with a range of acquired neurological problems. The term "non-specialised" is simply used to describe services that are not organised to manage challenging behaviour resulting from neurobehavioural disability, and are not arranged specifically to enable neurobehavioural principles to be operationalised to enable management of such disability.

POTENTIAL OBSTRUCTIONS MANAGING CHALLENGING BEHAVIOUR IN NON-SPECIALISED SERVICES

Some of the more frequent constraints which may potentially reduce opportunities for successful management of challenging behaviour found in non-specialised services include the following.

Limitations in the physical environment.   The rehabilitation environment should be as quiet as possible to minimise problems with distractibility. Physically, it should be as free from extraneous "clutter" as possible for the same reason. Many "traditional" rehabilitation units may be situated within large, bustling medical hospitals. They often incorporate a degree of open planning in their design. They may be a thoroughfare within the hospital through which many people pass. Distractions may be routinely present with the television or radio being continually left on. Telephones may frequently be heard. Several people may be undergoing individual therapy within close physical proximity. Simultaneous conversation may be a routine feature of the environment. Distractions of this kind will mitigate against new learning for people who have difficulties maintaining attention to task.

Lack of availability of specialised advice.   Advice on the assessment and treatment of neurobehavioural problems falls most often within the domain of appropriately experienced clinical neuropsychologists, neurologists, and neuropsychiatrists. Unfortunately, because there are so few neurobehavioural units (at least in the UK), and lack of specialised training in neurorehabilitation, there are comparatively few specialists available to fulfil this role.

Lack of clinicians experienced in brain injury rehabilitation. Neuro-behavioural interventions are reliant on the quality of those people who implement them. Again, the small number of specialised neurobehavioural units reduces the number of staff whose knowledge and experience are essential in making the interdisciplinary team work for the brain injured person.

Low expectations. The presence of challenging behaviour that is unsuccessfully managed may result in the rehabilitation team lowering its expectations regarding goals to be achieved in therapy (see Davis et al., 1994). For example, if patients with acquired brain injury, whose ability to tolerate frustration is low and who lack insight, are physically aggressive when attempts are made to engage them in physiotherapy, therapists may, not unreasonably, withdraw their input. The behaviour of both the person in rehabilitation and the therapy staff becomes reinforced. As a result, patients may acquire a reputation that leads to generalised reduction in the expectations placed on them, whilst they themselves acquire behaviours that are used purposefully to avoid or escape activities they do not want to engage in (Alderman, 1991).

Lack of routine. Within non-specialised rehabilitation environments the structure of the day may be poorly defined.

Poor communication within the multidisciplinary team. Not all therapy will necessarily take place within the rehabilitation unit. For example, the occupational or speech and language therapy departments may be situated some distance away. Whilst people may be taken from the rehabilitation unit for therapy, there may be no formal opportunities for members of the multidisciplinary team to meet and share their goals. The importance of clinical review meetings for this purpose cannot be overstated. Inconsistencies regarding functional and other expectations within the team can rapidly develop. For example, individuals are taught to sit and stand within physiotherapy using a particular method within sessions, whilst at other times other staff may use completely different techniques. This does little to help habit formation or generalise the beneficial effects of rehabilitation.

Insufficient staff numbers. Staffing levels may be insufficient to enable effective management of challenging behaviour. A ratio of one member of staff to every brain injured person during the therapy day is probably the minimum requirement.

Lack of training. Training opportunities for staff are often lacking. This may be because insufficient staffing means that the clinical team is overstretched and often struggles to ensure basic standards are maintained. Other reasons are the lack of availability of practitioners in neurobehavioural practice to facilitate such training, and the view that time away from patients for training cannot be justified on the grounds that "their treatment will suffer".

Patient mix.   It is known that people with acquired brain injury comprise a non-homogeneous group. Within a general rehabilitation unit this heterogeneity, particularly when somebody who has challenging behaviour is present, may be accentuated. Clearly, the needs of a passive elderly person who has had a stroke will be very different from those of an active young man in his late teens whose behaviour is disruptive as a consequence of TBI.

Poor understanding of the problems of acquired brain injury.   When members of the rehabilitation team are not acquainted with the neurobehavioural sequelae of acquired brain injury, the conduct of people who present with challenging behaviour may be inadequately interpreted, often according to some "common sense" view. Often the belief exists that behaviour exhibited by such people is always entirely under their control and that they are "doing it deliberately" or are "lazy". This leads to the formation of unhelpful and negative attitudes.

The concepts of "fairness" and ethics regarding behaviour modification. Considerable resistance from members of the interdisciplinary team to the use of behaviour modification methods can arise. Despite its emphasis on skill building and reinforcement it is, paradoxically, not uncommon for such interventions to be perceived as "unfair", "punishing" or "unethical".

Insufficient use of group work.   Whatever the focus of therapy, be it physical, cognitive or functional, delivering rehabilitation using groups is very advantageous in the management of challenging behaviour. Not only is this beneficial regarding the economical deployment of staff and the presence of immediate support, but it also allows opportunities for the team to redirect their attention from an individual who is being disruptive to those who are not. Use of peer pressure and the ability to begin to work with somebody who may feel threatened when treated individually provide further benefits to group work. However, in many rehabilitation units groups are not used. Not only are potential benefits missed, but the probability of reinforcement of escape and avoidance behaviour, together with decreasing expectations, are increased in individual therapy sessions. As a result, they can quickly become confrontational.

Positive reinforcement of challenging behaviour.   Within the context of a busy, under-resourced rehabilitation unit, there may be insufficient time to give people regular quality social contact. However, when an individual begins to engage in inappropriate behaviour, for example to shout, scream, masturbate, or be aggressive, staff attention will be rapidly directed to them in an effort to curtail such conduct. Frequently, people may be told "... don't do that". Unfortunately, under circumstances devoid of appropriate social contact, the attention received by the person, even when it is delivered in the form of criticism, may be welcome. Staff may thereby unwittingly reinforce challenging behaviour.

Thus, the presence of one or more of these factors may not only work against the successful application of behaviour modification techniques within non-specialised rehabilitation settings, but may also encourage and reinforce challenging behaviour. Absence of expert clinical leadership, deficiencies in expertise and knowledge regarding brain injury within the team, low expectations, and lack of structure (both within the physical environment and what happens within it), all help create conditions that work against people achieving their optimum rehabilitation potential.

What then are the necessary prerequisites for attempting to manage challenging behaviour within non-specialised services?

CLINICAL LEADERSHIP IN NON-SPECIALISED SERVICES

The first requirement is the availability of a neurobehavioural consultant (in practice, usually a clinical neuropsychologist). This person will provide the initial assessment of the problem, which should incorporate the observations of other members of the clinical team and, where possible, the views of the patient and his or her family. The neurobehavioural consultant will also impart knowledge regarding neurobehavioural sequelae to the team, and equip them with the necessary skills required to implement treatment interventions devised. He or she will steer the team through the process illustrated in Figure 9.1 and provide the necessary clinical leadership. In addition, the consultant may recommend input from other professionals.

Interaction between the brain injured person and his or her environment may often drive and maintain challenging behaviour. Expert assessment undertaken by the neurobehavioural consultant may demonstrate this and will have obvious implications for treatment. Space does not permit the range of assessment techniques available. However, the use of *analogue assessment* has particular advantages within neurobehavioural rehabilitation, although it has not seen widespread use within the field to date (Treadwell & Page, 1996). As well as using any neuropsychological data available to help determine the influence of underlying cognitive impairment on challenging behaviour, further clarification of brain–behaviour relationships may be possible by manipulating external antecedents and contingencies. The effect of these manipulations is evaluated by measuring the target behaviour. This approach is particularly helpful when attempting to determine reasons underlying behaviour in people who have global, severe cognitive impairment, and those who have significant communication problems.

Figure 9.2 illustrates the potential benefits of this approach. The individual concerned was a young man, CG, who had sustained a very severe head injury. As a result, he had acquired a wide range of physical and functional problems. Cognitive impairment was characterised by severe difficulties with memory and executive functioning. Speed of information processing was significantly reduced. Receptive and expressive communication difficulties were evident. At the time of assessment CG was receiving treatment in a non-specialised neurorehabilitation unit.

Staff observed that CG was routinely physically aggressive towards both objects and people. Their perception was that aggression characterised the majority of their interactions with CG. As a result, they were unwilling to work with him and the expectations levied against CG within rehabilitation were minimal. Analogue assessment was conducted as part of the investigation of CG's behaviour. The goal

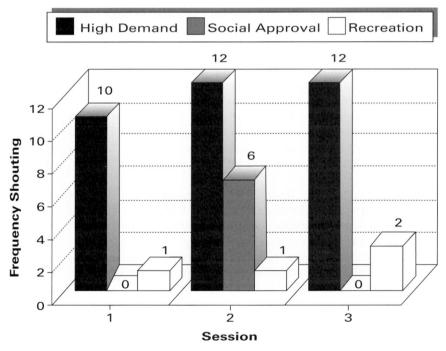

Figure 9.2.   Results of an analogue assessment carried out to investigate possible causes of CG's challenging behaviour. Note that each session lasted 15 minutes and that the order of conditions varied within each session.

was to observe and measure changes in CG's response pattern made in response to carefully controlled environmental manipulations.

The effect of three conditions was assessed over three separate assessment sessions. Each session lasted 15 minutes and was divided into three 5-minute trials. Each condition was implemented during one of the 5-minute trials within each session. The order of the conditions was varied across each of the three sessions. The assessor remained present throughout. As well as recording the target behaviour (physical aggression), she also implemented the environmental manipulations. The first condition was that of "recreation". Here, CG watched television: the assessor attempted social contact every 30 seconds, and interacted with CG whenever he initiated this. This was essentially a control condition. The second was that of "social approval". Its purpose was to determine to what extent staff attention reinforced aggression. No attention was given to CG unless he became aggressive: when this happened, he was given a 10-second social reprimand (along the lines of "... don't do that"). The final environmental manipulation was that of "demand". Its purpose was to determine if aggression served any escape or avoidance function by giving CG continuous verbal instructions whilst executing a peg-board game. These instructions were withdrawn for periods of 30 seconds in response to aggressive behaviour. Figure 9.2 clearly demonstrates that CG was more aggressive when high demands were placed upon him.

The results of this assessment were used to help dispel staff perception that aggression was a response to all interaction. This evidence was used to encourage staff to interact with him more throughout the day in order to help build positive relationships and reinforce appropriate behaviour, whilst a specific behaviour modification programme was implemented during formal rehabilitation sessions to help manage aggression and reduce opportunities for escape and avoidance.

Behaviour modification and the "three Cs"

Having conducted an assessment and analysis of challenging behaviour, it is helpful to measure its frequency and/or duration before implementing a treatment programme in order that the impact of the latter may be evaluated at some later stage through repeated measurement (see Wood, 1987, and Hersen & Barlow, 1984, for further details). Having obtained this pre-treatment baseline, the neurobehavioural consultant will formulate reasons underlying behaviour based on the clinical history, neuropsychological test data, mood, interaction with the environment, observations collected, and their specialised knowledge of acquired brain injury. An appropriate treatment intervention will then be devised.

The success of the treatment programme will be almost entirely dependent on the ability of those charged with executing it to implement it as intended. Education and support of the clinical team by the neurobehavioural consultant are paramount.

Anxieties and concerns about treatment must be diminished if intervention objectives are to be met. In the author's view, the clinical team must be encouraged to embark on treatment in the spirit of a collaborative venture, to which each individual can contribute through regular contact with the neurobehavioural consultant in which people are encouraged to express their concerns, views, and ideas. This greatly increases the probability that the intervention programme will be executed as intended as members of the clinical team are "on board" and fully understanding of its aims.

An important goal for the neurobehavioural consultant is to monitor not only the impact of the intervention on challenging behaviour, but also the efficacy with which the clinical team delivers it. To meet this goal, awareness of the "Three Cs" amongst the team is, in the author's view, paramount. The "Three Cs" refer to: Consistency; Clarity; and Contingencies. Briefly, these are as follows.

Consistency

It has been well established that responses to target behaviours must be consistent in order to obtain the intervention goal, and to avoid a paradoxical intermittent reinforcement schedule being set up that undermines the efficacy of the programme. This means that it is essential that all people who come into contact with the person exhibiting challenging behaviour react the same way in response to it, that is, *they adhere to the demands of the programme*. If this consistency is absent, for example, when nursing and therapy staff respond as per the programme, but domestic staff do not (a not uncommon situation), the resulting intermittent reinforcement schedule can actually result in the target behaviour becoming *more* resistant. This serves as a reminder that *all* members of the team need to be involved and on board with the intervention.

Clarity

A prerequisite for consistency is that of clarity regarding intervention. Objective operational definitions of what constitutes the target behaviour must be agreed between the neurobehavioural consultant and the clinical team: use of terms that lack specificity must be avoided. For example, "verbal aggression" would be insufficient as an operational definition of a target behaviour. Should this include swearing? Would aggressive references to a person who is not present result in the intervention being implemented? Unless the target behaviour is specified using concrete, objective, observable criteria, treatment will be implemented inconsistently.

The intervention procedure must also be written in sufficient detail to help reduce variability in how individual members of the clinical team implement it. An example of this is shown in Table 9.3.

Contingencies

The contingencies of the target behaviour, that is, what happens immediately afterwards, are crucial. Contingencies are delivered by the clinical team and must always be specified in the written procedure pertaining to any intervention. They constitute the "business end" of many behaviour modification programmes in the sense that achievement of the desired goal of an intervention is dependent on the response of the clinical team. There must always be a *consistent* response to the target behaviour; for this to happen, all members of the team must have *clarity* regarding the procedures used. The *contingencies* to behaviour are operationalised through implementation of these procedures.

The potential benefits to clinical teams employing the "three Cs" are illustrated in Figure 9.3. This demonstrates the positive impact on behaviour that can be obtained by utilising simple behaviour modification interventions.

Data in Figure 9.3 represent observational recordings concerning FA, a 35-year-old woman who had suffered a posterior communicating artery aneurysm three years previously. A computed tomography (CT) scan revealed an extensive subarachnoid haemorrhage, and also areas of cerebral infarction. FA subsequently demonstrated behavioural disturbance with episodes of agitation and disinhibition.

Neuropsychological assessment suggested the current level of intellectual functioning, as measured by the Wechsler Adult Intelligence Scale—Revised

TABLE 9.3

An example of how a target behaviour needs to be operationally defined, and an extract of the procedure used when implementing the intervention. The intervention used was response cost

Target behaviour
All directed verbal abuse, including:
1. May or may not have sexual content
2. May or may not be shouted
3. Must be clearly directed at another individual
4. Must not be non-specific, e.g., "… bloody hell" or "don't bloody know" does not constitute directed verbal abuse.

Procedure
Whenever the target behaviour is observed, the following procedure will be used.
1. Immediately stand in front of TJ, or if he is sitting, engage his attention from the side.
2. State clearly what the behaviour was that TJ had just engaged in that led to the programme being implemented.
3. Hold out your hand, palm up, and prompt TJ to hand over one of his tokens; if necessary, give up to two prompts—if the client does not comply after the second prompt, TOOTS assist one token away.
4. *Do not* give verbal praise when TJ hands over a token.
5. Remind TJ that it is in his interests to retain his tokens.
6. A 30-second "cooling off" period will normally commence following removal of any token: any target behaviour that occurs during this time will be TOOTS—if it continues beyond this time a further token is lost as above.
7. *Make the necessary recordings on the form.*

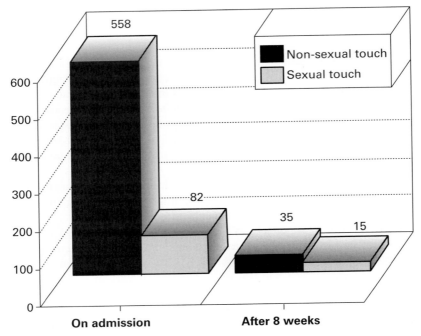

Figure 9.3. Reduction in FA's inappropriate touch over an 8-week period in which all appropriate behaviour was reinforced, and staff attention withdrawn contingent on the target behaviour. Note data reflects continuous frequency counts made of touch during the first 7 days after admission, and a further 7 days during the 8th week of admission.

(Wechsler, 1981) fell in the "impaired" range. In contrast her pre-morbid level was estimated to have been within "borderline" limits. Performance was severely impaired on both verbal and non-verbal tests. Functioning was poor on tests of executive skills, and she showed a considerable level of perseveration on a modified version of the Wisconsin Card Sorting Test (Nelson, 1976).

On admission to the Kemsley Unit, it was soon evident that one aspect of challenging behaviour that continued to prevent her accessing rehabilitation was that of disinhibited touching of staff, some of which appeared to be overtly sexual in nature. As a result, all touch FA initiated towards others was continuously recorded during the first seven days of her admission.

The subsequent intervention was simple and entirely consistent with the treatment philosophy of the Unit: to reinforce all appropriate behaviour through social attention, and to withdraw this whenever she initiated touching of staff. The effect of using "'time-out-on-the-spot' from positive reinforcement" (abridged to "TOOTS"; see Wood, 1987, and Burgess and Wood, 1990, for detailed discussion of this technique) against a therapeutic background of regular social approval for appropriate behaviour was assessed by repeating measurement of FA's touch for a further seven days, during the eighth week of her admission. Figure 9.3 demonstrates the significant reduction evident in this aspect of her challenging behaviour.

Whilst the intervention used was simple, it is most unlikely it would have successfully influenced FA's behaviour without the clinical team employing the "three Cs". They had *clarity* regarding the nature of the target behaviour and the procedures used within the interventions; they were *consistent* in the response made when the target behaviour occurred, and aware of the necessity to maintain conditions which emphasised achievement, success, and social approval when it did not; and the *contingency* to this behaviour, that is, the form this response took through withdrawing attention, was clearly understood and utilised by all members of the team.

STRUCTURE IN NON-SPECIALISED SERVICES

When a neurobehavioural consultant is available to provide clinical leadership, many of the other obstacles whose presence prevents successful management of challenging behaviour within non-specialised services may be eroded through the introduction of enhanced levels of structure.

The degree of structure inherent in a service may be conceptualised as a continuum: specialised neurobehavioural units lie at one end of this in that the service they provide is organised to maximise structure. Rehabilitation units whose clinical organisation has not considered the needs of people with challenging behaviour would fall at the opposite end of the continuum, and would be characterised by the range of obstacles to neurobehavioural work outlined earlier. Units that introduce greater levels of structure (in the sense that it has been described here) will move further along the continuum. The severity of challenging behaviour that could be effectively managed would thus be dependent on the position of any service on this continuum. For example, if a service rich in structure fell at one end it may have the capacity to manage severe physical aggression; alternatively, if a moderate level of structure was present, perhaps the most extreme form of challenging behaviour that could be managed would be verbal aggression.

What characterises this structure?

The *physical* structure of the environment has already been referred to. Additional levels of structure refer to *what happens* within this environment. This can be conceptualised at three levels, these being: the structure provided by the *interdisciplinary team*; that produced by the *routine imposed on the day*; and that imposed through the *behaviour modification interventions*. The first two of these will be briefly commented on, the third more substantially.

Structure provided by the interdisciplinary team

When the clinical team is interdisciplinary rather than multidisciplinary, many of the obstacles to neurobehavioural work will be overcome. Within an interdisciplinary team there is substantial blurring and sharing of roles. Ideally, therapists and nurses would work within the same physical environment. There are regular clinical meetings in which discipline-specific and shared goals are discussed. All members of the team are rehabilitation therapists. As behaviour is a shared goal, all members of the team act as behaviour therapists: all team members have equal responsibility for ensuring behaviour modification interventions are implemented as and when necessary. An interdisciplinary team facilitates good communication and a co-ordinated approach to rehabilitation and maximises consistency.

Structure provided by the routine imposed on the day

It is helpful to impose a timetable of events on the day to provide structure through routine. For example, the day may be divided into meal times, formal sessions, and "free"[2] time. Although the content of formal sessions varies, the routine imposed in terms of how the day is organised is identical. Thus, there may be two 1-hour rehabilitation sessions during the morning, and two in the afternoon. There are defined periods of "free" time between these. Similarly, meals are at designated times. Routine facilitates the establishment of timetables to meet individual needs and provides opportunities to practise skills throughout the day. It promotes consistency. It also creates an environment in which there is an expectation for people to attend sessions and participate at an appropriate level.

Structure imposed through behaviour modification interventions

The structure imposed by behaviour modification interventions can be seen as advantageous: it rewards appropriate behaviour and sufficient effort; it provides a framework that facilitates participation in the wider rehabilitation programme; and it ensures consistency.

These number amongst the most obvious benefits of using behaviour modification programmes. However, within neurobehavioural work there are additional advantages regarding this clinical population.

---

2   The term "free" time simply reflects periods away from formal therapy sessions. However, rehabilitation is a 24-hour process and during "free" time the interdisciplinary team would continue to have expectations about behaviour and functional activity, implementing treatment interventions as directed and continuing to establish good habits.

Systems of feedback

In order to understand the nature of these benefits it is useful to consider behaviour modification interventions within the context of feedback systems.

All behaviour has some impact on the environment: appreciation of the nature of these consequences must be mediated through awareness of feedback. Even when the consequence of a behaviour is not especially overt, most neurologically healthy people will utilise feedback from the environment independently and use this to help regulate subsequent output. As a more obvious example, an individual might become acutely aware that telling an embarrassing joke about somebody in the presence of that person's wife was inappropriate from the resultant range of non-verbal cues. In this instance the joke teller is able effectively to utilise a range of cognitive subsystems in order to register awareness of these cues through feedback: this information should almost certainly lead to a change in behaviour in an attempt to retrieve the situation. However, when these subsystems are impaired, for example, through acquired brain injury, the ability to monitor the environment will deteriorate, with the result that many social cues whose presence informs us it is time to change behaviour will be missed. When this occurs, inappropriate behaviour may persist and more overt systems to deliver feedback will be necessary (Alderman, 1996; Alderman, Fry, & Youngson, 1995).

For people with acquired brain injury who have difficulty perceiving these sorts of social cues, an alternative may be for them to become aware of the inappropriateness of their behaviour through another person giving them explicit verbal feedback (see Chapters 4 and 6). When, because of monitoring difficulties, it is necessary to deliver feedback at such an explicit level in an effort to effect behaviour change, a further important consideration regarding feedback systems must also be made in relation to this population. This concerns the division of such systems into those that are "naturalistic" or spontaneous, and those that are programmed. In both cases, it is usual for feedback about behaviour to be given by another person.

Spontaneous ("naturalistic") feedback systems. Spontaneous feedback systems are reliant upon the personal desire of an individual to provide it. They are therefore notoriously *inconsistent.* For example, when a person engages in challenging behaviour within a non-specialised rehabilitation service, they may or may not receive verbal feedback as a result; in addition, the content of the message given may vary significantly.

Within a multidisciplinary team there are invariably one or two people who are able to form positive relationships with a person who exhibits challenging behaviour, and as a result are able to deliver verbal feedback that may have a beneficial impact. However, these benefits are dependent on their presence. Such "person dependency" renders spontaneous feedback systems vulnerable.

When a patient exhibits challenging behaviour, the response of many team members may well be to avoid contact with them. Systems of spontaneous feedback therefore discourage social interaction. This may well encourage the development of an environment that actually encourages challenging behaviour. When people with acquired brain injury are routinely ignored, they may consequently deliberately engage in aggressive acts in order to get attention, even if this attention is delivered in the form of criticism. When subjected to such behaviour, the natural response of many members of a clinical team may be to respond with phrases such as "... don't do that". Spontaneous feedback systems may therefore create conditions that reinforce challenging behaviour.

Programmed feedback systems. A critical task for the neurobehavioural consultant working within a non-specialised service will be to replace this spontaneous system of feedback with one that provides *programmed* feedback. By now the reasons for this should be clear: Programmed feedback will help circumvent difficulties with monitoring that drive aspects of challenging behaviour; and programmed feedback will change and systematise the behaviour of the clinical team, which otherwise may inadvertently encourage challenging behaviour.

In essence, behaviour modification interventions constitute programmed feedback systems through the implementation of contingencies. These interventions provide suitable vehicles to deliver consistent feedback: the nature of this feedback will be selected by the neurobehavioural consultant as being that which will most support the likelihood that desirable learning will occur.

When the "three Cs" are applied, feedback given in response to challenging behaviour is *consistent*, as all members of the clinical team are responsible for implementing the contingencies of the intervention. For the same reason, programmed feedback is less vulnerable as it is not person dependent. The imposition of programmed feedback should always attempt to turn the negative contingencies operating within spontaneous systems around, in that specific interventions are conducted against a therapeutic background that *encourages positive interaction*. Finally, such systems reinforce desirable conduct whilst ensuring that appropriate feedback follows challenging behaviour.

Varieties of programmed feedback. The essence of programmed feedback is its consistency: it is always given to an individual after he or she has engaged in challenging behaviour. The form this feedback takes will be specified in the procedure pertaining to that behaviour modification intervention, and operationalised within its contingencies. For example, at the simplest level, the consequence of challenging behaviour is the implementation of "time-out-on-the-spot" against a background of social approval: under this scheme feedback is withdrawal of attention. It is important to note that feedback may not always be verbal.

Whilst the immediate contingency to challenging behaviour may be TOOTS, additional programmed feedback may be given at regular intervals using other operant approaches including the token economy (Wood, 1987) and interventions based on the principles of differential reinforcement (Alderman & Knight, 1997; Alderman, Shepherd, & Youngson, 1992). Conversely, explicit verbal feedback may form part of the immediate contingency to challenging behaviour, such as with discriminatory time-out (Wood, 1987), response cost (Alderman & Burgess, 1994; Alderman & Ward, 1991), and self-monitoring training (Alderman, Fry, & Youngson, 1995).

Whilst the intent of any intervention is to eliminate challenging behaviour, the initial goal of the neurobehavioural consultant when implementing behaviour modification interventions within non-specialised services is to change the environment. Of course, this should always be attempted in the spirit of a collaborative venture with the clinical team. From the above, it is hoped the reader will appreciate that spontaneous feedback systems which characterise such environments increase the likelihood of the clinical team behaving towards people in rehabilitation in a manner that supports and encourages challenging behaviour. *Implementation of programmed feedback systems through behaviour modification interventions changes the behaviour of those people working with a patient.* In this sense, although the programme goals of such interventions are to modify challenging behaviour exhibited by the patient, their initial aim will be to change the behaviour of the clinical team: without this prerequisite the primary goal is unlikely to be achieved.

CONCLUDING REMARKS

In this chapter, an attempt has been made to describe how challenging behaviour attributable to acquired brain injury may be managed.

Initially, the nature of challenging behaviour was discussed. Definitions from the area of learning difficulties reflect that such behaviour is not merely limited to physical aggression, but includes conduct that prevents access to community resources. The benefits of post-acute rehabilitation for people with acquired brain injury are well established, but may be prevented by the presence of challenging behaviour: its definition was therefore expanded to reflect this.

Following this, the prevalence and type of challenging behaviour likely to be observed with this clinical population were described. Outcome studies reflect longevity of neurobehavioural problems and these may constitute significant barriers to rehabilitation and community reintegration. Despite the prevalence of challenging behaviour, rehabilitation services in the UK are insufficiently organised to manage these effectively.

Next, a range of possible treatment methods was reviewed. Cognitive impairment, or indeed the presence of challenging behaviour itself, limits the use of psychotherapy. Whilst it is inevitable that nearly all people who present with challenging behaviour will come into contact with medical services, shortage of experienced neuropsychiatrists within the UK may mean that the potential contribution of medication to appropriate management is under-exploited. Sedation should not be seen as the long-term management option of first choice, and treating neurobehavioural sequelae of head trauma as purely psychiatric phenomena is mistaken.

By contrast, behaviour modification approaches have much to offer this clinical population, especially when combined with principles borrowed from neurology and neuropsychology. The resultant neurobehavioural paradigm provides clinicians with a methodology that attempts to clarify the nature of behaviour that has its origins in complex interactions between the individual, the nature of the organic damage sustained, the cognitive problems acquired, and the environment.

Services must be organised to circumvent cognitive barriers to learning if rehabilitation is to succeed. However, in order to manage challenging behaviour they must also be organised to support neurobehavioural practice. However, most neurological rehabilitation services are not organised in this way: unfortunately, not only do many services create conditions that are antagonistic to neurobehavioural practice, but they also may inadvertently create and maintain challenging behaviour.

Much of this chapter is concerned with suggesting how services could be organised to enable neurobehavioural principles to be operationalised within non-specialist settings. It is suggested that two essential conditions are necessary to facilitate this. The first is the provision of appropriate clinical leadership from an experienced neurobehavioural practitioner. The second is the establishment of an appropriate level of structure, through the interdisciplinary team, daily routine, and implementation of behaviour modification interventions. The sum purpose of these conditions is to replace spontaneous systems of feedback with a consistent programmed system. This aim reflects acknowledgement that aspects of challenging behaviour are driven by cognitive problems, especially difficulties with attention and monitoring, and by inconsistencies within the environment, including the behaviour of the clinical team itself.

Whilst there is acknowledgement in the literature regarding the prevalence and severity of neurobehavioural disorders, which include challenging behaviour, the literature pertaining to management of these within non-specialised services is not extensive (as reviewed earlier in this chapter). Whilst there is potential to purposefully manage and change challenging behaviour within non-specialised services, operationalising neurobehavioural principles and maintaining those conditions necessary to facilitate these are vulnerable and consequently difficult to sustain. If such work is to be upheld, services must be reorganised with the explicit aim of being able to manage challenging behaviour within a broader rehabilitation programme. Furthermore, considerable additional resources need to be directed within such services. The sum outcome of these requirements is that such work can never be undertaken casually.

An additional and important consideration is that the severity of challenging behaviour that can be effectively and safely managed must be acknowledged by any service. Unfortunately, insufficient numbers of clinicians trained and experienced in neurobehavioural methods within the UK exist at this time to enable substantial reorganisation of services in this way. Until this situation is resolved, the proportion of people who achieve their rehabilitation potential through successful management of challenging behaviour will not increase, and the bottleneck that exists for specialised services.

REFERENCES

Alderman, N. (1991). The treatment of avoidance behaviour following severe brain injury by satiation through negative practice. *Brain Injury, 5*, 77–86.

Alderman, N. (1996). Central executive deficit and response to operant conditioning methods. *Neuropsychological Rehabilitation, 6*, 161–186.

Alderman, N., & Burgess, P. (1994). A comparison of treatment methods for behaviour disorders following herpes simplex encephalitis. *Neuropsychological Rehabilitation, 4*, 31–48.

Alderman, N., & Knight, C. (1997). The effectiveness of DRL in the management and treatment of severe behaviour disorders following brain injury. *Brain Injury, 11*, 79–101.

Alderman, N., Shepherd, J., & Youngson, H.A. (1992). Increasing standing tolerance and posture quality following severe brain injury using a behaviour modification approach. *Physiotherapy, 78*, 335–343.

Alderman, N., & Ward, A. (1991). Behavioural treatment of the dysexecutive syndrome: Reduction of repetitive speech using response cost and cognitive overlearning. *Neuropsychological Rehabilitation, 1*, 65–80.

Alderman, N., Fry, R.K., & Youngson, H.A. (1995). Improvement of self-monitoring skills, reduction of behaviour disturbance and the dysexecutive syndrome: Comparison of response cost and a new programme of self-monitoring training. *Neuropsychological Rehabilitation, 5*, 193–221.

Alderman, N., Davies, J.A., Jones, C., & McDonnell, P. (1999). Reduction of severe aggressive behaviour in acquired brain injury: Case studies illustrating clinical use of the OAS–MNR in the management of challenging behaviours. *Brain Injury, 13*, 669–704.

Ben-Yishay, Y., Rattock, J., Lakin, P., Piasetsky, E.B., Ross, B., Silver, S., Zide, E., & Ezrachi, O. (1985). Neuropsychologic rehabilitation: Quest for a holistic approach. *Seminars in Neurology, 5*, 252–258.

Booream, C.D., & Seacat, G.F. (1972). Effects of increased incentive in corrective therapy. *Perceptual and Motor Skills, 34*, 125–126.

Broe, A. et al. (1981). The nature and effects of brain damage following severe head injury in young subjects. In T.A.R. Dining & T.J.Connelly (Eds.), *Head injuries* (pp. 92–97). Brisbane: Wiley. Reprinted in part in Walsh, K.W. (1985), *Understanding brain damage: A primer of neuropsychological evaluation* (p. 145). London: Churchill Livingstone.

Brooks, D.N., McKinlay, W., Symington, C., Beattie, A., & Campsie, L. (1987). The effects of severe head injury upon patient and relative within seven years of injury. *Journal of Head Trauma Rehabilitation, 2*, 1–13.

Burgess, P.W., & Alderman, N. (1990). Rehabilitation of dyscontrol syndromes following frontal lobe damage: A cognitive neuropsychological approach. In R.Ll. Wood & I. Fussey (Ed.), *Cognitive rehabilitation in perspective*. London: Taylor & Francis.

Burgess, P.W., & Wood, R.Ll. (1990). Neuropsychology of behaviour disorders following brain injury. In R.Ll. Wood (Ed.), *Neurobehavioural sequelae of traumatic brain injury*. London: Taylor & Francis.

Burke, H.H., Wesolowski, M.D., & Lane, I. (1988). A positive approach to the treatment of aggressive brain injured clients. *International Journal of Rehabilitation Research, 11,* 235–241.

Carberry, H., & Burd, B. (1983). Social aspects of cognitive retraining in an outpatient group setting for head trauma patients. *Cognitive Rehabilitation, 1,* 5–7.

Cope, D.N. (1994). Traumatic brain injury rehabilitation outcome studies in the United States. In A.L. Christensen & B.P. Hazzell (Eds.), *Brain injury and neuropsychological rehabilitation: International perspectives*. Hillsdale, NJ: Lawrence Erlbaum.

Corrigan, J.D., Arnett, J.A., Houck, L.J., & Jackson, R.D. (1985). Reality orientation for brain injured patients: Group treatment and monitoring of recovery. *Archives of Physical Medicine and Rehabilitation, 66,* 626–630.

Davis, J.R., Turner, W., Rolinder, A., & Cartwright, T. (1994). Natural and structured baselines in the treatment of aggression following brain injury. *Brain Injury, 8,* 589–597.

Diller, L., & Weinberg, J. (1977). Hemi-inattention in rehabilitation: The evolution of a rational remediation program. In E.A. Weinstein & R.P. Friedland (Eds.), *Advances in neurology*, Vol. 18. New York: Raven Press.

Eames, P. (1988). Behaviour disorders after severe head injury: Their nature and causes and strategies for management. *Journal of Head Trauma Rehabilitation, 3,* 1–6.

Eames, P., & Wood, R.Ll. (1985). Rehabilitation after severe brain injury: A follow-up study of a behaviour modification approach. *Journal of Neurology, Neurosurgery and Psychiatry, 48,* 613–619.

Emerson, E., Barrett, S., Bell, C., Cummings, R., McCool, C., Toogood, A., & Mansell, J. (1987). *Developing services for people with severe learning difficulties and challenging behaviours*. University of Kent at Canterbury, Institute of Social and Applied Psychology.

Foster, H.G., Hillbrand, M., & Chi, C.C. (1989). Efficacy of carbamazepine in assaultive patients with frontal lobe dysfunction. *Progress in Neuro-Psychopharmacology and Biological Psychiatry, 13,* 865–874.

Fussey, I., & Giles, G.M. (Eds.) (1988). *Rehabilitation of the severely brain injured adult: A practical approach* (1st edn.). London: Croom Helm.

Gentry, M., McDonnell, A., & Cory, S. (1991). *Code of practice*. South Warwickshire Challenging Behaviour Team, Warwick: South Warwickshire NHS Trust.

Geva, N., & Stern, J.M. (1985). The mourning process with brain injured patients. *Scandinavian Journal of Rehabilitation Medicine, Supplement No.12,* 50–52.

Giles, G.M., & Clark-Wilson, J. (1988). Functional skills training in severe brain injury. In I. Fussey & G.M. Giles (Eds.), *Rehabilitation of the severely brain injured adult: A practical approach* (1st edn.). London: Croom Helm.

Giles, G.M., & Clark-Wilson. (1999). *Rehabilitation of the severely brain-injured adult: A practical approach* (2nd edn.). Cheltenham: Stanley Thornes.

Goll, S., & Hawley, K. (1988). Social rehabilitation: The role of the transitional living centre. In R.Ll. Wood & P.G. Eames (Eds.), *Models of brain injury rehabilitation*. London: Chapman & Hall.

Goodkin, R. (1966). Case studies in behavioural research in rehabilitation. *Perceptual and Motor Skills, 23,* 171–182.

Goodkin, R. (1969). Changes in word production, sentence production and relevance in an aphasic through verbal conditioning. *Behaviour Research and Therapy, 7*, 93–99.

Greenwood, R.J., & McMillan, T.M. (1993). Models of rehabilitation programmes for the brain-injured adult: I. Current provision, efficacy, and good practice. *Clinical Rehabilitation, 7*, 248–255.

Halligan, P.W., & Marshall, J.C. (1996). The wise prophet makes sure of the event first: Hallucinations, amnesia, and delusions. In P.W. Halligan & J.C. Marshall (Eds.), *Method in madness: Case studies in cognitive neuropsychiatry*. Hove: Psychology Press.

Hersen, M., & Barlow, P.H. (1984). *Single case experimental designs: Strategies for studying behaviour change* (2nd edn.). New York: Pergamon.

Hirsch, J. (1993). Promising drugs for neurobehavioural treatment. *Headlines*, March/April, 10–11.

Ince, L.P. (1976). *Behaviour modification in rehabilitation medicine*. London: Williams and Wilkins.

Jackson, W.T., & Gouvier, W.D. (1992). Group psychotherapy with brain-damaged adults and their families. In C.J. Lang & L.K. Ross (Eds.), *Handbook of head trauma: Acute care to recovery*. New York: Plenum Press.

Johnson, R., & Balleny, H. (1996). Behaviour problems after brain injury: Incidence and need for treatment. *Clinical Rehabilitation, 10*, 173–181.

Johnston, S., Burgess, J., McMillan, T, & Greenwood, R. (1991). Management of adipsia by a behavioural modification technique. *Journal of Neurology, Neurosurgery and Psychiatry, 54*, 272–274.

Kanfer, F.H., & Goldstein, A.P. (1986). *Helping people change: A textbook of methods* (3rd edn.). New York: Pergamon Press.

Leer, W.B. (1986). Brain injured activity group for cognitive retraining in a rehabilitation setting. Abstract, Proceedings of the 5th Annual Meeting of the National Academy of Neuropsychology. *Archives of Clinical Neuropsychology, 1*, 55.

Leer, W.B., & Sonday, W.E. (1986). Brain injured client coping skills group in a rehabilitation setting. Abstract, Proceedings of the 6th Annual Meeting of the National Academy of Neuropsychology. *Archives of Clinical Neuropsychology, 1*, 277.

Lincoln, N.B. (1979). *An investigation of the effect of the effectiveness on language retraining methods with aphasic stroke patients*. Unpublished doctoral dissertation, University of London.

Luria, A.R. (1963). *Recovery of function after brain injury*. New York: Macmillan.

Luria, A.R., Naydin, V.L., Tsvetkova, L.S., & Vinarskaya, E.N. (1969). Restoration of higher cortical function following local brain damage. In P.J. Vinkin & G.W. Bruyn (Eds.), *Handbook of clinical neurology* (Vol. 3). Amsterdam: North-Holland.

McGuire, T.L., & Sylvester, C.E. (1990). Neuropsychiatric evaluation and treatment of traumatic brain injury. In D. Bigler (Ed.), *Traumatic brain injury: Mechanisms of damage, assessment, intervention and outcome*. Austin, TX: Pro-ed.

McKinlay, W.W, Brooks, D.N., Bond, M.R., Martinage, D.P., & Marshall, M.M. (1981). The short term outcome of severe blunt head injury as reported by the relatives of the injured person. *Journal of Neurology, Neurosurgery and Psychiatry, 44*, 527–533.

McMillan, T.M., Papadopoulas, H., Cornall, C., & Greenwood, R.J. (1990). Modification of severe behaviour problems following herpes simplex encephalitis. *Brain Injury, 4*, 399–406.

Medical Disability Society (1988). *Report of the working party on the management of traumatic brain injury*. London: Royal College of Physicians.

Miller, H. (1966). Mental after-effects of head injury. *Proceedings of the Royal Society of Medicine*, *59*, 257–261.

Miller, L. (1994). Traumatic brain injury and aggression. *Journal of Offender Rehabilitation*, *2*, 91–103.

Miller, E., & Cruzat, A. (1981). A note on the effects of irrelevant information on task performance after mild and severe head injury. *British Journal of Social and Clinical Psychology*, *20*, 69–70.

Mooney, G.F. , & Hass, L.J. (1993). Effect of methylphenidate on brain injury-related anger. *Archives of Physical Medicine and Rehabilitation*, *74*, 153–160.

Nelson, H.E. (1976). A modified card sorting task sensitive to frontal lobe defects. *Cortex*, *12*, 313–324.

Oddy, M. (1984). Head injury and social adjustment. In D.N. Brooks (Ed.), *Closed head injury: Social and family consequences*. Oxford: Oxford University Press.

Patterson, C.H. (1986). *Theories of counselling and psychotherapy* (4th ed.). New York: Harper & Row.

Powell, G.E. (1981). *Brain function therapy*. Aldershot, UK: Gower Press.

Power, P.W., & Dell Orto, A.E. (1980). Approaches to family intervention. In P.W. Power & A.E. Dell Orto (Eds.), *Role of the family in the rehabilitation of the physically disabled*. Baltimore: University Park Press.

Prigatano, G.P. (1986). Psychotherapy after brain injury. In G.P. Prigatano, D.J. Fordyce, H.K. Zeiner, J.R. Roeche, M. Pepping, & B.C. Wood (Eds.), *Neuropsychological rehabilitation after brain injury*. Baltimore: John Hopkins University Press.

Prigatano, G.P. (1987). Psychiatric aspects of head injury: Problem areas and suggested guidelines for research. *BNI Quarterly*, *3*, 2–9.

Prigatano, G.P., Fordyce, D.J., Zeiner, H.K., Roueche, J.R., Pepping, M., & Wood, B.C. (1984). Neuropsychological rehabilitation after closed head injury in young adults. *Journal of Neurology, Neurosurgery and Psychiatry*, *47*, 505–513.

Rarapta, M., Herrmann, D., Johnson, T., & Aycock, R. (1998). The role of head injury in cognitive functioning, emotional adjustment and criminal behaviour. *Brain Injury*, *12*, 821–842.

Sazbon, L., & Groswasser, Z. (1991). Time-related sequelae of TBI in patients with prolonged post-comatose unawareness (PC-U) state. *Brain Injury*, *5*, 3–8.

Stern, B., & Stern, J.M. (1985). On the use of dreams as a means of diagnosis of brain-injured patients. *Scandinavian Journal of Rehabilitation Medicine, Supplement No.12*, 44–46.

Symonds, C.P. (1937). Mental disorder following head injury. *Proceedings of the Royal Society of Medicine*, *30*, 1081–1092.

Tadir, M., & Stern, J.M. (1985). The mourning process with brain injured patients. *Scandinavian Journal of Rehabilitation Medicine, Supplement No. 12*, 50–52.

Taylor, G.P., & Persons, R.W. (1970). Behaviour modification techniques in a physical medicine and rehabilitation centre. *Journal of Psychology*, *74*, 117–124.

Thomsen, I.V. (1984). Late psychosocial outcome in severe blunt head trauma. *Brain Injury*, *1*, 131–143.

Treadwell, K., & Page, T.J. (1996). Functional analysis: Identifying the environmental determinants of severe behavior disorders. *Journal of Head Trauma Rehabilitation*, *11*, 62–74.

Wechsler, D. (1981). *The Wechsler Adult Intelligence Scale—Revised*. San Antonia, TX: The Psychological Corporation.

Weddell, R., Oddy, M., & Jenkins, D. (1980). Social adjustment after rehabilitation: A two year follow-up of patients with severe head injury. *Psychosocial Medicine, 10*, 257–263.

Weinberg, J., Diller, L., Gordon, W.A., Gerstman, L.J., Lieberman, A., Lakin, P., Hodges, G., & Ezrachi, O. (1979). Training sensory awareness and spatial organisation in people with right brain damage. *Archives of Physical Medicine and Rehabilitation, 60*, 491–496.

Wilson, B. (1989). Injury to the central nervous system. In S. Pearce & J. Wardle (Eds.), *The practice of behavioural medicine.* Oxford: Oxford University Press.

Wood, R.Ll. (1987). *Brain injury rehabilitation: A neurobehavioural approach.* London: Croom Helm.

Wood, R.Ll. (1988). Management of behaviour disorders in a day treatment setting. *Journal of Head Trauma Rehabilitation, 3*, 53–62.

Wood, R.Ll. (1990). Conditioning procedures in brain injury rehabilitation. In R.Ll. Wood (Ed.), *Neurobehavioural sequelae of traumatic brain injury.* London: Taylor & Francis.

Wood, R.Ll., & Eames, P. (1981). Application of behaviour modification in the rehabilitation of traumatically brain injured patients. In G. Davey (Ed.), *Applications of conditioning theory.* London: Methuen.

Youngson, H.A., & Alderman, N. (1994). Fears of incontinence and its effects on a community based rehabilitation programme after severe brain injury: Successful remediation of escape behaviour using behaviour modification. *Brain Injury, 8*, 23–26.

CHAPTER TEN

Rehabilitation of the dysexecutive syndrome

J.J. Evans
Oliver Zangwill Centre for Neuropsychological Rehabilitation, Ely, UK

INTRODUCTION

The dysexecutive syndrome includes difficulties in problem solving, planning and organisation, self-monitoring, initiation, error correction, and behavioural regulation. In characterising this syndrome, Baddeley and Wilson (1988) drew on the work of Rylander (1939), who described how individuals who suffer damage to the frontal lobes have impairments in attention (being easily distracted), difficulties grasping the whole of a complicated state of affairs (an abstraction problem), and whilst they may be able to work along routine lines, they have difficulties in new situations. Baddeley (1986) coined the term dysexecutive syndrome as a replacement for the term "frontal lobe syndrome". He wanted to move away from an anatomically based description for a set of cognitive impairments, in favour of a common cognitive or functional link between the diverse set of problems that can occur after frontal lobe damage. He emphasised the importance of the underlying processes served by the frontal lobes, including that of the "central executive" component of the working memory model. Baddeley suggested that impairment in the central executive results in a "dysexecutive" syndrome.

ATTENTIONAL CONTROL AND PROBLEM SOLVING

Baddeley (1986) said that the concept of the central executive is similar to that of the supervisory attention system (SAS), described by Norman and Shallice (see Shallice, 1988). They discussed the control of action in terms of two levels of control: an automatic schema-driven level (involving a non-conscious automatic control process referred to as contention scheduling) and the more conscious level referred to in terms of the SAS. The SAS was described as being required in five different situations: those that involve (1) planning or decision making; (2) error correction or troubleshooting; (3) responses that are not well learned or where they contain novel sequences of actions; (4) dangerous or technically difficult decisions; and (5) situations that require the overcoming of a strong habitual response or resisting temptation. A task clearly illustrating the distinction between automatic and conscious control of action is driving a car. When learning to drive a car, co-ordinating a complex set of actions requires conscious attention, to the point that any distraction (e.g., somebody talking or the radio being on) can seriously impair functioning. However, with repetition, a level of skill develops such that most tasks can be carried out without conscious attention being required so that the driver can drive and hold a conversation, listen to the radio and so forth, without any significant impact on performance. Even for the skilled driver though, novel or at least unusual situations will arise that require conscious attention to action and some form of problem solving.

More recently, Shallice and Burgess (1996) have argued that the SAS can be fractionated into a set of basic subcomponents, or subprocesses, and present evidence (based on neuropsychological dissociations and functional brain imaging) for the fractionation. They argue that responding appropriately to novelty requires three processes, each of which consists of a further set of subprocesses. Within their model (see Shallice & Burgess, 1996, p. 1407) they posit the need for (1) a process that results in the creation of a temporary new schema (since routine behaviour is governed by existing schemas, novel behaviour will require the creation of a new schema), (2) a special-purpose working memory that is required for the implementation of the temporary new schema, and (3) a system that monitors, evaluates, and accepts or rejects actions depending upon their success in solving the novel problem.

Shallice and Burgess's model is essentially a detailed problem-solving framework relating closely to Luria's (1966) conception of problem-solving (which he also characterised as a major role of the frontal lobes), which includes the three phases of strategy selection, application of operations, and evaluation of outcomes. Each stage of the problem-solving framework requires the contribution of a number of underlying cognitive processes for effective functioning. Indeed, problem solving might be conceptualised as an emergent property of the co-ordinated interaction of more basic cognitive processes. For example, adequate attentional skills are required in order to notice that a problem exists. The ability to use existing episodic and semantic memory (see Dritschel et al., 1998) is required to identify potential actions. Effective working memory is required to hold in mind and evaluate potential solutions and evaluate an implemented solution. The role of mood and motivation must be considered in any assessment of a client's ability to solve problems. Low or anxious mood and poor motivation are common consequences of brain injury and inevitably have an impact on the probability of an individual effectively solving problems (Evans, Williams, O'Loughlin, & Howells 1992).

Shallice and Burgess (1996) argue that the subprocesses of the SAS dissociate. Patients with brain injury may have difficulty with one or more of the processes, whilst others remain intact. Clinically this is evident. For example, some patients appear to be aware that a problem exists, but have difficulty planning and evaluating potential solutions. Consequently the patient may respond to a problem with inappropriate (impulsive) actions. Indeed, impulsivity is a relatively common consequence of brain injury, particularly where the frontal lobes have been involved. The individual appears to "act without thinking", doing the first thing that comes to mind, failing to think of alternative solutions to a problem, and failing to anticipate the consequences of the chosen action.

This was particularly evident in one client who had suffered a severe head injury. He had made a relatively good recovery and was hoping to return to work as a senior manager in a financial services company. What became clear from formal testing and observation two years post-injury was that when he was prompted to use residual problem-solving skills he could be successful in dealing with novel problems. However, when not prompted he tended to act impulsively and make errors. In contrast, some patients are able to generate a plan, but an intention to act may not be translated into action (see case RP described by Evans, Emslie, & Wilson, 1998).

Problem solving seems to be dependent upon three broad processes. The first relates to the ability to notice or be aware that a problem exists, and to monitor and evaluate solution implementation (i.e., online monitoring). The second relates to the development of a plan of action (i.e., planning), whilst the third relates to the initiation of action (i.e., translation of intention into action). Impairments at any stage can cause devastating social handicaps, as described in the classic cases of Phineas Gage and patient EVR (Eslinger & Damasio, 1985). Similarly, the social impact of specific problems with planning and organisational skills is well illustrated by the cases described by Shallice and Burgess (1991) who, like EVR, have impaired executive ability and disastrously organised lives but adequate general intellectual ability. Patient RP (Evans et al., 1998) similarly showed adequate general intellectual and memory functioning but impaired attention and executive skills. As a consequence, RP was unable to translate intention into action, to plan ahead, and sustain attention whilst carrying out tasks. She was unable to work or effectively manage the household and required constant support and supervision from her husband, who had to give up his job to care for her. Crepeau and Schertzer (1993) provide further evidence of the social handicap caused by dysexecutive syndrome. They describe the results of a meta-analytic study of factors that predict return to work following traumatic brain injury, which showed that the presence of impairments in executive functioning was a significant factor predicting return to work.

KEY ISSUES IN ASSESSING DYSEXECUTIVE PROBLEMS

The lack of a widely accepted theory of executive functioning has limited the development of tests based on theoretical constructs. As a consequence, the main validation data for many tests is that impaired performance correlates with the presence of frontal lobe lesions. The emphasis has therefore been on detecting frontal pathology, rather than executive dysfunction *per se*. Furthermore, many of the so-called "frontal tests" are simply not sensitive to the everyday problems experienced by patients (see Powell & Wood, Chapter 4, this volume). As Shallice and Burgess (1991) noted, the problem with many traditional frontal lobe tests is that "the patient typically has a single explicit problem to tackle at any one time, the trials tend to be short …, task initiation is strongly prompted by the examiner and what constitutes successful trial completion is clearly characterised" (pp. 727–728). By contrast, most of life's everyday problems are relatively unpredictable, have more than one possible "correct" solution, and may require actions to be carried out over a long period of time. A further difficulty in assessing an individual's ability to solve a novel problem is that what is novel to one individual may be entirely routine for another.

It is proposed here that that a problem-solving framework provides a way of structuring assessment and rehabilitation. The cognitively intact individual does not of course respond to every novel situation in a slow, deliberate fashion, carefully planning the solutions to problems before implementing action. Depending on the nature of the problem, the process of problem solving might be very rapid, and the implemented solution may be subject to a series of revisions (via a trial, error, and error-correction sequence) as a monitoring process reveals that the implemented solution is not effective. Nevertheless the framework, and in particular the three processes (on-line monitoring, planning, and initiation) seen as underlying the various stages, provides a useful starting point for thinking about what we are actually trying to assess.

Wherever the process of problem solving breaks down, the consequence is essentially the same in that the individual fails to deal effectively with novel situations. However, if we are to use our understanding of a person's difficulties to guide our interventions we need to establish the nature of the impairment in terms of the stages in the process of problem solving. This point was made by Crepeau, Scherzer, Belleville, and Desmarais (1997), who demonstrated dissociations in impairments at different stages of the problem-solving process amongst a group of brain injured individuals. They used a four-stage model: (1) analysis of the problem, (2) formulation of a general solution, (3) planning of the specific stages, and (4) monitoring during execution. Unfortunately, the study was based on improvements on psychometric tests. When they tried to validate this approach by comparing performance on these tests with performance on a set of "real-life" photocopying tasks, designed to require the same stages of problems solving, there was little correlation. However, Crepeau et al. (p.160) noted: "The results thus strongly suggest that more attention should be directed to the assessment of the components of executive functions rather than relying on a global score ... [since] ... use of a single score may lead to the conclusion that the patient has little or no residual executive capacities when in fact only one of the components is disrupting the capacity. This is particularly important for rehabilitation as the identification of an individual's strength constitutes the first step towards the remediation of deficits in problem-solving."

Assessment can be conducted either at the level of the basic cognitive skills (e.g., attention, memory) or at the level of problem solving itself (e.g., by presenting specific problems to be solved, in the form of standardised psychometric tests or via more functional practical tasks). Individuals with impaired cognitive functions will fail to solve problems unless they compensate in some way for the impaired process. However, if there is minimal or no impairment of critical underlying specific processes, there may be an impairment in the co-ordinated use of these processes, so one must assess problem solving directly. Whilst assessment should be aimed at identifying which stage of problem solving is impaired, instead of trying to assess specific stages of problem solving with specific tests (as Crepeau and colleagues were attempting), it may be necessary to rely on a systematic analysis of how an individual's performance on more complex tests fails. Examples of such tasks include the Modified Six Elements and Zoo Map tasks from the Behavioural Assessment of the Dysexecutive Syndrome Battery (Wilson et al., 1996). Tasks such as these may be failed for a variety of reasons, but by analysing the similarities in performance (or errors) across the tests it is possible to establish at what stage the problem-solving process breaks down.

The ability to solve problems can also be assessed through the use of observation of the client in functional situations. The processes of noticing problems and translating intention into action are perhaps best assessed in such functional settings. Most standard tests present problems rather directly to the patient and prompt task completion, so there is little demand on the ability to "notice" or define the problem, nor to self-initiate task completion. The individual may not be aware that there is a gap between an intended goal (either self or externally generated) and the individual's ability to achieve that goal (i.e., not notice there is still a problem to be solved). In our centre we frequently use the task of planning and preparing an unfamiliar meal as an example of a complex task that requires at least some, and often a lot, of problem solving.

MANAGEMENT AND TREATMENT OF DYSEXECUTIVE PROBLEMS

Assessment should guide treatment, but helping patients with a dysexecutive syndrome is not an easy task. In 1982 Craine wrote "recognising and attempting specific remediation of frontal lobe dysfunction is of relatively recent origin, and has proved to be a rather difficult and frustrating task" (p. 239). This statement remains largely true today, although in the intervening years there have been a number of attempts at rehabilitating executive impairments, with varying degrees of success.

As with any area of cognitive rehabilitation, one of the key issues is whether interventions should be aimed at treating the executive impairment (i.e., restoring the lost function) or seeking to provide clients with strategies that enable them to compensate for the impairment. If both approaches were successful and required equal time, then it might not matter which approach was taken. However, at present there is little evidence for the effectiveness of either approach. The treatment approaches that have been tried can be divided into interventions that (1) explicitly aim to restore or retrain impaired executive functioning, (2) use internal or external aids or strategies, or (3) modify the environment to bring about a change in behaviour.

Interventions aimed at restoring or retraining impaired executive function

Evidence that executive dysfunction can be returned to normal is slim, if not non-existent. Placebo-controlled single-case studies of the drug Idazoxan (Sahakian, Coull, & Hodges 1994) in patients diagnosed with frontal lobe dementia are promising. However, it is not clear that frontal lobe dementia is a good model for non-progressive, single-event brain damage. Nevertheless, this work clearly needs expanding so that the potential benefit of pharmacological interventions is adequately assessed. Further work must also address the extent to which improvement of performance on specific tests of planning, such as those used in studies to date, generalises to everyday problem solving.

Retraining approaches to rehabilitation make the assumption that practising a particular cognitive function through tasks and exercises will enable that function to return, in a more or less normal fashion. For example, von Cramon, Matthes-von Cramon, and Mai (1991) and von Cramon and Matthes-von Cramon (1992) describe a group-based training programme described as "problem-solving therapy". Problem-solving therapy is seen as a retraining approach. However, it is debatable as to whether the treatment restores lost problem-solving skills or provides patients with a combination of internal and external strategies enabling them to achieve success in solving problems (i.e., the means of problem solving may be different from their pre-morbid style). This point may seem academic and perhaps the most important questions are: what does the treatment involve and does it work?

von Cramon and colleagues note that the broad aim of problem-solving therapy is to provide patients with "techniques enabling them to reduce the complexity of a multi-stage problem by breaking it down into more manageable portions. A slowed down, controlled and step wise processing of a given problem should replace the unsystematic and often rash approach these patients spontaneously prefer" (von

Cramon et al., 1991, p. 46). The therapy approach adopts a problem-solving framework that draws on the work of d'Zurilla and Goldfried (1971). The specific aims of the therapy are to enhance the patients' ability to perform each of the separate stages of problem solving, through practice on tasks that are designed to exercise the skills required for each of the separate stages. von Cramon and colleagues document examples of the exercises they use to enhance the ability to (1) identify and analyse problems, (2) separate information relevant to a problem solution from unimportant and irrelevant data, (3) recognise the relationship between different relevant items of information and if appropriate combine them, (4) produce ideas/solutions, (5) use different mental representations (e.g., verbal, visual, abstract patterns such as flow charts) in order to solve problems, and (6) monitor solution implementation and evaluate solutions.

To illustrate the type of training task used, exercises for working on the ability to separate information relevant to a problem from unimportant or irrelevant data include practice at formulating "wanted" small ads and telegrams, where the need for only including relevant information is at a premium. Practice at generating ideas is gained from tasks such as completing unfinished stories, for-and-against discussions of current affairs, and practice brainstorming sessions. Patients are encouraged to monitor solution implementation via the use of work books, and group activities where a patient is asked to be a co-therapist during a game (e.g., Mastermind), drawing other players' attention to mistakes, irregularities, and unnecessary moves. Therapy runs for a period of about six weeks with an average of 25 sessions. Each group involves four to six clients who initially work independently, but as soon as possible two clients work together on an assignment, with the division of labour being clearly explained. Finally, task-orientated groups are established in which each individual in the group takes on the responsibility for finding the solution to the part of a project (e.g., organising a visit to a museum in the city centre).

The question as to whether problem-solving therapy works has been addressed in one study. von Cramon et al. (1991) compared a group of patients who received problem-solving therapy ($n = 20$), with a group of patients who received a control memory therapy ($n = 17$). The control group allowed for the possibility that clients might benefit from general advice and group activity, rather than specifically from the tasks aimed at exercising executive skills. They showed that patients who underwent problem-solving therapy showed some improvement in tests of general intelligence and problem solving (Tower of Hanoi) compared with controls. von Cramon and colleagues demonstrated some generalisation of problem-solving skills to untrained test tasks but there was no evidence of generalisation to everyday situations. Evidence for the latter is hard to obtain because of measurement difficulties but it is clearly important that some evidence is obtained of generalisation to situations outside of formal test sessions (see Powell & Wood, Chapter 4, this volume). von Cramon and colleagues also noted that a small number of patients actually deteriorated on tests. They hypothesised that this was due to an increased awareness of the complexity of problems on the part of the patient, leading to confusion about how to respond. By contrast, such patients had a pre-treatment propensity towards premature or ill-considered actions, some of which would have been correct by chance.

Whether problem-solving therapy is a restoration or compensation rehabilitation approach remains a matter of debate. Furthermore, emphasis on training separate stages of the problem-solving process may make it difficult for some clients to develop an understanding of the whole process of problem solving. It could be argued that this is important for success, especially if the treatment works by providing patients with a structure or problem-solving routine to use when faced with a problem.

Internal strategies

A number of interventions aimed at helping clients with executive difficulties might be considered as "internal" strategies. Typically this means that the client is using a mental routine or self-instructional technique. Cicerone and Wood (1987) provide a good example of the use of the self-instructional technique in a 20-year-old man with a severe head injury. He was described as functioning relatively independently, but impulsively interrupted conversations and generally appeared not to think before he did something. They used the Tower of London Test as a training task, asking the client to state each move he was about to make while attempting to solve the problem and then to state the move while he performed it. In stage two the patient was asked to repeat the first stage except to whisper rather than speak aloud. Finally, in the third stage he was asked to "talk to himself" (i.e., to think through what he was doing). This approach was successful in improving performance on the trained task, but more importantly, there was generalisation to two other untrained tasks. In addition, with some generalisation training, there were improvements in general social behaviour, rated by independent raters. The main change brought about by this simple self-instructional technique was that it helped the patient to slow his approach to the task in hand and, in effect, develop a habit of thinking through his actions rather than responding impulsively.

As discussed earlier, the concepts of attention and executive functioning are inextricably linked, and attentional problems may underlie difficulties with problem solving at a number of different points in the process. Robertson et al. (1995) describe another self-instructional training method for sustained attention and unilateral neglect. Their rationale is that the system mediating sustained attention has an important modulating effect on the posterior spatial orienting system. In cases of persisting unilateral neglect it is hypothesised that there is a combination of deficits in both of these systems. Thus, if it is possible to improve sustained attention, this may have a knock-on effect on the orienting system and neglect may be reduced. The intervention was essentially a self-alerting technique to enhance sustained attention. Patients were assessed on tests of neglect, sustained attention, and control tasks (i.e., tests where performance was not expected to improve as a result of training). During the training procedure, individuals practised tasks that required sustained attention skills for successful completion. The rationale for the training was explained and whilst the patient carried out the task the trainer would rap sharply on the desk at unpredictable intervals (between 20 and 40 seconds) and say "attend" in a loud voice. After several repetitions, the patient was asked to say "attend" (or some other alerting statement) when the trainer rapped on the table. In the next step, patients were cued to rap the desk themselves and say "attend"; then the patient rapped the desk and said "attend" subvocally, and finally the patients were required simply to signal whenever they were mentally knocking the desk and saying "attend" to themselves. They were also given instructions about the usefulness of trying to apply this self-alerting strategy habitually in everyday life situations. Significant improvements were found on both neglect and vigilance tasks, with (as predicted) no changes on the control tests. It seems likely that this method works both by increasing the client's level of alertness or arousal and also by ensuring that the client frequently reviews what he or she is doing and keeps on task. The idea of patients developing a "checking routine" is an important aspect of the development of internal strategies for coping with problem-solving situations.

von Cramon and Matthes-von Cramon (1994) provide another example of an internalised external check-list routinely applied to compensate for executive deficits. They describe GL, a 33-year-old physician who had a traumatic brain injury at the age of 24, resulting in bilateral frontal lobe damage. Despite the injury, GL passed his medical exams post-injury (although after several failures). He was described as having "drifted" through several jobs in neurosurgery, pathology, and the pharmaceutical industry. His problems were characterised as involving a lack of overview and being dependent upon meticulous instructions. He was unable to benefit from feedback, spending too much time on routine activities and being unable to adapt himself to the requirements of novel or changing situations. In the study, a protected work trial was established in a hospital pathology lab and he was provided with prototypical reports on autopsy. It was noted that he tended to jump to conclusions about diagnosis and he was therefore taught a set of rules/guidelines for the systematic process of diagnosis. These rules were initially provided in the form of a written check-list, which, over time, GL learned and was able to apply without the need to refer to the check-list. GL improved his ability to diagnose correctly and to write reports. However, there was no generalisation to a novel planning task.

This study demonstrates that one approach to tackling executive impairments is to identify the specific tasks that patients need to be able to do, but which their executive deficits prevent them from doing. The patient is then supported in learning to perform the task. What starts off as a novel task requiring appropriate problem-solving skills becomes a routine task. The limitation of this approach is that there is unlikely to be generalisation to other problem-solving situations. Nevertheless this may be the most effective approach for situations where the client is attempting to achieve a major personal goal.

EXTERNAL AIDS

To-do lists and appointment diaries are used by most of us to support planning, organisation, and memory. One of the most effective rehabilitation approaches for clients with executive impairments (and of course memory impairments) is to help them make use of memory aids that are employed by a large portion of the non-brain injured population. This is often much easier to achieve with clients who have previously made use of such aids; others may be more reluctant to try. Burke, Zencius, Wesolowiski, and Doubleday (1991) describe six case studies where check-lists were used in order to help clients develop and carry out plans. For example, the case of a 38-year-old man who had problems with sequencing steps in a task, such as planing timber in the wood shop. Using a multiple baseline across tasks procedure, it was demonstrated that introduction of check-lists improved performance, which was maintained even after the check-lists were withdrawn. This suggests that, as for patient GL, the client had learned a task routine. Significantly, the client was also better at a task for which the check-list had not been introduced. The authors concluded that he was able spontaneously to generalise the use of a structured approach to the new situation. What was perhaps critical was the fact that the structured check-list approach was introduced not just for one task, but across a range of tasks in a systematic fashion, encouraging the client to learn both specific tasks and a general approach to new situations. The use of NeuroPage, an external alerting and reminding system, in the context of executive dysfunction is described later in this chapter.

ENVIRONMENTAL MODIFICATION

For some patients with executive impairment, the main opportunity to intervene may lie in changing some aspects of their environment (either the physical or social environment). Work with family, friends, and colleagues is important and might be considered an environmental modification approach. Helping relatives and carers to understand the nature of the client's executive difficulties can be extremely important in minimising negative responses to problems arising from a dysexecutive syndrome. For example, one of the hardest things for families to appreciate is that an initiation difficulty is not laziness. Another is that the person may remember some things and not others due to attentional problems rather than not bothering to remember. Thus education can have an important role in helping families both to understand and modify their own behaviour in relation to clients (for a case example see O'Brien, Prigatano, & Pittman, 1988). For some people, particularly those with very severe executive impairments or with a combination of executive and other difficulties, the use of retraining methods, internal or external aids may simply not be possible. Such individuals may be unable to deal with complexity, or severe learning difficulties may prevent them from making use of strategies. A combination of difficulties can result in problem behaviour such as aggressive or stereotyped behaviour, each of which may prevent the client from participating in other rehabilitation activities and cause significant disruption for family, friends, and carers. In this situation, it is often necessary to provide a highly structured environment with the opportunity for very frequent feedback in order to help clients to shape and modify their behaviour. The work of Alderman and colleagues (Alderman & Burgess, 1990, 1994; Alderman & Ward, 1991) illustrates the use of behaviour modification techniques, originally developed in the context of work with people with complex patterns of neurobehavioural disability which are relevant in the context of the combination of memory and executive impairments in this client group (see Chapter 9, this volume).

AN APPROACH TO REHABILITATION DERIVED FROM THE PROBLEM-SOLVING FRAMEWORK

A post-acute rehabilitation programme, delivered by a multidisciplinary team at the Oliver Zangwill Centre, uses both individual and group activities to improve problem-solving abilities. Clients attend the programme for 6–14 weeks full-time, followed by 6–14 weeks of community integration involving part-time attendance at the centre. The programme is based on a similar programme developed by Prigatano (1986) and aims to address cognitive, emotional, and physical problems within a highly integrated, or holistic approach (Wilson et al., 2000). The programme aims to help clients compensate for impairments in problem solving, rather than trying to restore lost functions. Although it is clear that there are different stages to the problem-solving process and these may be selectively impaired, it is usually not felt appropriate to focus separately on just one aspect of the process. In both individual and group work, a problem-solving framework is utilised, with the focus on the solving of "complete" problems. However, depending on the nature of a client's problems, different aspects of the framework and different strategies will be emphasised.

The treatment group, referred to as the attention and problem-solving (APS) group, is an adaptation of von Cramon's problem-solving therapy group and runs for about 8–10 weeks, depending on progress. The group runs twice a week, for about an hour. Each group member also has at least one additional individual session (of approximately 40 minutes per week) focusing on individual issues arising from the group. The first few sessions primarily address attentional difficulties and the later sessions are used to introduce the problem-solving framework to the clients. This framework is presented as a paper-based check-list (see Figure 10.1) with an accompanying template (see Figure 10.2), but clients are encouraged, through practice at using the framework with the template, to internalise the framework so that in time its use becomes automatic.

Although the group and individual work takes a "whole-problem" approach to work on problem solving, different stages in the process will be highlighted depending on the specific nature of an individual's difficulties.

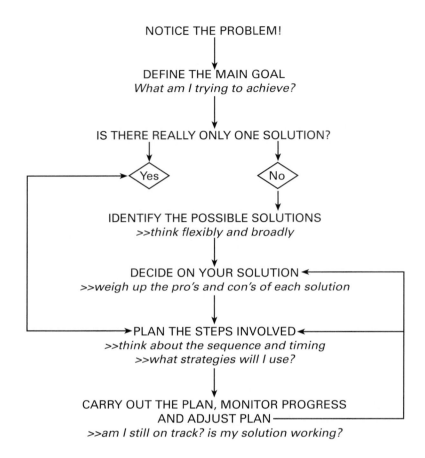

NOTICE THE PROBLEM!

DEFINE THE MAIN GOAL
What am I trying to achieve?

IS THERE REALLY ONLY ONE SOLUTION?

Yes   No

IDENTIFY THE POSSIBLE SOLUTIONS
>>think flexibly and broadly

DECIDE ON YOUR SOLUTION
>>weigh up the pro's and con's of each solution

PLAN THE STEPS INVOLVED
>>think about the sequence and timing
>>what strategies will I use?

CARRY OUT THE PLAN, MONITOR PROGRESS
AND ADJUST PLAN
>>am I still on track? is my solution working?

OVERALL EVALUATION
*>>was it a success, what went well, what went
badly?*

Figure 10.1.   The problem-solving and planning framework presented to clients in an attention and problem-solving group.

Problem awareness, monitoring, and evaluation. Many clients with difficulties in problem solving show some lack of awareness of their own difficulties and the way in which these affect everyday tasks. For many clients, early group work focuses on increasing ability to self-monitor, particularly (and perhaps ironically) for difficulties in attention and problem solving. Clients are given a self-monitoring sheet, which they are asked to complete on a daily basis. Staff also keep a monitoring sheet and the staff and client sheets are compared in an individual session with the

Date: ....

1. **Main goal** ———————————————

2. **If there is really only one obvious solution go to section 5 and plan the steps. If there is more than one possible solution go to section 3.**

3. *Alternative solutions*	*Pros*	*Cons*

4. **Decision** ———————————————

5. **Plan**

	Steps	Strategies	Done ✓ or ✗
1.			
2.			
3.			
4.			
5.			
6.			

Remember to monitor and evaluate! Are things going well? if not, do you need to change your plan?

Figure 10.2.   A template for use by clients to structure their problem solving.

client. Clients also attend a group called understanding brain injury, which aims to educate clients about the nature and the common consequences of brain injury in a way that promotes insight. Within the APS group there are also a series of games and tasks illustrating different types of attentional demand.

With a developing awareness of the nature of attention and problem-solving difficulties, the APS group focuses on specific strategies for managing attention, including managing the environment (e.g., reducing external distractions) and managing attentional demand by time management or task scheduling (e.g., doing one thing at a time, working in short bursts and the taking a break). Emphasis is placed on developing a mental checking routine (e.g., Am I doing what I should be? Am I on track? Do I still have my main goal in mind?). This might be facilitated through the use of an alarm (such as a watch alarm) sounding at intervals. This might be combined with a cue card containing the client's own self-monitoring statement.

Developing a plan.   Many clients have no difficulty in noticing that a problem exists, but may jump to hasty, and inappropriate solutions. Use of the problem-solving framework helps replace this impulsive response with a more effective one. In group sessions, clients practise using the problem-solving framework on both hypothetical and genuine problems from their own life. As with most group treatments, one of the most effective components is the discussion between clients of how they solve problems. Within sessions there may be specific practice at generating alternative solutions (illustrating to the clients the importance of divergent thinking) and weighing up the pros and cons of solutions. A key element of the process is not just identifying the stages of a plan, but the strategies required to ensure that the stages are completed. Clients are encouraged to think about strategies learned from other aspects of the programme (such as the use of external memory aids). This is illustrated in Figure 10.3, which shows a problem-solving framework template completed by a young head injured man (BC) in response to a hypothetical problem.

It is anticipated that practice with both hypothetical and "real-life" problems enables clients to internalise this structured approach to problem solving, and use it in everyday life. The client mentioned above noted, "I can use the framework in my head for small problems, but for bigger problems where my plan will take a while I have to write it down on the template otherwise I'll forget". The final group sessions involve planning and carrying out a half-day activity at the centre and then a full-day activity away from the centre. The group ends when clients become practised and proficient in using the framework, although clients are encouraged to use the framework throughout the rehabilitation programme.

Initiating action.   Patient RP, who was described earlier, is an illustration of someone who has difficulty translating intention into action (see Evans et al., 1998). She was distractible and had difficulty completing tasks. Despite adequate memory

Problem: You're in charge of organising transport for a youth football team. On Saturday they play 60 miles away. You usually go by bus. Kick off is at 3 p.m. It is Friday. Everyone knows to meet at your home football ground for 12 noon. The bus company phoned to say that all their drivers are on strike. What do you you?

Main Goal: To get to the football match.

Alternative solutions	Pros	Cons
Cancel game	Time to arrange alternative transport Extra practice and rest time	Arranging suitable time to play game to fit in with other games. Letting other people know before they leave, other team and fans.
Phone alternative bus company	Get to game. Won't let fans down. Should make it on time	Finding another bus company at short notice. Cost of using another company. Might be a bit late arriving at game.
Ask some of the playersif they can give lifts if they can drive.	Should get to the game on time. Save on bus hire	Getting enough cars. All cars knowing the way and not getting lost.
Play at own football pitch	Won't have to arrange transport	Other teams being able to get to football ground. Letting fans down.

Decision: Phone alternative bus company

Plan:

1. Find local yellow pages
2. Search through for bus and coach companies
3. Phone companies to get best deal
4. Choose bus company to use
5. Tell company to be at ground for 12 noon
6. Meet at football ground at 12 noon with everyone else and leave

Strategies: Use problem-solving framework, using breathing technique to relax when talking to bus company, write down details of bus companies and costs, use alarm on electronic organiser to remind me to be on time.

Remember: Monitor and Evaluate!

Figure 10.3.   Illustration of the use of a problem-solving framework template by a young head injured man (BC) for a hypothetical problem.

and intelligence, RP's combination of executive and attentional deficits had a significant impact on her level of functioning. Her husband reported that although she could accurately say what she had to do, she needed to be prompted to do many things (e.g., take her medication, go to her voluntary job). She was highly distractible (having set off to do one task she would be very frequently distracted by something else along the way and fail to return to the original task, and she took an excessive amount of time to get things done). There was also evidence of general organisation and planning difficulties so that she had great difficulty cooking a family meal. The intervention, used very successfully with RP, was a paging-based reminder system known as NeuroPage. This system was developed by Hersh and Treadgold (1994) and it was evaluated with a group of people with memory problems by Wilson, Evans, Emslie, and Malinek (1997). The system utilises radio paging technology and involves the patient wearing an alphanumeric pager. Reminders of things to do are entered onto a central computer using NeuroPage software. This automatically sends out the message via a modem to a paging company, which then sends out the message to the patient's pager, which bleeps and delivers a text message. In the case of RP this system was evaluated via a single-case experimental design demonstrating that it was highly effective in helping her to complete tasks she needed to do on time. Evans et al. (1998) noted that there appeared to be two important aspects to the success of the paging system. The first was the presentation of an external text message that appeared to be important for RP and prompted behaviour in a way that an internal intention to act failed to do. The second aspect was the bleeping of the pager, which provided an attentional boost to facilitate RP's initiation of tasks and help her sustain attention during task completion. If the latter element was the critical one, then it should be possible for RP to benefit from a simple alarm (e.g., watch alarm) delivering an alerting bleep at the right time. Use of such a tool was not attempted with RP, because she was reluctant to give up what had become a very effective aid. However, use of such alarms could be helpful for certain clients and be used in the development of mental checking routines described earlier.

For individuals with initiation or problem-solving difficulties, the learning of specific task routines via check-lists and so on is important. The establishment of daily routines can also be a means of enabling clients to function more effectively. In effect, a structure is being provided for the client, who is unable to cope in unstructured situations. One critical aspect of following daily routines is the transition from one part of a routine to another. It is at these times that clients are vulnerable to distraction and/or poor initiation, which may prevent maintenance of the routine. So when developing a routine, it is important to establish how the end of one part of a routine may act as a trigger for the next part.

Sometimes difficulty translating intention into action is not so much an initiation problem than a failure of prospective remembering. Where a plan of action to solve a problem involves steps that take place over several hours, days, or weeks, it is possible that individuals will fail to carry out the necessary action at the correct time (because, for example, they fail to notice that the time to act has arrived, or fail to recall what action is required). A straightforward, but essential part of the process of training clients to use a problem-solving framework, is to ensure they plan just how they will remember to carry out the steps. Often this means that there is a need to use memory aids.

CONCLUSIONS

The prospects for developing better rehabilitation techniques for dysexecutive problems are good. Progress is dependent upon advances being made in the theoretical understanding, modelling, and assessment of executive functioning. The term dysexecutive syndrome is likely to become redundant as evidence emerges for the cognitive and anatomical fractionation of the syndrome. More sophisticated assessment needs to identify deficits in specific processes, although this will not necessarily be done through process-specific tests. As has been argued earlier, impairments may only be revealed in complex test situations (i.e., novel multistage tasks). In this situation identifying deficits is dependent upon careful analysis of patterns of results across tests. Virtual reality technology may have a role to play in the construction of tasks that are sufficiently like the complex everyday situations that people find themselves in, whilst maintaining sufficient control to be able to compare one individual's performance with another.

There is only a handful of well-controlled intervention studies in the literature that have examined the efficacy of interventions for executive dysfunction. More are needed. The role of pharmacological interventions remains to be clarified. Robertson and Murre (1999) raise the tantalising prospect of cognitive interventions targeted at rescuing partially damaged neural circuits. Whether this can be done for complex executive processes dependent upon disparate neural circuits or only for highly specialised functions associated with discrete brain regions remains to be seen. Functional imaging (PET and fMRI) could have an important role in helping us understand what changes as a result of interventions: brain or only behaviour. For many patients any form of restoration of function will be unrealistic. Compensatory approaches will always be a necessary element of rehabilitation of executive deficits. Whether through restoration or compensation techniques, we must improve the targeting of our interventions. However, in devising treatments that are better targeted at areas of deficit, we must be careful to ensure that those interventions bring about changes that are meaningful to those for whom they are designed. The allure of designing impairment-specific treatments is great, but if we are not helping people to function independently, obtain or sustain work or maintain personal relationships, then our efforts are likely to be wasted.

REFERENCES

Alderman, N., & Burgess, P.W. (1990). Integrating cognition and behaviour: A pragmatic approach to brain injury rehabilitation. In R.Ll. Wood & I. Fussey (Eds.), *Cognitive rehabilitation in perspective* (pp. 204–228). London: Taylor & Francis.

Alderman, N., & Burgess, P. (1994). A comparison of treatment methods for behaviour disorder following herpes simplex encephalitis. *Neuropsychological Rehabilitation, 4*, 31–48.

Alderman, N., & Ward, A. (1991). Behavioural treatment of the dysexecutive syndrome: Reduction of repetitive speech using response cost and cognitive overlearning. *Neuropsychological Rehabilitation, 1*, 65–80.

Baddeley, A.D. (1986). *Working memory*. Oxford: Oxford University Press.

Baddeley, A.D., & Wilson, B.A. (1988). Frontal amnesia and the dysexecutive syndrome. *Brain and Cognition, 7*, 212–230.

Burke, W.H., Zencius, A.H., Wesolowski, M.D., & Doubleday, F. (1991). Improving executive function disorders in brain injured clients. *Brain Injury, 5*, 241–252.

Cicerone, K.D., & Wood, J.C. (1987). Planning disorder after closed head injury: A case study. *Archives of Physical Medicine and Rehabilitation, 68*, 111–115.

Craine, J.F. (1982). The retraining of frontal lobe dysfunction. In L. Trexler (Ed.), *Cognitive rehabilitation: Conceptualisation and intervention* (pp. 239–262). New York: Plenum.

Crepeau, F., & Scherzer, P. (1993). Predictors and indicators of work status after traumatic brain injury: A meta analysis. *Neuropsychological Rehabilitation, 3*, 5–35.

Crepeau, F., Scherzer, P., Belleville, S., & Desmarais, G. (1997). A qualitative analysis of central executive disorders in a real-life work situation. *Neuropsychological Rehabilitation, 7*, 147–165.

Dritschel, B.H., Kogan, L., Burton, A., Burton, E., & Goddard, L. (1998). Everyday planning difficulties following brain injury: A role for autobiographical memory. *Brain Injury, 12*, 875–886.

d'Zurilla, T.J., & Goldfried, M.R. (1971). Problem-solving and behaviour modification. *Journal of Abnormal Psychology, 78*, 107–126.

Eslinger, P.J., & Damasio, A.R. (1985). Severe disturbance of higher cognition after bilateral frontal lobe ablation: Patient EVR. *Neurology, Cleveland, 35*, 1731–1741.

Evans, J.J., Emslie, H., & Wilson, B.A. (1998). External cueing systems in the rehabilitation of executive impairments of action. *Journal of the International Neuropsychological Society, 4*, 399–408.

Evans, J., Williams, J.M.G., O'Loughlin, S., & Howells, K. (1992). Autobiographical memory and problem solving strategies in parasuicidal patients. *Psychological Medicine, 22*, 399–405.

Hersh, N., & Treadgold, L. (1994). Prosthetic memory and cueing for survivors of traumatic brain injury. Unpublished report obtainable from Interactive Proactive Mnemonic Systems, 6657 Camelia Drive, San Jose, California.

Luria, A.R. (1966). *Human brain and psychological processes*. New York: Harper and Row.

O'Brian, K.P., Prigatano, G.P., & Pittman, H.W. (1988). Neurobehavioural education of a patient and spouse following right frontal oligodendroglioma excision. *Neuropsychology, 2*, 145–159.

Prigatano, G. (1986). *Neuropsychological rehabilitation after brain injury*. Baltimore: Johns Hopkins University Press.

Robertson, J.H., & Murre, J. (1999). Rehabilitation of brain damage: Brain plasticity and principles of guided recovery. *Psychological Bulletin, 125*(5),

Robertson, I.H., Tegner, R., Tham, K., Lo, A., & Nimmo-Smith, I. (1995). Sustained attention training for unilateral neglect: Theoretical and rehabilitation implications. *Journal of Clinical and Experimental Neuropsychology, 17*, 416–430.

Rylander, G. (1939). Personality changes after operations on the frontal lobes. *Acta Psychiatrica et Neurologica,* Supplementum XX. Copenhagen: Ejnar Munksgaard.

Sahakian, B.J., Coull, J.J., & Hodges, J.R. (1994). Selective enhancement of executive function in a patient with dementia of the frontal lobe type. *Journal of Neurology, Neurosurgery and Psychiatry, 57,* 120–121.

Shallice, T. (1988). *From neuropsychology to mental structure.* Cambridge: Cambridge University Press.

Shallice, T., & Burgess, P. (1991). Deficits in strategy application following frontal lobe damage in man. *Brain, 144,* 727–741.

Shallice, T., & Burgess, P. (1996). The domain of the supervisory process and temporal organisation of behaviour. *Philosphical Transactions: Biological Sciences, 351,* 1405–1412.

von Cramon, D., & Matthes-von Cramon, G. (1992). Reflections on the treatment of brain injured patients suffering from problem-solving disorders. *Neuropsychological Rehabilitation, 2,* 207–230.

von Cramon, D., & Matthes-von Cramon, G. (1994). Back to work with a chronic dysexecutive syndrome? (A case report). *Neuropsychological Rehabilitation, 4,* 399–417.

von Cramon, D., Matthes-von Cramon, G., & Mai, N. (1991) Problem-solving deficits in brain injured patients: A therapeutic approach. *Neuropsychological Rehabilitation, 1,* 45–64.

Wilson, B.A., Alderman, N., Burgess, P., Emslie, H., & Evans, J.J. (1996). *The behavioural assessment of the dysexecutive syndrome.* Flempton: Thames Valley Test Company.

Wilson, B.A., Evans, J.J., Emslie, H., & Malinek, V. (1997). Evaluation of NeuroPage: A new memory aid. *Journal of Neurology, Neurosurgery and Psychiatry, 63,* 113–115.

Wilson, B.A., Evans, J.J., Brentnall, S., Bremner, S., Keohane, C., & Williams, W.H. (2000). The Oliver Zangwill Centre for Neuropsychological Rehabilitation: A partnership between health care and rehabilitation research. In A.-L. Christensen & B.P. Uzzell (Eds.), *International handbook of neuropsychological rehabilitation* (pp. 231–246). New York: Kluwer Academic/Plenum Publishers.

PART THREE

Models of service delivery

CHAPTER ELEVEN

The effectiveness of neurorehabilitation

G.M. Giles
Crestwood Behavioral Health Inc.,
and Samuel Merritt College, Oakland, CA, USA

INTRODUCTION

Traumatic brain injury (TBI) is the leading cause of death for citizens of the US under the age of 45. There are 56,000 deaths and 373,000 hospital admissions annually, 99,000 of which result from moderate to severe brain injury. Annual costs associated with TBI in the US are estimated to be over $25 billion. The majority of the costs are paid for by taxpayers. Individual lifetime costs can exceed $4 million (Brooks, Lindstrom, McCray, & Whiteneck, 1995). Improved early medical management has improved outcome following severe traumatic brain injury (Baxt & Moody, 1987) but evidence for positive effects of treatment after acute medical rescue has been difficult to obtain. Central questions for those involved in rehabilitation should be: (1) Is rehabilitation effective? and (2) Do the benefits outweigh the costs?

Although post-acute rehabilitation is strongly advocated by practitioners, many equally fervently held beliefs have proved erroneous when subjected to rigorous scrutiny. The efficacy of TBI rehabilitation is particularly difficult to establish because of:

1. The nature of the injury.
2. The nature of recovery.
3. The diversity of the patient's problems.
4. Ethical considerations.

As a result, all of the available studies that address TBI rehabilitation have been methodologically limited and their findings must be interpreted with care.

In the US a number of factors, including the growth of managed care, have led to significantly increased scrutiny of TBI rehabilitation in general and post-acute service provision in particular (Committee on Government Operations, 1992; Giles, 1994). Long-standing pessimism regarding TBI rehabilitation amongst medical professionals further jeopardises the acceptance of social rehabilitation by third party payers and statutory agencies (see Eazell, Chapter 12).

Given the limitations on resources it is neither practical nor ethical to ignore the efficiency and cost of services. Consequently, this chapter reviews evidence for the effectiveness of TBI rehabilitation, at the acute and post-acute stages of recovery, by examining published studies that predominately concern TBI. Single-case and small series designs are included if they highlight an "active ingredient" of treatment or provide collateral support on key issues in studies that comprise a large cohort, but are methodologically weak. Evidence for the effectiveness of social rehabilitation is discussed in relation to cognitive impairment, challenging behaviour, and community integration. Problems in the interpretation of findings are discussed. Due to space limitations discussion of vocational rehabilitation is omitted.

THE EFFECTIVENESS OF ACUTE REHABILITATION SERVICES

Acute rehabilitative services are provided in a hospital setting following emergence from coma and medical stabilisation. Treatment planning is usually led by a physician and follows a multidisciplinary model. Rehabilitation in this setting is expensive and therefore cost-effectiveness must be compared to clinical outcomes. Many studies indicate that exposure to acute rehabilitative intervention following brain injury leads to functional improvement (Carey, Seibert, & Posavac, 1988; Heinemann et al., 1990). Carey et al. examined the functional gains made by 6194 general rehabilitation inpatients (TBI, cerebrovascular accident, orthopaedic, etc.) at 22 rehabilitation facilities and found that patients with TBI made the largest functional gains of any disability group. Other descriptive pre-test post-test design studies have found that patients in multidisciplinary acute rehabilitation programmes show improvements in multiple areas of functioning (Sahgal & Heinemann, 1989) and that these gains are maintained at follow-up (Carey et al., 1988; Heinemann et al., 1990). The design of these studies does not allow the attribution of improvement to specific programme elements or distinction between changes caused by therapy or spontaneous recovery. However, early admission to rehabilitation and higher pre-morbid educational attainment were correlated with improved outcome within the study populations.

In a retrospective study, Putnam and Adams (1992) examined 100 randomly selected persons with severe TBI served by a no-fault serious injury claims office in Michigan. The study was unique because only patients deemed to be "catastrophically" injured by the insurance carrier were included and because there was no financial limit on rehabilitation. Unfortunately, severity of injury was confounded with expenditure, meaning that patients who received the most treatment also were the most impaired, making it difficult to evaluate the effectiveness of treatment. As might be expected, the most severely injured persons received the most treatment. Despite this, the amount of physical therapy (PT), occupational therapy (OT), and speech therapy (ST) provided to patients was correlated with the degree of functional independence at discharge.

Although not a study of rehabilitation *per se*, Wade et al. (1998) report a prospective randomised control trial of psychological and educational support services offered to patients admitted to hospital for head injury. All adults ($N = 314$) admitted to hospital after a head injury of any severity were prospectively randomised into a trial group who received additional support services provided by a specialist team ($N = 184$) or a group who received the standard hospital management and no specialist follow-up services. Patients were assessed six months after discharge using the Rivermead Head Injury Follow Up Questionnaire (Crawford, Wenden, & Wade, 1996) and the Rivermead Post-Concussion Symptoms Questionnaire (King et al., 1995), providing measures of social disability and post-concussion symptoms, respectively. Each patient in the trial group was contacted 7–10 days after injury and offered assessment, information, support, and advice as needed. Forty-six percent of the trial group also received further outpatient intervention. At 6-month follow-up the trial group had significantly less social disability and significantly fewer severe post-concussion symptoms than the control group. The majority of patients were in the mild to moderate severity categories (73%) and post-traumatic amnesia (PTA) exceeded 7 days in only 10% of cases. The main benefit of treatment may have been in minimising the effect of a vicious cycle of anxiety exacerbating post-concussion symptoms and vice versa. The more severely injured patients appear not to have benefited from the service.

The timing of rehabilitation is another important consideration. Cope and Hall (1982) retrospectively studied patients with severe TBI in an acute rehabilitation setting and divided a total of 36 cases into early and late rehabilitation admission groups (admitted before and after 35 days post-injury). Two groups of 16 and 20 patients were matched for length of coma, age, level of disability, and neurosurgical intervention. Late-admission patients required twice as much time in rehabilitation to reach standard discharge criteria as the early-admission group. Outcome was comparable at 2-year follow-up. It is not clear why the late group were not admitted to rehabilitation earlier (Cope & Hall, 1982) but obviously the reasons for this may have affected outcome.

Spettell et al. (1991) found that severity of TBI predicted both duration of rehabilitation stay and outcome (as measured by the Glasgow Outcome Scale, GOS). However, duration of acute hospital stay was superior to severity of TBI alone in predicting duration of rehabilitation. Spetell et al. suggest that it is the combination of TBI severity and severity of multiple trauma that predict the length of inpatient rehabilitation. These findings suggest a possible reinterpretation of the results of Cope and Hall (1982) because severity of TBI, combined with severity of non-brain injuries and medical complications, influence both length of acute hospitalisation (and consequently the timing of rehabilitation admission) as well as the duration of rehabilitation, whereas at the 2-year follow-up stage, only severity of TBI influences outcome (Cope & Hall, 1982; Spettell et al., 1991). In a study of 27,699 patients of mixed diagnosis undergoing initial rehabilitation Heinemann et al. (1994) suggested that patients who are transferred to rehabilitation more promptly may be relatively healthier and have fewer complications and therefore be ready to tolerate and benefit from comprehensive inpatient rehabilitation.

Tuel et al. (1992) retrospectively examined the records of 49 patients with severe TBI readmitted to an inpatient rehabilitation facility more than 12 months post-injury. Pre- and post-rehabilitation Barthel Index scores (Mahoney & Barthel, 1965) revealed improvement in 53% of patients. Gains were highly correlated with length of readmission but not with patient age, length of coma, time since injury, or the duration of any previous rehabilitation. Patients with mid-range admission Bartel index scores (21–85) demonstrated the largest gains.

Consideration must also be given to whether specialised rehabilitation is more effective than traditional forms of treatment. Rehabilitation outcome studies have mainly addressed the external parameters of treatment, such as hospital or community based (Willer, Button, & Rempel, 1999), early or late, intensity of treatment (Blackerby, 1990), or length of treatment (McLaughlin & Peters, 1993). In a rare attempt to examine the influence of the type of acute rehabilitation on the outcome of severe brain injury Mackay et al. (1992) compared outcome in 21 patients from 10 different hospitals with no formal TBI programme (TBI-NF) to that of 17 patients who received a formal TBI programme (TBI-F). Criteria for inclusion in the study were a Glasgow Coma Scale (GCS) score of 3–8 indicating severe TBI and discharge from the same rehabilitation facility. Injury Severity Score (ISS), Rancho Los Amigos Scale (RLAS; Hagen, Malkamus, & Durham, 1977), and GCS score did not differ between the two groups. The TBI-F group differed from the TBI-NF group in that the former received OT, PT, and ST, and were involved in structured multisensory stimulation to increase motor and cognitive skills. Outcome data for the two programmes revealed a 33% drop in the duration of coma and length of rehabilitation in the TBI-F group compared to the TBI-NF group. Cognitive outcome was superior in the TBI-F group, resulting in more discharges to home rather than extended care facilities.

These results suggest that an early formal programme significantly reduces morbidity. However, this finding depends on treating coma duration as a dependent variable and not regarding it as evidence of failure to establish comparable samples. GCS scores are available shortly after injury. However, coma duration may be a more sensitive measure of injury. If we assume no treatment effect then the outcomes are readily explainable as a result of the more extended period of coma of the TBI-NF group.

Blackerby (1990) examined treatment intensity versus length of stay for patients in a coma stimulation programme and patients in acute rehabilitation at two hospitals. Service delivery models at the hospitals changed from providing 5 hours to 8 hours of therapy per day. There was an associated decrease in length of stay; this was clearly evident in three of the programmes and marginal at the fourth programme. No real evidence is offered that length of stay is an isolated dependent variable and so the study is difficult to interpret. Other factors such as more focused goal setting or more intensive family training might have led to reduced treatment duration irrespective of the number of hours of therapy.

McLaughlin and Peters (1993) investigated the cost-effectiveness of a "step up" programme in which highly functional patients spend the later weeks of their inpatient stay in a transitional living setting. The step up programme was compared to a conventional inpatient programme. Costs were calculated using hospital daily charges. Patients' cognitive status was measured using the Rancho Los Amigos Scale and functional status by the Bartel Index. At discharge both groups were rated the same for cognitive status but the step up patients were rated as more functionally independent than the patients in the conventional programme. The authors concluded that the transitional living scheme was more cost-effective than the conventional programme. However, the sample size was too small to detect statistically significant results.

There is general agreement across studies that skills acquired at the acute stage of rehabilitation are durable (Ashley, Persel, Clark, & Krych, 1997; Carey et al., 1988; Heinemann et al., 1990). However, Cifu et al. (1999) found a 20–22.5% annual re-hospitalisation rate during the first, second and third years following TBI in patients treated at four medical centres in the federally funded Traumatic Brain Injury Model Systems. Approximately half of the re-hospitalisations were for elective reasons (such as for orthopaedic or reconstructive surgery). However, the frequency of readmission for seizure disorder and psychiatric problems did increase annually over the 3-year follow up period.

POST-ACUTE REHABILITATION

Programmes for cognitive impairments

Prigatano et al. (1984) described the effects of 6 months of intensive post-acute rehabilitation for severely traumatically brain injured young adults (coma duration was assessed retrospectively but was a minimum of 24 hours and a maximum of "several weeks") (mean time post-injury 21.6 months). The study consisted of a comparison of 18 treated patients and 17 untreated controls. The treatment group showed a slightly greater improvement over controls on neuropsychological measures. Psychosocial adjustment was substantially improved in the treatment group versus the controls. In their discussion the authors suggest that the patients most likely to benefit are those with problems in coping with disability, and with a good work history prior to brain injury. Patients with residual impairments, who can be taught strategies to overcome their problems, make the best candidates for rehabilitation (Prigatano et al., 1984).

Fryer and Haffey (1987) compared the effects of an outpatient cognitive rehabilitation programme and a residential programme designed to help patients redevelop domestic and community activities of daily living skills (ADL). The outpatient cognitive retraining programme is reviewed here and the residential programme is described below. The cognitive retraining programme drew inspiration from Luria's functional systems approach. The underlying assumptions were that the social behaviours necessary to achieve community re-adaptation were dependent on a hierarchy of cognitive skills and that a training programme to improve attention, perceptual discrimination, information integration and retrieval, and executive control would result in community re-adaptation. The treatment group comprised 18 persons with TBI with a mean age of 29.8 years and a mean coma duration of 29 days (range 2–180 days). The majority of patients had a coma duration of less than one week. The training programme consisted of 30 sessions over a 10-week period (the average session lasting 40 minutes). The purpose of training was to achieve the cognitive performance thought necessary to support community re-adaptation. Outcome was measured using the Disability Rating Scale (DRS; Rappaport et al., 1982) and an unpublished rating scale. Patients were divided into success and non-success groups based on achieving a criterion level by the end of the programme. Follow-up data were gathered at one year post-discharge.

There was a strong relationship between achieving criterion, particularly in executive functioning, with disability rating at follow-up. Both severity of injury and severity of disability at admission predicted both response to the programme and community re-adaptation. Spontaneous recovery was also clearly involved in the recovery of function, with the mean time between onset and treatment for the nine patients who achieved community re-adaptation being 12.7 months (SD = 1.1 months, range 12–15 months), while the time for the non-success group averaged 28.0 months (SD = 18.6). The outcome of this study led the authors to re-examine the appropriateness of the model for the most severely impaired patients.

Ruff et al. (1989) describe the first study to compare "neuropsychological" treatment with a non-structured treatment which controlled for equivalent professional attention and psychosocial support. Forty subjects with moderate to severe TBI at least one year post-injury were randomly assigned to the treatment or control protocol. Every patient received 160 hours of input over an 8-week period. The neuropsychological treatment included computer-assisted training modules on selective attention, spatial integration, memory, and problem solving. The control treatment included supported group therapy, computer games, coping skills training and didactic exercises and work book sessions on daily living skills and recreational activities. Comparison of pre- and post-treatment data on cognitive functioning demonstrated that both groups showed significant improvement. The fact that all participants were one year post-injury and the incorporation of an 8-week baseline period suggested that the change was unlikely to be a result of spontaneous recovery. However, there was no significant difference between the improvement of the treatment and the control group.

This study is methodologically superior to that of Prigatano et al. (1984) in that the control group received a comparable amount of attention and staff contact. This is of interest because it is important to attempt to establish what it is about treatment that is helpful. If the effect is generated by staff helping the patient focus attention on his or her problems, non-specific support or encouragement to change habits, or to expose themselves to new experiences, then these elements could be included in a relatively low-cost programme with only limited involvement of high-cost staff. Interestingly, the level of improvement described by Ruff et al. and Prigatano et al. appear comparable, despite the much shorter treatment duration described by Ruff et al.

Scherzer (1986) reported the results of a programme of cognitive retraining following the model of Yehuda Ben-Yishay (Ben-Yishay & Diller, 1981). Patients were aged 16–60 years (average 27 years), were at least a year post-injury at intake evaluation (average time post-coma was 59 months), and had an average coma duration of 46 days. Treatment lasted for 30 weeks and consisted of cognitive retraining; basic attention and orientation, memory exercises, visuomotor co-ordination and visual information processing, verbal comprehension, communication, and reasoning skills. The content served as a vehicle for the transmission of strategies. The strategies were intended to have practical value in everyday life. In addition to the cognitive retraining, participants were provided with problem-solving training, personal counselling, relaxation, physical exercise, and prevocational training and were involved in weekly therapeutic community and social skills groups. The author reported that patients showed improvement in tests of attention, visual information processing, memory, and complex reasoning, whereas verbal IQ and academic skills did not improve. Unfortunately, many of the tests used to assess outcome were also used as training tasks so improvement might have resulted from practice effects. It was not possible to establish functional gains that corresponded to the cognitive improvements (Scherzer, 1986).

Mills, Nesbeda, Katz, and Alexander (1992) reported the functional outcome of 42 persons with TBI (average coma duration 22 days, range 0–90 days, SD = 39 days) following outpatient cognitive rehabilitation. Mean time post-injury was 50.3 months (range 6–403, SD = 73). The programme consisted of a minimum of 6 weeks treatment and emphasised psychological support and the development of practical skills. The functional evaluations focused on a range of skills such as use of public transportation, self-care, leisure, and money management skills. Treatment goals were individually established; examples include "establish the use of a time planner as a memory aid of daily activities" and "speak slowly and clearly so that others can understand". Improvement was measured by the extent to which the patients met their pre-established goals and on cognitive measures. There was improvement in the functional measures after treatment but no change in cognitive functioning over baseline. Functional improvement was independent of age, injury severity, and time post-injury (however, pre-morbid educational accomplishment predicted better outcome). Follow-up at 6, 12, and 18 months showed that the majority of patients maintained or improved their functional status, with vocational status showing the greatest risk of deterioration. No information is provided regarding the theoretical models used. However, there is no mention of learning theory, so a behavioural approach to skill development does not appear to have been adopted. It would be interesting to know how structured and consistent the retraining programmes were.

Programmes for challenging behaviour

Eames and Wood (1985a, b) described the first use of a token economy for patients with severe TBI. The patients' disturbed behaviours prevented them from benefiting from standard therapy to reduce physical, behavioural, and functional skills deficits. The methods used are similar to those used in the management of severe behaviour disorders in other populations, but had not been previously used with this population. Treatment was based on positive reinforcement of appropriate behaviours (social reinforcement, attention, and praise plus tangible reinforcement, e.g., chocolate, soft drinks, or privileges). To avoid reinforcing inappropriate behaviour by social interaction a "time-out-on-the-spot" (TOOTS) procedure was used. TOOTS is an extinction method based on removing from the subject the opportunity of gaining positive reinforcement contingent upon the subject producing an unwanted behaviour and is adapted from the behavioural procedure of time-out (Giles & Clark-Wilson, 1999; Ullmann & Krasner, 1969). Episodes of physical aggression led to time-out for 5 minutes in a time-out room. Patients were taught positive behaviour and skills to increase their performance and quality of life.

A follow-up study examined 24 patients treated consecutively on this unit. Mean interval between injury and admission to the unit was 4 years, and the condition of all patients on admission was considered static. Time since discharge ranged from 6 to 39 months (mean 18 months). The principal outcome measure used was a hierarchical scale of placements ranked in terms of quality of life for the patient (Eames & Wood, 1985a). Study results demonstrated durable improvement in patient behaviour and subsequent placement.

Burke, Wesolowski, and Guth (1988) described the outcome of a specialised programme for individuals with behavioural or emotional disturbances following brain injury. Outcome data from 44 clients discharged from the programme during one year were analysed. Clients were generally single males between the ages of 18 and 25 years, injured in motor vehicle accidents with coma duration of over 6 weeks. The clients were post-acute and were admitted more than 4 years post-injury. Average length of stay was 204 days. The general philosophy of the programme was applied behavioural analysis—similar to that of Eames and Wood but with the addition of vocational training. Following treatment 69% of clients were placed in a less restrictive setting and 67% were in some type of employment. At 3–12-month follow-up 59% of the clients continued to live in the community and 50%

maintained employment. The client population is unusually homogeneous in terms of severity of injury (all clients were severely injured) and acuity (all patients were post-acute). Gains were of similar magnitude irrespective of injury severity and chronicity.

Eames et al. (1995) describe the results of intensive long-term behaviourally focused intervention for 55 adults with TBI. Patients were treated at a single programme specialising in the rehabilitation of individuals with severe disorders of social behaviour. Of 77 patients who completed rehabilitation 55 agreed to follow-up. Patients treated had severe behaviour disorder and all had sustained extremely severe TBI as indicated by coma duration (mean 5.2 weeks, range 0.14–52, SD = 8.3). Mean length of time from injury to admission was over 41 months (range 1–180, SD = 47.9, median 20). Mean length of stay was 11.0 months (range 1.3–33.9, SD = 8.17, median 9.3). Follow-up consisted of a factual interview to elicit information such as placement, amount of supervision, advice and help required, employment, social activities, and residual behaviour and cognitive problems. The primary outcome measure was a placement hierarchy of gradated levels based on the resident's placement and the supervisory needs. Outcome indicated that 63% of patients had improved placements on discharge and in 40% of cases the discharge placements were considerably improved. Outcome of the patients who were admitted within the first year post-injury were better than outcome of those admitted after one year. This early group also had shorter coma duration. However, long delays between injury and treatment were still compatible with worthwhile achievements in independence.

Wood, McCrea, Wood, and Merriman (1999) report a community-based programme, treating patients who were more severely impaired than persons typically treated in community programmes in the US. This report (and the programme it describes) therefore occupies an intermediate position between the reports of behaviour disorder programmes and community integration programmes. The authors attempted to assess both the clinical and cost-effectiveness of intervention with a group of 76 individuals treated at various sites who underwent social rehabilitation for a minimum of 6 months and in whom cognitive and behavioural problems had previously prevented community living. Most of the participants were young adults (average age 27), were 12 months or more post-injury and most were injured in motor vehicle accidents with a mean PTA of 23.5 days (SD = 41.2, range 3–168). Pre-admission, discharge, and follow-up data, the latter obtained from telephone interview, were analysed. Clients were divided into three groups according to time from injury to admission: group 1, 0–2 years ($n =$ 18), group 2, 2–5 years ($n = 30$), and group 3, 5 years or more ($n = 28$). Interventions were neurobehavioural, and used both behavioural and cognitive–behavioural approaches. Programmes were led by psychologists, included other licensed healthcare workers but relied heavily on facility-trained care workers. Outcome was assessed by examining changes in living situation, employment status, hours of care, persistence and intrusiveness of neurobehavioural problems, and projected cost of care. Consistent with other studies using a one-year cut-off for early versus late rehabilitation more improvement was found in all outcome measures for the early admission group, and the least improvement was found in the 5-year plus group. None the less, group 3 showed significant reduction in disability and cost projections. There was significant reduction in the percentage of clients in high-dependency living situations. Over 60% of clients were in some type of vocational or educational placement post-rehabilitation, in contrast to 4% prior to rehabilitation. Behaviour problems were reduced in frequency and severity although 13.6% of clients continued to have problems that made it difficult to retain in-home support workers. Many clients continued to improve after discharge and so were performing more independently at follow-up than at the time of discharge. Wood et al. (1999) concluded that community-oriented neurobehavioural intervention is effective in ameliorating the social and behavioural skills deficits of patients with TBI. The most benefit was obtained by those admitted 2 years or less post-injury but it was suggested that those 5 years or more post-injury may benefit. The authors noted that the deficits of the very severely injured group were often not evident early after emerging from coma and typically became evident by one year post-injury. This report is notable in that the group of patients treated were very severely injured and severely impaired, were significantly post-acute, showed considerable improvement, and the improvement continued post discharge (Wood et al., 1999).

Programmes for community reintegration

Fryer and Haffey (1987) described a residential programme to help patients redevelop domestic and community ADL skills. The focus of the intervention was to increase patient competency in task performance rather than to improve cognitive skills. The programme used a residential community re-entry model and was located in houses in a community setting close to shops and other amenities. Residents participated in all aspects of daily living, including self-care, cooking, cleaning, shopping, and so on. Fourteen male patients with TBI comprised the study participants. Mean age at injury was 29.1 years and mean injury to admission interval was 20 months. Average length of stay was 9 months and follow-up averaged 15 months post-discharge. At discharge five patients were considered to have good outcome (living at home requiring no ongoing supervision and engaged in many residential activities). Four patients had fair outcome, required less than 8 hours of supervision, and were engaged in many residential activities. Three patients had poor outcomes, continuing to require 24-hour supervision and assistance with self-care and mobility, and two patients had very poor outcome. Admission DRS score was a powerful predictor of outcome. There was improvement between discharge and follow-up and the authors speculated that the patients may have been able to apply compensatory strategies to novel demands. However, it was suggested that the key to community re-adaptation was the degree of mastery rather than improvement *per se*, with acknowledgement that the principles of social learning theory were not fully integrated into the treatment programme.

Cope, Cole, Hall, and Barkans, (1991a, b) reported the outcomes obtained by a group of post-acute community-based treatment programmes. The programmes included specialised behaviour disorder, residential community reintegration, day, outpatient, and home programmes. Treatment components included behavioural management, activities of daily living, self-management, substance abuse, social, academic, and vocational skills training, but varied from programme to programme and from patient to patient. A population of 173 persons with TBI were considered to have participated in the programme for long enough (greater than 45 days) to show clinical effect and, of these, 145 cases were available for follow-up (83.8%). Telephone interviews were conducted 6, 12, or 24 months post-discharge with the client or family member if this was deemed appropriate. Measures of outcome included residential status, level of activity, and hours a day of attendant care or supervision required. A subanalysis was performed of individuals who were admitted to the programme a year or more post-injury and were not admitted from another facility.

In the total sample there were significant improvements in the numbers of patients living independently and working, and a very significant reduction in the number of individuals requiring attendant care. However, 29% of patients were admitted less than 3 months post-injury and 75.8% of the total sample were admitted 1 year or less post-injury. The authors note that without a matched control group identifying treatment effects was problematic. The authors addressed this issue by analysing the data for the 24.2% of patients who were admitted more than 1 year post-injury. The evidence for improvement is more equivocal for this group. There was a reduction in the number of patients living at home, with an increasing tendency for patients to live in board and care homes and skilled nursing facilities. On the other hand there was an increase in the number of individuals in competitive employment and a very significant increase in the numbers engaged in some type of vocational activity. The number of people requiring attendant care also decreased, as did the duration of the attendant care required. These results are unlikely to be the result of spontaneous recovery alone. However, patients in the analysis were predominantly early post-acute and had mostly mild to moderate impairment. The heterogeneity of the sample makes it difficult to assess the effect of treatment. Given the high cost of providing them post-acute services might be restricted to those patients who would not improve independently. The sample heterogeneity also makes cost–benefit analysis difficult because it is reasonable to assume that most of the patients treated at the beginning of the treatment period would not have needed the same level of assistance by the end of the treatment period, simply by virtue of spontaneous recovery. Stability of outcome is also difficult to interpret as the heterogeneity may mask loss of independence in the most severely affected group when different treatment cohorts are analysed.

Johnston and Lewis (1991) and Johnston (1991) have reported the outcomes of a group of community re-entry programmes. The sample was obtained from a list of patients discharged during the first quarter of 1988, omitting those cases treated for less than 45 days. The patient sample consisted of 82 persons from nine facilities. Level of functioning at or before admission was compared with outcomes of telephone interview one year post-discharge. A means of inferring injury severity (i.e., GCS, coma, or PTA duration) was not provided. The areas examined were independent living and productive activities. Because this was a case-managed, goal-driven system, outcomes were assessed in terms of the goals that had been established for each client. Average length of stay was 8.8 months and average cost $106,000. Clients admitted less than 6 months after injury improved substantially more than the remainder of the sample. Levels of supervision were rated on a 5-point scale from 0 (needs 24-hour supervision) to 4 (independent, needs virtually no help or supervision). Cases admitted soon after onset experienced a greater decrease in supervision than those admitted later. The median decrease in supervision level was four steps for cases admitted less than 180 days after onset, three steps for cases admitted 180–364 days, and one step for those admitted in the second or subsequent year. Improvements were still significant for those admitted after one year. Although much of the improvement was seen in those less than one year post-injury, there was substantial improvement in those patients admitted after one year. Return to paid employment remained difficult for many clients, with only 23.5% of the total sample being in paid work at follow-up. Interestingly major improvements in client functioning occurred in areas not stated as explicit outcome goals. Decreases in supervision and improvements in household management were rarely stated as goals but these were clearly important areas of improvement for clients in these programmes. In clients who were admitted with deficits in self-care and mobility there were major improvements. Participation in the programme did not prevent the later emergence of emotional and behavioural problems, with approximately 24% developing new emotional or behavioural problems (consistent with the findings of Brooks & McKinlay, 1983, and the suggestion of Wood et al., 1999). Anticipated outcomes were not attained as frequently as expected and teams had difficulty in anticipating the ways in which clients were likely to benefit. There was no association between length of stay and improved outcome, and in fact the longer the stay the less the patient improved overall.

Re-entry programmes deliver a variety of different interventions over a wide range of clients. Some of the interventions, although expensive, may well be no more effective than unspecialised supportive care. Others may be highly effective and produce major and enduring effects not attainable in other ways. It is important to know which are which. Harrick et al. (1994) report a 3-year outcome of patients treated at a transitional living centre for post-acute TBI patients. The subjects were the first 21 people who completed the programme of a single transitional living centre and were available for 3-year follow-up. Participants in the study had all sustained severe TBI (mean 28.1 days, range 3–90, SD = 24.7). Participants were an average of 37.1 months post-injury (range 30–168, SD = 42.1), with many having participated in inpatient medical rehabilitation prior to admission to the transitional living centre. Mean length of stay was 25.5 weeks (range 8–56, SD = 11.2). Treatment included behaviour management, activities of daily living retraining, counselling, and academic and vocational retraining, all provided in the context of a group residential facility with a community living focus. Guiding concepts included the importance of self-awareness to adapting to community life, and the use of compensatory strategies and modification of the physical and social environment so as to reduce disability. Functional status was measured by participation in productive activity, need for financial support, place of residence, and level of supervision required. Improvements observed at one-year follow-up remained stable or had improved at three-year follow-up. Loneliness and depression increased over time to become the problems reported most frequently at follow-up.

Willer et al. (1999) compared the outcomes of individuals with severe TBI treated in a post-acute residential rehabilitation programme ($n = 23$) with a matched sample of individuals receiving limited services in their homes or on an outpatient basis. The treatment groups included all persons admitted consecutively over a 3-year period, none had a coma duration of under 3 days and 18 of the 23 had a coma duration of over 21 days. The control group was obtained from the local brain injury support group. The treatment and the control group were matched for gender, length of coma, time since injury, and level of disability. Treatment subjects showed a greater improvement in both cognitive and motor outcome than the control group. The treatment subjects also improved more significantly in community integration as measured by the CIQ (Community Integration Questionnaire), although this may be accounted for by the treatment groups' more impaired scores at the start of treatment.

METHODOLOGICAL ISSUES

Interventions and outcome criteria change over the course of recovery from TBI. Early management focuses on medical rescue and physiological interventions to establish medical stability. Early interventions are intended to facilitate patient recovery and prevent complications (Giles & Clark-Wilson, 1999). Later interventions focus on non-physiological factors, such as cognitive status, functional adaptability, and behavioural control. Outcome in such cases is usually described in terms of self-sufficiency in community living. When learning is the intervention and outcome is measured by incremental rather than profound behavioural change, intervention is by necessity protracted and many confounding influences can obscure the factors that actually underlie behavioural improvement.

Researchers have established a variety of methods to prevent confounding factors from threatening the validity of research. However, few authors have systematically examined threats to internal and external validity in relation to research in TBI rehabilitation, presumably believing that they are too obvious or well known to warrant detailed discussion. This explanation is, however, belied by the absence of serious discussion, or in some cases, recognition of major methodological problems in studies that are widely claimed as evidence for one point or another (see, for example, Cope & Hall, 1982; Mackay et al., 1992). The research design that is most effective in minimising the potential for confounding factors to bias results is the randomised pre-test post-test control group design (Campbell & Stanley, 1966). Other designs control for confounding variables to some degree but none as effectively. To date no randomised pre-test post-test control group studies have been conducted of TBI rehabilitation. Some studies of the effectiveness of acute rehabilitation have used a non-equivalent control group design (Aronow, 1987; Mackay et al., 1992). Most post-acute studies have failed to use any type of control or comparison group (with the exception of Eames & Wood, 1985; Prigatano et al., 1984; and Willer et al., 1999).

A number of factors have contributed to this lack of the randomised pre-test post-test control group. Most individuals who work in rehabilitation would consider it unethical to withhold treatment from an individual in the acute stage of recovery from TBI, although there are many individuals who do not receive inpatient rehabilitation who might benefit from it. However, due to unavailability of services or for financial reasons, such individuals are not available to researchers for control purposes. Prospective randomised trials are costly and financial constraints may have played a part in impeding this type of research. An alternative approach is to compare different types of rehabilitation. Treament comparisons have been used in examining treatment effects following CVA (Basmajian et al., 1987; Kalra & Eade, 1995) but have been largely neglected in TBI research, probably for logistical reasons and because the nature of cerebral pathology and recovery patterns are less predictable in TBI. Many of the follow-up reports of treatment were from pilot projects or entrepreneurial endeavours where obtaining comparison groups may be problematic.

Spontaneous recovery

Another important factor is spontaneous recovery. In the US some of the largest studies of post-acute rehabilitation have included more patients who were less than 12 months post-injury than were more than 12 months post-injury (Cope et al., 1991a, b). As in other countries, in the US acutely injured people are more likely to be funded for rehabilitation than those later in recovery. Studies of costs associated with TBI have shown that on average more money is spent on the first 12 months of treatment than after this period (Brooks et al., 1995; Sakata, Ostby, & Leung, 1991). The selection bias (acutely ill people in the acute stage of recovery) may interact with the type of treatment provided to mislead us about what constitutes effective treatment. If patients in the early stages of recovery will improve (at least to some extent) regardless of the treatment type, then we may be misled into believing that a treatment was effective when it was not.

Fifty five percent of individuals with severe TBI survive the month following trauma and of these the majority show improvement in many areas of functioning over the first 6–12 months (Jennett & Teasdale, 1981). In some contexts clinicians recognise that following life-saving neurosurgical interventions most of the improvement demonstrated in the early stages of recovery is spontaneous, i.e., results from the natural processes of healing. Despite the claims by many of its advocates that coma stimulation enhances the extent of recovery following TBI, many patients have recovered without this type of intervention (Lewin, Marshal, & De Cad Roberts, 1979; Rader, Alston, & Ellis, 1989).

Spontaneous recovery may also account for much of the improvement in the community-oriented post-acute reports. A variety of methods have been used to distinguish the effects of treatment from the improvement that may occur spontaneously. The most frequently used procedure is to set a 12-month cut-off, after which the patient is considered post-acute (i.e., has entered a chronic stage) and after which no further spontaneous improvement is expected. Unfortunately, although 12 months may be a good average cut-off, improvement is known to continue past this period in some more severely injured patients (Mackworth, Mackworth, & Cope, 1982). At 12 months post-injury an individual recovering from an injury with 7 days of coma may be at a very different point in the hypothetical slope of recovery than someone with a 6-month history of coma.

In post-acute rehabilitation, treatment periods tend to be extremely long. The time from injury to admission is often shorter than the period of time that the person spends in treatment. It is not unusual for the patient to be in treatment for 12 months and the longer the period of treatment the more difficult it is to establish that the patient's improvement is a response to the treatment and not a natural process of recovery. The relationship between time since injury and the severity of injury is complex. Many people who are more severely injured are likely to enter post-acute treatment later; therefore, worse outcomes for this group may relate to injury severity and not time when rehabilitation started. Therefore, continued improvement in those admitted after 12 months post-injury does not necessarily indicate an effect of treatment versus spontaneous recovery.

Injury severity

Severity of injury is an important predictor of outcome. There remains no absolute measure of severity of TBI, and views vary as to how it should be defined. Glasgow Coma Scale (GCS) score, duration of coma, and length of post-traumatic amnesia (PTA) are the most accepted criteria (Jennett & Teasdale, 1981). Severe brain injury has been defined as leading to GCS score of 3–8, coma in excess of 1 hour (Aronow, 1987) or of 6 hours or to PTA in excess of 24 hours (Jennett & Teasdale, 1981; Russell & Smith, 1961). Mild and moderate head injury are variously defined. There is a correlation between duration of coma and length of PTA and both are correlated with severity of brain trauma. However, the two criteria may produce different indicators of severity. Patients who are initially assigned a mild or a moderate injury severity using GCS or coma duration may be reassigned to the severe group when PTA duration becomes available (Williams, Levin, & Eisenberg, 1990). When attempts are made to determine the effectiveness of treatment by the use of a comparison group, differences in severity become a major threat to internal validity.

Aronow (1987) compared the outcomes of a group of patients provided with acute rehabilitation at a regional centre of excellence, with patients matched for injury severity from a neurosurgical unit in an area of the US where comprehensive TBI rehabilitation was unavailable. The two groups of patients were selected retrospectively by chart review using a single criteria set. All patients had sustained severe brain injury (coma duration of 1 hour or more) were aged 5–80 years, had an acute hospital stay of at least 15 days, and were not comatose at the time of acute hospital discharge. In the rehabilitation group the charts of 107 consecutive patients were reviewed and 68 of the patients met the criteria. To obtain the comparison group 1400 cases of TBI were screened and only 61 met the criteria, the vast majority of the neurosurgical patients having only mild head injury requiring hospitalisation of only short duration. Outcome measures were collected by telephone interview and included questions about living arrangements, amount of ADL assistance needed, vocational status, social isolation, etc. At follow-up, data were collected on duration of PTA. Over two-thirds of the rehabilitation group (69.8%) were found to have PTA duration of 4 months or more, while 73.5% of the non-rehabilitation group had PTA duration of 1 month or less. Despite attempts to control for severity using the acute measures available, referral to a nationally known centre of excellence was not independent of injury severity and selection bias remained even after attempts to match for injury severity had been used. Unfortunately, statistical attempts to control for the differences in severity assume that patients of different severity will show similar patterns of response to treatment and that severity itself is a unitary concept; both of these assumptions are quite dubious. The findings that both groups had comparable outcomes on the majority of measures is essentially uninterpretable given the methodological difficulties.

Patient selection

Whether or not the patients described in a study are representative of TBI patients generally must also be considered. For example, researchers who exclude individuals with substance abuse problems, history of previous TBI, or psychiatric impairment may be excluding a significant proportion of the total TBI population, making their sample unrepresentative. In terms of the published outcome studies, it is questionable whether patients seen at commercial post-acute TBI programmes in the US are truly representative of the population of brain injured people. There may for example be considerable cultural variations in the patients typically referred for post-acute rehabilitation in different industrialised nations. If the experimental population is not truly representative of the total population then it may be that treatment that is effective with the selected population is less effective or ineffective with an unselected population. An example of this might be the highly selected population studied by Ben-Yishay and associates (1987).

Measures of outcome

Another potential threat to straightforward interpretation of research findings is the effect of instrumentation. TBI outcome data is often derived from observation or rating scales and these are often prone to unnoticed changes in criteria or "instrumentation drift" (e.g., a patient's behaviour is rated as being more or less present or exaggerated as staff become more familiar with the patient or the behaviour; Giles & Clark-Wilson, 1993). Another important consideration is measurement precision. All measures are prone to error. The less discriminating the measure needs to be, the less the potential for error. However, choosing accuracy over the risk of error can result in highly reliable information that fails to provide the needed information. Standard outcome instruments may be insensitive to outcome in the post-acute continuum (Kilgore, 1995). Most instruments are designed to measure the types of changes that occur in acute rehabilitation, i.e., measures that capture improvements of the magnitude that occur during the period of greatest spontaneous recovery. These instruments may be insensitive to the subtle but important changes that may occur with rehabilitation in the post-acute recovery period. Measures need to be appropriately targeted to the range of behaviours that significantly affect outcome in the specific treatment setting or context of concern. Observers, either staff or family members, may change as a result of interaction with the patient, whilst ratings may change because staff become experienced in handling the patient, mature in the caregiver or staff role, or have more relaxed or more stringent standards. Differences may also occur if different raters are used for pre-test, post-test, or follow-up measures or if these measures have different sources of information (Anderson et al., 1993; Menegazzi, Davis, Sucov, & Paris, 1993).

Hall et al. (1996) examined the characteristics of the FIM (Functional Independence Measure), FIM+FAM (Functional Assessment Measure), DRS (Disability Rating Scale) and CIQ, focusing on ceiling effects after rehabilitation discharge. The authors were interested in the extent to which the scales could measure meaningful changes after discharge and the residual deficits of TBI survivors that might compromise full community integration. Data were analysed from the model system traumatic brain injury database. The authors identified a substantial ceiling effect of the FIM, which was evident even by the time of discharge from acute rehabilitation (one-half of the cases had an average score of 6–7 across the 18 FIM items). The addition of the FAM added some useful information but a ceiling effect was still present in one-third of cases. The DRS showed less ceiling effect than either the FIM or the FIM+FAM at discharge and one and two-year follow-up but also provided very little information; depth was sacrificed in return for brevity. The CIQ had a ceiling effect on both home and social integration subscales when compared with scores from a sample of persons without disability. However, the productivity subscale showed greater sensitivity. The FIM, FIM+FAM, and two of the three CIQ subscales were not sensitive to impairments that may have affected functional status in the community. This lack of sensitivity at the high end results in an inability to assess changes that may occur in the community. Reliability and validity are not sufficient criteria for assessing the appropriateness of the scale: the measure must also address the factors that remain significant issues for individuals' post-acute rehabilitation.

Describing the independent variable

Often the reader (and we might suspect the author of the report) has very little idea what treatment was actually provided. The method section in published reports is intended to describe procedures in sufficient detail to allow for the replication of the intervention. Very minimal programme descriptions are provided in most reports, making it difficult to know what protocols were applied across the patient population. A number of the programmes described have been based on innovative and powerful leadership from a single individual or group of individuals. It is difficult to establish if these person-driven programmes can actually be replicated. Is it the treatment itself or the cult status that welds a treatment team into producing an especially effective set of interventions? Can this be replicated in ordinary programmes that can be set up in multiple sites?

Describing and measuring the dependent variable

Outcome is difficult to quantify for many patients. When discharge placement is the outcome variable it is difficult to know if the treatment was effective or if very effective case management is maintaining the living situation. If what is important is a sustained level of functioning in living situations or vocational placement then when and how often follow-up is performed is important. One-shot follow-up often fails to capture the patient's problems. Outcome measures may be so general that they fail to capture clinically and functionally relevant changes as a result of treatment. For example, the GOS may not capture clinically meaningful patient improvement (Putnam & Adams, 1992). Ceiling effects on measures used to assess outcome may also obscure meaningful improvement.

Multiple treatment interference

The same individual may be the target of multiple types of treatment either sequentially or at the same time. Some of the treatment may not even be recognised as treatment. For example, a cognitive retraining programme may impose increased demands on patients' functional behaviours, making it difficult to determine the active ingredient of treatment.

Lack of homogeneity of subjects

The heterogeneity of the samples makes it very difficult to ascertain the effect of treatment. When looking at subjects with different times since injury, different severity of injury and at different points on the recovery curve, it is hard to determine what intervention had what effect. Patients may have a differential response to a non-specific treatment effect, a specific treatment, or to the application of multiple treatments. Lack of homogeneity in injury severity in combination may pose the greatest single threat to the interpretation of the quasi experimental designs used in TBI outcome research. For example, the subjects in the study of Mills et al. (1992) have a coma duration ranging from 0 to 90 days (SD = 39.9) and entered the programme from 6 to 403 months post-injury (SD = 73.0).

Interaction of history and treatment

Many of the transitional living follow-up studies describe treatment that occurred in the US between 1984 and 1992. The majority describe work carried out between 1986 and 1992. As in other countries, in the US this was a period of rapid growth of post-acute rehabilitation. Many of the programmes that were described opened rapidly and have since closed (Giles & Clark-Wilson, 1999). Much of the data was gathered for the purposes of marketing. In the US the financial support for these programmes is now far more constricted (Giles & Clark-Wilson, 1999). Many of the patients treated in these programmes would probably not be funded in the current climate. It is therefore possible that the specific historical context of the treatment provided what would at other times prove to be an unrepresentative sample of individuals attending post-acute rehabilitation services.

DISCUSSION

The results of programme-based outcome studies present findings that, for methodological reasons, are difficult to interpret. A certain amount of stimulation appears necessary to maximise recovery and delays in rehabilitation may have negative consequences for a significant proportion of patients. However, patients may continue to respond to rehabilitative interventions for a long time post-injury and there is no evidence for a definitive cut-off point after which improvement is no longer possible. Studies of general rehabilitation that include a functional component are consistent in demonstrating a positive response to treatment in both the acute and post-acute stages of recovery. Studies that show the largest improvements in functioning are confounded by spontaneous recovery effects. The largest group studies in both the acute and post-acute stages offer little by way of guidance regarding the types of intervention that are most likely to be effective. At the acute stage of rehabilitation improvements are made in multiple areas of functioning. At the post-acute stage, however, whatever the theoretical model or the intervention strategy used, what seems to improve most is functional skills. This is both encouraging and discouraging at the same time as it is evident that something is working to improve patients' competencies, but we are not sure what it is. In the absence of large-scale comparisons of different types of treatment other methods are required to determine the types of interventions most likely to be effective.

Not surprisingly the development of assessment tools has followed the progress of the service delivery system. The first measures developed were acute measures and gross long-term outcome measures. As acute rehabilitation became more common, acute rehabilitation measures (e.g., FIM) developed with the level of precision appropriate to the changes patients made during this period. Functional measures that capture the degree of change in the post-acute period are needed.

Studies of individuals or small groups allow a range of alternative methods to control for maturation and other threats to internal validity. Multiple baselines within and between individual designs are receiving increased attention. ABAB and other multiple treatment or reversal designs offer potent methods to examine the effects of treatment on individuals.

Researchers have addressed the question of whether or not it is possible to achieve robust behavioural change in TBI rehabilitation. Lloyd and Cuvo (1994) reviewed the literature and found that patients with TBI both maintained and generalised functional behaviours after appropriately designed training. Similarly, patients who are many years post-injury have been shown to respond to treatment. The range of behaviours that have been addressed is wide, ranging from continence to behavioural aspects of social behaviours. Given that it is possible to achieve robust behavioural change in individual patients, does individual piecemeal behavioural engineering result in behavioural change important enough to affect outcome in terms of long-term care cost and quality of life? No review has specifically addressed this issue, but with major change in the amount of care required of some patients and with change in living environment made possible by these changes it is difficult to see how there could fail to be a change in the cost of care.

The major problem with individual or small group designs relates to external, particularly population, validity. The population of patients reported in the literature is often the *good responders* (i.e., only those for whom the intervention worked). No definitive evidence is available to address this issue. However, it does often seem that rather than the easiest cases, it is the most problematic patients whose problems are systematically addressed and reported (Manchester, Hodgkinson, & Casey, 1997). Not all TBI patients require the same type of treatment but it is important to know whether a specific intervention is likely to be effective with a group of roughly similar patients with roughly similar problems. Giles, Ridley, Dill, and Frye (1997) described the application of specific ADL training to all patients in a consecutive series of patients admitted to a transitional living centre. It is important to know the injury and referral pattern for the entire group of patients as well as the patients treated to understand the likely applicability of the approach. Individual patients who receive a treatment should be described in detail. Eventually, this type of approach could allow for the development of specific targeted interventions for specific problems and the development of detailed descriptions of the patients' characteristics associated with a particular intervention being effective.

What are the characteristics of post-acute social rehabilitation programmes that make them successful? What are the sizes, staffing and geographic catchment areas? Should they be satellites of local hospital or regional specialised centres? When is placement in the community to take place? What are the specialised support services needed to maintain gains achieved? These are fundamental questions to which we have as yet no answer.

The single programme outcome study has provided us with some information about the efficacy of post-acute rehabilitation. However, to add new information to the current body of knowledge changes are needed in the way clinical research is carried out. The following recommendations are offered as a potential way forward in improving the scientific rigour and hence our ability to interpret findings.

1. Increasing emphasis should be placed on reporting the severity of injury with as much precision as possible. The source of referrals should be described and in post-acute social rehabilitation efforts should be made to obtain acute records and to estimate from collateral sources the duration of PTA (when this information is not obtained prospectively).
2. The independent variable should be described in sufficient detail to distinguish it from other types of intervention and so that it can be replicated. It is important to be able to compare the applicability of different models of treatment to persons with different severities of injury and different functional levels at the time of admission to the post-acute programme. Treatment durations should be analysed to help determine the point at which an intervention begins to show diminishing returns.
3. Specific interventions should be developed and applied to all patients in a series who have deficits in the targeted area. In this way we can begin to estimate both the general applicability of an intervention and the interventions appropriate to the target population in terms of severity of impairment, etc.
4. The effect of rehabilitation should be assessed with a core set of measures that are appropriate for the patient's deficits and the goals of rehabilitation. Current measures used in the post-acute period lack precision or are insensitive to achievable changes. While participation is important and can be a direct focus of intervention, much of post-acute intervention is directed

at patients' abilities, so functional behaviours need to be measured. Functionally relevant measures, appropriate for the degree of change possible in post-acute rehabilitation and which capture the change in targeted behaviour, need to be developed (Giles, 2000).

5. Specific targeted interventions are important in social rehabilitation but the milieu itself is also believed to be an active part of treatment. We need to define, operationalise, and compare social rehabilitation milieu and delivery methods.

REFERENCES

Anderson, S.I., Housley, A.M., Jones, P.A., Slattery, J., & Miller, J.D. (1993). Glasgow Outcome Scale: An inter-rater reliability study. *Brain Injury, 7,* 309–317.

Aronow, H.U. (1987). Rehabilitation effectiveness with severe brain injury: Translating research into policy. *Journal of Head Trauma Rehabilitation, 2,* 24–36.

Ashley, M.J., Persel, C.S., Clark, M.C., & Krych, D.K. (1997). Long-term follow-up of post-acute traumatic brain injury rehabilitation: A statistical analysis to test for stability and predictability of outcome. *Brain Injury, 11,* 677–690.

Basmajian, J.V., Gowland, C.A., Finlayson, M.A.J., Hall, A.J., Swanson, L.R., Stratford, P.W., Trotter, J.E., & Brandstater, M.E. (1987). Stroke treatment: Comparison of integrated behavioral–physical therapy vs traditional physical therapy programs. *Archives of Physical Medicine and Rehabilitation, 68,* 267–272.

Baxt, W.G., & Moody, P. (1987). The impact of advanced pre-hospital emergency care on the mortality of severely brain injured patients. *Journal of Trauma, 27,* 365–369.

Ben-Yishay, Y., & Diller, L. (1981). Rehabilitation of cognitive and perceptual defects in people with traumatic brain damage. *International Journal of Rehabilitation Research, 4,* 208–210.

Ben-Yishay, Y., Silver, S.M., Piasetsky, E., & Rattock, J. (1987). Relationship between employability and vocational outcome after intensive holistic cognitive rehabilitation. *Journal of Head Trauma Rehabilitation, 2,* 35–48.

Blackerby, W.F. (1990). Intensity of rehabilitation and length of stay. *Brain Injury, 4,* 167–173.

Brooks, C.A., Lindstrom, J., McCray, J., & Whiteneck, G.G. (1995). Cost of medical care for a population-based sample of persons surviving traumatic brain injury. *Journal of Head Trauma Rehabilitation, 10,* 1–13.

Brooks, D.N., & McKinlay, W.W. (1983). Personality and behavioral change after severe blunt head injury – a relative's view. *Journal of Neurology, Neurosurgery, and Psychiatry, 46,* 336–344.

Burke, W.H., Wesolowski, M.D., & Guth, M.L. (1988). Comprehensive head injury rehabilitation: An outcome evaluation. *Brain Injury, 4,* 313–322.

Campbell, D.T., & Stanley, J.C. (1966). *Experimental and quasi-experimental designs for research.* Chicago: Rand McNally.

Carey, R.G., Seibert, J.H., & Posavac, E.J. (1988). Who makes the most progress in inpatient rehabilitation? An analysis of functional gain. *Archives of Physical Medicine and Rehabilitation, 69,* 337–343.

Cifu, D.X., Kreutzer, J.S., Marwitz, J.H., Miller, M., Hsu, G.M., Seel, R.T., Englander, J., High, W.M., & Zafonte, R. (1999). Etiology and incidence of rehospitalization after traumatic brain injury: A multi center analysis. *Archives of Physical Medicine and Rehabilitation, 80,* 85–90.

Committee on Government Operations (1992). *Fraud and abuse in the head injury rehabilitation industry.* Thirty-fifth Report of the Committee on Government Operations, House Report 102-1059. Washington, DC: US Government Printing Office.

Cope, D.N., & Hall, K. (1982). Head injury rehabilitation: Benefits of early intervention. *Archives of Physical Medicine and Rehabilitation, 63,* 433–437.

Cope, D.N., Cole, J.R., Hall, K.M., & Barkans, H. (1991a). Brain injury: Analysis of outcome in a post-acute rehabilitation system. Part 1: General analysis. *Brain Injury, 5,* 111–125.

Cope, D.N., Cole, J.R., Hall, K.M., & Barkans, H. (1991b). Brain injury: Analysis of outcome in a post-acute rehabilitation system. Part 2: Subanalyses. *Brain Injury, 5,* 127–139.

Crawford, S., Wenden, F., & Wade, D.T. (1996). The Rivermead head injury follow up questionnaire: A study of a new rating scale and other measures to evaluate outcome after head injury. *Journal of Neurology, Neurosurgery, and Psychiatry, 60,* 510–514.

Eames, P., & Wood, R. (1985a). Rehabilitation after severe brain injury: A follow-up study of a behaviour modification approach. *Journal of Neurology, Neurosurgery, and Psychiatry, 48,* 613–619.

Eames, P., & Wood, R. (1985b). Rehabilitation after severe brain injury: A special-unit approach to behaviour disorders. *International Rehabilitation Medicine, 7,* 130–133.

Eames, P., Cotterill, G., Kneale, T.A., Storrar, A.L., & Yeomans, P. (1995). Outcome of intensive rehabilitation after severe brain injury: A long term follow-up study. *Brain Injury, 10,* 631–650

Fryer, L.J., & Haffey, W.J. (1987). Cognitive rehabilitation and community readaptation: Outcomes from two program models. *Journal of Head Trauma Rehabilitation, 2,* 51–63.

Giles, G.M. (1994). The status of brain injury rehabilitation. *American Journal of Occupational Therapy, 48,* 199–205.

Giles, G.M. (2000). *Reliability and validity of a functional outcome measure for persons with brain injury.* Unpublished doctoral dissertation, California School of Professional Psychology, Alameda, California.

Giles, G.M., & Clark-Wilson, J. (1993). *Brain injury rehabilitation: A neurofunctional approach.* London: Chapman and Hall.

Giles, G.M., & Clark-Wilson, J. (Eds.). (1999). *Rehabilitiation of the severely brain injured adult: A practical approach* (2nd ed.). Chichester, UK: Stanley Thornes.

Giles, G.M., Ridley, J., Dill, A., & Frye, S. (1997). A consecutive series of brain injured adults treated with a washing and dressing retraining program. *American Journal of Occupational Therapy, 51,* 256–266.

Hall, K.M., Mann, N., High, W.M., Wright, J., Kreutzer, J.S., & Wood, D. (1996). Functional measures after trumatic brain injury: Ceiling effects of FIM, FIM+FAM, DRS, and CIQ. *Journal of Head Trauma Rehabilitation, 11,* 27–39.

Harrick, L., Krefting, L., Johnston, J., Carlson, P., & Minnes, P. (1994). Stability of functional outcomes following transitional living program participation: 3 year follow up. *Brain Injury, 8,* 439–447.

Heinemann, A.W., Linacre, J.M., Wright, B.D., Hamilton, B.B., & Granger, C. (1994). Prediction of rehabilitation outcomes with disability measures. *Archives of Physical Medicine and Rehabilitation, 75,* 133–143.

Heinemann, A.W., Sahgal, V., Cichowski, K., Tuel, S.M., & Betts, H.B. (1990). Functional outcome following traumatic brain injury: Translating research into policy. *Journal of Neurologic Rehabilitation, 4,* 27–37.

Jennet, B., & Teasdale, G. (1981). *Management of head injuries.* Philadelphia, PA: F.A. Davis.

Johnston, M.V. (1991). Outcomes of community re-entry programs for brain injury survivors. Part 2: Further investigations. *Brain Injury, 5,* 155–168.

Johnston, M.V., & Lewis, F.D. (1991). Outcomes of community re-entry program for brain injury survivors. Part 1: Independent living and productive activities. *Brain Injury, 5,* 141–154.

Kalra, L., & Eade, J. (1995). Role of stroke rehabilitation units in managing severe disability after stroke. *Stroke, 26,* 2031–2034.

Kilgore, K.M. (1995). Measuring outcome in the post-acute continuum. *Archives of Physical Medicine and Rehabilitation, 76,* SC21–SC26.

King, N.S., Crawford, S., Wenden, & F.J., Moss, N.E., & Wade, D.T. (1995). The Rivermead post concussion symptom questionnaire: A measure of symptoms commonly experienced after head injury and its reliability. *Journal of Neurology, 242,* 587–592.

Lewin, W., Marshal, T.F., & De Cad Roberts, A.H. (1979). Long term outcome after severe head injury. *British Medical Journal, 2,* 1533–1538.

Lloyd, L.F., & Cuvo, A.J. (1994). Maintenance and generalization of behaviors after treatment of persons with traumatic brain injury. *Brain Injury, 8,* 529–540.

Mackay, L.E., Bernstein, B.A., Chapman, P.E., Morgan, A.S., & Milazzo, L.S. (1992). Early intervention in severe head injury: Long-term benefits of a formalized program. *Archives of Physical Medicine and Rehabilitation, 73,* 635–641.

Mackworth, N., Mackworth, J., & Cope, D.N. (1982). Towards an interpretation of head injury recovery trends. In *Head Injury Rehabilitation Project: Final report* (pp. 1–66). San Jose, CA: Santa Clara Valley Medical Center Institute for Medical Research.

Mahoney, F.I., & Barthel, D.W. (1965). Functional evaluation: The Barthel Index. *Maryland State Medical Journal, 14,* 61–65.

Manchester, D., Hodgkinson, A., & Casey, T. (1997). Prolonged, severe behavioral disturbance following traumatic brain injury: What can be done? *Brain Injury, 11,* 605–617.

McLaughlin, A.M., & Peters, S. (1993). Evaluation of an innovative, cost effective programme for brain injury patients: Response to a need for flexible treatment planning. *Brain Injury, 7,* 71–75.

Menegazzi, J.J., Davis, E.A., Sucov, A.N., & Paris, P.M. (1993). Reliability of the Glasgow Coma Scale when used by emergency physicians and paramedics. *Journal of Trauma, 34,* 46–48.

Mills, V.M., Nesbeda, T., Katz, D.I., & Alexander, M.P. (1992). Outcomes for traumatically brain-injured patients following post-acute rehabilitation programs. *Brain Injury, 6,* 219–228.

Prigatano, G.P., Fordyce, D.J., Zeiner, H.K., Roueche, J.R., Pepping, M., & Wood, B.C. (1984). Neuropsychological rehabilitation after closed head injury in young adults. *Journal of Neurology, Neurosurgery and Psychiatry, 47,* 505–513.

Putnam, S.H., & Adams, K.M. (1992). Regression-based prediction of long-term outcome following multidisciplinary rehabilitation for traumatic brain injury. *Clinical Neuropsychologist, 6,* 383–405.

Rader, M.A., Alston, J.B., & Ellis, D.W. (1989). Sensory stimulation of severely brain injured patients. *Brain Injury, 3,* 141–147.

Rappaport, M., Hall, K.M., Hopkins, K., Belleza, T., & Cope, D.N. (1982). Disability rating scale for severe brain trauma: Coma to community. *Archives of Physical Medicine and Rehabilitation, 63,* 118–123.

Ruff, R.M., Baser, C.A., Johnston, J.W., Marshall, L.F., Klauber, S.K., Klauber, M.R., & Minteer, M. (1989). Neuropsychological rehabilitation: An experimental study with head-injured patients. *Journal of Head Trauma Rehabilitation, 4,* 20–36.

Russell, W.R., & Smith, A. (1961). Post-traumatic amnesia in closed head injuries. *Archives of Neurology, 5,* 16–29.

Sahgal, V., & Heinemann, A. (1989). Recovery of function during inpatient rehabilitation for moderate traumatic brain injury. *Scandinavian Journal of Rehabilitation Medicine, 21,* 71–79.

Sakata, R., Ostby, S., & Leung, R. (1991). Functional status, referral and cost of treatment for persons with traumatic brain injury. *Brain Injury, 5,* 411–419.

Scherzer, B.P. (1986). Rehabilitation following severe head trauma: Results of a three year program. *Archives of Physical Medicine and Rehabilitation, 67,* 366–374.

Spettell, C.M., Ellis, D.W., Ross, S.E., Sandel, M.E., O'Malley, K.F., Stein, S.C., Spivak, G., & Hurley, K.E. (1991). Time or rehabilitation admission and severity of trauma: Effect on brain injury outcome. *Archives of Physical Medicine and Rehabilitation, 72,* 320–325.

Tuel, S.M., Presty, S.K., Meythaler, J.M., Heinemann, A.W., & Katz, R.T. (1992). Functional improvement in severe head injury after readmission for rehabilitation. *Brain Injury, 6,* 363–372.

Ullman, P., & Krasner, L. (1969). *A psychological approach to abnormal behavior.* Engelwood Cliffs, NJ: Prentice Hall.

Wade, D.T., King, N.S., Wenden, F.J., Crawford, S., & Caldwell, F.E. (1998). Routine follow up after head injury: A second randomized controlled trial. *Journal of Neurology, Neurosurgery, and Psychiatry, 65,* 177–183.

Willer, B., Button, J., & Rempel, R. (1999). Residential and home-based postacute rehabilitation of individuals with traumatic brain injury: A case control study. *Archives of Physical Medicine and Rehabilitation, 80,* 399–406.

Williams, D.H., Levin, H.S., & Eisenberg, H.E. (1990). Mild head injury classification. *Neurosurgery, 27,* 422–428.

Wood, R.Ll., McCrea, J., Wood, L.M., & Merriman, R. (1999). Clinical and cost effectiveness of post-acute neurobehavioral rehabilitation. *Brain Injury, 13,* 69–88.

CHAPTER TWELVE

Service provision for social disability and handicap after acquired brain injury

T.M. McMillan
University of Glasgow, Gartnavel Royal Hospital, UK

M. Oddy
Brain Injury Rehabilitation Unit, Wadhurst, UK

INTRODUCTION

Traumatic head injury is the most common form of acquired brain injury in the young adult. In the first few months after injury almost all patients will have returned home—even those who had suffered a severe head injury. Beyond this time, the incidence of severe disablement that prevents return to the community without the need for supervision is low. The small numbers of cases who are unable to return home within a few months are necessarily demanding of specialist resources. In others who return home quickly after a severe head injury, their disablement is less obvious to clinicians, relatives, and to themselves but nevertheless long-term disadvantage results (McMillan & Greenwood, 1993).

Studies in Glasgow and elsewhere have shown how the stress and burden felt by relatives increases over time (Brooks et al., 1987a, b; Oddy, Coughlan, Tyerman, & Jenkins, 1985). This may be because relatives become aware of rapid improvement in physical abilities in the first 6–12 months after injury, and recognise recovery of cognitive and other functions in the first 2 years or so, but between 2 and 5 years realise that further change is unlikely. Disablement, particularly arising from cognitive impairment, and even subtle changes in personality, result in the family becoming socially isolated and experiencing continuing conflict in the home and persisting financial stringencies (Oddy, 1993). There is also the likelihood that some people with a head injury deteriorate over time, becoming more disabled after discharge from rehabilitation (Gualtieri & Cox, 1991), highlighting the need for routine and repeated follow-up. A mechanism for deterioration in the community is not difficult to find. Given structure and support people with head injury may function relatively well in post-acute rehabilitation. They are usually motivated by a strong desire to return home and to go back to work, with the implication for them that they will then have "recovered". This is easier and more palatable than having to incorporate a new and less able "self" into their psyche. However, they are less able to function without structure and support; they may return to work but are unable to sustain employment for many reasons (Wehman et al., 1990, 1993). In more disabled cases, reduction in drive and motivation results in an erosion of daily routine and self-care.

For many years service provision in the UK centred around the more disabled and were based in inpatient rehabilitation centres (Greenwood & McMillan, 1993). During the 1990s there was a growing trend generally in the UK towards community-based care (Griffiths, 1988). Neurorehabilitation is no exception, but the development of services has generally lacked co-ordination. In the late 1980s it was found that people with head injuries could fall through the "net" of rehabilitation services at almost every conceivable step (Murphy et al., 1990) and there is little evidence to suggest that this has changed. Poor co-ordination of existing services, inadequate or absent discharge plans, absence of follow-up, and deficiencies in some services that do exist mean that the concept of a "seamless service" rarely exists. Of even greater concern: In one recent study it was found that 25% of severe and 67% of mild–moderate head injury patients admitted to a hospital did not have the fact that they had sustained a head injury recorded in their notes (Moss & Wade, 1997).

In this chapter the concept of a model service, discussed elsewhere (McMillan & Greenwood, 1993a, b; Oddy et al., 1990) is developed from the viewpoint of social reintegration, and the dangers from "service mirages" are discussed.

THE SIZE OF THE PROBLEM

It may seem surprising, at the beginning of a new millennium, that the incidence of traumatic brain injury and the prevalence of chronic disablement in the UK is simply not known. Earlier studies suggest an incidence of about 300 in 100,000 of the population who are admitted to hospital, with over 90% of these being minor head injuries (Field, 1973; Miller & Jones, 1985,). The prevalence of disability was estimated to be 100–150 per 100,000 in a study in the west of Scotland (Bryden, 1988). Bryden suggests that there are two new cases per 100,000 per annum contributing to prevalence, and that the average general practitioner might have two of these cases on his register.

These figures may by now be inaccurate. Road casualties and deaths have fallen dramatically in recent times (Jennett, 1985). Broughton (1997) reported the rate of accidents, deaths, and injuries in the UK between 1943 and 1993 expressed per million vehicle kilometres travelled per annum. The rate for death/serious injury fell more than threefold between 1973 and 1993. There have been improvements in safety likely to reduce the incidence of severe head injury such as seatbelts, use of bicycle helmets, and traffic restrictions (Thompson et al., 1996). There have been improvements in medical care and treatment, including published guidelines for trauma care, the availability of computed tomography (CT) scanners in local hospitals, early transfer to neurosurgery, and the continuing development of pharmacological treatments such as neuroprotective agents (Teasdale, 1995). Indeed a recent survey in the US reports much lower hospital discharge rates (103 per 100,000) than anticipated (National Center for Health Statistics, 1997).

Good epidemiological studies are, however, difficult to carry out. The rubrics for coding head injury apply also to facial injury, and some individuals receive more than one code, which can lead to erroneous and duplicate counting (Jennett, 1996). Some individuals receive no code but have clearly suffered significant head injuries (Moss & Wade, 1997). There are also local variations in incidence which can make generalisation from regional or national studies dangerous in terms of service planning. Tennant et al. (1995) reported data on incidence from the north-west region of England collected in 1986. Overall the incidence of 295 cases per 100,000 was in keeping with earlier published studies. However, in the 19 districts comprising that region, the incidence (discharged cases) ranged from 88 to 886 per 100,000 and only one in five districts had an incidence within 20% of UK regional or national figures.

It is obvious that in order to plan a service the size of the problem must be identified. What is also clear is that the figures from studies in the 1970s and 1980s may no longer be accurate, and systematic studies that overcome the difficulties described above are now required in the UK. What is more, local provision of services should reflect need estimated locally and not automatically use regional or national guidelines.

SERVICE NEEDS AND SERVICE PROVISION

The range of disablements that the service must provide for is immense. It extends from patients with minor head injuries who may require short-term advice and guidance, to severely brain injured individuals who are completely dependent for all care. An essential aspect of a high-quality service is the flexibility of its delivery, in order that the needs of the heterogeneous population that comprises acquired brain injury are met. Such a service should provide a seamless programme of rehabilitation that fits the key needs of patients at the time that they need them, and to do this sophisticated organisation and routine follow-up are required. A poor service will have no specialist facilities or will simply "slot" patients routinely into parts of the service independent of the patient's needs. The service needs to be patient-centred, with formal goal setting. Components of the model service shown in Figure 12.1 are developed from earlier work (see Oddy et al., 1990 and McMillan & Greenwood, 1993a).

Early rehabilitation. There has been a long-standing view that neurorehabilitation should start as early as possible (Cope & Hall, 1982), and indeed evidence is growing to support this view (see Wilson, 1998, and Chapter 13). The earliest possible intervention is during coma. There is limited evidence that intervention at this point can reduce coma duration or have any effect on longer-term outcome in terms of disability (see Wilson & McMillan, 1993), although the results of one or two studies are interesting (Mackay et al., 1992; Mitchell, Bradley, Welch, & Britton, 1990). Resources are inevitably limited, and at this time it is difficult to recommend that they should be directed towards intensive neurorehabilitation when the patient is in coma. Further research is required, however, and the use of relatives as "rehabilitation therapists" at this time should be considered. Post-coma, early rehabilitation should be geared towards the patient being in a safe environment, and where consideration of confusion and fatigue together with the development of avoidable physical problems such as contractures is paramount. Relatives may be in crisis and at this time need to be advised about the likely phases of recovery and be supported (Soderstrom et al., 1988). There should be a designated ward for people with an acquired brain injury, and who are in an acute phase of rapid recovery. This ward requires input from staff experienced with this patient group. It is unhelpful for the confused patient to be admitted to any ward where there is a bed, given the lack of constancy of patients and staff to be found on a general ward in a large hospital and the fact that such staff themselves may have no experience or understanding of the post-acute effects of traumatic brain injury, including post-traumatic amnesia (PTA). The concept of providing sensory regulation for coma patients that avoids over-stimulation or under- stimulation (Wood, 1991) is likely to apply equally to these confused patients. It is not uncommon for even mildly agitated patients with PTA to be given strong sedative medication at this time for these reasons. Especially in more severely injured cases, inappropriate management at this time can lead to the development of difficult behaviour which may persist (Johnson & Balleny, 1996). It is not that these patients do not learn, simply that their learning and judgement are impaired (Wilson, Baddeley, Shiel, & Patton, 1992). Relatives may be given no understanding that after coma there will be confusion and disorientation, and that memory for recent events during this time will be very poor. Indeed staff on general wards may themselves confuse PTA with psychosis and prescribe major tranquillisers. In the acute phase after injury, these designated wards play a key role as the first stage of rehabilitation but this requires active management. There needs to be clear arrangements for the onward transfer of patients when they are medically stable, in order to avoid a static situation developing in which new patients cannot be admitted and an inappropriate service is provided for those with profound brain injuries.

Inpatient brain injury rehabilitation centres. The size and number of units of this kind will depend on population and geographical area; however, typically there should be a 24-bedded inpatient unit serving a population of 2–3 million people (McMillan & Greenwood, 1993a; Pentland & Barnes, 1988). Traditionally their emphasis has been on physical rehabilitation and cardiac fitness, especially of stroke

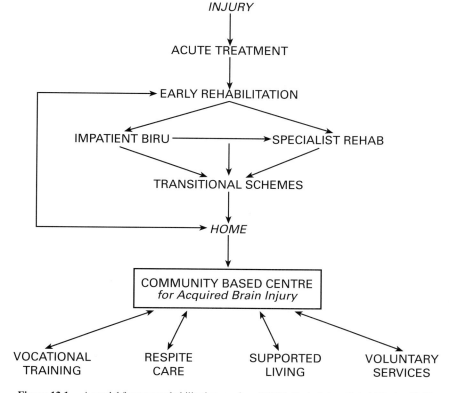

Figure 12.1. A model for neurorehabilitation services (BIRU; Brain Injury Rehabilitation Unit).

and head injury (see McMillan & Greenwood, 1993b). The fact that physical complications such as bed sores, joint contractures, frozen shoulders, and infections of the bladder and urinary tract which were once common (Rusk et al., 1966, 1969) and are now rare is a tribute to the work of these units. Increasingly they offer services to a wider range of cases including maintenance of physical ability in multiple sclerosis, running programmes for chronic back pain, admitting slower stream cases prior to discharge to home, admitting cases in post-traumatic amnesia for management, and developing programmes aimed at reducing the impact of cognitive impairment and personality change in people with minimal physical problems.

Specialist units.   In the UK, hospital-based acute services are always run by the National Health Service and rehabilitation services, which include physical disablement or community-based teams, usually are. With only a very few notable exceptions, specific and specialist rehabilitation for cognitive or behavioural problems, specialist slow-stream rehabilitation and specific supported living schemes for acquired brain injury people tend to be found in the independent sector. There is no reason in principle why the NHS should not develop behaviour treatment units or the independent sector community teams. There are encouraging trends for NHS and independent sector services to work hand in hand and work towards model or "seamless" services.

Behaviour management and treatment.   It is mistaken for local services to believe that they can treat persisting and severe behaviour problems (less expensively) in a non-specialist unit or that such a unit can easily be created locally. For change requiring *treatment,* a programme that allows immediate and consistent responses to inappropriate behaviour is required, in an environment which itself operates as a therapeutic milieu. This is especially the case where the individual has little or no insight into the inappropriateness of his or her behaviour. At best, some neurorehabilitation units that do not specialise in behaviour treatment can *manage* difficult behaviour during its natural course of recovery (e.g., during resolution of PTA) by providing a safe and understanding environment and a programme of care geared towards this end. An exception is the rare case where the individual has a behaviour problem that is not especially disruptive or dangerous to others, and who also has insight and is motivated to change (Johnston, Burgess, McMillan, & Greenwood,1991). When specialist intervention is provided this can often need a year or more of intensive work (Eames & Wood, 1985). Relatively few specialist behaviour treatment units are needed, but the quality of their intervention must be intensive and high. There is evidence that these units can effectively treat cases with persistent and difficult behaviour, and reduce social disability and dependence (Alderman, Fry, & Youngson, 1995; Alderman & Knight, 1997; Eames et al., 1995).

The number of cases with severe, persisting behaviour problems after brain injury are relatively few with an incidence of perhaps 0.3 per 100,000 per annum (Greenwood & McMillan, 1993), although almost 10 times this number might have persistent behaviour problems which are less severe, and have adverse consequences for day-to-day life (Johnson & Balleny, 1996), but may not demand inpatient treatment.

Cognitive rehabilitation.   Many people with acquired brain injury, especially those with traumatic brain injury or anterior communicating artery aneurysms, have little or no physical disability but have significant and disabling impairment of cognitive function. There is a need for services designed specifically for rehabilitation of cognitive deficits for a number of reasons. It is more common for people with cognitive deficits to lack awareness of their deficits and hence to underestimate their need for rehabilitation. Different methods are required to enable them to benefit from the learning experience of rehabilitation because their learning abilities are commonly compromised. Cognitive impairment has a different impact and leads to a different form of dependency than does physical disability. For example, cognitive impairment tends to have a more pervasive influence on ability to return to work than physical impairment. The impact on an individual's sense of self and on the way he or she is perceived by significant others is very different. Furthermore, cognitive deficits are often associated with changes in motivation which therefore have to become a prime focus of rehabilitation in their own right.

Only a very limited number of services specifically designed for this group currently exists in the UK and Europe. The US and Israel have been the pioneers of these types of service. Four broad approaches are common in cognitive rehabilitation. One is the milieu approach (Ben Yishay, 1996; Prigatano and Fordyce, 1986), another is often referred to as the functional approach (Mills et al., 1992; Ponsford, et al., 1995), and the others are based on cognitive neuropsychology (Riddoch & Humphreys, 1994) and theory-driven research aimed at reducing cognitive impairment (Robertson, North, & Geggie, 1992; Robertson, Hogg, & McMillan, 1998).

These approaches are by no means mutually exclusive. The milieu approach emphasises the need for a structured and mutually supportive physical and interpersonal environment. It is often argued that a *prosthetic* environment is as important for someone with cognitive disabilities as it is for a physically disabled person. However, the nature of the modifications required is very different. The functional approach focuses upon enabling people to overcome their deficits in a range of practical situations by use of strategies. Cognitive neuropsychology is primarily an attempt to develop theories of cognitive function by studying the impact of brain injury on cognitive function but which has the spin-off of proposing methods of ameliorating cognitive deficits. For many years it has been thought that little can be done to ameliorate cognitive impairment using neuropsychological treatments, but recent work is suggesting that some impairments, such as those of language and attention, might be remediable to an extent. These theory-based treatment techniques are not widely used as yet (Robertson et al., 1992, 1998; Taub et al., 1993; Tallal et al., 1996).

If cognitive rehabilitation is to be delivered effectively and if progress is to be made in this specialised area, dedicated services are required. These may take the form of residential units although much of this work can be achieved on a day rehabilitation basis.

Transitional rehabilitation units

These post-acute units may be day or residential and are designed to act as a bridge between hospital and community. They concentrate on improving function and not on reducing impairment. Length of attendance is often around 12 months. Although professional staff are normally involved in a supervisory role, most direct work with clients is carried out by specially trained assistants. The emphasis is on ordinary activities rather than therapeutic sessions. Relatively few are found in the UK and there is little evidence regarding their effectiveness (Boake, 1990; Harrick, et al., 1994). For non-residential cases, this role could be absorbed by a community centre for acquired brain injury.

The community centre for acquired brain injury

Given that patients with severe head injury may receive rehabilitation for up to a year in hospital inpatient units, that a high proportion of them are young adults in their early 20s with persisting disablement and a life span that is virtually unaffected, it is obvious that rehabilitation needs to continue in the community and may be needed intermittently for many decades. Where the community is geographically dispersed over a wide area, or where there are few specialists in head injury, or where an individual requires a care regime, a case management system may be effective in monitoring and maintaining the individual in the community. More usually a community-based neurorehabilitation service is required.

The service should have a day centre base, which allows the option of clients being seen at home or at the centre, and in this way makes the best use of clinical time. It should be the "hub" for a number of smaller or more specialised services (the "spokes") and have various roles. These roles include establishing demand by having a register of all admitted head injuries and offering follow-up to them, direct clinical involvement, liaison with other services including enhancing communication and developing services, providing a critical staff mass, training new staff and professional updating of existing staff, instigating and encouraging research, and audit of both input and change.

1. The establishment of a log of all cases admitted to hospital after head injury is crucial. This can allow a service to be provided to all head injuries, including the minor cases. The log, in combination with collaboration from local hospitals in terms of coding of head injuries, would be the first step in preventing individuals from falling through the net of rehabilitation services. Wade et al. (1998) found that a limited/brief intervention for less severe head injuries admitted to hospital led to fewer symptom complaints and reduced social disability at follow-up in a study using a randomised control design.

2. The clinical service would involve routine follow-up which would, in the case of more severe head injuries, continue over the longer term. This means that cases are actively followed-up, *not* that follow-up is available on request. It would involve support and advice to relatives. It would offer clinical interventions designed not only to monitor and maintain function (including managing changes in circumstance), but also where realistic to reduce disability using rehabilitation techniques embedded in a client-centred goal-planning system (McMillan & Sparkes, 1999). In this way deterioration in function and the development of

new problems might be minimised and successful treatments should be best placed to generalise to the actual environment in which the individual normally lives rather than an artificial hospital or "hotel"-based setting.

3. It is not unknown for a service to be developed by the energies and enthusiasm of an individual with the support of a small team, only to wither when that individual leaves. The concept of a critical staff mass means that there are sufficient experienced and senior staff to allow for random variations in recruitment and retention without the service deteriorating catastrophically. Having this at the centre means that in principle less experienced staff can be recruited at the "spokes" and be given professional support and training from the centre which allows that service to be maintained.

4. The liaison role is important in ensuring continuity of input and that the right input is provided at the right time, and is a key feature of the case management role of the centre. By establishing local need and auditing outcome, arguments for the development of services can be made.

5. Professional training is often insufficiently specialised for optimum work with people who require neurorehabilitation. There is a need for specific training, some of which has to take place locally. There is also a need for training of staff at the "spokes" who may work with a variety of client groups. Finally there is a need for ongoing continuing professional development, some of which would occur in house, but some at a regional level, perhaps organised at the level of a detailed national curriculum for neurorehabilitation which is then dispersed.

6. Purchasers of services must be encouraged to consider costs in terms of value. This requires audit of clinical input as well as measurement of outcome. The other non-specific activities such as information giving and staff training must also be accounted for. Specific research issues should be addressed, such as the effectiveness of new treatment techniques.

Case managers

In the US, the use of case managers is widespread (Dixon, Goll, & Stanton, 1988). In that context they can be employed via a number of sources, but tend to have financial empowerment to purchase services (Deutsch & Fralish, 1988). In the UK case managers for brain injury began to appear in the late 1980s, with a role often confused with, but distinct from, social workers or key workers (McMillan et al., 1988). In general terms, case management as a co-ordinating tool for community services was recommended in the Griffiths report (Griffiths, 1988). Whereas there is evidence for effectiveness in improving service provision and reducing costs of care and time off work (Challis & Davies, 1986; Leavitt et al., 1972; Perlmann et al., 1985, Wasylenski et al., 1985) there have been few studies in brain injury. Greenwood et al. (1994) reported a controlled study of case management versus routine services in severe head injured patients followed up for up to two years. The case-managed group received more services, but outcome was not improved.

The authors conclude that brain injury case management is not recommended as a routine NHS service, but that independent case management of specific individuals with severe and complex disablements is likely to be helpful.

Vocational rehabilitation

Following severe head injury return to competitive employment is significantly reduced (Johnson, 1998; McMordie, Barker, & Paolo, 1990; Ponsford, 1995; Wehman et al., 1995). Supported employment schemes have been successful in returning head injured people to work, even when they have previously failed, and in some cases when they were not employed pre-injury (Kreutzer, Wehman, Morton, & Stonnington, 1988; Wall et al., 1998; Wehman et al., 1990, 1993). Key elements of this approach include assessment of potential, on-site job coaching, and matching the demands of the job to the residual capacities of the individual, fitting both the job to the person and the person to the job.

In the UK supported employment schemes are only rarely found in the NHS, but are increasingly being developed by the independent sector, social services departments, and occasionally by the Department of Employment.

Supported living

If the severely head injured person is not able to live with complete independence, and cannot return home because there is insufficient support from relatives or carers, options tend to revolve around group-based homes for mental health patients, reformed drug abusers, or people with congenital learning difficulties. It is rare for these facilities to be ideal for the head injured person who has the unique combination of personality change, cognitive impairment and intact memory for a "normal" lifestyle pre-injury. The independent sector provides a number of warden-supported, group-based homes for brain injured people, but these are rare and little is provided in such a specific way by statutory services in the UK.

The situation is similar for day centre provision. In addition to the above groupings, there is provision for the physically disabled, but little specifically for those with head injuries. An important exception are Headway Houses, organised via the National Head Injuries Association, which are charitably funded. Day centres at the very least help to provide a daily activity for patients, which helps to maintain a routine and an, albeit brief, respite for relatives.

Respite care

One of the most important services, yet one of the most difficult to provide, is respite care. The ability to spend time apart is a vital and normal part of family life that can be extremely difficult for a person with a brain injury and their family. Day centres, sheltered employment, and sporting and leisure facilities for the disabled can provide regular such opportunities. Longer periods apart can be difficult to achieve. Holiday centres providing breaks for people with brain injury are one means of achieving this. Facilities used to provide respite for people with other disabilities is another option but has the disadvantage that staff may not be familiar with the particular needs of the person with a brain injury. For specialist services, it is difficult to provide an economically viable service for respite care, given the intermittent nature of the demand, which tends to be concentrated during certain periods of the year. It is also difficult to provide a responsive respite care service for times of family crisis, or a service that enables relatives of those with cognitive and behavioural difficulties to have regular evening breaks.

Whatever the difficulties, this issue needs to be addressed as respite can enable those who wish to continue to provide care for their family member to do so despite the immense pressures involved. The alternative is normally residential care, which is expensive and often far less satisfactory for the person with the brain injury.

Voluntary agencies

These have a variety of roles, including information giving, networking and support for head injured people and their families, providing day centres, reducing social isolation and as lobby groups to local and national government which can eventuate advantageous changes in legislation and service provision.

ROGUE ELEPHANTS AND SERVICE MIRAGES

Cost containment is a key element of health policy that is unlikely to change in the medium term. This means that new developments in service provision tend to occur at the expense of existing services. Neurorehabilitation is no exception. A danger from the point of view of the consumer is that new developments may be cost-cutting, less specialist, and less effective (but perhaps more local) than existing services. Examples of this include the establishment of brain injury rehabilitation centres in district hospital wards. This reduces the number of cases that can be referred to a regional centre (as the contract has been reduced in size), but the district service is essentially staffed on a part-time basis, and at worst may simply be a collection point for these patients in part of a ward so designated, with little more access to therapy than they would have had elsewhere in the hospital.

A second example can be the establishment of community rehabilitation teams, which may be understaffed, rarely include a clinical psychologist, tend not to have a day centre base and hence can only see patients in their home. In one survey, 34 out of 35 community teams in south-east England, which serve a population of about 15 million people, rarely saw *any* head injured patients. This is understandable and not a criticism of these teams, because their remit is usually physical disability, including elderly stroke patients and some patients with progressive neurological conditions and because their work load is high (McMillan & Ledder, submitted).

Service mirages of this kind are doubly destructive if purchasers believe that they provide a comprehensive service for traumatic head injury and hence that they should replace more intensive or specialised neurorehabilitation. In the short term this could easily lead to an erosion of the critical staffing mass at regional/specialist centres via cost savings, and to an extent from which they are unable to recover.

LEADERSHIP AND STAFFING

The type of leadership required depends on the nature and size of the particular rehabilitation service. There are of course several leadership roles. Except perhaps in very small services, it makes sense to separate management from clinical leadership. The former, which includes responsibilities such as financial management, personnel issues, and administration, is usually seen as a set of generalised, transferable skills. Clinical leadership, which involves clinical decision making, service philosophy, and design and motivation of the working team, requires a different set of skills. These skills essentially concern clinical/professional and scientific knowledge of brain injury and credibility in the eyes of colleagues to play a lead role in team decisions. Whilst management is based on formal authority, successful clinical leadership depends on sapiential authority. Because brain injury rehabilitation is a new and developing field such skills and knowledge are in short supply. Traditionally in health care the senior medical doctor has taken on this role. Whilst in some contexts this is still the most appropriate arrangement (e.g., in the early stages of recovery soon after injury) it should not be an automatic assumption in all brain injury rehabilitation. This is particularly the case where time since injury increases and the patient is approaching or has already been discharged to the community. At this time when cognitive and emotional problems are often the most salient, medical training is often not the most relevant. Nor will the medical practitioner be the most experienced in such rehabilitation. There are a number of precedents, in the US, in the UK and elsewhere in Europe, for non-medical clinical leadership (Ben Yishay, Silver, Piasetsky, & Rattock, 1987; Prigatano and Fordyce, 1986; Teasdale, Christensen, & Pinner, 1993; Wood, McCrea, Wood, & Merriman, 1999). Even in those contexts where there is a major medical role in the team it has been demonstrated that the medical practitioner can fulfil an important role without being the clinical leader (Oddy, 2000).

The staff mix of a team is another issue that has to be addressed in any service. Some reports (Medical Disability Society, 1998) have suggested ratios of particular clinical professionals to patients. Whilst attempts to set standards are laudable, such an exercise is extremely questionable since the requirements will depend on the nature and aims of the service and the way in which duties are organised.

At present, the professions most commonly involved include physiotherapists, speech and language therapists, occupational therapists, medics, nurses, social workers, and clinical psychologists. In addition, staff without a professional background are frequently employed, given in-house training and assist qualified members of the team. In some locations other designations have been given, such as "cognitive rehabilitation therapist". There has also been the suggestion that there should be a new, "generic brain injury therapist" who combines the skills, at least of the three therapy professions, but is trained from the outset in brain injury rehabilitation. Whilst this has certain attractions (e.g., elimination of aspects of training not relevant to brain injured people and the creation of specialists who will be dedicated to this field), it might cause yet more inter-professional "boundary disputes" and may restrict the development of brain injury rehabilitation by making it too inward looking a field of endeavour.

What is crucial to the success of any brain injury service is that the staff have the opportunity to specialise in this role, obtain further and continuing post-qualification training, and secure promotion without having to leave the field.

CONCLUSIONS

Although there are some general principles concerning the nature of services required for brain injury rehabilitation the systems of service delivery will inevitably vary from country to country depending on the organisational structures in existence. There are undoubtedly more services for brain injury than there were 10 or 15 years ago, notwithstanding the fact that in the US the "bubble" of service expansion in the 1980s has burst (Wood, 1996). A problem in the UK is that some existing services have not been designed in a way that is likely to lead to efficient and effective delivery and there are few, if any, parts of the world where one can be sure of receiving a seamless service from acute care through to long-term follow-up.

Acquired brain injury appears to have a higher profile now than 10–15 years ago, but services have not necessarily become more specifically targeted. If anything, in the UK there appears to be an increasing trend to provide a single service for disparate groups of individuals. Brain injury rehabilitation is best conducted in services dedicated to those with acquired brain injury, for the majority of whom personality changes and cognitive impairments are the primary disabilities. Very few services exist for this group despite the fact that the nature of the service that they require is very different from other groups.

In the UK at least, there is still a tendency to establish either inpatient facilities or non-specific community teams. It is our contention that the middle road of day rehabilitation should be the cornerstone of brain injury rehabilitation.

REFERENCES

Alderman, & N., & Knight, C. (1997). The effectiveness of DRL in the management and treatment of severe behaviour disorders following brain injury. *Brain Injury, 11,* 79–101.

Alderman, N., Fry, R.K., & Youngson, H.A. (1995). Improvement of self-monitoring skills, reduction of behaviour disturbance and the dysexecutive syndrome. *Neuropsychological Rehabilitation, 5,* 193–222.

Ben-Yishay, Y. (1996). Reflections on the evolution of the therapeutic milieu concept. *Neuropsychological Rehabilitation, 6*, 241–360.

Ben-Yishay, Y., Silver, S., Piasetsky, E., & Rattock, J. (1987). Relationship between employability and vocational outcome after intensive holistic cognitive rehabilitation. *Journal of Head Trauma Rehabilitation, 2*, 35–49.

Boake, C. (1990). Transitional living centres in head injury rehabilitation. In J.S. Kreutzer and P. Wehman (Eds.), *Community integration following traumatic brain injury* (pp. 115–124). Baltimore: Paul. H. Brookes.

Brooks, D.N., McKinlay, W.W., Symington, C., Beattie, A., & Campsie, L. (1987a). Return to work within the first seven years of severe head injury. *Brain Injury, 1*, 5–19.

Brooks, D.N., Campsie, L., Symington, C, et al. (1987b). The effects of severe head injury on patient and relative within seven years of injury. *Journal of Head Trauma Rehabilitation, 2*, 1–13.

Broughton, J. (1997). Road accident statistics. In M. Mitchell (Ed.), *The aftermath of road traffic accidents* (pp. 15–32). London: Routledge.

Bryden, J. (1988). How many head injured? The epidemiology of post head injury disability. In R.Ll. Wood & P. Eames (Eds.), *Models of brain injury rehabilitation*. London: Chapman Hall.

Challis, D., & Davies, B. (1986). *Case management in community care*. Aldershot: Gower.

Cope, D.N., & Hall, K.M. (1982). Head injury rehabilitation: Benefits of early intervention. *Archives Physical Medicine Rehabilitation, 63*, 433–437.

Deutsch, P.M., & Fralish, K.B. (1988). *Innovations in head injury rehabilitation*, (pp. 3.22–3.26). Mathew Bender.

Dixon, T.P., Goll, S., & Stanton, K.M. (1988). Case management issues and practices in head injury rehabilitation. *Rehabilitation Counselling Bulletin, 31*, 325–343.

Eames, P., & Wood, R. (1985). Rehabilitation after severe brain injury: A follow-up study of a behaviour modification approach. *Journal of Neurology, Neurosurgery and Psychiatry, 48*, 616–619.

Eames, P., Cotterill, G. Kneale, T.A., Storrar, A.L., & Yeomans, J. (1995). Outcome of intensive rehabilitation after severe brain injury: A long term follow-up study. *Brain Injury, 10*, 631–650.

Field, H.J. (1976). *Epidemiology of head injuries in England and Wales with particular reference to rehabilitation*. London: HMSO.

Greenwood, R.J., & McMillan, T.M. (1993) Models of rehabilitation programmes for the brain injured adult I: Current service provision. *Clinical Rehabilitation, 7*, 248–255

Greenwood, R.J., McMillan, T.M., Brooks, D.N., Dunn, G., Brock, D., Dinsdale, S., Murphy, L., & Price, J. (1994). Effects of case management after severe head injury. *British Medical Journal, 308*, 1199–1205.

Griffiths, R. (1988). *Care in the community*. London: HMSO.

Gualtieri, C.T., & Cox, D.R. (1991). The delayed neurobehavioural sequelae of traumatic brain injury. *Brain Injury, 5*, 219–232.

Harrick, L., Krefting, L., Johnston, J., Carlson, P., & Minnes, P. (1994). Stability of functional outcomes following transitional living programme participation: 3 year follow-up. *Brain Injury, 8*, 439–447.

Jennett, B. (1996). Epidemiology of head injuries. *Journal of Neurology, Neurosurgery, and Psychiatry, 60*, 362–369.

Johnson, R. (1998). How do people get back to work after severe head injury? A 10-year follow up study. *Neuropsychological Rehabilitation, 8*, 61–80.

Johnson, R., & Balleny, H. (1996). Behaviour problems after brain injury: Incidence and need for treatment. *Clinical Rehabilitation, 10,* 173–181.

Johnston, S., Burgess, J., McMillan, T.M., & Greenwood, R.J. (1991). Management of adipsia by a behavioural modification technique. *Journal of Neurology, Neurosurgery and Psychiatry, 54,* 272–274.

Kreutzer, J.S., Wehman, P., Morton, M.V., & Stonnington, H.H. (1988). Supported employment and compensatory strategies for enhancing vocational outcome following traumatic brain injury. *Brain Injury, 2,* 205–223.

Leavitt, S.S., Beyer, R.D., & Johnston, T.L. (1972). Monitoring the recovery process *Industrial Medicine, 41,* 25–30.

Mackay, L.E., Bernstein, B.A., Chapman, P.E., Morgan, A.S., & Milazzo, L.M. (1992). Early intervention in severe head injury. *Archives of Physical Medicine Rehabilitation, 73,* 635–643.

McMillan, T.M., & Greenwood, R.J. (1993a). Models of rehabilitation programmes for the brain injured adult II: Model services and suggestions for change in the UK. *Clinical Rehabilitation, 7,* 346–355.

McMillan, T.M., & Greenwood, R.J. (1993b). Head injury. In R.J. Greenwood, M. Barnes, T.M. McMillan, & C. Ward (Eds.), *Neurological rehabilitation* (pp. 437–450). Edinburgh: Churchill Livingstone.

McMillan, T.M., & Sparkes, C. (1999). Goal planning and neurorehabilitation: The Wolfson Neuro-Rehabilitation Centre approach. *Neuropsychological Rehabilitation, 9,* 241–252.

McMillan, T.M., & Ledder, H. (submitted). Services provided by community neurorehabilitation teams in south-east England.

McMillan, T.M., Greenwood, R.J., Morris, J.R., Brooks, D.N., Murphy, L., & Dunn, G. (1988). An introduction to the concept of head injury case management with respect to the need for service provision. *Clinical Rehabilitation, 2,* 319–322.

McMordie, W., Barker, S.L., & Paolo, T.M. (1990). Return to work (RTW) after head injury. *Brain Injury, 4,* 57–69.

Medical Disability Society (1988). *Report of a working party on the management of traumatic brain injury.* London: The Development Trust for the Young Disabled.

Miller, J.D., & Jones, P.A. (1985). The work of a regional head injury service. *Lancet,* 1141–1144.

Mills, V.M., Nesbeda, T., Katz, D.I., & Alexander, M.P. (1992). Outcome for traumatically brain injured patients following post-acute rehabilitation programmes. *Brain Injury, 6,* 219–228.

Mitchell, S., Bradley, V.A., Welch, J.L., & Britton, P.G. (1990). Coma arousal procedure: a therapeutic intervention in the treatment of head injury. *Brain Injury, 4,* 273–279.

Moss, N.E.G., & Wade, D.T. (1996). Admission after head injury. *Injury, 27,* 159–161.

Murphy, L.D., McMillan, T.M., Greenwood, R.J., Brooks, D.N., Morris, J.R., & Dunn, G. (1989). Services for severely head injured patients in North London and environs. *Brain Injury, 4,* 95–100.

National Centre for Health Statistics (1997). *Data file documentation, National Hospital discharge survey, 1980–1995.* Rockville, MD: National Center for Health Statistics, Centre for Disease Control and Prevention.

Oddy, M. (1993). Psychosocial consequences of brain injury. In R.J. Greenwood, M. Barnes, et al. (Eds.), *Neurological rehabilitation* (pp. 423–436). Edinburgh: Churchill Livingstone.

Oddy, M. (2000). Taking the lead in brain injury services. *The Psychologist, 13,* 21–23.

Oddy, M., Bonham, E., McMillan, T.M., Stroud, A., & Rickard, S. (1990). A comprehensive service for the rehabilitation and long term care of head injury survivors. *Clinical Rehabilitation, 3*, 253–259.

Oddy, M., Coughlan, T., Tyerman, A., & Jenkins, D. (1985). Social adjustment after closed head injury: A further follow-up seven years after injury. *Journal of Neurology, Neurosurgery and Psychiatry, 48*, 564–568.

Pentland, B., & Barnes, M. (1988). Staffing provision for early head injury rehabilitation. *Clinical Rehabilitation, 2*, 309–313.

Perlmann B.B., Melnick, G., & Kentera, A. (1985). Assessing the effectiveness of a case management programme. *Hospital Community Psychiatry, 36*, 405–407.

Ponsford, J. (1995). Mechanisms recovery and sequelae of traumatic brain injury. A foundation for the REAL approach. In J. Ponsford, S. Sloan, & P. Snow (Eds.), *Traumatic Brain Injury* (pp. 1–31). Hove, UK: Lawrence Erlbaum Associates Ltd.

Ponsford, J.L., Sloan, S., & Snow, P. (1995). *Traumatic brain injury: Rehabilitation for everyday adaptive living.* Hove, UK: Lawrence Erlbaum Associates Ltd.

Prigatano, G.P. (1986). Psychotherapy after brain injury. In G.P. Prigatano (Ed.), *Neuropsychological rehabilitation after brain injury,* Baltimore: Johns Hopkins University Press.

Prigatano, G.P., & Fordyce, D.J. (1986). *The neuropsychological rehabilitation program at Presbyterian Hospital, Oklahoma City.* Baltimore: Johns Hopkins University Press.

Riddoch, M.J., & Humphreys, G.W. (1994). *Cognitive neuropsychology and cognitive rehabilitation.* Hove: Lawrence Erlbaum Associates Ltd.

Robertson, I.H., Hogg, K., & McMillan, T.M. (1998). Rehabilitation of visual neglect: improving function by contralesional limb activation. *Neuropsychological Rehabilitation, 8*, 19–29.

Robertson, I.H., North, N.T., & Geggie, C. (1992). Spatiomotor cueing in unilateral neglect: Three case studies of its therapeutic effects. *Journal of Neurology, Neurosurgery and Psychiatry, 55*, 799–805.

Rusk, H.A., Block, J.M., & Loman, E.W. (1969). Rehabilitation following traumatic brain damage. *Medical Clinics of North America, 53*, 677–84.

Rusk, H.A., Loman, E.W., & Block, J.M. (1966). Rehabilitation of the patient with head injury. *Clinical Neurosurgery, 12*, 312–323.

Soderstrom, S., et al. (1988). A program for crisis intervention after traumatic brain injury. *Scandinavian Journal of Rehabilitation Medicine (Suppl.), 17*, 47–49.

Tallal, R., Miller, S.L., Bedi, G., Byma, G., Wang, X.Q., Nagarajan, S.S., Schreiner, C., Jenkins, W.M., & Merzenich, M. (1996). Language comprehension in language-learning impaired children improved with acoustically modified speech. *Science, 271*, 81–84.

Taub, E., Miller, N.E., Novack, T.A., Cook, E.W., Fleming, W.C., Nepomuceno, C.S., Connell, J.S., & Crago, J.E. (1993). Techniques to improve chronic motor deficit after stroke. *Archives of Physical Medicine and Rehabilitation, 74*, 347–354.

Teasdale, G. (1995). Head injury. *Journal of Neurology, Neurosurgery and Psychiatry, 58*, 526–539.

Teasdale, T.W., Christensen, A.-L., & Pinner, E.V. (1993). Psychosocial rehabilitation of cranial trauma and stroke patients. *Brain Injury, 7*, 535–542.

Tennant, A., MacDermott, N., & Neary, D. (1995). The long term outcome of head injury. *Brain Injury, 9*, 595–605.

Thompson, D.C., Rivera, F.P., & Thompson, R.S. (1996). Effectiveness of bicycle safety helmets in preventing head injuries. *Journal of American Medical Association, 276*, 1968–1974.

Wade, D.T., King, N.S., Wenden, F.J., Crawford, S., & Caldwell, F.E. (1998). Routine follow-up after a head injury: A second randomised controlled trial. *Journal of Neurology Neurosurgery and Psychiatry, 65,* 177–183.

Wall, J.R., Rosenthal, M., & Niemczura, J.G. (1998). Community based retraining after acquired brain injury. *Brain Injury, 12,* 215–224.

Wasylenski, D.A., Goering, P., & Lancee, W. (1985). Import of a case manager on psychiatric after care. *Journal of Nervous Mental Disease, 17,* 303–308.

Wehman, P., Kregel, J., Sherron, P., Kreutzer, J., Fry, R., & Zasler, N. (1993). Critical factors associated with the successful supported employment placement of patients with severe traumatic brain injury. *Brain Injury, 7,* 31–44.

Wehman, P.H., Kreutzer, J.S., West, M.D., Sherron, P.D., Zasler, N.D., Groah, C.H., Stonnington, H.H., Burns, C.T., & Sale, P.R. (1990). Return to work for persons with traumatic brain injury: A supported employment approach. *Archives of Physical Medicine Rehabilitation, 71,* 1047–1052.

Wehman, P.H., West, M.D., Sherron, P., & Kreutzer, J.S. (1995). Return to work for persons with severe traumatic brain injury: A data-based approach to program development. *Journal of Head Trauma Rehabilitation, 10,* 27–39.

Wilson, B.A. (1998). Recovery of cognitive functions following non-progressive brain injury. *Current Opinion in Neurobiology, 8,* 281–287.

Wilson, B.A., Baddeley, A., Shiel, A., & Patton, G. (1992). How does post traumatic amnesia differ from amnesic syndrome and chronic memory impairment? *Neuropsychological Rehabilitation, 2,* 231–243.

Wilson, S.L.W., & McMillan, T.M. (1993). A review of the evidence for the effectiveness of sensory stimulation treatment for coma and vegetative states. *Neuropsychological Rehabilitation, 3,* 149–160.

Wood, R.Ll. (1991). Critical analysis of the concept of sensory stimulation for patients in vegetative states. *Brain Injury, 5,* 401–410.

Wood, R.Ll. (1996). Ten years of post-acute brain injury rehabilitation: (A view from the independent sector). *Personal Injury,* 203–211.

Wood, R.Ll., McCrea, J.D., Wood, L.M., & Merriman, R.N. (1999). Clinical and cost effectiveness of post-acute neurobehavioural rehabilitation. *Brain Injury, 13,* 69–88

Commentary on service provision for social disability and handicap after acquired brain injury: An Australian perspective

J.L. Ponsford
Monash University and Bethesda Rehabilitation Centre, Melbourne, Australia

As in the UK and the USA, the number of road deaths and traumatically head injured survivors in Australia appears to have declined gradually over the past two decades, due to improved road safety measures and better systems of trauma management, although there is a lack of accurate national figures. Australian outcome studies indicate that whilst physical mobility and independence in personal care tend to be restored in more than 90% of cases, there are continuing problems with cognitive function and behaviour. These have a significant negative impact upon work or study, leisure activities, and personal and social adjustment in the majority of those with severe traumatic head injury. Reported problems tend to increase between two and five years post-injury, with growing levels of social isolation, anxiety, and depression (Olver, Ponsford, & Curran, 1996).

Despite differences in the structure and funding of health care and accident compensation systems between the UK, US, and Australia, there have been many parallels in the development of services for individuals with traumatic head injury. There has been a growing realisation of the need for specialised services, which focus more upon cognitive, behavioural, and social problems, rather than the traditional rehabilitation focus upon mobility and independence in daily activities. However, the different funding systems for rehabilitation in Australia do impact upon the nature and availability of services, resulting in some variability in the nature and quality of service provision from one state to another.

Most Australians with brain injury do not receive rehabilitation funded by private health insurance. They are treated either in government-funded programmes, or in private programmes funded by no-fault accident insurance schemes existing in some states, such as Victoria. Under the Transport Accident Commission and Work Cover schemes in Victoria, individuals sustaining injuries in motor vehicle or work-related accidents are automatically covered for hospital and rehabilitation costs, as well as loss of earnings, regardless of fault. There is also entitlement to funding for supported work trials, integration support for students, attendant care, and respite care. Some specialised services for head injury rehabilitation have been developed within the private sector as a result of these schemes. They allow for more rapid access to services without monetary cost to the injured person or family. They also ensure access to comprehensive rehabilitation services across a broader spectrum of injury severity than appears to be the case in the UK, and with greater equity than appears to be the case in the USA. Services also tend to be somewhat less time-limited than in the US and the UK. Victoria, New South Wales, South Australia, and Western Australia also have government-funded networks of brain injury rehabilitation services, based in capital cities. A few of the larger rural centres have developed support networks. The South Australian support network makes use of teleconferencing to provide therapeutic input to clients in isolated rural areas. However, as in the UK and the USA, there are wide variations in the quality and availability of programmes in different parts of the country. There is still a need for greater equity of access and better integration of services. Some individuals receive only standard inpatient and possibly outpatient therapy in a general rehabilitation setting. Availability of follow-up support varies greatly. Services in rural areas are particularly limited.

Acute management tends to take place in neurosurgical wards of major hospitals, some of which now have specialised trauma units catering specifically for the needs of brain injured individuals. There remains a significant need for better communication and support for families during this phase. Specialised inpatient brain injury rehabilitation facilities funded by the government and/or private centres now exist in most capital cities, with approximately one such 12–15-bed unit per million population. Many very severely brain injured patients from country areas receive inpatient rehabilitation in these city-based units.

Historically, and in many centres to the present time, brain injury rehabilitation has been delivered according to an inter- or multidisciplinary model, with the majority of therapy being carried out at the rehabilitation centre. With increasing evidence of long-term difficulties experienced by head injured individuals in the community, there has been a gradual shift towards the more client-focused model of service delivery outlined by McMillan and Oddy. This involves setting goals with involvement of the brain-injured person and family, and conducting therapy in community settings, with a focus on tasks and roles of direct relevance to the injured individual. Active involvement of family, friends, employers, and teachers is also being sought to a greater degree than previously, with the realisation of the essential role they play in implementing compensatory or other management strategies and continuing the rehabilitative process over the longer term.

It is increasingly recognised that there is a significant need for psychological support for the person with head injury and close others. Whilst important at all stages of recovery, this seems to be particularly necessary after the injured person has left inpatient care, and begins to experience the impact of major changes in lifestyle and ability levels. Development of adjustment difficulties and substance use problems is common at this time. Family members also tend not to focus upon lasting behavioural or personality changes until some time after the injured person has returned home. Availability of skilled psychological support services is still rather limited in Australia, even within specialised units. There has also been a growing awareness of the importance of follow-up contact to continue over many years, in order to provide support in dealing with the problems as they arise. Only a few centres are able to offer continuing follow-up, however. In this regard the concept of the community centre for acquired brain injury, which has a register of all brain-injured individuals in the local area and routinely makes follow-up contact, providing assistance as necessary, is a very good one.

Transitional living programmes have been established in association with many of the specialised brain injury rehabilitation programmes, in order to provide individuals with traumatic head injury with the experience of living in a shared house or an apartment within a residential community. Intensive training can be provided in personal care, and domestic and community-based activities.

There is an opportunity to deal with interpersonal difficulties, to develop and practise anger management strategies and other interpersonal problem-solving skills and to receive psychological support. Use of leisure time is another important focus of these programmes. Support is given in moving to a permanent place of living, either finding new accommodation or re-establishing roles and relationships in a previous place of living, establishing independence; and developing social and recreational activities and emotional supports within the local community. Follow-up assistance is essential in order to deal with new problems as they arise.

In those cases where funding is available, an attendant carer may be employed and trained to support the person with brain injury to live independently. Attendant carer roles may vary from the provision of assistance or supervision with personal, domestic, or community activities, to assistance in accessing work, study, or recreational activities, to facilitating the development of a social network. The use of attendant care support provides invaluable respite for families and enables many injured individuals to live in the community.

Outcome data from the Transitional Living Centre at Bethesda Rehabilitation Centre (Olver & Harrington, 1996) in Australia have demonstrated that, whereas 15% of clients required assistance with domestic and community activities on commencement of the programme, on completion more than 80% were independent in light domestic tasks, cooking, laundry, shopping, banking, and public transport, and more than 50% were independent in heavy domestic tasks, household organisation, and financial management. While only 2% were able to live independently on entry to the programme, 58% were able to live independently afterwards, 22% required some supervision, and 19% continued to need active assistance.

Another model of service provision that has evolved in Australia over the past few years has been that of a community-based team. The composition of such teams varies, but most comprise a case manager, co-ordinating the services of occupational therapy, speech pathology, clinical and/or neuropsychology, and physical therapy and/or social work, as needed. Vocational counselling and educational assessment is also typically available. All team members would not necessarily be involved with a given individual. Assessment, goal-setting, and interventions are carried out within the relevant settings in the community. Intervention may involve training to establish routines, development of compensatory strategies, or modification of the task or environment to maximise successful task performance. The aim is to harness a range of local community resources and natural supports in order to attain goals, and to facilitate the establishment of a support network of family, friends, and others. The case manager or specific team members ideally maintain follow-up contact to ensure that the network is maintained and to deal with any difficulties arising. However, the extent to which this is possible is limited by the resources of the teams, which typically carry extremely heavy workloads. Although therapists working in these teams and their clients feel this service model is more effective, there are no comprehensive data available as yet to indicate the relative costs and outcomes from these programmes, as opposed to centre-based programmes.

It would appear that rehabilitation services are more readily available across a broader range of injury severity in Australia than in the UK. Perhaps because of this, there is considerable emphasis in the Australian system on returning to work or study. However, support for the process of return to work or school in Australia varies somewhat with sources of funding. For those covered by no-fault compensation schemes there is funding for supported work trials, and integration support and/or tutoring for those in secondary or tertiary education. There is also a government-funded vocational rehabilitation service available nationally. A detailed analysis of job or study requirements is carried out to determine what limitations the person may have in fulfilling these and what modifications need to be made to the work or study regime to accommodate these limitations. Education of employers and teachers and frequent communication are vital components of this process. Usually the employee returns to work initially on a part-time, trial basis with their salary paid by the insurer. A therapist may spend time in the workplace facilitating work performance and assisting in the development of strategies to overcome difficulties. For those who do not have a job to return to, the process is more complex. Assistance is required in evaluating work skills, developing a résumé and job interview skills, networking suitable employers, and supporting the employee in learning to cope with the job. Outcome data indicate that there is considerable movement in and out of employment between 2 and 5 years post-injury. In view of this, continuing follow up after return to employment is essential in order to circumvent or deal with problems which arise, often due to interpersonal conflict or changing demands in the workplace. Availability of such follow-up contact is limited.

Behaviour management remains the biggest challenge to service providers. Several states have specialist units for managing severely disturbed brain-injured individuals. Victoria also has a government-funded community-based support team for individuals with severe, long-term behaviour problems who have no access to compensation. This team of clinical psychologists and neuropsychologists offers education, secondary and tertiary consultation to institutions (e.g., nursing homes, schools) or caregivers, as well as direct intervention in relevant community settings. There is no doubt that such specialised services are essential to the management of persisting severe behaviour problems.

The majority of those with severe head injuries live with their families in the long term, often ageing parents. However, a growing number of group homes are being set up for brain injured individuals in Australia. These are funded either through one of the no-fault insurance schemes, which are encouraging such arrangements, or from financial settlements of those injured and living in the houses. These situations usually involve more than one head injured person living together, sharing attendant care support. In others, the injured person lives alone, with attendant care support, or with non-injured house mates. Those living in these houses are generally supported by case managers and require a considerable amount of therapeutic support to set up and maintain the household. Having more than one brain injured person living together causes conflicts at times. Nevertheless, the benefits to quality of life, and frequently also behavioural and functional levels, are immense.

Few activity programmes have been established to provide opportunities for those with brain injuries to explore interests and mix socially. One such recreational programme has recently been established using the facilities of one of the universities in Melbourne. Only those with very severe injuries tend to want to be involved in such day programmes. There are very few day programmes in Australia which cater specifically for young brain injured people. In general an attempt is made to integrate those with head injuries into activities in their local communities. This is not always successful or sustainable, however. Ongoing case management is necessary in order to maintain these arrangements. For those with compensation, funding is available for respite care. However, options for provision of respite care are extremely limited.

The Head Injuries Council of Australia, Headway, and other state brain injury organisations provide invaluable services in advocating for the rights of those with brain injury, providing information regarding resources, and above all supporting those injured and their families. Their resources appear to be more limited than those of Headway UK or the National Head Injuries Foundation in the USA, due to a relative lack of government funding support.

REFERENCES

Olver, J., & Harrington, H. (1996). Functional outcome after a transitional living programme for adults with traumatic brain injury. In J. Ponsford, P. Snow, & V. Anderson (Eds.), *International perspectives in traumatic brain injury* (pp. 359–361). Bowen Hills: Australian Academic Press.

Olver, J.H., Ponsford, J.L., & Curran, C.A. (1996). Outcome following traumatic brain injury: A comparison between 2 and 5 years after injury. *Brain Injury, 10*, 841–848.

Commentary on service provision for social disability and handicap after acquired brain injury: An American perspective

D.E. Eazell
Past Chairman, American Medical Rehabilitation Providers Association, USA

In this chapter McMillan and Oddy accurately depict the circumstances to which a person with acquired brain injury will be exposed in many industrialised nations throughout the world. The findings in their review of the literature on the incidence of acquired brain injury trending down appear supported in the US. Their observation that "seamless rehabilitation" is the most desirable method for the provision of recovery services to the person having acquired brain injury is a need not only in the UK but every industrialised nation in the world.

In the US one can find the multitude of services described by the authors. There are acute specialised rehabilitation hospitals and units within hospitals, transitional living units, long-term specialised residential centres, day care, home health care, vocational, and recreational programmes for persons with acquired brain injury. The one common issue among these services is that, generally, they are not seamless and their availability is subject to the person with brain injury having the financial resources that permit access to the service. If, after an injury, fault is conceded by another party (e.g., employer or insurance liability carrier) and financial reimbursement follows via the courts, access to rehabilitation services from the acute phase through to community re-entry services becomes a likely option. In all other circumstances, specialist rehabilitation services may be hard to access. Further, the geographic region in which a person resides will determine the availability of different types of rehabilitation service.

The Rehabilitation Services Administration, a department of Health and Human Services of the US government, published a paper entitled *Vocational rehabilitation service coordination for persons with traumatic brain injury* (1998). The conclusions of the paper support the idea that "seamless rehabilitation" remains a distant hope in the USA. The conclusions reached included the following:

1. There is no co-ordinated system of care and community re-entry.
2. The State Vocational Rehabilitation Agency, as a time-limited service provider, does not allow for ongoing lifelong support required by the person with acquired brain injury.
3. Rural areas present significant challenges in bringing necessary services for persons with brain injury.

To complicate the challenge of achieving "seamless rehabilitation", the USA is on a relentless mission to reduce the cost of health care through managed care. The result of the managed care effort demonstrates itself by reducing lengths of stay in acute hospitals and transitional living centres from months to days. Accordingly, the family is the unit of treatment on which the patient must rely for recovery. In the US the majority of family units have two persons working to support the family lifestyle. As a result, when a traumatic injury is visited upon a family unit, major financial, psychological, and social disruptions are commonplace. Further, managed care companies are authorising rehabilitation services to be provided in lower-cost skilled nursing facilities, so that costs for medical care can be contained. The rehabilitation consumer often cannot distinguish between types of services needed or required for their recovery. If the physician in the managed care organisation recommends skilled nursing, versus hospital care, the consumer will generally abide by the physician's recommendation.

State and federal government reimbursement to skilled nursing facilities was converted in the late 1990s to a prospective payment system. This method of reimbursement has generally reduced the financial resources paid to the skilled facilities for rehabilitation services. The federal government, through the Health Care Financing Administration (HCFA), is designing a similar reimbursement system for acute care rehabilitation hospitals and units, such that a likely reduction in the financial means to provide rehabilitation services will occur for this group of providers. By statute, the reduction cannot be less than 2% of the current reimbursement paid to hospitals. The American Medical Rehabilitation Provider Association (AMRPA) is working with HCFA in an attempt to achieve some measure of equitable payment for patients needing rehabilitation. It is too soon to comment regarding the results of the negotiations. However, the agenda of HCFA is to reduce cost while the intention of the provider group is to protect rehabilitation services for the disabled. AMPRA is analysing several data sources that may justify rehabilitation interventions at the acute level in relationship to functional outcomes within the community. The data will not include transitional living services or community re-entry options, as HCFA does not cover such services.

The availability of reimbursement to provide recovery from the acute phase of rehabilitation to community-based services (seamless rehabilitation) for the person with acquired brain injury is complicated by insurance policy language and differing agenda's among the major insurance agencies. For example, if one is injured by an uninsured motorist in a state that does not operate a "no-fault" insurance plan, and if the injured party is without the financial means to pay for rehabilitation, then insurance cover for rehabilitation would be provided by the federal/state governmental plan called Medicaid. In the State of California, the injured party would receive, at best, a few weeks of acute rehabilitation in a speciality hospital. Only 20% of the cost of outpatient services would be paid and this might only include a few sessions of speech, occupational, and physical therapy. The California/federal governmental insurance policy will not provide community-based neurobehavioural rehabilitation or other transitional living experiences offered by community centres designed for such treatment. The injured party, upon discharge from the outpatient setting, would have to apply for financial support from another agency, vocational rehabilitation from still another agency, and would probably need to live with a family member who will assist in their recovery. At a time when support is needed by the family and recovering patient, it is unfortunate that numerous negotiations and prolonged waiting for decisions permitting assistance is the rule and not the exception.

Under circumstances wherein the injured party can hold another party liable and the insurance company is accountable for a lifetime of expense, the person should be able to access services that offer seamless rehabilitation. The insurance company liability for lifetime medical care and living expenses encourages that company to reduce the cost of that lifetime care by facilitating maximum independence. When the liability is great, one often finds case managers co-ordinating the recovery of the injured party from the acute phase to full community re-entry services.

Still another insurance scenario could result in medical care being provided by a managed care insurance company. The managed care insurance policy generally will not cover community re-entry services. As a result, the managed care company will only provide physical recovery interventions and thus the insured and his or her family will have to travel the road of negotiation for living expenses and community re-entry services from the myriad or scant governmental and non-profit agencies in their respective community.

Usually, the resolution to the problem of creating "seamless rehabilitation" for persons with acquired brain injury boils down to the issue of money and who manages it. We may one day discover that sufficient financial resources exist to operate a seamless system. However, reaching agreement with the powers that currently consume and/or control the financial resources in a disjointed delivery system will delay the implementation of an effective rehabilitation process and life management system for persons with acquired brain injury.

The US has centres of excellence in a few geographic locations. These are heavily supported by voluntary donations from the community. The leaders in such organisations must have the vision for seamless rehabilitation. This may require them to dissociate themselves from the role of ensuring the financial survival of their centre. The information required to create the appropriate services is available in published journals relating to acquired brain injury. There are knowledgeable professionals in the field who can assist in designing appropriate programmes for persons with brain injury. Observations of the family associated with the person experiencing the brain injury often reveal the services needed by that family and injured party. However, a review of current literature could lead one to conclude that the traditional services and clinical structures operated in the USA are obsolete because they were constructed within a framework where method of payment had to be secured as a priority for every case and the facility had to be perceived as appropriate by paying agents (often insurance companies). Balancing risk between continuing with historically accepted services, for which payment sources have been established, and risking the development of new and more effective treatment innovations for which payment is not established, is no easy task for the managers of these centres.

There are bright and knowledgeable minds in the US that have the capacity to formulate the service needs for persons with acquired brain injury, so why then does the US often relegate this population to a meagre and dysfunctional system of service? Perhaps the answer is to be found in the system of health care itself. Major insurance carriers, governmental agencies, professionals, and consumers and providers of rehabilitation interventions seem unable to reach agreement regarding an appropriate system of care for the person with acquired brain injury. The data to support a co-ordinated system of care in the US is much like the services provided— it exists in bits and pieces. Medical insurance companies, employers, and the numerous governmental service divisions that serve persons with acquired brain injury would probably not endorse and, in fact, would probably strenuously oppose a co-ordinated system of care in which each would perceive a possible loss of financial resource and/or control of that resource. The future for a rehabilitation provider in the US will continue to have payment sources demand more efficient and effective methods of delivery. Those insurance companies that cover only the initial rehabilitation recovery phase (i.e. managed care) will look to rehabilitation providers to collect data that demonstrates future cost reductions in lifetime medical care as a result of the rehabilitation interventions. Those insurance companies that have a broader liability for the injured party will likewise require data demonstrating a correlation between rehabilitation intervention and cost-effective community living outcomes. The numerous providers of rehabilitation services in the US will become fewer due to financial resource restrictions, while those providers left will strenuously compete for the remaining limited funds.

The National Association for Brain Injury in the US has advocated that co-ordinated services be provided to persons with brain injury. The effort to bring a more effective and co-ordinated service for their constituency has been a challenging one. The author is not optimistic that a lobbying effort of sufficient magnitude can be mobilised to create a seamless rehabilitation system in the US. There are too few people who care about persons with acquired brain injury to mobilise the personal commitment necessary to modify the bits and pieces of rehabilitation provided for this minority. We currently have a system in which (1) there are a relatively small group of patients whose problems are not obvious to the layman and which do not attract sympathy in the way that other deserving groups might (e.g., the disabled child); (2) those who provide rehabilitation cannot agree about the needs of people with acquired brain injury; (3) major groups that could influence public policy would probably oppose the development of a "seamless service". Consequently, whilst centralised management for major trauma, with the financial authority to take the person from the acute phase of rehabilitation to community living, would be desirable for the confused consumer, a national system reflecting the characteristics of seamless rehabilitation for persons with acquired brain injury is unlikely to become a reality in the US, at least in the foreseeable future.

Seamless rehabilitation has been defined and can theoretically be made operational. It is the personal commitment of the many, wanting to help the few, combined with the release of financial control by the many to the few, that will make seamless rehabilitation a reality in the US. The needs of persons with acquired brain injury for methods that facilitate their inclusion into the community will remain a pressing issue for this population in the US. McMillan and Oddy are to be commended for framing a solid direction that can be considered for a seamless rehabilitation system long overdue. Perhaps one day the US will "use" the service design proposed by them.

SOURCES OF INFORMATION

Vocational Rehabilitation Service Coordination for Persons with Traumatic Brain Injury (1998). Rehabilitation Services Administration, through The National Institute on Disability and Rehabilitation Research, http://www.naric.com.

Zollar, Carolyn, Executice Vice President Public Policy, American Medical Rehabilitation Providers Association, Washington, DC.

Parrette, Anne, Director of Public Policy, National Brain Injury Association (biausa.org).

CHAPTER THIRTEEN

Future directions:
Brain injury services in 2010

M. Oddy
Brain Injury Rehabilitation Unit, Wadhurst, UK

T.M. McMillan
University of Glasgow, Gartnavel Royal Hospital, UK

INTRODUCTION

At the time of writing we look ahead into the new millennium. In this chapter we have the freedom to gaze into our crystal ball and anticipate developments that may have occurred by the year 2010. To do this we will look at (1) scientific and technological developments, (2) service systems, and (3) staff training over the next 10 years. We intend to consider what may happen, what we can hope will happen, and what it will take to achieve these changes. Looking back over the last 10 years there have certainly been changes in each of these three areas. Perhaps some of the most significant developments are those that provide tools to make further advances. An example is the development of functional imaging from its infancy in the 1980s. Much work has been carried out over the last decade in cognitive neuropsychology although this perhaps has yet to reach its full potential. Further studies evaluating the efficacy of brain injury rehabilitation generally have appeared during the last decade. New and more sophisticated neuropsychological tests have been developed. Indeed with the advent of the Wechsler Adult Intelligence Scales III, rather few tests remain from the neuropsychologist's test battery of 10 years ago. Computer technology and its accessibility has developed in leaps and bounds during the 1990s. Yet this does not appear to have had as great an impact as was expected (Ager, 1991). Perhaps there is a time lag and the next decade will see full exploitation of the technological advancements made in the last decade.

Services have altered over the last 10 years. In the US there has been a retraction of inpatient services following a dramatic increase in the 1980s, whereas in Britain and Europe, new dedicated services for brain injury have been introduced. These services have appeared in a number of different forms, but perhaps the greatest development has been in community-based services.

As far as professional developments and the training of staff are concerned there have been no major changes over the last decade. However, a number of suggestions have been made, for example, that there should be a new professional "breed" of generic brain injury therapists (Wood, 1996) or neurocognitive therapists or trainers. Some developments have occurred within the existing professions. For example, speech and language therapists trained over the last decade have had a thorough grounding in cognitive neuropsychology. Post-qualification courses in rehabilitation taking entrants from a range of professional backgrounds have emerged. In medicine the number of those trained in rehabilitation medicine has considerably increased during the last decade. In psychology the number of clinical psychologists specialising in neuropsychology has increased and two new subdivisions of applied psychology have appeared (health psychology and counselling psychology). As yet, these developments have had little impact on brain injury rehabilitation. Health psychologists focus on health-related research and evaluation but usually do not engage in direct work with individual clients. Interest from counselling psychologists is growing, but by and large they have yet to apply their skills to those who have suffered a brain injury (Judd & Wilson, 1999). Professionalism in clinical neuropsychology has continued to develop whether as a distinct discipline (e.g., Australia, South Africa, Holland) or as a specialism after qualifying in clinical psychology (UK) .

SCIENTIFIC AND TECHNOLOGICAL DEVELOPMENTS

Prevention

This is always likely to remain the surest means of avoiding the difficulties and distress caused by brain injury. The last two decades have seen greater emphasis on vehicle safety, including increased usage of seatbelts, air bags, side impact bars, and bicycle helmets; the continuing separation of pedestrians from traffic; vehicle calming methods; more effective drink driving campaigns; and more stringent criteria for passing driving tests. Although there is little direct evidence for a change in the incidence of traumatic brain injury overall (see McMillan & Oddy, Chapter 12, this volume), it is likely that improvements in safety have reduced morbidity from the level that would have been reached without their introduction. It is imperative for all, including institutions such as government and insurance companies, that safety measures continue to develop in this millennium. However, there may well be developments in other areas of accident prevention. Research on driver behaviour suggests that inexperienced drivers differ from more experienced drivers in their ability to anticipate hazards (McKenna & Horswill, 1999). This finding in itself could be translated into improved training for learner/inexperienced drivers. Greater use of driving simulators might improve the skills of inexperienced drivers before they are let loose on the road. Sensor systems fitted to cars could automatically enforce speed restrictions or otherwise reduce reliance on the driver's reaction to a hazard. Eventually it may be possible simply to key in a destination (or "speak in" a destination) and the vehicle will automatically transport its passengers, eliminating the possibility of driver error. Formula One motor racing cannot fail to impress and surprise, when drivers step nimbly out of a wrecked car that a few seconds before was travelling at over 100 miles per hour. It seems that the design of these cars gives considerably more protection to their occupants than that of commercially available cars. It is to be hoped that relevant technology used in motor sports will become an integral part of commercial car design by the year 2010.

Improved outcome after brain injury is also likely to follow improved care at the scene of the accident and in the acute stages of care. Improved scanning and access to scanners has meant that the early detection of some secondary effects of brain injury is possible and research has continued into methods of reducing and preventing the cascade of secondary and tertiary effects following a brain injury. Over the next decade we may look forward to improved chemical management of acute brain injury, and to developments in techniques for detecting complications, and perhaps (currently) more controversial interventions, such as artificially cooling the brain might become standard. Improvements in the speedy and effective delivery of acute services can also be achieved—but these will be discussed in the section on service developments.

Treatment and rehabilitation

Recently there have been some preliminary indications that the adult brain may be capable of supporting the genesis of neurones. Traditionally, it has been accepted that although axons and dendrites may regenerate, if the cell body is damaged the cell dies and in adults cannot be replaced. This has been challenged by animal research for some time, but recently evidence for neurogenesis in the brains of adult humans has been reported (Eriksson et al., 1998). The practical implications of this work are as yet unclear, but if neurorehabilitation, perhaps in concert with medication, could stimulate genesis of neurones then recovery after brain injury might attain new horizons (see McMillan, Robertson, & Wilson, 1999). Over the last decade there has been a significant trend away from attempts at remediation of cognitive impairment towards functional rehabilitation. This has been based on the premise that it is not possible to enhance recovery at the level of cognitive impairment, and hence that rehabilitation must focus on training people to use strategies to achieve goals. However, the finding by Eriksson et al. (1998) together with recent evidence for effectiveness of rehabilitation directed at some specific cognitive impairments (see McMillan & Oddy, Chapter 12 this volume) suggests that the next decade could see the development of treatments that reduce *impairment* after brain injury.

Another development over the past 25 years has been the implantation of foetal or neural tissue grafts into areas including the hippocampus and striatum. In addition to extensive animal research, clinical trials have included Parkinson's and Huntington's disease patients with some evidence for improved motor control in the former (Dunnett, in press). This is clearly an exciting advance which might in time be considered for severe brain injury. It is likely that in order for such replacement tissue to lead to maximal recovery of function, optimal environmental conditions and rehabilitation procedures will need to be identified.

An area that has been all but ignored during the last decade is that of enriched environments. There is a considerable body of research on animals indicating that it is possible to design external as well as internal environments that stimulate the recovery of the brain following injury. For example, experimental work with laboratory rats has demonstrated that greater interaction with the environment results in a more highly developed and more efficient brain. Increased environmental interaction has also been shown to enhance behavioural and cognitive recovery following many types of brain damage in animals. This work has yet to be meaningfully applied to rehabilitation following brain injury in humans. Although complex, the notion that external environmental conditions could be set to enhance recovery from brain injury is of interest, particularly if neurogenesis and brain implants prove to be clinically effective in acquired brain injury cases. Rose and Johnson (1996) suggest that virtual reality technology may provide a means of designing and controlling a person's interaction with the environment and hence become a powerful rehabilitation tool. By the year 2010 we may be able to specify more closely the nature of the interaction required by people with different types and severity of brain injury at different stages in their recovery to optimise outcome and it might be possible to use virtual reality technology as a vehicle to provide this.

In a series of experiments on unilateral left visual neglect, Robertson and North (1992, 1993) and Robertson, Hogg, and McMillan (1998) found that voluntary left-hand movements in left hemi-space reduce visual neglect. This improvement in attention extended to far space and was not confined to reaching space but did not improve attention in other modalities. Experiments such as these have the potential to identify mechanisms of recovery that may be neglected in current rehabilitation practice. They demonstrate that a careful experimental approach that examines theoretical models (Rizzolatti & Camarda, 1987) can suggest new methods of improving function following brain injury. Work of this kind has considerable potential for major advances over the next 10 years and once again holds out the possibility of improving brain function by providing appropriate, directed stimulation.

Traditionally, rehabilitation has fundamentally been an educational process. A different approach has been to search for ways of enhancing learning in those with brain injury. Baddeley (1993) has emphasised that a theory of learning that applies to those who have cognitive deficits following brain injury is fundamental to rehabilitation endeavour. Practical examples arising from cognitive psychology include errorless learning and vanishing cues techniques, and many others have been based on learning theory. The development of such methods over the next 10 years offers further scope for improvement in our ability to rehabilitate following brain injury.

Advances in functional imaging and other measures of physiological activity are providing new insights into the mechanisms of recovery and restoration of function following brain injury. So far such techniques have focused primarily on the recovery of motor functions. Compared to healthy controls increased cortical activity has been found in stroke patients, particularly in the unaffected hemisphere and in the sensory motor cortex. For example, Cramer, Nelles, Benson, and Kaplan (1997) found that in stroke patients carrying out a finger-tapping task with their unaffected hand there was a reduction in the activation of the sensory motor cortex of the unaffected hemisphere, whereas there was increased activation in this area when the affected (ipsilateral) hand was carrying out the task. Hence it appears that there is some reorganisation of function between hemispheres following injury. Studies such as these hold promise of greater understanding of the natural processes of recovery and a means of directly observing the effects of intervention. This could result in both greater ability to predict the nature and extent of recovery and also direct therapeutic efforts more precisely. Clearly there is a great leap to be made between the relatively simple functions such as finger tapping and complex cognitive processes, but given our ever-increasing ability to process information, such methods could be applied to these functions as we begin the new millennium.

Specific pharmacological advances may also produce considerable gains. One area would be improved anticonvulsants, particularly ones that cause minimal cognitive impairment. There is also scope for more judicious and less indiscriminate use of these. The advent of new major tranquillisers and antidepressants has had a significant impact in recent years. Behavioural changes continue to be a highly significant consequence of brain injury for many individuals. Many drugs used to combat these changes have significant side-effects such as increasing the likelihood of epileptic fits. The development of drugs that avoid these side-effects has been and may continue to be a significant advance. Reduced motivation is yet another disabling consequence of brain injury and recent studies with bromocryptine have confirmed that improvements in some cases can be achieved (Powell, Al-Adawi, Morgan, & Greenwood, 1996).

Considerable attention has been directed towards the pharmacological enhancement of memory and other cognitive functions. Neurotransmitters play a critical role in the brain circuits involved in various aspects of memory and cognition (Iversen, 1998). Cholinergic replacement therapy is already being used in Alzheimer's disease and the study of other neurotransmitters may eventually provide means of therapeutic intervention. Preliminary studies of the administration of oxygen and glucose have also reported positive effects on memory performance in healthy adults, especially when given in combination (Winder & Borrill, 1998).

Advances such as those described above will not occur unless there are sufficient financial and manpower resources for underlying research. Such study needs to be supported across the spectrum of recovery and rehabilitation. As indicated above, concentration on more technical aspects of research such as cell transplantation is unlikely to result in its full potential being reached, unless there is concomitant research directed at the nature of the rehabilitation environment and procedures required to enable useable function to be regained.

SERVICE SYSTEMS

The most dramatic scientific and technological advances will only benefit those who have suffered brain injuries if they are systematically incorporated into service systems. Indeed many of the potential advances outlined above will only occur if both research funding and clinical services exist. In Chapter 12 we describe the development of brain injury services in recent years and our view of the optimal system of services that should exist now. The same general structure should be able to incorporate any scientific and technological advances during the next decade but clearly the exact service specification will need to take these advances into account. For example, advances in our understanding of how to provide an enriched environment could lead to changes in the way services are offered, including a suitable physical environment, adequate staffing, and suitable professional training.

Perhaps the most important issue is the need for dedicated brain injury services. The consequences of brain injury and the impact of these necessitate very different services from those with other rehabilitation needs. Those with predominantly cognitive, behavioural, and motivational deficits need a service that is designed differently from those with predominantly physical impairment. This point needs to be accepted by all those responsible for the design and provision of health and social care. Although some progress has been made in recent years, there is still a tendency to lump disparate service groups together for the sake of economy. Unless clinicians and researchers are able to concentrate on specific groups, developments will be inhibited and rehabilitation for those with a brain injury will be less effective.

Considerable advances have been made over recent decades in the initial care of those who have suffered brain injuries. Nevertheless considerable scope remains for preventing the cascade of negative consequences which typically occur following brain injury. Improvements in preventive techniques and in response times by the paramedical services at the scene of the accident are possible and of continuing significance. Increased use of imaging technology and the transmission of images from local hospitals to neurosurgical centres will also result in improved acute care. At present, it is typical in the UK for patients who have suffered a brain injury to be allocated to any one of a number of general or orthopaedic surgeons and placed in different locations within the hospital. The identification of one or two consultants and a particular ward or subward within the hospital would allow for greater expertise to be built up among staff and a more satisfactory environment for early recovery to be established. Such an arrangement would also make it easier to provide greater support to the family at this crucial stage in recovery. There is a danger, however, that such an arrangement can lead to patients being "collected" without adequate arrangements to ensure that their different needs are met as recovery progresses. Clearly the acute care should not only be designed with inpatient medical care *and* rehabilitation in mind, but should also be explicitly linked to services for post-acute rehabilitation. One perennial problem, particularly for those who later become the "walking wounded", is that where orthopaedic injuries coexist with brain injury the emphasis all too frequently falls on the physical injuries and the brain injury can be overlooked, or that post-discharge help is not arranged if the physical injuries resolve. Explicit criteria and satisfactory training of the inpatient team are required to avoid this danger.

It is frequently stated, but commonly forgotten, that brain injury is for life. The design of services clearly needs to reflect this. It is not currently possible to predict with any certainty which patients will encounter the greatest problems. Routine follow-up is essential. Since the most common and the most disabling consequences of brain injury are cognitive and personality changes, such follow-up should focus on these. Clinical neuropsychologists are the most appropriate speciality to carry out such routine reviews (Royal College of Surgeons, 1999). However, specially trained nurses or therapists could assist in this process.

The establishment of local community-based centres providing day rehabilitation could provide a well co-ordinated service for the local population in a cost-efficient way (see McMillan & Oddy, Chapter 12 this volume). The last decade has seen the community team as the focus of much brain injury rehabilitation. The present authors would hope to see this developed over the next decade to become community centres. The resources required for these are greater, but they would be able to provide a more comprehensive service, which would encompass the heterogeneous nature of acquired brain injury and different stages of rehabilitation in the community. As soon as the person is able to live at home a period of day attendance could begin. This would be time limited and geared towards achieving specific goals, but further involvement including active follow-up, further episodes of intervention, and overall case supervision would be provided. Such centres would clearly need to work closely with voluntary organisations such as the National Head Injuries Foundation to ensure that people with brain injuries and their families achieve the highest possible quality of life.

In Europe there are great inconsistencies between geographical locations in terms of provision of brain injury services. However, most individuals who sustain an acquired brain injury will not receive comprehensive intervention after the acute stage. Although service gaps have reduced over the last 10 years, brain injury services must expand further so that provision of a high-quality and comprehensive service will be the rule rather than the exception, regardless of type of injury or geographical location.

TRAINING OF STAFF

If services are to expand, then obviously the training of existing and new staff will need to keep pace with what will be a fast-developing area. The question of whether new breeds of professional are needed is less clear. The need for teamwork in brain injury rehabilitation is established, with none of the existing professional groups having a monopoly of the skills or knowledge required. The emergence of new professional groups such as cognitive rehabilitation therapists or generic brain injury therapists might lead to a reduction in the difficulty of attracting and retaining staff. However, this could also lead to the development of more, and unhelpful, professional boundaries. Career structures for these new professions may be truncated, causing discontent and retention problems. Further, the way new professions would relate to existing professions is unclear; for example, existing professional groups are already involved in the work that these new groups would cover, leading to potential disputes over roles, seniority, and responsibility that may be difficult to resolve. Perhaps more attention should be given to ensuring that sufficient numbers of existing professions are trained and can provide adequate staffing levels for the years ahead.

The continued development of post-qualification courses in brain injury rehabilitation might be a useful means of ensuring staff recruitment and retention in this field. Training courses for those who work as rehabilitation assistants, support workers, or care assistants are especially needed. At present there is no systematic training for these individuals, yet it is often this staff group who spend the greatest time in direct contact with patients. The importance of environmental conditions during recovery and the concept of the prosthetic environment in the longer term makes it imperative that such workers should be given adequate training, which should include a knowledge base about brain injury, how best to interact with a brain injured person, an understanding of behaviour management and treatment, and means of reducing the impact of cognitive impairment.

In the UK professional psychological services for people with acquired brain damage are mainly provided by clinical psychologists and in the next few years there will be a post-qualification training course in clinical neuropsychology for clinically qualified psychologists. This model is similar to a medical training model inasmuch that following an initial qualification a medic may then work in post and specialise in neurology. The UK model has the benefit that the *clinical neuropsychologist* will have extensive training, including in a range of therapeutic models and extensive clinical experience in training across the age range from child to elderly. This model also avoids competition for already scarce training resources, including clinical placements and funding of trainees (McMillan, 1997). In the US and Australia some graduates in psychology are trained directly as clinical neuropsychologists, with the advantages of reducing time and overall costs of training. In some countries such as the UK and US, clinical psychologists are fairly autonomous and able to accept referrals directly from general practitioners, social services or from lawyers, and may be found as directors of post-acute rehabilitation centres. This is an appropriate model, given that the post-acute effects of acquired brain injury that are most common and most commonly debilitating are psychosocial and not physical and this is the focus of their training. However, this is not the model adopted in some other countries in Europe where there is less autonomy and where direct referrals are not allowed and some supervision by medical practitioners is required.

CONCLUSION

The next 10 years promises exciting developments in neuropsychological rehabilitation, both through the greater application of recent developments in technology and neuroscience and through the new scientific and technological advances that the next 10 years will bring. However, the full benefits for clients will not be realised unless there is a concomitant political will to provide such services on a routine and equitable basis. This will necessitate an extension of training opportunities for staff, as well as the establishment of the range of clinical services indicated in Chapter 12. However, prevention of brain injury must continue to be the primary goal. Once again the application of existing technology could take us a long way, but implementation will require considerable determination to overcome reluctance based on cost and curtailment of "freedom".

REFERENCES

Ager, A. (Ed.) (1991). *Microcomputers and clinical psychology*. Chichester: Wiley.

Baddeley, A. (1993). A theory of rehabilitation without a model of learning is a vehicle without an engine: A comment on Caramazza and Hillis. *Neuropsychological Rehabilitation, 3*, 245–244.

Cramer, S.C., Nelles, G., Benson, R.R., & Kaplan, J.D. (1997). A functional MRI study of subjects recovered from hemiparetic stroke. *Stroke, 28*, 2518–2527.

Dunnett, S. (in press). Neural tissue transplantation. In R.J. Greenwood, M. Barnes, T.M. McMillan, & C. Ward (Eds.), *Handbook of neurological rehabilitation* (2nd ed.). Hove: Psychology Press.

Eriksson, P.S., Perfilieva, E., Bjork-Eriksson, T., Alborn, A.-M., Nordborg, C., Peterson, D.A., & Gage, F.H. (1998). Neurogenesis in the adult human hippocampus. *Nature Medicine, 4*, 1313–1317.

Iversen, S. (1998). The pharmacology of memory. *Comptes Rendus, de L'Academie des Sciences, 321*, 209–215.

Judd, D.P., & Wilson, S.L. (1999). Brain injury and identity: The role of counselling psychologists. *Counselling Psychology Review, 14*, 4–16.

McKenna, F.P., & Horswill, M.S. (1999). Hazard perception and its relevance for driver licensing. *IATSS Research, 23*, 36–41.

McMillan, T.M. (1997). The roles and training of clinical psychologists in the United Kingdom. *Zeitschrift für Neuropsychologie, 8*, 29–31.

McMillan, T.M., Robertson, I.R., & Wilson, B.A. (1999). Neurogenesis after brain injury: Implications for neurorehabilitation (editorial). *Neuropsychological Rehabilitation, 9,* 129–133

Powell, J.H., Al-Adawi, S., Morgan, J., & Greenwood, R.J. (1996). Motivational deficits after brain injury: Effects of bromocriptine in 11 patients. *Journal of Neurology, Neurosurgery and Psychiatry, 60,* 416–421.

Rizzolatti, G., & Camarda, R. (1987). Neural circuits for spatial attention and unilateral neglect. In M. Jeannerod (Ed.), *Neurophysiological and neuropsychological aspects of neglect* (pp. 289–313). Amsterdam: North Holland Press.

Robertson, I., & North, N. (1992). Spatio-motor cueing in unilateral left neglect: The role of hemispace, hand and motor activation. *Neuropsychologia, 30,* 553–563.

Robertson, I., & North, N. (1993). Active and passive activation of left limbs: Influence on visual and sensory neglect. *Neuropsychologia, 31,* 293–300.

Robertson, I.H., Hogg, K., & McMillan, T.M. (1998). Rehabilitation of visual neglect: Improving function by contralesional limb activation. *Neuropsychological Rehabilitation, 8,* 19–29.

Rose, F.D., & Johnson, D.A. (1996). Towards improved outcome. In F.D. Rose, & D.A. Johnson (Eds.), *Brain injury and after: Towards improved outcome* (pp. 73–95). New York: Wiley.

Royal College of Surgeons (1999). *Report of the Working Party on the Management of Patients with Head Injuries.* London: Royal College of Surgeons.

Winder, R., & Borrill, J. (1998). Fuels for memory: The role of oxygen and glucose in memory enhancement. *Psychopharmacology, 136,* 349–356.

Wood, R.Ll. (1996). Ten years of post-acute brain injury rehabilitation: (A view from the independent sector). *Personal Injury, 3,* 203–211.

Author index

297

Subject index